TENNESSEE & KENTUCKY

GARDEN GUIDE

The Best Plants for a Tennessee
or Kentucky Garden

D1636864

First published in 2012 by Cool Springs Press, an imprint of the Quayside Publishing Group, 400 First Avenue North, Suite 300, Minneapolis, MN 55401

Cool Springs Press titles are also available at discounts in bulk quantity for industrial or sales-promotional use. For details write to Special Sales Manager at Cool Springs Press, 400 North First Avenue, Suite 300, Minneapolis, MN 55401 USA. To find out more about our books, visit us online at www.coolspringspress.com.

To find out more about our books, visit us online at www.coolspringspress.com.

ISBN-13: 978-1-59186-537-7

Acquisitions Editor: Billie Brownell
Design Manager: Brad Springer
Layout: S. E. Anderson
Front Cover Design: Rob Johnson

Printed in China

10 9 8 7 6 5 4 3 2 1

TENNESSEE & KENTUCKY

GARDEN GUIDE

The Best Plants for a Tennessee or Kentucky Garden

Judy Lowe

Cool
Springs
Press

Growing Successful Gardeners™

MINNEAPOLIS, MINNESOTA

Dedication

To my dear husband, Carlyle, who makes life such a joy.

Acknowledgments

It's always a pleasure to once again work with Billie Brownell, the best—and most patient—editor a writer could ever have. I'm grateful beyond words for her kindness and guidance. Much appreciation is due Hubert (Hugh) Conlon, the book's horticultural advisor. He cheerfully kept us up-to-date with all the taxonomical changes to botanical names and offered invaluable advice. A very big thank-you to the countless Tennesseans and Kentuckians who answered my phone calls and e-mail messages asking for facts, advice, and recommendations. This would have been a much different guide—and not nearly as useful—without them.

Contents

Welcome to Gardening in Tennessee & Kentucky

Kentucky and Tennessee are great places to garden. But if you've moved here from another region, you may find yourself a bit confused. Maybe you aren't familiar with some of the plants you see around you because they didn't grow where you lived before, and you aren't sure how to plant or care for them. Or possibly you haven't been successful at growing plants here that were favorites in your previous region, and you wonder what went wrong. Why in the world don't your lilac bushes bloom as long and look as good in spring as those you grew in another state?

Gardening in a different part of the country—or becoming a new gardener—is a learning experience. But it doesn't have to be difficult. That's where this book comes in, showing you the best trees, shrubs, flowers, even vines and groundcovers, that are right for your part of Kentucky or Tennessee, and then explaining how to plant and care for them.

Once you have that simple knowledge—planting the right plants in the right places and caring for them in the way they prefer—you're well on your way to being a successful gardener in this region. And that means having a yard you're proud of without spending the majority of your waking hours working in it.

The advantages of gardening here include a long growing season, abundant rainfall (in most years), a mild climate in which many different kinds of plants thrive, and—for most of us—fertile soils. (Even clay is rich in nutrients.)

Rewards and Challenges

But, as is true everywhere, you will face some challenges. Our long, frost-free season often means battling more insects than gardeners do in colder climates. That clay soil can hold too much water and drown plants' roots. At the opposite extreme, rocky soils on mountains and hills drain so quickly that you may need to water two days after a downpour. While most of our winters are mild, they're rarely predictable—temperatures can fall from 80 to 20 degrees Fahrenheit in a single day. Plants don't like that any better than people do, and they suffer from such extremes. Rainfall may also be too much—15 inches in March—or too little—¼ inch in the heat of August. Still, any good gardener will tell you that the advantages of gardening in our states far outweigh the disadvantages.

Oak (Quercus)

Many homeowners believe that they need to have a green thumb in order to be a successful gardener. Not so. In reality, it's a matter of learning more about your yard and more about what plants want. No matter how much you like crape myrtle, for instance, it's not going to turn a shady yard into a sea of color. Crape myrtle's main need is *full* sun—provide that and it will be happy in your yard. If you have only four hours of daily sun to offer, it won't. Similarly, if you put moisture-loving impatiens in a hot, dry spot that's far from a water faucet, they're going to fail.

So, before you head to a nursery to buy plants, take time to learn more about your yard. Observe the amount of sunlight and shade in various sections at different times of day. Dig some holes to see what the soil is like—black and crumbly, hard and red, rock-filled, or somewhere in between. That gives you the knowledge you need to choose the plants that will be happiest in your landscape and the areas in which they'll thrive. When plants are happy—when they're placed in the conditions they prefer—they grow and bloom well, resist insects and diseases better, and look great. And that's what you're aiming for.

Designing a Landscape from Trees Down

Before you get too caught up in selecting individual plants, think about the overall effect of your yard, how everything works together. That's landscaping. If you've moved into a new house, or if you're starting a new landscape almost from scratch, choose trees first. They're the foundation of your garden; they provide the structure. Avoid the strong temptation to pick the fastest-growing trees you can find; these are almost always trees that have problems—and you'll always regret planting them. Instead, plant trees for posterity. If you want trees to grow as quickly as possible, water them regularly and fertilize them yearly, and they'll grow well.

Your second plant selections should be shrubs, probably a mix of evergreen and deciduous shrubs. Some should be flowering shrubs, and it's important to pay attention to when they bloom so that you can have flowers throughout the growing season, not just in spring. (Did you know that your yard could feature shrubs, such as witch hazel, in flower in *January*? That's one of the joys of gardening in our states.)

An important point is to look up the eventual height and spread of any shrub before you buy it. This is also true of trees and most other plants you buy, but ignoring shrubs' mature size can make a long-lasting difference. You understand why if you've ever had a shrub grow so that it blocks a living room window, and you've had to spend countless hours every summer cutting it back. Trust me on this one—those young shrubs will always look too tiny when you're planting them, but they don't stay small long. Then it will be a lot of work to have to constantly prune shrubs that are too large for the place in which they were planted or to have to dig them up and plant something that's the correct size. So often people will grumble about how they don't like forsythia, but the main complaint usually boils down to the fact that it wasn't planted somewhere that it has room to reach its mature size. Do it right the first time, and you'll be happier with the results.

After you've decided on trees and shrubs, it's time to think about flowers. Annuals provide the main floral show because they bloom for a long time. They're also colorful and relatively inexpensive (many can be grown from seed). Use them to fill containers and hanging baskets, as well as flower beds. But you may also want to add a border or bed of perennials. Unlike annuals these plants bloom for a shorter time and cost more individually, but they return year after year. You buy and plant them only once, and usually their numbers increase over the years. They add individuality to your garden.

Bulbs, corms, rhizomes, and tubers also produce popular flowers: daffodils, irises, dahlias, and more. Although easy to grow, they need care in planting, and not all return year after year; some must be dug up in fall, stored over winter, and replanted in spring.

If you find that grass has become difficult to grow in shade beneath trees no matter how often you reseed or fertilize, consider planting a shade-tolerant groundcover to provide texture and color without all the mowing that a lawn requires. It will look so much better and require much less work.

Nowadays, mentioning grasses doesn't necessarily mean fescue, Bermuda, zoysia, and the other common lawngrasses of our region, but increasingly includes tall, handsome ornamental species, which look good in the garden not only when they're green, but after frost when they've developed plumes and turned tan. If you want an almost foolproof plant—one that isn't bothered by insects or diseases and needs little water once it's established—a perennial type of ornamental grass will fill the bill.

Not everyone needs a vine, but keep in mind that they do serve many purposes, from hiding an eyesore to attractively covering a lamppost with flowers. They're also perfect in narrow spots where they can grow up instead of outward. Vines may be evergreen or deciduous, flowering or not. Many flowering vines are excellent for attracting butterflies and birds. Native vines are a natural part of a garden created for wildlife. And don't think that all vines grow like kudzu or Japanese honeysuckle. The best ones have excellent manners; they aren't bullies at all.

Finally, have you been thinking about joining the ranks of water gardeners? The appearance and sound of water in the garden has such a strong appeal that it's hard to resist. Water gardens can be any size to fit your yard—they don't have to be huge—and many companies now specialize in doing the hard work and installing them. After that, you can have the fun of planting and enjoying them.

If you've ever admired a beautiful yard but felt that you would never be able to do something similar in your own yard, I'll let you in on a secret: green thumbs aren't magically passed out to the fortunate few. They're the result of learning about plants and using common sense to landscape with them.

If you want to have an easy-care landscape, here are six steps to help you achieve that goal. If you've gardened at all, you probably already know—on some level—many of these "rules" for creating an attractive yard that requires only a little maintenance. They're simple, but they work.

How to Have a Good-Looking, Easy-Care Landscape

Rule 1

Use seasonal color and lots of it. Think of the yards that attract your attention in spring as you drive to and from work or errands. They may be undulating seas of yellow with rows of sunshiny forsythia and golden daffodils. Or they may be filled with fluffy white or pink clouds of ornamental cherry blossoms underplanted with red tulips.

In April, a garden that's a mass of dogwoods and azaleas is a floral fantasyland, and really, that's all you notice about the property. You don't see whether the house needs painting or the lawn could use some edging. Your eyes focus on the colorful flowers.

Mass planting of tulips and pansies

Rule 2

Groupings of any plant are more impressive than one or two single specimens. Three red azaleas, planted together, have more impact than one that's pink, one that's white, and one that's salmon. But take care to coordinate your colors. A row of either sunshiny forsythia or bright red flowering quince is eye-catching; but alternating the two shrubs in one row creates a jumbled effect. So does alternating boxwood and azalea. They look fine until spring, and then the azaleas' impact is diluted.

In the same way, tulips that are all the same color or that are planted so that drifts or blocks of the same color are together and flow into a drift of a complementary color are considerably more effective than multicolored mixtures. And watch out for masses of azaleas bought at different times. Make sure they're really all the same variety, because some colors—fuchsia and orangish-red—clash instead of coordinate. (Save your plant labels, so you know what you have. It also helps when you really love a plant and want to buy more in the future.)

Rule 3

Flowering trees and shrubs require much less effort on a homeowner's part than do annuals and perennials. You plant them once, keep them watered regularly for two years (until they're established and growing well), fertilize them yearly, and little more is needed. But they keep blooming year after year, even when you don't do a thing.

Beware, however, of creating a hodgepodge. One ornamental peach, two ornamental pears, a spirea, and a kerria—especially marching across the front of the property like so many decorated soldiers—don't attract much interest because the effect is too busy; there's no unity, no focal point.

Rule 4

Think beyond one season. If your yard currently looks best in spring, plant trees or shrubs that bloom in summer or that have especially colorful fall foliage. I always aim to have something in bloom or berry in my yard from spring until late fall—even into winter. These can be trees, shrubs, bulbs, perennials; it may surprise you how many seasonal variations you can find when you look. And it's getting easier to locate them, as breeders develop more plants that flower earlier and later and that bloom not just once a year but over and over. Some that have worked well for me in various places my husband and I have lived include deciduous magnolias, which may be grown as large shrubs or small trees and bloom very early in spring; Kousa dogwood (*Cornus kousa*), a beautiful flowering tree that blooms about a month later than the native dogwood and is generally not subject to anthracnose; ginkgo trees and named cultivars of red maple, which provide reliable fall color; and witch hazel, which brings a burst of blooms to the landscape in the middle of winter. Lenten roses provide more subtle and delicate winter beauty, so I plant them near the front walk. And I can't imagine my yard without red-berried hollies brightening the cold weather and attracting migrating birds.

Rule 5

Plant something different from what everyone else is growing. It will certainly attract attention. You need to be careful, though, to determine if there are reasons no one is growing the plant; maybe it isn't really hardy in your area or it's difficult to grow (meaning it may require more TLC than you have time for).

As you leaf through this book, you may discover that you haven't heard of some of the plants that are featured—red valerian, loropetalum, Japanese zelkova, and sweet box possibly among them. That's intentional. Many of the plants discussed are old favorites in our states, but others, which grow just as well, aren't as popular as they deserve to be. Consider giving some of them a try in your yard. They'll be reliable.

Rule 6

When it comes to bulbs, choose the ones that will come back each year and still look good. Daffodils and crocuses do; tulips sometimes don't. Daylilies do. So do bearded irises, but many of the newer cultivars are subject to many pests and may be harmed by cold weather. Siberian irises are trouble-free and don't need dividing often.

Paperbark maple (Acer griseum) *provides winter interest with its paperlike bark.*

From Theory to Practice

Since my family and I have moved around a great deal, I've had the opportunity to landscape more yards than most people. My first rule is that trees I plant will either flower, have berries, or be covered with colorful leaves in fall. They all have to do double duty—give summer shade and be eye-catching in at least one other season. In a small yard, I want the majority of shrubs to be evergreen and all of them to produce either flowers or berries. I try to space out the times when the shrubs are most colorful (that is, they won't all be spring-flowering azaleas). This means that my yard will have a year-round green foundation, and that— if I've planned well—there will be at least one, usually more, pockets of color in every month of the year. Of course, I add flowers—annuals, bulbs, perennials—as well as ornamental grasses to complement the shrubs and trees. But with just trees and shrubs, my yard will look attractive year-round. *That's* the way to do low-maintenance!

The Hardiness Zones and Why They Matter

For gardeners, "in the zone" doesn't mean a new diet or exercise program. Instead a gardening zone is one that describes a climate in which certain plants will thrive, and others won't. When learning about a plant, a gardener should always ask, "What zone does it grow in?"

This refers to the plant hardiness zone map developed by the U.S. Department of Agriculture (USDA). It's based on dividing the country into sections, or zones, depending on their average minimum winter temperatures, recorded at official weather stations over a period of years.

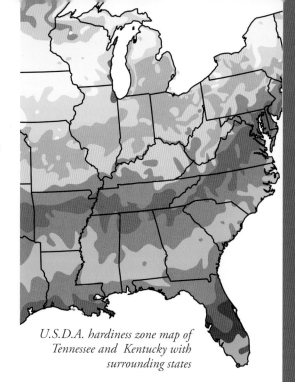

U.S.D.A. hardiness zone map of Tennessee and Kentucky with surrounding states

Until recently, we've been depending on a map that hadn't been updated for more than twenty years. Fortunately, that has changed.

The USDA's 1990 plant hardiness zone map placed most Kentucky residents in Zone 6a (average annual minimum temperature of -5 to -10 degrees Fahrenheit) or 6b (0 to -5), while a tiny portion were placed in Zone 5 (-10 to -15 degrees Fahrenheit). Most of Tennessee was in Zone 6, with the lower portion of the state in Zone 7a (0 to 5 degrees Fahrenheit), but the area around Memphis was Zone 7b (5 to 10 degrees Fahrenheit). But the 2012 map, based on low temperatures from 1976 through 2005, has moved most of us into a slightly warmer zone, as you'll see on the map on page 41.

How does this matter to you? It probably means that you'll be able to grow shrubs, trees, and perennial plants that you may not have considered cold-hardy in your area before. But a map based only on average low temperatures has obvious drawbacks. It doesn't offer foolproof guidance about what will—and won't—grow in our area, because tolerance to heat and humidity can be as big a factor in plant success in Tennessee and Kentucky as cold-hardiness. Many needled evergreen trees, for instance, do fine in very cold temperatures but die in our summer heat.

Another issue is that plants don't live by "average" temperatures. One winter with a low of 5 degrees Fahrenheit, another where it got to -5, and a third where the low was 0 may add up to an average minimum of 0 (Zone 7), but some plants that are rated for Zone 7 will die when temperatures fall to -5 during that one winter. You may want to be cautious about filling your yard with plants rated for the new, warmer zone. In an extra-cold winter (and we're still going to get them!), you're likely to lose a number of plants. Still, following the USDA Zone map works well if you realize its drawbacks.

A note to those who have moved here from the West Coast, particularly California, where the *Sunset* magazine climate zone maps are generally used instead of the USDA map: unfortunately, the *Sunset* maps aren't very helpful in the East. Use the maps shown here instead.

The Impact of Climate

Be aware that the official temperature at the airport may not help in telling you how chilly it gets in your backyard, since it's often miles away. Also recognize that every property has what are called microclimates, places where the climate and temperature are slightly different from surrounding areas. The south side of the house and spots next to expanses of paving are going to be warmer. Northern exposures will be cooler. Large trees and structures may provide shelter that helps retain heat at night. Slopes and especially low spots may be frost pockets that get colder than other nearby areas. Avoid planting spring-flowering plants in these vulnerable locations, because their blossoms will frequently be killed by late frosts.

Weather often plays an important part in whether or not frost nips spring flowers. An unseasonable warm spell in February can cause trees, shrubs, vines, and perennials to bud and begin to bloom sooner than usual. Then, when temperatures return to their normal chilly state, those premature blossoms are hit by frost. There's not much you can do about this except to try to place susceptible shrubs and trees in protected locations, where they won't be harmed. Or, in the case of shrubs, run out and cover them with a blanket or quilt (never plastic) when an unseasonable frost is forecast.

With perennials and bulbs, you can moderate the climate somewhat with the liberal use of mulch, which protects roots from winter cold. Mulch may also keep the soil cool in spring, to delay blooming until after damaging frosts have ended.

Our summer weather tends to be hot and humid. Some plants don't like this—Colorado blue spruce in Zone 7, for instance, or firs throughout the region. They're used to climates with cooler summers. Many needled evergreens react the same way, so if you want to grow one, it's important to select one that's adapted to our climate. Plants with silver or gray foliage are especially vulnerable to heat and humidity. When they've had enough, they collapse; gardeners call this melting out or melting down. It's just a fact of life here that some plants that thrive in northern climates won't do well in our region (lilacs that flower a short time, for instance). But so many more will be successful here that we would never have time—or space—to grow all the plant choices that are available to us.

What's in a Name? Decoding Botanical Names

Sometimes gardeners feel uncomfortable with botanical names. The words are unfamiliar and sometimes long and hard to pronounce. Why don't garden books just use common names instead?

There are several reasons that books and catalogs give both botanical and common names. Mostly, it's to avoid confusion. Common names for a plant vary from place to place. You and a neighbor, who grew up in a different state, may call the same plant by different common names. One plant may also have collected a number of different common names, adding to the confusion.

So every plant has a botanical name—usually Latin, occasionally Latinized Greek—that belongs to it and it alone. If you are looking for a particular plant at a local garden center or from a mail-order nursery, you'll find it by the botanical name. If you need to ask advice about a plant from the Extension service or another expert, they can readily identify your plant by its botanical name.

Another reason for using botanical names is that, once you look at them carefully, you'll pick up clues to what the plant is like. *Alba* means white, for instance. *Japonica* means the plant originated in Japan, while *Canadensis* tells you the plant was originally found in Canada. *Citrina* indicates lemony yellow. In leaf shapes, *lancifolia* is lance-leafed, *crispula* may be curled, *undulata* may be wavy, and *serrata* indicates serrated leaves. *Variegata* obviously indicates variegation. *Sempervirens* is evergreen. As part of a species name, *micro* means very small, *grandis* is large, and *gracilis* is slender.

The first word in a plant's botanical name (which is always capitalized and italicized) is the genus name; think of it as a family name. It's a group of plants that are closely related—*Hosta*, for instance. The second name (which begins with a lowercase letter and is also italicized) is the species, which identifies a distinct type of individual plant, such as *Hosta fortunei*. The third name (which may be more than one word) is the variety or cultivar name. In botanical terms, there are differences between varieties and cultivars, but in popular gardening parlance, they're used interchangeably. Cultivar stands for cultivated variety. It's a plant that was selected for its desirable qualities from a larger group of plants. The cultivar name is usually enclosed in single quotation marks. For example, *Hosta fortunei* 'Albopicta' further identifies our hosta as a particular cultivar.

But how do you pronounce all those tongue-twisting words? The pronunciation guides within each plant profile are provided to give you the confidence to ask for a plant and talk about it by its botanical name. Consider these a guide only. Different experts have varying ways of pronouncing some of these names. In most of the U.S., for example, we say "stokesia" as stow-KEY-zee-uh. In England, and among some professionals in this country, it's pronounced STOKES-ee-uh, after the man for whom the plant was named. So you'll hear it both ways.

Not to worry. You already know how to pronounce many more botanical names than you think. You're not so sure? Well, what about these—impatiens, petunia, salvia, begonia, zinnia, canna, crocus, dahlia, iris, zoysia, phlox, vinca, sedum, camellia, forsythia, hibiscus, nandina, rhododendron, viburnum, magnolia, hydrangea, and wisteria? See, you already have a head start on pronouncing botanical names.

Practically Guaranteed

If you have picked up this book out of a desire to beautify the corner where you live, read on—about soil, watering techniques, and fertilizer, as well as interesting plants that may be new to you. All the plants profiled in this guide have been selected because they'll thrive in your garden. They're practically guaranteed to make you look as though your thumb is bright green, whether you've gardened before or not. Just remember to match the plants to your yard's growing conditions, and you'll create a landscape to be proud of.

Gardening Basics

Gardening isn't difficult; even small children can be successful gardeners. But, as with other hobbies, gardening requires paying attention to the basics: soil, water, fertilizer, mulch, and weather. When you get those right you'll have a landscape to be proud of. All it takes is learning what you need to know.

Soil

It's hard to get excited about dirt. It's not as interesting as plants. It doesn't bloom; it just sits there, underfoot. But soil is the foundation for all your gardening. If the soil is good (either naturally or you've improved it), then plants are going to be happy. If the soil is poor, plants won't grow well and will develop problems. But there's a bit more to it than that. In order to grow well, specific plants need varying conditions—some like moist soil; others don't, for example—so the first step is to learn what your soil is like. A nearby neighbor who gardens can tell you; so can the Soil Conservation Service office in your county.

You've probably heard the advice about having your soil tested. That's wise counsel, although it's often ignored. It shouldn't be. Having your soil tested is easy. Just dig up small samples of soil from various parts of your yard, thoroughly mix them together, and turn them in to your county Extension service to be sent off for testing. The best time to do this is fall, when the labs aren't so busy and when—if your soil needs lime—there's plenty of time to apply it and have it begin to take effect. But if you haven't had your soil tested in a long time, or if you've added a substantial amount of amendments (fireplace ashes, wood chips, and so forth) to the soil since the last time it was tested, don't wait for the perfect time. Just go on and do it. It's relatively inexpensive and one of the most important things you can do to become a better gardener (and, consequently, have a better-looking yard).

When your soil test results come back, you'll learn if your soil is deficient in any nutrients that plants need (and therefore what kind and how much fertilizer to use) and also the pH of your soil. What's pH? It's the measure of acidity or alkalinity of your soil. A pH of 7 is neutral; below that is

If your compost pile is too wet and has an unpleasant odor, add more brown material and turn the pile so it can dry out.

acidic, above that is alkaline. Most of our soils are acidic, but some of us do live on properties with alkaline soil. Because plants have definite preferences for one type or the other, it's important to know your soil's pH level.

Because the ideal soil for most plants is moist and well drained, it's good to know whether your soil tends to stay wet or dry, and whether it drains well. Clay soils stay wet longer than loam; sandy or rocky soils drain much faster than other types of soil—which is often good—but they need watering more frequently. Plants that are able to live in especially wet or dry conditions are noted in the plants profiles in this book.

If you suspect that drainage is poor at a site in your yard, test to be sure. Dig a hole 6 to 12 inches deep and as wide. Fill the hole with water and time how long it takes for the water to drain completely. If it takes fifteen minutes to half an hour, drainage is good. Faster means the soil doesn't hold moisture well, and slower means you have clay.

The advice about improving your soil has been changing over the past few years, and there's no universal agreement on new rules. In the past, gardeners were told that just because their yards had a particular type of soil didn't mean they had to live with it. Instead, they could improve it with soil amendments. For example, organic matter (such as compost, rotted leaves, rotted sawdust, composted manure, fine bark, old mushroom compost, and peat moss) not only lightens heavy clay soil and improves its

drainage, but it also boosts the water-holding capability of lighter soil. When digging a new bed, gardeners would spread 3 or more inches of compost or other soil amendment on top of the soil and till it into the top 8 inches of soil. Or they would work soil amendments into the hole when they planted a new shrub or some bulbs.

For many people, that worked. But sometimes it created problems as the plants' roots had to grow from the "easy life" they had in loose, amended soil out into hard clay or whatever the native soil was. That's why most experts recommend planting trees in only the soil that's been removed from the hole; no added peat moss, fine bark, and so forth (see page 228.) Saying that soil amendments do no good for woody plants, some experts recommend planting shrubs the same way as trees. Not everyone agrees. At this point, amending soil is generally advised for perennials, annuals, bulbs, and so forth.

But two current movements that are catching on suggest that it's best for the soil *not* to rototill or dig it deeply. Learn more by reading *Teaming with Microbes: A Gardener's Guide to the Soil Food Web,* by Jeff Lowenfels, and *Lasagna Gardening,* by Pat Lanza. (The former is more about the science, the latter about growing the most popular plants.)

Water

How Much Is Enough?

The rule of thumb says that most garden plants need 1 inch of water per week in the growing season, and many need its equivalent all year long. Unfortunately, the amount of rain that fell at your city's airport or other official weather station may not be the amount that fell on your plants. The only way to know for sure is to put up a rain gauge that shows you what happened in your backyard. In summer, when "scattered showers" are always in the forecast, I find that the "official" rainfall and what fell on my yard are rarely the same. If I had watered—or not watered—on the basis of the totals given by the National Weather Service, I would almost always either overwater or underwater my plants. Instead, I save time and money—as well as protect my plants—by knowing exactly how much rainfall they receive.

To make sure you water your lawn enough, measure the amount of water your sprinklers spray during a specific amount of time.

When and How to Water

In general, plants respond best to thorough but occasional soakings rather than daily spurts of smaller amounts of water. This encourages plants to develop deeper roots, which provide greater stability; that's especially important for shrubs and trees. Deep roots also make plants more drought-tolerant. Shallow roots need more frequent watering.

The worst thing you can do for your plants in a drought is to stand over them with a hose for a few minutes each evening. Most of the water runs off instead of soaking in, and what does penetrate the soil doesn't usually go deeply enough. The soil should be wet to at least 8 to 10 inches deep for perennials and other flowers, 12 to 24 inches deep for trees and shrubs. Insert a dry stick into the soil to be sure how far the water has penetrated. It's impossible to say how long watering will take, because water absorption rates vary by soil type. An inch of water will penetrate fastest into sandy soil and slowest into clay. Time your watering the first few times and then you'll have a guide for future watering.

If you use sprinklers or an irrigation system, set out empty coffee cans at intervals to measure the amount of water delivered in thirty minutes. This will show you how long it takes the system to deliver an inch of water to your plants.

Too little water causes plants to perform poorly. Small leaves, pale or no flowers, stunted size, wilting, little or no fruit formation, and premature leaf drop can all be signs of water stress. Soil surfaces may dry out and even crack, destroying feeder roots near the surface; their loss can be fatal to annual flowers and vegetables. If watering seems adequate and plants still wilt daily, they may be located in too much sun. If such beds are deeply mulched, check to be certain that the water is getting down into the soil.

The best time of day to water is early morning; late afternoon is second best. No one wants to get up at 4 a.m. to turn on a lawn sprinkler. But there's an easy way out. Water timers can be attached to any hose or faucet to regulate sprinklers and soaker hoses. Digital timers are the hallmark of in-ground irrigation systems, but inexpensive manual timers work quite well for timing lawn watering or turning on trickle irrigation to the herb garden.

The Right Tools

As with all gardening activities, watering is more efficient with the right equipment. Small gardens and containers of plants can be watered efficiently with only a watering can and garden hose. Use a water-breaking nozzle to convert the solid stream of water into softer, smaller droplets that will not damage plants. When watering container plants, irrigate until water flows out the drain hole in the bottom of the pot, and then cover the soil with water once again. This practice ensures that all of the soil is completely moistened and keeps the root zone healthy by exchanging gases in the soil.

Larger garden beds require sprinklers, either portable or in-ground systems. Sprinklers spread plenty of water around and most of it gets to soil level; the rest is lost to evaporation but does provide

For efficient watering, use the right equipment.

a playground and essential moisture for birds. Adjustable sprinkler heads are a good investment; the ability to set the pattern specifically to make sure the water doesn't end up on the driveway or street gives the gardener more control over irrigation and saves money.

Where water is precious or pricey, drip watering systems (also known as trickle irrigation) and soaker hoses offer very efficient irrigation. They're especially useful around plants such as roses and zinnias, which develop mildew or other fungus diseases easily. These hoses apply much smaller amounts of water at one time than you may be used to. (Their slow watering is good for plants; it sinks into the soil right at the root zone.) If you leave a soaker hose on for the same time that you run a sprinkler, it will deliver much less water. Because delivery is slow, you need to leave it on longer. How long? To measure output, let the water run for an hour, then turn the soaker hose off. Dig down into the soil to see how deeply it is wet. That will help you gauge how long to keep soaker hoses or drip systems on. For the health of your plants, when watering this way, occasionally supplement with overhead watering (either sprinklers or hand-held hoses) to clean the leaves and deter insects.

Watering Plants in Containers

Container plants, especially hanging baskets and annuals in small pots, generally need watering once or twice a day in mid and late summer, when temperature and humidity levels are high. You can lessen this chore by choosing a potting soil that contains a super-absorbent polymer (the front of the bag usually says something like "holds more water"). Or you can buy one of these polymers and mix it into regular potting soil. They absorb moisture and then release it as the plants need it. Although they're pricey, only a tiny amount is needed (never use more than what is recommended, or you'll have a mess on your hands), and they last in the soil for up to five years. My experience is that they just about double the length of time between waterings. That is, if I would water a container plant without the polymer once a day, then, with the polymer, I can usually water every other day. That may not sound like a big deal, but in the dog days of August, it's a blessing! These super-absorbent polymers are sold under a number of trade names; ask for them at garden centers and nurseries.

Why Is Watering Important?

Water is vital because it makes up at least 95 percent of a plant's mass, and its timely supply is crucial to healthy growth. It is literally the elixir of life, moving from the root zone and leaf surfaces into the plant's systems, carrying nutrients and filling cells to create stems, leaves, flowers, and fruit. Without ample water for roots to work efficiently, nutrients go unabsorbed, growth is stunted, and plant tissues eventually collapse, wilt, and die. Ironically, too much water creates equally disastrous conditions. When soils are flooded, the roots suffocate, stop pumping water and nutrients, and the plant eventually dies.

Watering Tips

- Shrubs and other plants growing under the overhang of a roof may need more frequent watering than those planted out in the yard. Foundation shrubs often don't get much water from precipitation, and they also have to contend with the reflected heat from the house.
- Raised beds, berms, and mounds also need watering more often.
- Watch out for excessive runoff when watering. If the soil isn't absorbing the moisture, slow the rate of water application.
- Never fertilize without watering thoroughly afterward. Fertilizer salts can damage plant roots if moisture is lacking.

Fertilizer

Nutrition in appropriate amounts is as important as sunlight and water to plant growth. Three elements—nitrogen, phosphorus, and potassium—are essential to plants and are called macronutrients. Some of these macronutrients are obtained from the soil, but if they're not available in the amounts needed, the gardener must provide them through fertilizer.

Each nutrient plays a major role in plant development. Nitrogen produces healthy, green leaves, while phosphorus and potassium are responsible for strong stems, flowers, and fruit. Without enough of any one of the macronutrients, plants falter and often die. Other elements, needed in much smaller amounts, are known as trace elements, minor elements, or micronutrients. Included in most complete fertilizers (a "complete" fertilizer contains nitrogen, phosphorus, and potassium), the minor elements are boron, iron, manganese, zinc, copper, and molybdenum.

Fertilizers come from two basic sources: organic materials and manufactured ones. Organic sources include rocks, plants, and animals; fertilizers are extracted or composted from them. The advantages of organics affect both plants and people: centuries of history to explain their uses, slow and steady action on plants and especially soils, and the opportunity to put local and recycled materials to good use. Manufactured sources are the products of laboratories. Nutrients are formulated by scientists and produced in factories. The advantages of commercially prepared inorganic fertilizers are consistency of product, formula diversity, definitive analysis of contents, and ready availability. Some gardeners use a combination of the two, but purely organic enthusiasts use natural products exclusively.

Every fertilizer sold must have a label detailing its contents. Understanding the composition and numbers improves the gardener's ability to provide nutrition. The three numbers on a fertilizer label relate to its contents; the first number indicates the amount of nitrogen, the second number the amount of phosphorus, and the third, the amount of potassium. For example, if the numbers are 20-15-10, it means the product has 20 percent nitrogen, 15 percent phosphorus, and 10 percent potassium. Their relative numbers reveal their impact on plants—a formula high in nitrogen greens-up the plant and grows leaves; ones with lower first and higher second and third numbers encourage flowers and fruits.

A good rule of thumb is to use a balanced fertilizer (one where all the numbers are equal, as in 10-10-10) to prepare new soil. Then fertilize the plants with a formula higher in nitrogen at the beginning of the growing season to get plants up and growing; switch to special formulas (that is, those formulated specifically for flowers and fruiting) later in the season, if more than one feeding is needed. (You'll fertilize annuals, vegetables, and container plants more than you will shrubs or trees.)

Both organic and chemical fertilizers can be water-soluble or granular; both types have advantages and appropriate uses. Soluble formulas are mixed in water. They are available in very specific formulas, compact to store, fast acting, and can be used either as a soil drench or to spray the leaves (plants will absorb them through foliage or soil). Although solubles work quickly (leaves will often green up overnight—great if you want the yard to look good for a cookout), their effects

---

Ready to Use ①

FERTIFEED ②

All Purpose Plant Food ③

12-4-8 ④

FertiFeed Ready To Use All-Purpose Plant Food
Net Weight 4lb. 12oz. (2.15kg)

GUARANTEED ANALYSIS

Total Nitrogen (N).. ⑤ .12%
    12.0% Urea Nitrogen
Available Phosphate (P_2O_5).. ....4% ⑥
Soluable Potash (K2O).. ⑦ .8%
Manganese (Mn)..0.05% ⑧
    0.05% Chelated Manganese (Mn)
Zinc (Zn) 0.05%
    0.05% Chelated Zinc (Zn)
Inert Ingredients...76% ⑨

Information regarding the contents and levels of metals in this product is available on the Internet at http://www.regulatory-info-sc.com.

KEEP OUT OF REACH OF CHILDREN

1 Type of fertilizer
2 The fertilizer brand name
3 Intended use
4 Fertilizer analysis
5 Nitrogen content
6 Phosphorous content
7 Potassium content
8 Nutrients other than N-P-K
9 Other ingredients

Fertilizer label

Topdressing the soil

do not last long and they must be reapplied frequently. They are especially useful in growing container plants, which need more frequent watering as well as fertilizing.

Granular fertilizers can be worked into the soil when tilling or used as a top dressing around established plants. They incorporate easily into soils, and their effects may last for several weeks or even longer. Slow-release fertilizers, which may be pelleted, keep working for three to nine months depending on the formula. The coated pellets of these fertilizers (Osmocote™ is one that's readily available) decompose slowly with water or temperature changes over time. They cost more than granular fertilizers but save much time because they're usually applied just once a season. Their other big advantage over granular fertilizers is that it's almost impossible for gardeners to "burn" plant foliage when using them, whereas great care must be taken to keep granular fertilizers off plant parts.

Preparing to apply liquid fertilizer

Organic fertilizers also work slowly over a long period of time. They usually have lower ratios of active ingredients (nitrogen, phosphorus, and potassium) and so provide steady nutrition, rather than a quick green-up. Organic fertilizers that provide nitrogen are bloodmeal, fishmeal, soybean meal, and cottonseed meal. Organic phosphorous fertilizers include bonemeal and rock phosphate. To provide potassium, use greensand or sulfate of potash-magnesia. More and more common these days are organic fertilizers where the manufacturer has combined several ingredients in a product that's ideal for bulbs, shrubs, or trees. This makes using organic fertilizers much easier.

Although soil may contain many nutrients, some gardeners feel they need to do something more to help their plants. However, many tend to overdo it. Too much fertilizer can harm plants, just as too little does. Excessive nitrogen, for instance, often leads to attacks of aphids, which appreciate the tender young growth that's being produced, and to floppy stems in perennial plants.

Rules to Remember

- Never fertilize a plant in dry soil. Water plants the day before you fertilize, or at least several hours ahead of time.
- Always use products at the rate recommended on the label or a little lower. Never use more than what is recommended.
- Immediately rinse stray granules off plant leaves to prevent "burning" (sucking the moisture out of leaves).

Mulch

One important thing you can provide your plants—which may mean the difference between success and failure—is mulch.

Mulch is the most useful material in your garden. A blanket of mulch keeps soil warmer in winter and cooler in summer, prevents erosion, and doesn't allow the soil surface to develop a hard crust. When heavy rain or drought causes water stress, mulch ameliorates both situations, acting as a barrier to flooding and conserving water in dry soil. Mulch suppresses weed growth and prevents soil from splashing onto leaves (and thus reduces the spread of soilborne diseases). A neat circle of mulch around newly planted trees offers a physical barrier to keep lawnmowers and string trimmers away from tender trunks. (Such trunk damage is one of the leading causes of death for young trees.) Mulch also makes a garden look neater than it does with just bare soil.

What Is Mulch?

Mulch can be any material, organic or inorganic, that covers the soil's surface. Popular organic mulches include hardwood barks (ground, shredded, or nuggets), pine and wheat straws, shredded leaves and leaf mold, and shredded newsprint and other papers. Your excess grass clippings also make a great mulch, provided you let them age a week or so (until they're no longer hot) before using, so they don't burn plants. Organic mulches are especially beneficial, because they gradually break down and enrich the soil, gently providing nutrients to your plants.

If you can find a source of free organic material in your area—peanut hulls, ground-up corncobs, waste from an old cotton gin, or similar materials—so much the better. At one place I lived, I had a friend who was a high school industrial arts teacher, and several times a year he brought me enormous bags of sawdust, left over from his students' projects. After I let the sawdust rot, it became a wonderful no-cost mulch.

And, of course, don't overlook rotted leaves as excellent free mulch. I've often wondered why some homeowners lug bags of leaves to the curb in fall, then, in spring, turn around and spend money to buy bags and bales of mulch material from a nursery.

Inorganic mulches can be made from pea gravel, crushed lava rock, marble chips, crushed pottery shards, and clear or black plastic. Also available in garden centers to be used as mulch are rolls

Distributing pine straw mulch

of landscape fabric, which looks like a thick cloth. Both plastic and landscape fabric need to be covered with a layer of an organic mulch for appearance's sake, unless used in the vegetable garden.

In general, organic mulches are best around your yard's ornamental plantings. Black plastic and some landscape fabrics can prevent air, water, and nutrients from readily reaching the roots of your plants. They also cause shallow root growth, which makes the plants more susceptible to drought. And they're messy when they need to be replaced in a few years.

Because pea gravel and other stone mulches are difficult to move if you decide you don't like the way they look, you may want to try them in a small spot first. They're ideal, however, for pathways and other permanent areas, because they don't rot or float away.

Beyond practical considerations, you may want to think about what different mulch materials offer the landscape aesthetically. The color and texture of many mulches can be attractive and offer contrast to green plants and lawns. Used on walkways and paths, mulch should provide a comfortable walking surface in addition to weed control to high-traffic areas. Mulch adds definition to planting areas and can be extended to neatly cover thinning lawn areas under trees. Mulch also works as a landscape-unifying element—use the same mulch material throughout the garden to tie diverse plantings together visually and also reduce maintenance.

Mulch Dos and Don'ts

- When planting new trees and shrubs, apply mulch to a depth of about 3 inches (3 to 5 inches for pine needles, which quickly compress).
- Replenish mulch around perennials each year when tending established beds in spring or fall.
- Use pine straw to mulch plantings on slopes or hills, where other mulches may be washed away in hard rains.
- Don't pile mulch up against a plant's stem or trunk; that can cause damage. Instead, start spreading mulch about 2 inches away from the plant (6 inches away from a tree or shrub).
- Don't pile mounds of mulch around trees; it's not good for them.
- When setting out small bedding plants, you may find it easier to mulch the entire bed first, and then dig individual holes, rather than to try to spread mulch evenly around tiny seedlings.
- Don't spread mulch over weed-infested ground, thinking it will kill the weeds. Generally, they'll pop right through. Instead, weed before mulching.

- Add to the organic mulch around each plant yearly, 9 to 12 months after you originally mulched. Think of this mulch renewal not as a chore, but as a garden job that pays rich dividends.
- In fall always add more mulch around plants that may be damaged by an extra-cold winter.
- Wait until the soil has reliably warmed up (usually in May) before mulching heat-loving plants, such as perennial hibiscus, caladium, and Madagascar periwinkle. If they're mulched too early, the soil will remain cool and they'll get off to a very slow start.
- If the ground stays wet all the time, don't mulch; it only aggravates the situation.
- Don't overdo the mulch. More than 4 or 5 inches of mulch may prevent water and air from penetrating to the soil below.

Compost

Compost is a boon to your garden, your pocketbook, and the environment. It's one of the simplest and least expensive ways to add nutrients to your garden. And it puts yard and kitchen waste to good use, while also keeping it out of landfills.

Making compost can be as simple as piling up autumn's leaf harvest and leaving it behind the shrubs until it decomposes over the next year or so. The result will either be leaf mold (the leaves have rotted, but pieces are still distinguishable) or true compost, which has no distinct leaves remaining.

Better compost comes by mixing other organic materials with the leaves, then aerating and moistening the pile. In warm weather and with less than an hour's attention each week, a 3-foot pile of leaves can produce about 2 gallons of screened compost in fewer than three months. The average backyard composter builds a pile, tends it once a month, and has compost in six months. The choice is yours—slow and steady, or tending the pile for faster results.

Bins for making compost are available commercially and offer the advantage of being attractive and self-contained—a definite plus in many neighborhoods. But almost any material can be used to

Compost "ingredients" (grass clippings, kitchen scraps, newspaper, and dried leaves)

make a compost container so long as it holds a pile about 3 feet square (the smallest size that consistently heats up well), allows air and water to pass through, and offers some way to turn the pile. Wooden slats, rings of wire fencing, or recycled wooden pallets make practical and inexpensive compost bins. I've even used tomato cages made from concrete reinforcing wire.

Be a good neighbor about your pile. Many people put their compost at the far reaches of their yard, right up against the property line—next to the neighbor's yard. If you don't want to look at it, your neighbor won't either. Try moving it to a site that's handier for scooping out the compost and screen the bin with shrubs or vines to improve its appearance.

Care and Feeding of Compost

Yard materials appropriate for composting—besides fallen leaves—include lawn clippings (as long as the grass hasn't been treated with chemicals); frost-killed annuals, perennials, and vegetable plants; and rotting or damaged fruits or vegetables. Woody materials (pruned stems and branches from shrubs and trees) can be used in limited amounts if they're ground up. Small pieces always compost faster. Whenever possible, chop and shred materials before adding them to the pile.

The ideal ratio of materials for compost is two parts "brown" (or high carbon) material (such as leaves, hay, straw, sawdust, and chopped cornstalks) to one part green (or high nitrogen) material (such as kitchen scraps, grass clippings, fresh leaves blown down in a storm, fresh weeds, and fresh manure). This allows the material to decompose at an optimum rate. Layer the materials brown/green/brown and repeat. At every foot of height, sprinkle on a cup of good garden soil and half a cup of organic nitrogen to inoculate, or start, the pile "cooking." Kitchen debris—from vegetable trimmings to egg shells and coffee grounds—make excellent additions to the pile. Keep a stick handy and bury those wet materials deep in the compost pile. A good size for a pile is 4 feet high by 3 to 4 feet wide.

The composting process depends on organic materials working together in the presence of microorganisms and minimal amounts of nitrogen and water to produce heat. Active compost can measure up to 150 degrees Fahrenheit or higher at the center of the pile. This heating action sterilizes many pests, but there are still materials to leave out of the compost pile because they don't break down completely or they adversely affect the finished product. Avoid these materials in compost piles: animal waste, including cat litter; meat of any sort, raw or cooked; weeds with seedheads attached; diseased plant debris; and lawn clippings recently sprayed with weed-control products. Also, don't try to compost things—meat scraps, for example—that will attract rats or cause dogs to dig in the pile.

Tending the pile is a simple matter of turning the compost with a spading fork to aerate the mixture. A two-bin system simplifies this task (the gardener moves the mix from one bin into the other and back again), but so long as the compost is turned over or into another pile even briefly, aeration is accomplished. In the absence of regular rainfall, water the pile occasionally to keep it moist.

Occasionally, a pile that is left unturned or is built with excessive fresh, green matter will develop the unpleasant odor of anaerobic bacteria at work; turn the compost immediately and add some dry brown material or a sprinkling of horticultural lime to control the smell.

If you can't make enough compost for all your needs, purchasing bagged compost has three advantages. First, it is readily available on demand; unlike waiting for the backyard pile to mature, you can purchase bagged products at the garden center. Second, the material is consistent and thus reliable in its performance. Finally, bagged products have been analyzed for fertilizer content more precisely than homemade composts. That information reveals what nutrients will be available to growing plants and what additional fertilizer elements to add for balanced soil fertility.

A free alternative is the compost offered by some communities that collect yard and park waste, shredded tree trimmings, and so forth, let them rot, and give the end product to residents.

Pruning

While winter, when plants are dormant, is often seen as the ideal time to prune, both late and early spring are also good times to prune some plants.

General Pruning Guidelines

- Prune spring-flowering shrubs and trees as soon as they finish blooming.
- Prune shrubs that flower after July 1 in late winter or early spring.
- Prune broadleaf evergreens whenever their stems and branches are not frozen. December is an excellent time, as you may use prunings for holiday decorations.
- Prune berry-producing shrubs after the berries are gone.

Pruning with hand pruners

What to Prune in Early Spring

- Summer-flowering shrubs and trees that bloom on new growth
- Roses (hybrid teas, grandifloras, polyanthas, miniatures, and shrub roses)
- Winter damage from all shrubs and trees
- Shrubs that produce berries

What to Prune in Late Spring

- Spring-flowering shrubs
- Hedges (by shearing)

Pruning with long-handled loppers

Start pruning a tree by undercutting from beneath the limb with your bow saw or chain saw.

Finish the cut from above. This keeps the bark from tearing when the limb breaks loose.

Trim the stub from the limb so it's flush with the branch collar.

What to Prune in Summer

- Climbing or rambling roses (after flowering)
- Dogwood, maple, walnut, and yellowwood trees
- Hedges (by shearing)

What to Prune in Fall

- Trim back any extra-long rose canes that would whip in the wind over winter

What to Prune in Winter

- Shrubs with berries and evergreen shrubs for holiday decoration (if desired)
- Deciduous trees (except those noted under "Summer")

Pruning Roses

Start all rose pruning by cutting back diseased, deformed, broken, or winterkilled canes and stems. Also remove all stems that are smaller than the diameter of a pencil and all crisscrossing canes. Cut off any growth that's coming from beneath the bud union. Many roses are grafted onto the rootstock of another type of rose, usually one that's a vigorous grower. If different roses suddenly appear on your bush, they're from the rootstock and the canes on which they're growing should be removed immediately; otherwise, they will take over.

Always use clean, sharpened pruners or loppers, and make your cuts at a 45-degree angle about ¼ inch above an outward-facing swollen bud. The angle of the cut will help prevent the cane from rotting, and cutting above a bud that faces the outside of the bush will direct new growth in that direction. (Discourage growth toward the interior of the bush since it interferes with the air circulation that helps keep fungus diseases at bay.)

Seal the ends of all canes after pruning with shellac, white glue, candle wax, or commercial sealant. This prevents borers from getting into the canes and causing considerable damage.

When you finish pruning a hybrid tea rose, you should have three to six good-sized canes that are evenly spaced in a vase shape. Leave them about 18 to 24 inches tall. On floribundas and grandifloras, the rule of thumb is to cut the canes back to about half the size they were the previous summer. Or you may leave the canes about 24 inches high. If you have a lot of miniature roses, it's okay to save time and prune them with hedge shears after flowering.

When to Prune

- Prune hybrid teas, floribundas, shrub roses, miniatures, polyanthas, and species roses in early spring, about two months before you expect the first blooms (i.e., March 15 for flowers by May 15). Then remove faded flowers and prune back lightly after each blooming.
- Don't begin pruning climbing roses and ramblers until they're at least two to three years old. After that, prune as necessary after they finish blooming to keep them in-bounds.
- Prune shrub or old garden roses lightly to shape or shorten vigorous growth right after they finish flowering. If they bloom several times during the season, remove faded flowers and prune as needed after each flush of blossoms.

Blackspot

Pests and Diseases

Most gardeners see bugs as "the enemy." Sometimes that's true, but sometimes it isn't. Beneficial insects, such as ladybugs and praying mantis, often control other insects that do cause damage in the garden. (This is an area in which scientists—and home gardeners—are learning more.)

Applying deer repellent

In the not-so-distant past, the main decision about pest control was: Do I use an organic method, or do I spray with a chemical? Now, even those who don't consider themselves strictly organic gardeners may not pick up an insecticide from the start of the growing season until the end. There are so many other effective controls available that spraying may not be necessary.

There is often a simple solution for the problem, such as picking bagworms off shrubs by hand in the evening after the caterpillars have returned "home," or using physical barriers such as floating row covers to block insects' access to plants. Another example is placing tulip bulbs in a "cage" made of chicken wire so that moles and field mice can't dig them up.

An Ounce of Prevention

One solution that's often overlooked is prevention. If you keep lawn mowers and string trimmers away from the trunks of dogwoods, for instance, you probably won't have to worry about dogwood borers. And if you seal the ends of the canes (with white glue, shellac, or commercial sealant) when you prune roses, rose borers won't be able to tunnel into the stems.

But the biggest preventative of all is a healthy plant that's been placed in the conditions it prefers (sun or shade, moist or dry soil). A plant that needs sun isn't going to grow well in shade, and if you put a plant that needs well-drained soil in a spot that rarely dries out, the plant may develop root rot and die. If a plant is watered regularly and receives the nutrients it needs, insects and diseases are much less likely to be a problem.

Some plants are more susceptible to insects and diseases than others. The majority of plants listed in this book are seldom targets for insects or diseases. That's one reason they're included; few of us want to spend our time in the garden fighting pests. But that doesn't mean you have to avoid plants that are subject to a particular insect or disease. Instead, look for disease-resistant varieties of those plants. Find these by reading catalog and label descriptions, and ask knowledgeable gardeners, as well as nursery personnel. Why grow garden phlox, zinnias, and bee balm that look awful halfway through the summer because of powdery mildew when you can find cultivars that rarely develop it? Similarly, don't choose a rose just because it has a pretty flower; make sure it's resistant to blackspot—then you won't be spending your summer with a sprayer in your hands.

Cleanliness Is Next To . . .

Gardening practices can also make a big difference as to whether or not plants are free of diseases and insects. If you use a hose or overhead sprinkler to water plants that are subject to mildew, blackspot, and other fungal diseases, the wet leaves will probably become diseased. But if you water at the base of the plants (such as with soaker hoses), you may be able to prevent fungus problems.

In the same way, if a rose develops blackspot and sheds the affected leaves, the fungus spores will stay in the ground litter to trouble the plant again the next year—unless you rake up all the diseased leaves and remove them from the garden.

I recall a business management technique called "Managing by Walking Around." What it meant was that there was no substitute for what a manager saw and learned on daily visits to all parts of a company or office. This also applies to gardeners. Most good growers walk through their yards, looking at their plants, once a day or at least once a week. If something is wrong, they quickly notice and take care of it before it gets out of hand. (All insects and diseases, as well as weeds, are more easily controlled if caught early.)

Using Caution with Chemicals

No specific chemical controls are mentioned in this book, because the recommended products change frequently. Old products are taken off the market as new ones are developed. This is also true of organic products. Your local office of the Extension service will have the most up-to-date advice on any plant problem. Personnel at a good nursery often can point you to an effective control also.

But you have to do your part. You've heard it a million times, but how often do you actually read every word on the label of a pesticide? It's the smart thing to do—yes, even if it is an organic product—and it can save you from making mistakes. When you follow label instructions that tell you not to spray the product if temperatures are above 85 degrees Fahrenheit, for example, you can avoid needlessly damaging your plants. You'll learn some products are toxic to bees and, therefore, shouldn't be sprayed until dusk, when honeybees aren't likely to be in the garden. You'll also discover that insecticidal soap and horticultural oil are toxic to fish, so they shouldn't be used near a water garden.

Common Pests in Tennessee and Kentucky

Some problems pop up over and over in Tennessee and Kentucky gardens. Here are the most common insect and disease problems that you'll face, along with some possible solutions.

Insects

APHIDS

Description: Tiny, pear-shaped, juice-sucking insects (⅛- to ¼-inch long) that are found on new growth.
Signs: Foliage and flowers (particularly roses) may look distorted; plants become weakened. They exude a sticky, sweet substance on the plants (called honeydew), which attracts ants.
Prevention: Stop fertilizing. On roses, shrubs, or trees that have had continuing problems with aphids, spray with dormant oil in winter. Introduce ladybugs or green lacewings into the garden.
Control: Knock aphids off plants with a strong blast of water from the hose. Spray with insecticidal soap. (Both methods may need to be repeated.)

Aphids attacking leaf

BAGWORMS

Description: Caterpillars that reside inside a tiny conical-shaped brown bag that, in small numbers, look as though they are part of the needled evergreen on which they're found.
Signs: Little brown bags that resemble small pinecones; defoliated shrub or tree needles.
Prevention: None.
Control: In early evening, pick off and destroy all the bags you can find. Do this several nights in a row, because it's difficult to see them all. Afterward, check the affected shrub or tree (and those nearby) once a week. You can also spray with *Bacillus thuringiensis* (Bt), although you have to be sure the caterpillars are in the bags before spraying—they are usually "out" during the day.

CATERPILLARS

Description: There are many different caterpillars that munch their way through your yard. Remember, though, that caterpillars are future butterflies or moths, and decide accordingly if the damage is serious enough to warrant control.
Signs: Skeletonized leaves. Usually you will see the caterpillars, if you look carefully.
Prevention: None.
Control: Handpick them off. Spray with Bt.

JAPANESE BEETLES

Description: A ½-inch beetle with a metallic green coat and copper-colored wings. They emerge from the ground in late spring and return to the soil in late summer.

Signs: Groups of beetles; flowers and foliage eaten away.

Prevention: Kill the grubs, in the soil, that become beetles. Provide some shade (Japanese beetles are worse in full sun). Spread milky spore, *Bacillus papillae*, on the lawn to kill the larvae. (This is relatively expensive and takes several years to be fully effective, but one treatment lasts up to fifteen years. Best results are obtained when your neighbors use milky spore too.)

Control: Handpick beetles. Do **not** put up traps.

SCALE

Description: Small brown bumps on stems, leaves, or bark. Some have soft coatings; others have a hard coating that is difficult to penetrate with insecticides.

Signs: Leaves or needles turn yellow, then brown. A black sooty mold may be present, as well as a sticky substance called honeydew.

Prevention: Use dormant oil spray on susceptible plants in winter, and summer oil in the growing season.

Control: Scrape off scales with your fingernails, nail file, or a plastic dish scrubber. Or use light horticultural oil (sun oil) beginning in spring as growth begins and monthly throughout the growing season.

SLUGS, SNAILS

Using beer to eliminate slugs and snails

Description: Small mollusks with or without shells

Signs: Ragged holes in plant leaves and slimy trail they leave behind on the plants, the ground, and any nearby sidewalk.

Prevention: Encourage slug-eating birds to visit frequently. Put copper strips sold for slug control around containers and beds. Use prickly mulch—such as straw, cocoa hulls, or sharp stones—and save eggshells or wood ashes until you have enough to make a 2-inch barrier around plants that attract slugs and snails.

Control: Among the many ways to get rid of slugs and snails are: Apply Sluggo®, an organic slug and snail control. Wearing gloves, pick the slimy pests off plants by hand and crush underfoot. A 3- to 4-inch-wide band of lime on the ground dissolves slugs on contact (but adversely affects plants that need acid soil). Salt also dissolves slugs, but isn't good for plants, so use it only on sidewalks or driveways. Pour beer into a saucer or jar lids and place it in the garden where you've seen slug damage; remove drowned slugs each morning. Just as effective as beer is dissolving ¼ teaspoon yeast and 1 teaspoon sugar in 1 cup of water. Beer and yeast are most effective the first two days they're placed out. During rainy spells, use covered slug and snail traps sold at garden centers instead of jar lids, so your beer or yeast bait doesn't get diluted.

SPIDER MITES

Description: Spider mites are so small they're often confused with dust. To know if you have them, hold a piece of white paper beneath a leaf as you shake it; if dots show up on the paper, they're mites.

Signs: Speckled or yellowed leaves; buds that dry out instead of opening.

Prevention: Water plants regularly—particularly those in hot, dry locations—and hose down the foliage of susceptible plants weekly.

Control: Hit the undersides of leaves with a hard blast of water from the hose. Repeat as needed. Introduce ladybugs or green lacewings into the garden.

TENT CATERPILLARS

Description: These 2-inch-long blue-and-black caterpillars build white, gauzy nests where tree branches join the trunk.

Signs: You will see the tents before you notice any damage.

Prevention: Check the bark or twigs of fruit trees, ornamental fruit trees, and other susceptible plants in winter for egg masses and remove them.

Control: Remove caterpillars by hand (always wear gloves); spray nests in early evening with Bt (caterpillars leave the nests during the day). Do not burn the tents; this can harm the tree.

THRIPS

Description: Thrips are almost too tiny to see with the eye. They suck juices from foliage and flowers.
Signs: Leaf surface becomes silvery or bronzed and may be speckled; flowers are distorted or don't open; black flecks may appear on the undersides of leaves.
Prevention: Keep plants well watered and hose the foliage weekly (except on plants such as roses and zinnias, which develop mildew easily).
Control: Place sticky yellow traps (available at garden centers) near infested plants. Pick off affected flowers and remove them from the garden. Introduce beneficial insect predators, such as parasitic wasps or green lacewings.

WHITEFLIES

Description: Tiny, white flying insects.
Signs: When you brush against an infected plant, a cloud of whiteflies arises. Leaves may turn dappled yellow, and then curl up. You may notice a sticky substance on the foliage that turns black.
Prevention: No prevention.
Control: Place yellow sticky traps (available at garden centers) near infested plants. Hose down with a strong blast of water; spray with insecticidal soap or horticultural oil; or introduce natural enemies, such as parasitic wasps or green lacewings.

Diseases

BLACKSPOT

Description: Round black spots on leaves, and sometimes rose canes, caused by a fungus.
Symptoms: Spots increase; leaves turn yellow and fall off. (Leaves will grow back, but repeated loss and regrowth weakens the bush.)
Prevention: Plant roses that are resistant to blackspot. Grow them in full sun. Don't use sprinklers or other watering systems that splash water on leaves. In late fall, rake up and remove from the garden all leaves and mulch at the base of affected plants; replace with fresh, clean mulch. Spray plants with lime sulfur in winter. Grow plants farther apart to improve air circulation.
Control: Use a fungicide. (Note than some organic fungicides will burn leaves if used at what are normal summer temperatures in our area.)

Leaves with blackspot

POWDERY MILDEW

Description: White or gray splotches that eventually, if not checked, cover leaves and buds.
Symptoms: New growth is stunted; flowers may not open or will be covered with mildew.
Prevention: Plant mildew-resistant cultivars. Water at the base of the plant, so leaves don't get wet. Improve air circulation. Give plants more sun. Remove affected plant parts from the garden.
Control: Spraying Neem and potassium bicarbonate may help. Some gardeners also have had success with a homemade mixture of 1 tablespoon baking soda and 1 to 1½ tablespoons sun oil (sometimes called light horticultural oil) mixed in a gallon of water and sprayed on mildewed plants.

ROOT ROT

Description: Root rot can be the result of bacteria, a fungus, overwatering, or poor drainage.
Symptoms: Foliage, or entire plant, wilts and turns brown; stems and branches die. When plant is dug up, roots are rotting.
Prevention: Mix heavy clay soil with plenty of organic matter, such as fine bark, compost, or rotted leaves. Plant in raised beds. Don't crowd plants. Don't overfertilize. Don't buy damaged bulbs or tubers, and handle them carefully to prevent injuring them during planting. Don't replant in affected areas. Switch to plants that can tolerate wet soil.
Control: If excess water enters the area from downspouts or drainage pipes or ditches, divert the water flow and channel to other areas.

Weeds

An old saying points out the most important thing you need to know about weeds: "One year of seeds, seven years of weeds." If you let weeds go to seed, you'll have them around for years to come. For that reason, I've gone around the yard cutting off weed seedheads when I knew I wouldn't be able to weed for a few days, such as before a vacation.

Weeds Are Competitors

Weeds are the bullies of the garden. They compete with your desirable plants for water, space, sun, and nutrients. A few here and there probably won't make much difference, but if left unchecked, they can take over—making much more work for the gardener.

Like flowers, weeds may be annuals, perennials, or, occasionally, biennials. Crabgrass and chickweed are summer annuals, which sprout from seed that has lain dormant since the previous year. Henbit is a winter annual; it pops up in your yard in fall and drops its seeds over winter. Knowing this life cycle, it's easier for you to understand when it's critical to control weeds.

Perennial weeds—such as nutsedge, quackgrass, kudzu, plantain, and curly dock—are the hardest to control once mature. Get them out of the garden when they're young, and the job will be easier. If you hoe or dig weeds with deep taproots, be sure you grub out the entire thing; otherwise, the weed will sprout from even a tiny piece that was left in the ground.

Where do weeds come from? The wind may deposit them, birds drop the seeds, and you may bring them into the garden in straw mulch or fresh manure. Whenever you dig or till the soil, you bring weed seeds to the surface, where they can germinate and grow. (A thick layer of mulch can help prevent this.)

Getting Rid of Weeds

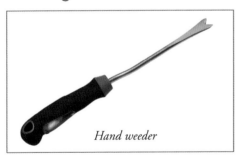

Hand weeder

Remove weeds by pulling, digging, or hoeing—it's better exercise than going to the gym! If you choose to use a chemical control, be certain that you understand how the product works (some are selective—they kill only weeds and not grasses; others kill everything they touch; still others prevent weed seeds from germinating, but don't affect weeds that are already present). Be cautious about using a fertilizer that contains weedkiller in a lawn that has trees or shrubs near. Gardeners have reported damage to good plants that absorbed the weedkiller through their roots.

Never spray a herbicide when there's the least little breeze stirring or when temperatures are high—you may damage nearby plants if you do. Also ask at your favorite full-service garden center about organic weedkillers and organic pre-emergent weed preventers. As of this writing, most organic weedkillers get rid of only the top of the plant, not the root, so they help only with annual weeds. But I think we'll see some breakthroughs.

Sowing and Starting Seeds

Thrifty gardeners enjoy growing plants from seeds—collected from plants grown the previous year, shared by friends, or purchased. If you want to get a head start on the season and have plants to set out as soon as the chance of frost has passed, you'll need to start them indoors in containers. But if you don't mind having flowers that begin blooming in midsummer, you can sow them directly in the garden where you want them to grow.

Starting Seeds Indoors

For indoor planting, use wooden or plastic flats, peat pots, cell packs, or any number of homemade containers, such as egg cartons, Styrofoam cups, or cut-down juice or milk jugs or cartons. Just about anything will work, as long as it's clean and you can punch drainage holes in the bottom. Soak used pots in a mixture of one part liquid bleach to nine parts water; rinse and then let dry for several days.

While any high-quality potting soil may be used for starting seeds, I use a commercial seed-starter potting mix because it doesn't contain perlite (which tends to float to the surface and get in the way). Always moisten the mix thoroughly with warm water at least a few hours ahead of time. Fill the container to within ½ to 1 inch from the top (leaving the larger amount of room on bigger containers) and pat down gently to level the surface.

Read the packet directions to see how deeply the seeds should be planted and if they should be covered or not (a few seeds require light to germinate). The packet will also tell you about how long it will take the seeds to grow into plants large enough to go outdoors into the garden. If it says eight weeks, then count back from your average date of last frost to see the best time to sow the seeds. Doing it too early generally leads to leggy plants (those that are tall and spindly) instead of the desired short and stocky.

Scatter the seeds evenly over the surface of the potting mix, or scratch light furrows or rows into the soil and sow the seeds in those.

Buy seed-starting tray kits at garden centers or home-improvement stores. Plant one or two seeds per section of the seed starting tray. Cover the seed starting tray with the plastic lid or with clear plastic wrap. Check the seeds as they're sprouting. If the top of the soil is dry, mist the sprouts or very lightly water them. When they have two or more sets of "true leaves," transplant them into larger containers.

Cover with clean builder's sand, press down gently, and then water lightly. Some gardeners like to cover the flat or container with plastic until the seeds germinate. Place the container where the temperature is about 70 degrees Fahrenheit. In a house that's kept cooler, try putting a few seed containers on top of a water heater or refrigerator. (You can also buy special heating mats to place under flats that will keep the soil warm.) Don't let the soil dry out, but don't let it get soggy either.

When the seeds sprout and start growing, give them strong light (from sun or fluorescent fixtures left on twelve to fourteen hours a day). Wait until they've developed their second set of true leaves (these will look different from the first set of leaves that develop) and transplant them into individual containers of moist potting soil into which you've poked small holes for the plants. Use a spoon or fork to gather up the small seedlings and place them in their new homes. If you have to touch the seedlings (to separate those that have become intertwined), always hold them by the leaves, never the stem—which can easily be crushed and kill the young plant. Again, keep the soil in the individual containers moist and provide plenty of light for the plants. Temperatures may be cooler than those needed for seed germination. Use water-soluble fertilizer at half-strength every other week.

Transplant seedlings into the garden as you would purchased bedding plants, after the chance of frost has passed—unless the plant is hardy and able to withstand cold weather.

Sowing Seeds Outdoors

In mid to late spring after the weather is warm, prepare a plot of ground by removing all weeds and grass; then till or dig the soil 8 inches deep. Add soil amendments (see pages 17–18) and granular or pelleted fertilizer, if desired, and till or mix again. Smooth the top of the soil, and water well. Wait a day before planting.

To make rows, scratch a line in the soil with the corner of a hoe. Drop the seeds in the row, trying to space them evenly. Next, using the hoe or your hands, pull a small amount of soil over the seeds (cover so that they're no deeper than twice the diameter of the seed). Firm the soil and water gently. When seedlings appear, thin them by pulling out the ones that are growing too close to others. If you didn't mix fertilizer with the soil before planting, feed the young plants after they have six leaves. Spread fertilizer no closer than 1 inch from the stems, and follow label instructions for the amount to use.

The easiest flowers to grow from seeds sown outdoors are cleome, cosmos, marigold, and zinnia. Many vegetables that have large seeds—beans, peas, cucumbers, melons, and squash, for example—are also very easy to start from seeds planted where they are to grow. Planting from seed is fun for both kids and adults.

Made in the Shade: Plants for Shady Spots

The two main things to remember about shade gardening are that all shade isn't equal, and that there's no standard definition of what shade is. Maybe, in thinking about your own yard, you've become confused by terms such as dappled shade, high shade, and bright shade. Dappled shade receives spotty sunlight through the leaves of trees. Bright shade and high shade refer to areas that receive no direct sunlight, but are brightly lit (in the case of high shade, because tree limbs have been removed to a height of 10 feet or more). Dense shade is heavy shade, such as beneath evergreen trees with low limbs.

A Note of Caution: Invasive Plants

No one wants to introduce a plant that's going to become a nuisance in his own yard or in the larger environment—remember kudzu!—so here are some things that are good to know about invasive plants.

According to the federal government, an invasive species is defined as "an alien species whose introduction does or is likely to cause economic or environmental harm or harm to human health." It is also defined as "a species that is non-native to the ecosystem under consideration and whose introduction causes or is likely to cause economic or environmental harm or harm to human health."

Each state has a group that determines the invasive plants within that state. The Kentucky Exotic Pest Plant Council and the Tennessee Exotic Pest Plant Council have online lists of alien plants that they consider invasive. The Tennessee organization also has an "alert" list of plants that have not been determined to be invasive in the state but may possibly become so. Its members will be gathering more information to make a determination, so you may want to think of it as a "caution" or "watch" list if you're considering buying any of the plants on the list. A person may use the word "invasive" to describe a plant that aggressively broadens its range, either by seeds or by spreading roots. But these may happen only in a specific region or in particular growing conditions. So if you hear or read that a plant is invasive or "takes over," see if it's on the lists of our states' exotic pest plant councils. A plant that's invasive in California or Maine often isn't in Kentucky or Tennessee.

Since common names can be misleading, find the correct botanical name when you're trying to determine invasiveness. (Out West, "ice plants" of one species are highly invasive; of another species, they're well behaved.)

Sometimes, botanists and horticulturists determine or believe that hybrids or cultivars of a plant may not become invasive, while the straight species is. That can get confusing for a layman, but I tend to go with what experts I trust say on the subject. (As an example, see page 183 for the plant profile of *Miscanthus*.)

But all this can change; plants that weren't invasive before can become so. It's a good idea to keep up with this issue so you can avoid having a plant bully in your yard or trying to take over nearby natural areas.

How to Use the *Tennessee & Kentucky Garden Guide*

Each plant profile in this guide provides you with information about the plant's unique characteristics, habits, and its basic requirements for active growth, as well as my personal experience and knowledge of it. All the information you need for landscape success is covered. You will find details such as mature height and spread, bloom period and colors (if any), sun and soil preferences, water requirements, fertilizing needs, pruning and care, and pest information.

Sun Preferences

Symbols represent the range of sunlight suitable for each plant. Full sun means full sun, all day, with the possible exception of an hour of shade in the morning or afternoon. Mostly sun is about six hours of direct sun during the day or four or five hours of only afternoon sun. Part shade is dappled shade or high shade with five or fewer hours of morning sun (three or fewer in the afternoon). Full shade is mostly shade all the time. Some plants can be grown in more than one range of sun, so you will sometimes see more than one sun symbol. The symbols are placed in order of my recommendation of sun exposure.

| Full Sun | Mostly Sun | Part Shade | Full Shade |

Additional Benefits

Many plants offer benefits that further enhance their appeal. The following symbols indicate some of the more important additional benefits:

 Attracts Butterflies, Moths, and/or Bees

 Bullet-Proof (resistant to adverse conditions, including drought)

 Attracts Hummingbirds

 Native Plant

 Produces Edible Fruit

 Good Fall Color

Garden Design

For most of the featured plants, I will share some design ideas, as well as suggestions for companion plants to help you achieve striking results from your garden. Landscape design is where many will find great enjoyment.

Try These

This section describes those specific cultivars or varieties that I have found particularly noteworthy. Give them a try, or perhaps you'll find your own favorites.

USDA Hardiness Zone Map

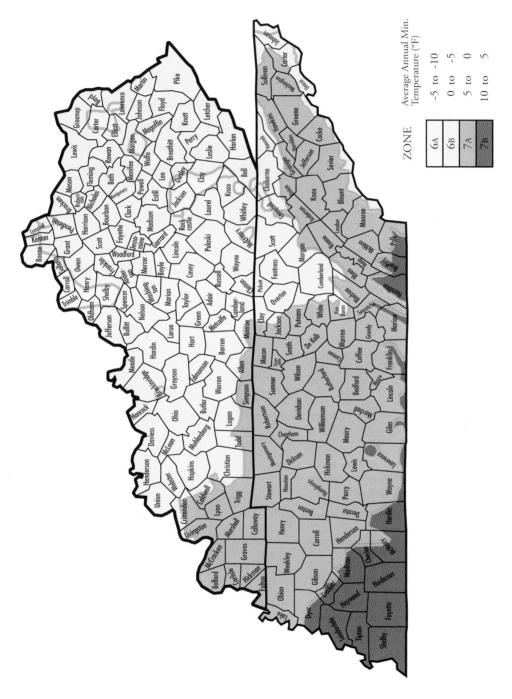

USDA Plant Hardiness Zone Map. 2012. Agricultural Research Service, U.S. Department of Agriculture. Accessed from http://planthardiness.ars.usda.gov.

USDA Hardiness Zones

Cold-hardiness zones indicate the minimum average temperature for an area. A zone assigned to an individual plant indicates the lowest temperature at which the plant can be expected to survive over the winter. All plants featured in this book will grow well in all our zones, unless noted otherwise.

Annuals

Annuals are the cheerful, uncomplaining workhorses of the garden. Most bloom or produce colorful foliage continually from spring until frost, asking only for regular watering, occasional feeding, and—sometimes, but not always—picking off old flowers as they fade.

Long-Lasting and Versatile Beauty

It's true that annuals—unlike perennials, shrubs, or trees—must be replanted every year, since they live out their life cycle in a season. But those other plants don't bloom as long as annuals do. So most gardeners feel that the extra effort of annual planting is worth it in return for such long-lasting and versatile beauty—in flower beds and borders, by the mailbox, in containers on decks, porches and patios, and wherever you'd like reliable and colorful flowers.

Celosia (Celosia)

Some annuals are perfect for those hot, sunny places in your yard. Others delight in the relative coolness beneath a shade tree. A few, wax begonia is a good example, will be happy in sun, shade, or anything in between. There are even annuals that are grown just in the cool-weather months.

When you shop for annuals, you'll find some types that will trail over the edges of pots, others that give off a pleasant perfume, some (such as coleus) that are grown more for their intriguing foliage than for flowers, tropical plants that laugh at the hottest temperatures summer can produce, and more flower and foliage colors than in a rainbow. That usefulness is why every landscape needs annuals.

Before You Buy Plants

Success with annuals starts with the proper selection. When choosing annuals to beautify your yard, here's what you need to think about before you head to the garden center:

- **Planting conditions:** Check the light, soil, and moisture conditions in the place where you plan to plant. Most annuals are sun lovers, so if your yard contains many trees, look for the ones that prefer shady spots. Also pay attention to areas where the soil stays particularly dry or wet. While some annuals won't be happy in those conditions, you'll find a number of

Begonia (Begonia) in a container

attractive and easy-to-grow plants that tolerate or even like those types of soil. Only a few annuals will grow in poor soil, so to enhance your chances of success, mix organic matter with the soil you have. (See pages 17–18.)

- **Color:** Choose colors that coordinate with your house (maybe matching the shade that the shutters are painted) or other plantings in the yard. Among other choices, some gardeners like to plant beds that contains different types of flowers in only one color (an all-blue, all-red, all-yellow, and so forth garden). Some people prefer to stick with pastel shades, while others enjoy a combination of hot colors (orange, yellow, gold). Growing annuals is a good way to enjoy your favorite colors outdoors. But don't get so carried away with color that you forget to watch such combinations as gold marigolds and red-flowered annuals such as salvia, which generally clash. White and light colors are especially good in areas where you can see them in the evening—around patios, for instance. Groups of plants in a single color have a more sophisticated and polished look than a mixture, which may have one red bloom, one pink, one yellow, and so forth.

- **Mature height:** Most annuals sold today are short—a foot tall or less. To add interest to your flower beds, search out plants that grow smaller or taller than that, placing the taller ones near the backs of the beds and the dwarf varieties toward the front.

- **Cut flowers:** Gardeners grow annuals because they look good in the garden for a long time. But the flowers of many annuals are easily cut and brought indoors to be enjoyed in vases and arrangements. If you don't like the idea of removing flowers from prominent spots in the yard, plant a special cutting garden in an out-of-the-way spot.

What Next?

When you buy annuals, look for strong stems, and peek beneath leaves for any signs of insects. Check the plant's roots—you should be able to see them, but roots shouldn't completely cover the soil in a thick web (this is called being rootbound, and it prevents plants from adapting well to their new home).

If the bedding plants you bought were growing in a greenhouse, they'll need to be "hardened off" before planting. This is the process of acclimating plants to outdoor conditions. (If annuals are taken from a warm, humid greenhouse, where they are protected from the elements, and suddenly have to contend with wind, cold, and full sun, they *will* struggle.) First, place the plants in a shaded, sheltered spot during the day, bringing them indoors at night if outdoor temperatures are predicted to fall below 50 degrees Fahrenheit. Then gradually increase their exposure to sun and other natural conditions until they're ready to live outside. This may take a week in mild weather or up to two weeks if nights remain cool.

It's difficult for most people to believe, but annuals that haven't yet started blooming when you buy them are a better bet to be successful in your garden than plants that are flowering like crazy. The reason is that in order to ensure the best summer-long performance, the young plants need to develop good root systems. If they're putting their energy into producing flowers instead, root growth (so important as the basis of later plant and flower growth) suffers. Many experts suggest pinching off flowers and buds just before you plant.

*Annual ornamental cabbage (*Brassica oleracea*) interplanted with perennial mums pair well in garden designs.*

Now You're Ready to Plant

Few of us have what could be considered ideal soil. Maybe your soil is rocky and alkaline, or hard clay that's difficult to penetrate except with a pick. Most annuals are going to have a difficult time living up to their potential in those kinds of situations. But you can help them by tilling or digging the soil about a foot deep and mixing organic matter, such as finely shredded pine bark, rotted leaves, peat moss, or compost, into the top 8 inches of soil before planting.

The best times to plant annuals are in early evening and on cloudy days. Several hours before you plan to plant, water the plants and the soil in the flower bed thoroughly. Place the plants in the ground at the same depth they grew in the pots, spacing them as recommended on the label. In hot weather, you may

Celosia (Celosia) closeup

need to provide some shading for a few days, to protect the young seedlings. And remember that those tiny root systems will need frequent watering for the first few weeks after planting; they simply aren't big enough in the beginning to fend for themselves. That's true even of plants touted as "drought-tolerant."

How to Start Annual Plants from Seed

Starting bedding plants from seed instead of buying them is fun, and you can grow intriguing plants that may not be carried in local garden stores. Read the seed packet to see how soon seeds need to be started before the date they are to be set outdoors. For a typical annual, it's usually six to eight weeks. But seeds of some popular annuals—such as geranium, Madagascar periwinkle, and wax begonia—need at least three to four months to germinate and grow to a good size.

The first step is to count back from the average last frost date in your area and write down when you need to start various types of seeds. Then don't start them before that date. Seeds that grow too long indoors are likely to get leggy. See page 37 for specific advice.

Care of annuals is simple. Even a child can do it. Just water regularly, fertilize occasionally (frequently for plants in containers, because nutrients are washed out the bottom of the pot by repeated watering), keep weeds pulled out, and remove faded flowers if they don't fall off by themselves. Pinching off blossoms that are past their prime is important not just for neatness, but because it causes the plants to bloom more and longer.

Annuals are a joy because they give you an almost instant flower garden and—best of all—an easy-to-grow garden filled with spectacular color for months on end.

Ageratum

Ageratum houstonianum

There are many reasons that blue blooms are greatly appreciated in the flower garden. Often, though, they aren't easy to find. What to do if you want to create a red, white, and blue flower bed? Look to ageratum, or floss flower. It's available in two sizes. Low-growing cultivars, which form a neat mound, are perfect to edge those patriotic beds where you've planted red and white annuals. Taller ageratum cultivars (24 to 30 inches high) often aren't available as bedding plants but can be grown from seed and make nice cut flowers. Ageratum is deer resistant. Its main drawback is that it stops blooming in high temperatures, but, if you remove the spent flowers, it reblooms when the weather cools.

Botanical Pronunciation
ah-jer-AY-tum hous-tone-ee-AN-um

Bloom Period and Seasonal Color
Summer flowers of blue, pink, white, or lavender

Mature Height × Spread
5 to 30 inches × 6 to 16 inches

When, Where, and How to Plant
Experienced gardeners can start ageratum from tiny seeds indoors in a warm room (70 to 75 degrees Fahrenheit) eight to ten weeks before the average last frost. Or buy bedding plants. When all chance of frost is past, plant dwarfs 6 inches apart (taller cultivars 9 to 12 inches) in well-drained soil that you've enriched with compost, peat moss, or fine pine bark. (See pages 37 and 45 for more details on planting annuals.) Ageratum does better in our region when given morning sun and afternoon shade rather than being grown in full sun.

Growing Tips
Regular watering is the key to keeping ageratum blooming. Never let the soil dry out. Fertilize twice a month with a water-soluble fertilizer for blooming plants or twice a season with a slow-release fertilizer for flowering plants.

Care
Keep the plants mulched to conserve moisture in the soil. If the blooms turn brown during the hottest part of summer, shear them off. New blossoms will appear when temperatures become more moderate. Watch out for spider mites, which make the leaves look grayish (see page 34 for control advice). Watch out for powdery mildew in shade. Consult the Extension service for advice.

Garden Design
I plant blue ageratum with white or pink cosmos and with clear yellow marigolds or coreopsis. A patriotic combination is white cosmos in the back, red petunias in the middle, and low-growing blue ageratum in front. A combo suggested by Proven Winners® that I've enjoyed is *Euphorbia* 'Diamond Frost', Supertunia 'Raspberry Blast', and 'Artist' blue ageratum. Taller cultivars of ageratums are excellent for flower arrangements. Try short cultivars in a rock garden.

Try These
The flowers of 'Southern Cross' are white in the center and blue on the outside. It's a good container plant. The Hawaii Series, which includes plants with white, pink, or blue flowers, is quite heat-tolerant. I especially like 'Blue Hawaii'.

Angelonia
Angelonia angustifolia

When, Where, and How to Plant
In late spring, after the soil has warmed up, plant angelonia in full sun (a little afternoon shade is fine in Zone 7). Moist but well-drained soil that contains ample organic material is ideal, but angelonia can tolerate both wet and dry soils. Space plants 12 to 14 inches apart. Because it's a heat-loving plant, angelonia can easily be planted up through midsummer, if you need to. Mix compost with the soil before planting, and add half the label-recommended amount of organic slow-release fertilizer for flowering plants or pelleted timed-release fertilizer. (See page 37 and 45 for more details on planting annuals.)

Growing Tips
Water angelonias in containers regularly when the top few inches of soil begin to dry out. Plants in beds will bloom better if watered deeply when rainfall is less than an inch a week, but mature angelonias can tolerate dryness. Fertilize plants grown in the garden and in containers about twice a month using liquid seaweed or a water-soluble fertilizer, according to package directions. Too much fertilizer causes an abundance of foliage growth and few flowers.

Care
Angelonias are very easy-care plants; the flowers don't need deadheading. Aphids may sometimes be a problem, and powdery mildew may occasionally appear (see page 35 for control advice). If it does, cut back on watering and consult the Extension service about what to do.

Garden Design
Angelonia is a long-lasting cut flower that's excellent in arrangements, so if you often bring flowers indoors, you'll want to add a few angelonia plants in various colors to a cutting garden. In the landscape, plant purple-flowered cultivars with plants of the colorful culinary herb Tricolor sage (*Salvia officinalis* 'Tricolor').

Try These
The Serena series is attractive, reliable, and disease-resistant. I especially like Serena Blue. The flowers of Angelmist Purple Stripe are quite eye-catching; the plant grows 2 feet tall. Angelface Dresden Blue has blooms with appealing color and form.

Angelonia is often called "summer snapdragon" because it's an excellent summer substitute for snapdragons, which prefer cooler weather. And if you look at the flowers closely, you'll see the resemblance between the two plants, although angelonia is showier. It's quite an addition to container gardens and flower beds, where it blooms all summer and well into fall. It's also a long-lasting cut flower. Angelonia loves hot weather and looks its best in the dog days of July and August. Mature plants are also drought-tolerant. And if that's not enough, angelonias are fragrant. Someone has compared the scent to grape soda; another says the foliage has an aroma like apples. Either way, it's a nice bonus for a great annual.

Botanical Pronunciation
an-jell-OWE-nee-uh an-gus-ti-FOE-lee-uh

Bloom Period and Seasonal Color
Flowers from spring until fall in white, pink, purple, or blue flowers

Mature Height x Spread
12 to 24 inches x 12 to 24 inches

Angel Wing Begonia
Begonia hybrids

Because I grow so many flowers in large pots, I've long considered angel wing begonia to be a heavenly container plant—always attractive, undemanding, and usually insect- and disease-free. Some have reddish leaves and others sport green leaves blotched in silver. My favorite angel wing flowers are scarlet, but you'll find plants with pink and white blossoms too; they're like the ones on wax begonias but appear in cascading clusters. Some plants of angel wing begonia grow as big as 3 feet tall and 3 feet wide, although many end up 2 feet by 2 feet, or slightly smaller. Either way, one plant will often fill an entire container. They're perfect for a shady porch, but some cultivars have been bred for full sun.

Botanical Pronunciation
bee-GO-nee-uh

Bloom Period and Seasonal Color
Flowers from spring through fall in red, pink, or white

Mature Height x Spread
1 to 3 feet x 1 to 2 feet

When, Where, and How to Plant
In spring after the last-frost date, fill a large pot or tub to within 2 inches of the rim with moistened, good-quality commercial potting soil. Mix the soil with compost, if available, and a pelleted slow-release fertilizer, according to package directions. (But first check to make sure the potting mix doesn't already contain fertilizer; some do.) Place the plant in the container at the same depth it grew in its pot and water thoroughly until the excess drains out the bottom hole. Place in a shaded or partly shaded location. Angel wings also thrive in large hanging baskets—try the big, moss-lined ones—and will grow nicely in a shady flower bed that has moist, well-drained soil. Don't crowd them; they like good air circulation.

Growing Tips
Let the top inch or two of the soil dry out between waterings. If you mixed a slow-release fertilizer with the soil at planting time, apply a second dose in midsummer. Otherwise, use a water-soluble fertilizer once a month.

Care
Mildew can be an occasional problem, often caused by too-wet weather or overwatering. If foliage develops a few leaf spots, remove the affected leaves from the plant and destroy. Mealybugs (white cottony masses) may be banished by a spray of insecticidal soap. For other problems, consult the Extension service.

Garden Design
Angel wing begonias are usually grown in containers. Mix plants that have red and white blooms, pink and white, or red and pink. Add *Euphorbia* 'Diamond Frost' or a white Supertunia (or both) to a large pot with a red-flowered angel wing.

Try These
Begonia hybrida 'Dragon Wing Red' tolerates sun as well as shade and performs beautifully not just in containers but also in flower beds. 'Dragon Wing Pink' is also heat-tolerant and has 3-inch flowers. Both are supposed to grow about 15 inches high and 12 inches wide, but mine grew larger (and therefore, more impressive).

When, Where, and How to Plant

Sow seed indoors 10 weeks before the last frost date in a sunny, moderately warm environment (65 degrees Fahrenheit). (See pages 37 and 45 for more details on starting annuals from seed.) Space seedlings or purchased plants 6 to 18 inches apart (depending on type) outdoors, after the chance of frost has passed and the soil has warmed. All types perform best in average, well-drained garden soil that receives sun all or most of the day. Add a pelleted slow-release fertilizer to the soil at planting time. (See page 45 for more tips on planting annuals.)

Growing Tips

Red salvia demands consistent moisture, wild scarlet sage likes dry soil (although it blooms better with some added moisture), and mealycups prefer to dry out between waterings. Fertilize every two weeks with liquid seaweed or a water-soluble fertilizer for flowering plants.

Care

Keep faded flower spikes picked off *Salvia splendens* so new flowers will continue to form. If you leave the bare flower stalks on the plant, cut the plant back in midsummer to encourage new growth. Pinch back mealycups after they bloom to maintain their bushy habit and keep more flowers coming. Slugs and snails may be a problem (see page 34 for advice on their control). If leafhoppers or aphids become troublesome, spray with insecticidal soap or, for severe infestations, ask the Extension service to recommend a control. *Salvia coccinea* reseeds itself, making it a perennial in your garden. If you don't want that, dig out the new plants in spring and replant elsewhere.

Garden Design

Edge a bed of red salvia with white alyssum, or plant red salvia with white Madagascar periwinkle. Plant wild scarlet sage and mealycup sage close to white roses. Give blue mealycups a home in the perennial border near yellow-flowering plants.

Try These

Salvia coccinea 'Lady in Red' is, hands down, my favorite annual. The foliage of pineapple sage (*Salvia elegans*) really does smell like fresh pineapple.

Some homeowners choose the same annuals every year because they always grow well and look good. So you may be a long-time fan of Salvia splendens, which is popularly referred to red salvia. After all, it's a good-looking, easy-care flower. But there are other salvias that you might enjoy planting. They aren't all red (look for pink, purple, blue, and white too), and the familiar spiked blooms aren't the only form. Among annual salvias, Salvia coccinea (wild scarlet sage) sports a stalk of delicate red, white, or pink blooms; and mealycup sage (Salvia farinacea, a perennial in hot climates) comes in white and shades of blue. All are simple to grow, like heat and sun, bloom until frost, and attract hummingbirds. (For perennial salvias, see page 167.)

Botanical Pronunciation

SAL-vee-ah

Bloom Period and Seasonal Color

From late spring through frost in bright red, pink, purple, salmon, blue, or creamy white

Mature Height × Spread

8 to 36 inches × 12 to 20 inches

Bat-Faced Cuphea
Cuphea llavea

What kind of a plant has the name "bat-faced"? Sounds rather dark and scary. Although another name, 'Tiny Mice' cuphea (QUE-fee-uh), is cuter, it may not be more appealing. Those are imperfect attempts to describe a spectacular flower—brilliant scarlet and beautiful purple—that's a bit of an unusual shape. But once you see the bold blooms, the common names won't matter a bit. It sure doesn't to hummingbirds and butterflies! Even nicer, bat-faced cuphea (much like the more familiar cigar plant species of cuphea) loves sun and heat and blooms from spring until frost, with no deadheading necessary. Some—but not all—cultivars are drought-tolerant. (If that's important to you, carefully read the label before you buy.)

Botanical Pronunciation
QUE-fee-uh LAY-vee-uh

Bloom Period and Seasonal Color
Spring to fall in red and purple

Mature Height x Spread
10 inches to 3 feet x 1 to 3 feet

When, Where, and How to Plant
Bat-faced cuphea prefers fertile, moist, but well-drained soil, but also grows well in containers placed in sunny spots. After chance of frost in spring, plant according to directions on page 45 and mix a slow-release fertilizer, according to package directions, with the soil when planting. Avoid soils that stay wet, because they can cause root rot. Space plants 1 to 2 feet apart. After planting in well-drained soil or in a container, mulch with 2 inches of organic matter, such as rotted leaves.

Growing Tips
Fertilize monthly during the growing season with liquid seaweed or a water-soluble fertilizer, or apply pelleted timed-release fertilizer halfway through the summer. Some cultivars are drought-tolerant, needing only occasional watering, and others need regular watering (much as you would water petunias). Read the plant label to find out what type you have and water as recommended.

Care
Deadheading isn't needed because flowers fall off on their own. Root rot will occur if the plants are overwatered or placed in poorly draining areas. If you see a white powdery-looking substance on the leaves or stems, that's powdery mildew. Consult the Extension service to ask for help. Aphids and whiteflies may also appear on the plants (see pages 33 and 35 for control advice).

Garden Design
This is a great plant for a cottage garden. In containers and beds, it's attractive near your favorite plants that have lavender, or bluish lavender, blooms—scaevola, lavender, petunias, angelonia, and so forth.

Try These
We're seeing more cultivars being introduced of this attractive, mound-forming annual. Among my favorites so far are 'Georgia Scarlet' (1 to 2 feet tall and 2 feet wide), 'Flamenco Samba' (1 to 3 feet tall and the same width), and 'Totally Tempted' (10 to 12 inches tall and about as wide). 'Tiny Mice' is drought-tolerant. 'Flamenco Rumba' has more red and less purple in the blooms; it gets about 16 inches high.

Bracted Strawflower
Bracteantha bracteata

When, Where, and How to Plant

To grow from seed, start six to eight weeks before the expected last frost. (See pages 37 and 45 for more about growing plants from seed.) Wait until May, when temperatures are reliably warm, to set out homegrown seedlings or purchased plants in a sunny location that has moist, well-drained soil. Mix a few inches of compost into the garden soil. Space the plants about a foot apart. (Page 45 has all the details on planting annuals.) If you want to fertilize at planting time, use an organic product that's low in phosphorous (the second of the three numbers on a fertilizer label), such as 5-3-3. In containers, use commercial potting soil mixed with compost.

Growing Tips

Although some bracted strawflowers are drought-tolerant, most need soil that's kept moist but not wet. Water whenever the top inch of the soil becomes dry. These plants don't need much fertilizer. An application of compost in mid-summer should be fine for those in flower beds. In containers, use liquid seaweed mixed with water twice a month.

Care

The more you pick the flowers, the more the plant blooms. There should be few insect or disease problems, with the possible exception of root rot in poorly drained soil.

Garden Design

Plant yellow-flowered bracted strawflower in a large container along with dwarf purple fountain grass, a sun-loving coleus that has variegated green leaves, and, along the rim of the pot, an ornamental sweet potato vine with either purple or lime-green foliage trailing over the edge. Or, for a colorful fall combo, plant bracted strawflower with 'Toffee Twist' carex (a short grass) and 'Sedona' coleus, which has orangish leaves. Remember to include some *Bracteantha bracteata* in the cutting garden so you have them to use in fresh or dried arrangements.

Try These

Sundaze Flame has yellow and red flowers that don't need deadheading. It grows 14 inches tall and is drought-tolerant.

When a plant is called a strawflower, you know that it's going to have daisylike blooms that are easily dried and the plants will be happiest in well-drained soil. All this is certainly true for bracted strawflower, an Australian native that's sometimes referred to as paper daisy or golden everlasting. This is a plant that loves hot weather and is a nice choice for gardens planted to attract wildlife, since it's popular with butterflies. Not only are the flowers good dried for winter arrangements, they're also long-lasting in fresh flower arrangements. Whether you cut any of the flowers or not, you'll enjoy the prolific flowering. Because of its colors and long-blooming habit, this is an excellent plant to showcase in fall containers and garden beds.

Botanical Pronunciation
brac-tee-AN-tha brac-tee-A-ta

Bloom Period and Seasonal Color
Late spring to fall in yellow, orange, pink, cream, or purple

Mature Height x Spread
14 inches to 3 feet x 10 to 24 inches

Cape Daisy
Osteospermum hybrids

Cape daisy is a cheerful, flowering plant that's native to South Africa. Its daisylike blooms are available not only in yellow but white, vivid purple, lavender, orange, white, cream, and pink. Some have intriguing "spooned" petals. For summer flowers, Cape daisy may do best in eastern Kentucky and mountainous areas elsewhere in our region. Although some of the new cultivars are more heat-tolerant than the species, many won't bloom well unless nights are cool, so those in Zones 6 and 7 may want to consider it mostly for spring and fall color, unless the plant label specifies heat-tolerant. Cape daisy has several common names, such as African daisy, which it confusingly shares with other plants, so it's best to remember the botanical name Osteospermum.

Botanical Pronunciation
ah-stee-oh-SPUR-mum

Bloom Period and Seasonal Color
Spring and fall flowers of yellow, orange, white, pink, and purple

Mature Height x Spread
6 to 14 inches x 1 to 2 feet

Zones
Zone 6a: spring-fall; Zones 6b, 7: fall and spring

When, Where, and How to Plant
Nurseries sometimes have plants of Cape daisy for sale in early fall, which is an excellent time to plant it in the warmer parts of Kentucky and Tennessee. You may also plant in spring just after the date of the expected last frost. Cape daisies need well-drained soil, so anyone with clay will need to mix it with organic matter such as finely shredded bark and rotted compost, or plant in a raised bed. Mostly sunny spots (especially in Zone 7) or areas with full sun will suit the plants best. Space plants 8 to 12 inches apart. Mix a slow-release fertilizer with the soil before you plant. (See page 45 for more details on planting annuals.)

Growing Tips
Water young plants to keep soil moist if weekly rainfall is less than an inch. After that, you may let the top inch or so of soil dry out before watering again. Fertilize monthly with a water-soluble fertilizer or liquid seaweed.

Care
Whiteflies, leaf miners, and fungal diseases may bother these plants. Get advice from the Extension service on controlling these problems. Keeping water off the foliage can help control leaf spots. Remove faded flowers.

Garden Design
When planting in containers, place the pots where viewers will be looking down on Cape daisy flowers; they're best seen from above. In spring, plant Cape daisies with snapdragons or perennial dianthus that have flowers in complementary colors; all of these plants will flower nicely in cool temperatures.

Try These
'Soprano Lilac Spoon' has amazing purple-lavender blooms as long as nighttime temperatures aren't too warm. 'Asti White' has pristine white petals with a purple center. It grows in both hot and cool summers and doesn't close its flowers at night or cloudy days. The flowers of 'Lemon Symphony' feature clear yellow petals with a blue center. It's drought-tolerant. 'Mara' is a bicolored peach selection that grows 10 inches high.

When, Where, and How to Plant

It's easy to start celosia from seed sown inside in flats or containers or outside in the garden where the plants will grow. Sow seed indoors about eight weeks before you plan to set them out; sow seed outdoors two weeks after the average last-frost date. (See pages 37 and 45 for helpful hints on seed starting.) Plants grown from seed sown outdoors won't bloom until July, but they make good replacements for purchased plants that didn't perform well. Set out nursery-bought plants after soil has warmed. Celosia likes sun and doesn't mind average, well-drained soil, although it prefers fertile soil that holds moisture but doesn't stay soggy. Space plants 9 to 12 inches apart. Mix slow-release fertilizer or an organic fertilizer for flowering plants in the planting hole.

Growing Tips

Water young plants regularly to keep the soil moist. Once they're established, little watering is needed, since celosia is relatively drought-tolerant. Fertilize twice a month with a liquid plant food.

Care

Pinching back the first flowers that appear will cause the plant to be bushier and produce more flowers, but continued pinching makes the plants top-heavy, so most people don't bother. For appearance's sake, remove the flowers as they fade. If a plant turns completely yellow, it's diseased; remove it from the bed and destroy. Otherwise, celosia should have few pests.

Garden Design

Plumed celosia adds a strong vertical accent to flower beds. Plant white petunias in front of any color celosia, or plant red celosia near the base of a white-flowered clematis.

Try These

The plumed flowers—in rose-pink, scarlet, and yellow—of Century Mix don't fade as the blooms get older. 'Fireglow' and 'Prestige Scarlet' are excellent cultivars of cockscomb; they won All-America Selections awards. Because the golden blooms of 'Fresh Look Gold' don't fade to brown, the plants look neater. 'New Look' has reddish leaves as well as red plumes.

Celosia isn't for folks who prefer pastel colors in the garden. It demands attention because of the brilliant colors of its flowers. There are three types. Most common is plumed celosia (C. argentea plumosa), well known for its spiky fire-engine red blooms (although you can also buy plants with yellow, orange, or pink blooms). Bright red also seems to be the color of choice in old-fashioned cockscomb (C. argentea cristata), which produces velvety, convoluted blooms that resemble a rooster's comb on steroids. Spiked cockscomb, also known as wheat celosia (C. spicata), grows 3 to 4 feet tall and produces numerous spikes in more muted colors. All these members of the amaranth family tolerate heat and drought and are excellent fresh or dried in flower arrangements. It may self-seed abundantly.

Botanical Pronunciation

seh-LOW-see-uh

Bloom Period and Seasonal Color

Summer to frost in red, yellow, orange, and pink

Mature Height × Spread

8 inches to 3 feet × 8 to 12 inches

Cleome
Cleome hassleriana

Annuals such as cleome had plenty of advantages for gardeners in the past. The plants were tall and made a nice row alongside the front or edge of the property. They reseeded, which meant that they came back year after year for free. The flowers were fragrant; and the plants were no trouble at all to grow. But garden fashions change. Now most homeowners buy bedding plants, which grow to a uniform height—relatively short— instead of growing flowers from seed. And today's gardeners don't want to take time to remove faded flowers. So, cleome (also called spider flower) wasn't grown much. But now it's made a well-deserved comeback. In midsummer, it gives the yard a gracious feeling that harks back to the best of yesteryear.

Botanical Pronunciation
klee-OH-mee hass-ler-ee-AH-nuh

Bloom Period and Seasonal Color
Midsummer until frost in shades of pink, rose, purple, and white

Mature Height × Spread
3 to 6 feet × 12 to 18 inches

When, Where, and How to Plant
Refrigerate cleome seeds overnight, and then plant in a sunny spot in the garden after the last expected frost date in spring. Or sow seeds six to eight weeks earlier in a warm, indoor environment for transplanting outdoors after the chance of frost is past. Thin, or set plants 18 to 24 inches apart in average, well-drained soil. Avoid windy locations. When planting, mix compost, an organic fertilizer for flowering plants, or a pelleted slow-release fertilizer with the soil. Mulch with 1 inch of pine needles.

Growing Tips
After cleome is established, it can tolerate some drought, but it's best to water often enough to prevent wilting—once dried out, the plant may not grow or bloom well from then on. Fertilize with weekly applications of a water-soluble plant food. Because cleome reseeds itself, use only a light mulch around the plants if you want the seeds to germinate and produce new plants.

Care
When plants are a foot tall, pinch an inch off the tip of the main stem to encourage branching. The plants attract few pests, but if aphids appear, spray with insecticidal soap. Occasionally leaf spot will develop. Pick off the affected leaves and dispose of them. If leaves mildew, consult the Extension service for advice. If you don't want cleome to sow seeds (and it can be an aggressive self-sower), pick off the seedpods before they turn brown and open.

Garden Design
Good for a butterfly garden or an area designed to attract wildlife. Cleomes also look nice, because of their height, in shrub borders, among foundation plantings, along fences (especially picket or split-rail fences), and with large ornamental grasses. Place at the back of a flower border to disguise any legginess.

Try These
Spirit Appleblossom has delicate pink and white blooms; it's very heat-tolerant. 'Senorita Rosalita', which has pink flowers, is heat-tolerant, doesn't self-sow, and doesn't need deadheading.

Coleus
Solenostemon scutellarioides

When, Where, and How to Plant
Set out plants after chance of frost has passed in spring. Coleus appreciates moist, well-drained soil; amend soil with organic matter to help it hold moisture. Some varieties tolerate more sun than others; check the plant label to be sure whether shade or sun is indicated. Usually the leaf colors appear more intense in shade or partial shade. Space plants 6 to 18 inches apart, depending on mature size. Mix pelleted slow-release fertilizer with the soil in the planting hole.

Growing Tips
Feed once a month with a water-soluble fertilizer, such as 20-20-20. Pay attention to the water needs of coleus in containers and hanging baskets; don't let them dry out.

Care
Pick off flowers as they appear. Once flowers open, the plants begin a natural decline. Watch out for snails and slugs (see page 34 for ways to control them). Begin lightly pinching the tips of the stems of upright coleus when they are 4 to 6 inches tall to encourage branching, and continue pinching occasionally as needed to prevent legginess. It's easy to take cuttings of coleus in August or September and root them; you can grow them indoors on a sunny windowsill all winter, pinching the young plants back only once or twice. When warm weather arrives in spring, gradually move your coleus back outdoors (see page 44 for details on "hardening off"). This enables you to save, from year to year, varieties that you particularly like.

Garden Design
Grow red coleus with silver-leaved dusty miller. Match other colors of coleus with perennial flowers or geraniums of the same shade. Gold and chartreuse coleus looks nice with yellow and green hostas, gold hakone grass, or orange New Guinea impatiens.

Try These
The leaves of 'Versa Lime' are a lovely solid green and combine beautifully with multicolored coleus cultivars. It tolerates sun. 'Versa Green Halo' has foliage with yellow centers edged in lime green; it will grow well in full sun or full shade.

I've always thought of coleus as a nice old-fashioned plant for shade, one favored by my mom and grandmother. But those ideas of coleus as low-key and shade-loving have flown out the window the past few years. Coleus has become a darling of plant breeders, and in the process has changed so much that my grandmom would be amazed. Every year new varieties are introduced with more and more brilliant color combinations—and leaf shapes—that will knock your socks off! And most of these new cultivars, propagated from cuttings instead of seed, don't bloom, saving you the chore of pinching off the tiny flowers all summer. Many will also tolerate a fair amount of sun, even in our climate. (Look for those called Sun Coleus.) When it comes to plants that are versatile and can take the heat, coleus now comes through with shining colors.

Botanical Pronunciation
sol-eh-no-STEH-mon scoo-tuh-LOID-eez

Bloom Period and Seasonal Color
From spring until frost, foliage in shades of red, pink, gold, chartreuse, and bicolors

Mature Height × Spread
6 inches to 4 feet × 8 inches to 3 feet

Cosmos

Cosmos species and hybrids

I adore flowers that seem cheerful—informal and brightly colored. Even nicer is if they're easy to grow. Cosmos bipinnatus (called cosmos or Mexican aster) and C. sulphureus (yellow cosmos) are all that and more. Yellow cosmos has red and orange as well as yellow daisylike blooms. C. bipinnatus has fernlike foliage and flowers that are white or some shade of pink. They may grow to 6 or 7 feet tall, although numerous cultivars are shorter. Cosmos thrives in poor soil, rarely needs watering once it's established, and doesn't require fertilizer. The reward for this benign neglect is armloads of blooms in the flower garden and full vases indoors from summer until frost. That makes me feel as cheerful as the cosmos look.

Botanical Pronunciation
KOZ-mose bi-pin-NAY-tus

Bloom Period and Seasonal Color
Midsummer to frost in yellow, orange, red, white, pink, rose, and fuchsia

Mature Height × Spread
2 to 7 feet × 1 to 2½ feet

When, Where, and How to Plant
Cosmos are easy to grow from seed (see pages 37 and 45 for directions for starting seed indoors). Begin six weeks before the last expected frost; sow in single pots rather than flats to prevent disturbing roots during transplanting. Or, after all chance of frost is past, sow seeds outdoors in a sunny spot where they are to grow. Plant in well-drained, poor to average soil. (When grown in soil rich with ample organic matter, stems will be weak and the plants will fall over or need staking.) Space homegrown or purchased plants 12 to 18 inches apart. Avoid putting tall cosmos in windy sites.

Growing Tips
Fertilize sparingly—one application of a water-soluble plant food at midseason is plenty. Once the plants are established, little watering will be needed, but if you do need to water during long dry spells, soak the soil thoroughly each time.

Care
To encourage branching and maximum flower development, pinch tall varieties when they reach 12 to 18 inches in height. Snap off faded flowers to keep cosmos blooming a long time and to prevent excessive reseeding. The plant typically experiences few insects or diseases, but can attract aphids. Spray them with insecticidal soap or a blast of water (see page 33 for more control advice). If you see more foliage than flowers, the soil is too rich, or you may be fertilizing too much.

Garden Design
Yellow cosmos makes an excellent addition to a wildflower meadow. Both it and Mexican aster are ideal additions to cottage gardens and are right at home in natural landscape styles. Put shorter types at the front of flower beds; use tall varieties for vertical interest at the rear.

Try These
The 'Ladybird Dwarf' series (red, orange-red, yellow, or gold flowers) grows about 12 to 16 inches tall. I particularly like 'Ladybird Dwarf Lemon', which is always covered with flowers.

Cup Flower
Nierembergia scoparia

When, Where, and How to Plant

To grow cup flowers from seed, start them indoors in spring 6 to 8 weeks before the expected last frost (see pages 37 and 45 for more about growing plants from seed). Just after the frost-free date has passed, place seedlings or purchased plants in a sunny or partially sunny spot, spaced 8 to 12 inches apart. The plants' preferred soil is rich and moist but well drained, but it typically adapts to less than ideal conditions (See page 45 for more details on planting annuals.) Mix a slow-release fertilizer with the plantingsoil. Mulch the soil with organic matter such as pine needles.

Growing Tips

Let the soil dry slightly between waterings. In containers, slightly moist soil will be welcome, but generally the plants are fairly adaptable. Water more often in the hottest weather. Fertilize monthly with liquid seaweed or a water-soluble fertilizer, according to package directions.

Care

Pinch tips of stems as needed to promote bushiness. If flowering slows in the summer heat, trim the plants to encourage new growth when temperatures become more moderate. Few insects or diseases are a problem, but keep an eye out for snails and slugs (see page 34 for ways to control them).

Garden Design

Let cup flowers spill out of beds to soften sharp edges. Because it has a trailing habit, cup flower is good along the rims of containers, hanging baskets, and window boxes. It's especially nice for containers attached to the rails of decks or fences. Also consider cup flower for rock gardens.

Try These

'Augusta Blue Skies' actually has lavender blooms with yellow centers; it's heat-tolerant. 'Mont Blanc' has white flowers and grows 6 to 12 inches tall. 'Purple Robe' is small—3 to 9 inches tall, spreading 6 to 12 inches; 'White Robe' is a similar size. 'Summer Splash' is an upright grower (24 to 30 inches tall) with white or pale blue blooms.

So many low-growing edging plants are neat but nondescript; they don't add much "oomph" to the flower garden. Cup flower, or broom cup flower, is an exception. It's neat, low-growing, and a nice edging plant—but it also has lovely lavender or white flowers that add beauty to the garden. Cup flower is also adaptable as to soil and moisture needs, nice for those with less than ideal conditions. This annual may be perennial in Zone 7 (and may return after mild winters in Zone 6), but consider it an annual in both zones until you see how it does for you. Some cup flowers don't bloom as much in the hottest part of summer, but many newer cultivars don't mind the heat.

Botanical Pronunciation

nee-rem-BER-gee-uh sko-PAY-ree-uh

Bloom Period and Seasonal Color

Spring to fall in white or lavender

Mature Height x Spread

3 to 12 inches x 6 to 24 inches

Diamond Frost Euphorbia

Euphorbia graminea 'Diamond Frost'

I've never been overly fond of white flowers. I know the reasons to grow them, and still, I'm tepid about them at best. Give me bright colors! So it amuses me how enthusiastic I've become about Euphorbia 'Diamond Frost'. Because both the flowers and the leaves are tiny, this isn't a plant that will put on a spectacular show. Instead, its greatest feature is how well it combines with other plants and makes them look better. It's considered a "filler," but in my container gardens, this airy annual has become an essential accent. 'Diamond Frost' looks dainty as it creates an ethereal cloud of delicate blooms, but it's tough—heat-tolerant, drought-tolerant, and deer-resistant—and keeps on going until frost. Then you can grow it indoors.

Botanical Pronunciation
u-FOR-bee-uh gruh-MIN-ee-uh

Bloom Period and Seasonal Color
Spring until fall with white flowers

Mature Height x Spread
1 to 3 feet x 1 to 3 feet

When, Where, and How to Plant
In spring, after chance of frost is past, plant 'Diamond Frost' in containers filled with moistened commercial potting soil or in flower beds that have moist but well-drained soil (see page 45 for more details on planting annuals). It's fine in both rich and moderately poor soils, but doesn't like wet areas. A spot that receives part sun—about 6 hours a day (morning sun is excellent)—is ideal in most of the region. The plant grows well in shade but doesn't bloom as profusely. In Zone 6a, you may give 'Diamond Frost' full sun or part sun.

Growing Tips
Water when the top inch of the soil dries out. In beds mature plants are relatively drought-tolerant but will bloom better if not allowed to dry out completely; in pots they will need regular moisture, although the soil surface should dry between waterings.

Care
Spider mites and aphids may occasionally attack plants (see pages 33 and 34 for advice to control them). If other problems appear, contact the Extension service for help. If you have a latex sensitivity, wear gloves when pruning 'Diamond Frost' so the sap does not get on you. Little fertilizer is needed and no deadheading is required.

Garden Design
The joy of white flowers is how well they combine with other colors—red, purple, orange, blue. It's fun to experiment. Try 'Diamond Frost' in a basket with blue scaevola, in a container with purple petunias and a purple-leaved ornamental sweet potato, or a container filled with nothing but 'Diamond Frost'. Combine with Supertunia Cotton Candy (a lovely pink) for an attractive baby shower or engagement party decoration.

Try These
Obviously, 'Diamond Frost' is my favorite, but there are other good choices. 'Hip Hop' flowers abundantly. 'Stardust White Sparkle' grows a compact 8 inches tall and wide. 'Stardust Pink Shimmer' has flowers with a pale pink tinge. 'Stardust Pink Glitter' has dark foliage and blooms with pink bracts.

Geranium

Pelargonium species and hybrids

When, Where, and How to Plant

Plant in the garden or in containers after the last frost. Most geraniums prefer morning sun and afternoon shade, but ivy geraniums need mostly shade, especially in hot summers. Use a high-quality packaged potting mix for containers and good moist soil but well drained if planting in the ground. Amend garden soil with compost or other organic matter to create a rich mixture that also drains readily. Work a pelleted slow-release fertilizer into the soil as you plant. Space geraniums 1 to 2 feet apart depending on type so that air circulates between them. Mulch lightly. (See page 45 for more tips on planting annuals.)

Growing Tips

Fertilize geraniums that are growing in containers once a week with a water-soluble fertilizer made for blooming plants, or with liquid seaweed. Place more pelleted slow-release fertilizer on top of the soil around bedding geraniums in midsummer; water well and place mulch on top. Keep the soil slightly moist—don't let it dry out, but don't let it get soggy either.

Care

As my mom did, pinch or cut back stems so the plants don't get leggy. If stems rot, get rid of the plants. If leaves turn yellow (and insects or disease aren't present), spray with chelated iron. Consult the Extension service about mildew or other problems. Remove old flowers to encourage new blooms. Geraniums root easily in fall; take cuttings, pot up, and overwinter on a sunny windowsill or in a greenhouse.

Garden Design

Line the stairs to the front door with clay pots of salmon-colored geraniums mixed with dusty miller, letting variegated ivy or *Vinca major* trail over the edges. (Get rid of the trailing plants in fall; they can be invasive.)

Try These

Caliente® 'Coral' has been exceptional for me and is a charming color. I've had excellent success in Zone 6 with the 'Tornado' series of ivy geranium (coral was best, but there's red, white, pink, and orange).

My mother always grew the best-looking geraniums. When people asked why hers were so much more impressive than theirs, she explained that she regularly pinched back the stems. That made the plants bushier and more compact, and they produced more flowers—all of which looked great. I would guess that most geraniums are grown in containers rather than in beds. But you may want to look for seed-grown geraniums in interesting colors that are inexpensive enough to grow as bedding plants (they will usually be sold in packs of four or six instead of in larger individual pots). In the cooler areas of the region, do try delicate-looking ivy geraniums in hanging baskets. I loved growing these when my family lived in Germany.

Botanical Pronunciation
pel-ar-GO-nee-um

Bloom Period and Seasonal Color
Spring until fall in red, orange, salmon, pink, lavender, and white; some are mottled or bicolored

Mature Height × Spread
12 inches to 3 feet × 14 to 24 inches

Globe Amaranth
Gomphrena globosa

I judge the success of my flower gardens in late August. Flowers that look as good, or even better, at the end of the summer than they did in May or June—especially if we've had a long hot spell marked by high humidity and little rain—are winners that I'll be sure to plant the next year. Globe amaranth (still called gomphrena by some) is one of those plants that laugh in the face of the hottest weather. It doesn't look like a typical bedding plant— it has a rounded shape and is topped all summer with little ball-like flowers that remind me of the ones on red clover. These will dry right on the plant and can be saved for winter arrangements.

Botanical Pronunciation
gom-FREE-nah glow-BOE-sah

Bloom Period and Seasonal Color
Summer to fall in white and shades of purple, pink, orange-salmon, and red

Mature Height × Spread
10 to 24 inches × 12 to 16 inches

When, Where, and How to Plant
You may grow globe amaranth from seed sown indoors eight to ten weeks before the expected last frost. The seeds germinate best at cool temperatures (60 to 65 degrees Fahrenheit), but grow better where it's warm (see pages 37 and 45 for more details on starting annuals from seed). Or buy bedding plants. Wait to plant outdoors until after the weather is consistently warm—generally not before May. Place in a sunny spot that has average to poor soil that drains rapidly. Space plants a foot or so apart. Mix pelleted slow-release fertilizer into the soil in the planting hole. (See page 45 for more details on planting annuals.)

Growing Tips
Once a plant's roots are established, water only during dry spells. If you used a timed-release fertilizer when planting, you shouldn't have to feed plants again. But if leaves look pale, apply a single application of water-soluble fertilizer, such as 20-20-20.

Care
Globe amaranth attracts few pests, but watch out for spider mites. To prevent spider mites, spray water once a week under the lower leaves of the plants (see page 34 or consult the Extension service for control advice). Globe amaranth dries easily. Cut the stems at the base just as the flowers completely open and hang them upside down in a warm place.

Garden Design
Edge a driveway or sidewalk with globe amaranth, or fill medium to large clay pots with plants for the deck. The pink and lavender shades of globe amaranth look nice combined with white-flowered annuals or perennials.

Try These
Gomphrena 'Audray Bicolor Rose' has a two-toned flower, mostly pinkish rose but white on top. The Las Vegas series (white, pink, purple) has been an outstanding performer. I love the unusual blooms of 'Fireworks', which are quite showy; the dense plant grows 3 to 4 feet tall and 1 to 2 feet wide, so it's not for small containers.

Impatiens
Impatiens walleriana

When, Where, and How to Plant

After chance of frost is past, plant impatiens in a shady spot about 10 to 12 inches apart in moist, well-drained garden soil. Enrich clay or rocky soils with compost, fine bark, or other organic matter. Partial shade is fine, but the more sun the plants receive, the more you'll have to water them. Mix an organic fertilizer for flowers or a pelleted slow-release fertilizer into the planting soil. Top with a 2-inch layer of organic mulch. (See page 45 for more details on planting annuals.)

Growing Tips

Ample water and frequent fertilization are the keys to success with impatiens. Keep the soil moist, and every two weeks during the season, apply a water-soluble fertilizer made for blooming plants. Water beds of impatiens with soaker hoses.

Care

Pests may include slugs in wet weather and spider mites in very dry weather (see page 34 for ways to control them). Downy mildew has become a big problem on impatiens in some other areas, so keep an eye out in wet, cool weather for yellowed and mottled leaves, and consult the Extension service immediately. Pinch plants back anytime they look leggy; cuttings will root easily to increase your collection. Some impatiens reseed, but the flower color may not come true to the parent plant.

Garden Design

Use brightly colored impatiens to surround trees and liven up a flower bed that contains ferns and hostas. Plant white or pastel shades *en masse* for viewing from the patio or deck at dusk. Pair white impatiens with red coleus and red impatiens with white caladiums.

Try These

Rockapulco 'Coral Reef' has double flowers. I like the cultivars in the Super Elfin XP series that have flowers with a contrasting "eye" in the center of the blooms. 'Cherry Splash', my favorite, has pale pink flowers with a deeper pink center and grows 8 to 10 inches high and 12 to 14 inches wide.

Anyone who has a shady yard needs no introduction to impatiens. It's long been the go-to annual to provide reliable, summer-long color in wooded areas. It's attractive, easy to grow, covered with flowers from the time you plant it until it's struck down by frost, and just as good in containers as in flower beds. Hybrids are available in a variety of heights, but you may find that in a rainy summer, they'll all grow tall and make an impressive show. There are so many varieties of impatiens that it's sometimes difficult to tell them apart. One solution: when you buy the plants, save the plant labels, so that if one variety was especially successful, you'll know what you to look for next spring.

Botanical Pronunciation

im-PAY-shens wall-er-ee-AY-nuh

Bloom Period and Seasonal Color

Mid-spring to frost in white, pink, lavender, red, orange, and bicolors

Mature Height × Spread

6 to 36 inches × 8 to 24 inches

Madagascar Periwinkle
Catharanthus roseus

When I plant a bed or container of annuals in spring, I want to know that they're going to be impressive in June and even early September. I don't want to be stuck in July or August with awful looking plants that need to be pulled out and replaced. That's why I plant perky Madagascar periwinkle. No matter how high the heat and humidity climb, its glossy green leaves and simple flowers always look neat. And it blooms all season long. Anyone who has tired of the white and pastel blooms will be pleased to know that now you can find bright orange, red, and even navy. When you go to the nursery, don't confuse it with the perennial groundcover vinca, which is also called periwinkle.

Botanical Pronunciation
cath-ah-RAN-thus ROE-see-us

Bloom Period and Seasonal Color
Spring to fall in white, pink, and lavender; some are accented by darker eyes

Mature Height × Spread
4 inches to 2 feet × 8 inches to 1½ feet

When, Where, and How to Plant
Don't rush to put Madagascar periwinkle outside in spring. It's a heat-loving plant, and its leaves may turn yellow when temperatures are below 70 degrees Fahrenheit. (If this happens, spray the plants with chelated iron mixed in water, according to label instructions, and the foliage will green up.) Plant 10 inches apart in a sunny area with moist, well-drained soil or in containers filled with a commercial potting mix. In a flower bed, mix a timed-release fertilizer into the soil, according to package directions. If the container potting mix doesn't already contain a slow-release fertilizer, add some (see page 45 for more details on planting annuals).

Growing Tips
In early August, sprinkle more pelleted slow-release fertilizer around the plants, and water well, or you can fertilize once a month with liquid seaweed or water-soluble 20-20-20 fertilizer. Mature plants won't need much watering in flower beds, but do water potted plants often enough that they don't wilt.

Care
To encourage branching, pinch the tips of the stems occasionally. Watch out for slugs and snails (see page 34 for ways to deter them). If mature, well-cared-for plants develop yellow leaves during warm weather, this is a sign of disease; dig up and remove the affected plants from the garden.

Garden Design
"Eyed" periwinkles look nice paired with snapdragons and wax begonias that have flowers the same color as the eyes. Look for trailing types to plant in hanging baskets and window boxes in sunny spots.

Try These
I've been impressed by the exciting new colors. 'Jams 'N Jellies Blackberry' has deep purple blooms on a plant that grows 16 inches tall. The large flowers of 'Pacifica Orange' almost glow. Pacifica XP 'Cherry Red Halo' is a nice bright color. Nirvana 'Cascading Rose' is semi-trailing. 'Titan Red Dark' has good-sized flowers. All are carefree. A pretty pastel is Norvana 'Pink Blush', which has a rosy center.

When, Where, and How to Plant

Marigolds are easy to grow from seed planted indoors one month before you want to set them outside (see pages 37 and 45 for more details on starting annuals from seed). You may also sow seeds outdoors in average garden soil from just after the last frost date until mid-June. Place the seeds or purchased bedding plants in full sun. In clay or rocky soils, mix some organic matter—such as compost, peat, or fine pine bark—into the soil before planting. Thin seedlings or space plants 6 to 10 inches apart, depending on the type (see page 45 for more details on planting annuals).

Growing Tips

Let soil dry out slightly between waterings, and fertilize about once a month with a liquid plant food for blooming plants—too much water and fertilizer contribute to excessive leaf growth with few flowers and may promote leaf diseases or root rot. Avoid overhead sprinklers and watering late in the day.

Care

Pinch plants as they grow to promote branching and more flowers. Keep faded flowers picked off to prolong bloom time. Slugs will devour tender young marigolds, especially in damp weather. In hot, dry areas, watch out for spider mites. (See page 34 for control advice.)

Garden Design

Use dwarf varieties along edges of containers that also hold zinnias, Madagascar periwinkle, short ornamental grasses, and other plants that appreciate a dry environment. Plant taller varieties in mixed flower and herb beds.

Try These

'African Taishan Gold' is my favorite yellow African marigold now. I grow 'Inca II Primrose' from seed because it's a long-time favorite I often can't find as a bedding plant. 'Primrose Lady' is another winner with yellow flowers. Durango Bolero is a dwarf with large yellow and red blooms. If you don't like the odor of marigold foliage, 'Lemon Gem' is a signet marigold with ferny leaves that has a citrus scent.

Anyone—even preschoolers—can grow marigolds, either from seed or plants. The most popular ones are dwarfs (called French marigolds), and who am I to argue with that? They're cute, although I find the orange-gold color that's most often seen hard to mix with other flowers. But I'd like to encourage more people to grow what are referred to as African marigolds (although they originated in the Americas). These are taller—10 to 24 inches—and have flowers 2 to 5 inches in diameter. Some varieties of African marigolds have clear yellow blooms, my favorites because they combine so beautifully with other colors. Despite the size of the plants and flowers, most stand up to thunderstorms just as well as dwarfs, if not better.

Botanical Pronunciation
tah-gee-teez

Bloom Period and Seasonal Color
Summer until fall in shades of yellow, burgundy, orange, and cream

Mature Height × Spread
6 inches to 3 feet × 10 inches to 3 feet

Melampodium
Melampodium paludosum

I keep waiting for melampodium to develop a popular common name, so it will be easier to ask for and talk about. It's sometimes called African zinnia and gold medallion flower, but neither name has caught on. Still, it's worthwhile learning to pronounce melampodium (all together now, mel-am-POE-dee-um) because this is one of the easiest summer flowers to grow—tolerant of heat, humidity, and drought. Its apple green leaves are an attractive contrast to the abundance of small yellow daisy-like blooms, it's low-maintenance, and you can even collect seeds to sow for the next year. Melampodium is compact and low-growing, but does spread up to 2 feet, a quality that I like because it means I can get by with purchasing fewer plants to fill my flower beds.

Botanical Pronunciation
mel-am-POE-dee-um pal-you-DOE-sum

Bloom Period and Seasonal Color
Summer in shades of golden yellow

Mature Height × Spread
8 to 20 inches × 14 to 24 inches

When, Where, and How to Plant
Melampodium seeds sprout easily; start indoors six weeks before the last expected frost, or seed directly into average garden soil after it warms up (see pages 37 and 45 for more details on starting annuals from seed). Purchased plants make great "instant color" in garden beds or pots in full sun. Space transplants or thin seedlings to 10 to 16 inches apart, and incorporate a pelleted slow-release fertilizer into the soil (see page 45 for more tips on planting annuals). Mulch lightly. Melampodium forgives poor soil and forgetful watering and grows fastest in hot weather, making it an excellent candidate for late planting and replacement of other annuals.

Growing Tips
Water regularly until plants are established, and then allow the soil to dry out between waterings. After that, little watering is needed. Feed once or twice a month with liquid plant food.

Care
Slugs can be a problem, but their invasion also indicates that conditions are too wet. Aphids and whiteflies occasionally appear. (See pages 33 and 35 for control of these pests.) Melampodium is such a carefree plant that it branches without pinching. The daisy-shaped flowers also dry up and shed readily, then quickly replace themselves without deadheading. Watch out, though: Melampodium reseeds prolifically unless thick mulch suppresses the process.

Garden Design
This is a perfect plant for massing. Try it with Shasta daisies, orange zinnias, black-eyed Susans, or sunflowers or in front of medium-sized ornamental grasses. It also makes a nice "perennial" in a bed of its own because it reseeds, *sometimes aggressively*, and produces new plants each year.

Try These
The ones I've tried are 'Showstar', 'Million Gold', and 'Medallion'. All have bloomed prolifically and with no work on my part. 'Million Gold' reaches a foot tall, 'Showstar' grows 12 to 18 inches high, and 'Medallion' is about 15 to 18 inches at maturity. They can be intermixed to make a "wavy" grouping that undulates up and down.

Million Bells
Calibrachoa hybrids

When, Where, and How to Plant
In spring, after chance of frost has passed, plant in containers filled with a good commercial potting mix. If the mix doesn't already contain fertilizer, combine it with pelleted timed-release fertilizer or with an organic slow-release fertilizer, according to package directions. If growing in beds, slightly acid soil is best; alkaline soil can result in yellowed leaves. To avoid root rot, make sure drainage is excellent; if you have clay soil, grow in raised beds. Million Bells and Superbells prefer full sun or a location that's in morning sun but offers a bit of afternoon shade. Place them at the same soil level they grew at in their containers and space 12 to 16 inches apart. Mix pelleted slow-release fertilizer with the soil before you plant.

Growing Tips
Fertilize calibrachoas in containers with a water-soluble 20-20-20 fertilizer once a week. In beds, a topdressing of compost twice a season should be ample. Let the top inch of the soil dry between waterings. Soil that's kept too wet can result in root rot.

Care
Aphids can attack new growth (see page 33 for advice to control them). In late summer, if the plant isn't as compact as before, take a pair of handpruners or even scissors and give the plants an all-over trim, stems and flowers. This will encourage new growth and flowers. Or, you can pinch them back a bit several times during the summer. But if the plants need that, it may be that they're not getting enough light; move them to more sun.

Garden Design
This is mostly a container plant. You may want to mix several shades of *Calibrachoa* in a hanging basket, or grow Minifamous Double Blue *Calibrachoa* with *Euphorbia* 'Diamond Frost'.

Try These
I really like the color of the flowers on Superbells Blackberry Punch—deep purple irregularly edged with lighter purple. The blooms on Minifamous Double Yellow are double, not like petunias at all. Superbells Peach flowers are bicolored.

My least-favorite garden chore is deadheading, pinching faded flowers off annuals. Like dusting or washing dishes, it has to be done over and over. The reason for deadheading is to keep plants producing more flowers and blooming longer. But for many years, I avoided growing petunias simply because I didn't want to be stuck removing dead blooms all summer. So when Million Bells—and Superbells (also a Calibrachoa hybrid)— were introduced, I immediately became a big fan. The main reason? These plants, covered with smaller, petunia-like flowers from spring until frost, didn't need to have the old flowers removed. Hooray! They are also rain- and heat-tolerant and disease-resistant. Grow them just as you do petunias—they're especially nice in baskets—but forget deadheading.

Botanical Pronunciation
kal-ih-brac-COE-uh

Bloom Period and Seasonal Color
Spring until fall frost in orange, salmon, red, yellow, white, pink, and lavender

Mature Height x Spread
6 to 12 inches x 24 to 48 inches

New Guinea Impatiens

Impatiens hawkeri

It's easy to tell by the flowers that this is a relative of the familiar shade-loving impatiens. But New Guinea impatiens are grown as much for their jazzy variegated foliage as for the showy colors of their flowers. Place them where you want plants that generate a festive feeling and say, "Look at me!"—near the swimming pool, for example, or in big pots scattered across a large deck. Unlike Impatiens walleriana, New Guinea impatiens—which were introduced into this country in the 1970s— is not a full-shade plant. In Zones 5 and 6, it's right at home in a spot that's mostly in sun all day. In Zone 7 and in hottest summers, give plants morning sun and at least some afternoon shade.

Botanical Pronunciation
im-PAY-shens HAWK-er-eye

Bloom Period and Seasonal Color
Summer to first frost with blooms in white, red, pink, lavender and salmon; leaves are green or red-bronze; some are variegated with creamy yellow

Mature Height × Spread
12 to 20 inches × 1 to 2 feet

When, Where, and How to Plant

Plant New Guinea impatiens 12 to 15 inches apart in slightly acidic garden soil that has been enriched with plenty of organic material, or place three plants in a 3-gallon container filled with a high-quality peat-based potting mix that you've amended with compost. You may need to experiment with the best sun exposure. In the cooler parts of the region and during moderate summers, the plants perform best where they're in sun all or most of the day. In hot summers and Zone 7, four to six hours of afternoon shade will be welcome. Add pelleted slow-release fertilizer, according to label directions, to the soil or the container's potting mix before planting.

Growing Tips

In beds, keep the soil mulched to hold in moisture. New Guinea impatiens prefer soil that's lightly moist but not soggy. Little fertilizer is needed; in fact, the plants are sensitive to excess fertilizer salts, so watch out in containers. Use a water-soluble fertilizer, such as 20-20-20, once a month. Fertilize twice a month if leaves begin to pale or turn yellow (unless foliage is supposed to be yellow).

Care

Pinch plants one time when they are 4 inches tall, then pinch stem tips as needed to keep the plant bushy. Flowers usually fall off on their own; if they don't, brush them off so the faded flowers won't develop mold. You should encounter few if any insects or diseases on New Guinea impatiens, with the exception of spider mites in hot weather and, occasionally, aphids and thrips (see pages 33, 34, and 35 for control advice, or consult the Extension service).

Garden Design

Grow New Guinea impatiens near cannas and agapanthus for instant tropical texture. These are ideal for containers and look nice in hanging baskets.

Try These

'SunPatiens Lavender' is a pretty color and it grows well. 'SunPatiens Compact Orange' is an easy-care showstopper. Infinity 'Lavender Imp' is a wonderful color.

Ornamental Cabbage and Kale

Brassica oleracea var. *acephala*

When, Where, and How to Plant

To grow from seed, start in summer. Sow in a sunny spot with well-drained garden soil, making sure you keep the seeds moist until they sprout. If you buy plants from a nursery in fall, do it as early as they're available. The sooner they're planted in well-drained soil and have developed a good root system, the more winter-hardy they'll be. Mix clay soil with compost or fine bark to improve drainage. Thin the seedlings or space purchased plants 1 foot apart; be sure the plant's crown sits directly at ground level, not above. Mix slow-release fertilizer with the soil at planting time. Mulch with shredded leaves or pine needles to moderate soil temperatures and retain moisture. (See page 45 for more details on planting annuals.)

Growing Tips

If rainfall is low, water young plants to keep the soil moist but not wet, until they are established or the ground freezes.

Care

Insects attracted to this plant include cabbage-worms, slugs, snails, and cutworms. For the last three, surround plants with collars to prevent them. Exclude egg-laying butterflies with insect barrier fabric or spray with Bt to control cabbage-worm larvae when they hatch. Caterpillars and most other pests will be problems mostly in fall; they disappear after cold weather arrives.

Garden Design

Plant ornamental cabbages and kale where they can be admired close-up and from above in winter. Grow them in a row along the top of a low wall, edging a bed of taller ornamental grasses, or in large containers.

Try These

Ornamental kales and cabbages usually aren't labeled with cultivar names at garden centers, so I'd choose by appearance. But should you find cultivars, I've liked the 'Color Up' series—in pink, white, or red—which has intense color-ation. And 'Flamingo Plumes' (magenta and purple) is so spectacular you may need only one plant.

Once, when you wanted plants to provide fall color after summer annuals had faded, mums were the main choice. Then pansies began to grow in popularity. Both are fine, but those looking for something that's not the same-old, same-old are turning to ornamental cabbage and kale (the latter has lacy, fringed leaves) to brighten the landscape. It's true that these plants aren't as hardy as pansies—they may not make it through the entire winter—but the reason to grow them is their drop-dead-gorgeous foliage in eye-catching combinations that range from green leaves veined with white along the outside of the plant and brilliant red centers, to plants with magenta centers edged by purple leaves to white contrasted against blue-green. That really brightens winter!

Botanical Pronunciation

BRASS-ih-kah ohl-er-AY-cee-uh variety a-SEF-uh-luh

Bloom Period and Seasonal Color

Mid to late fall and winter; grown for fringed leaves of green, white, red, pink, and purple

Mature Height × Spread

6 to 12 inches × 8 to 12 inches

Ornamental Pepper
Capsicum annuum

Every time summer temperatures are extra hot, I wonder why more gardeners aren't growing ornamental peppers. These decorative little plants are colorful, love heat, and produce edible peppers in colors that range from traditional red and orange to purple and cream (often on the plant at the same time). Sounds weird; looks wonderful. The taste will be appreciated by "pepperheads"—hot, hot, hot. But they're great even if you never use the peppers, because steamy weather causes them to thrive. They grow well in containers as well as any spot where you might raise tomatoes. I often place small ornamental pepper plants in a large container of heat-loving herbs (rosemary, sage, chives) on the patio, giving me a useful little edible garden near the grill.

Botanical Pronunciation
CAP-sih-come AN-you-um

Bloom Period and Seasonal Color
Summer to frost with white or purple flowers followed by peppers that ripen to red, purple, white, yellow, or orange

Mature Height × Spread
4 inches to 3 feet × 6 inches to 2 feet

When, Where, and How to Plant
Start seeds indoors using a packaged potting mix; place flats in a very warm (70 degrees Fahrenheit), sunny environment six weeks before the last frost (see pages 37 and 45 for more details about starting plants from seed indoors). Homegrown seedlings or small purchased plants don't like soil temperatures below 60 degrees Fahrenheit, so wait to plant outside until the soil has warmed up (often May). Peppers thrive in moderately rich soils that stay evenly moist. Amend sandy and clay soils with organic matter; mulch well. Space plants 10 to 16 inches apart. Work a pelleted slow-release fertilizer into the soil when you plant (see page 45 for more details on planting annuals).

Growing Tips
Use a water-soluble fertilizer, such as 20-20-20, once a week, especially if growing in containers. Water as needed; peppers that are grown in containers may need water daily in the heat of the summer to prevent wilting. Plants stunted by lack of water will not fruit, but in moist soil and moderate rainfall, watering may not be needed.

Care
Whitefly can be a serious pest (see page 35 for controls). Plants received as gifts in December (when they're called Christmas peppers) should be kept on a sunny windowsill a warm, bright room until frost-free weather arrives. Repot in a peat-based potting mix and grow outdoors for the summer.

Garden Design
Grow ornamental peppers with heat-loving white Madagascar periwinkle for eye-catching color all summer. They're ideal in containers of herbs or at the base of potted miniature tomatoes. But keep them away from children who might be tempted to put the peppers in their mouths—they're *very* hot.

Try These
The slightly shiny, purplish black foliage of 'Black Pearl' is the perfect foil for the round and glossy black fruits that ripen to bright red. 'Tricolore garda' produces conical peppers that go from purple to cream to orange and then red on a plant that's 16 inches tall.

Pansy

Viola × wittrockiana

When, Where, and How to Plant

Buy pansies in early fall; choose plants that have few flowers but plenty of buds. To get the maximum effect from pansies in beds or borders, plant them 5 to 7 inches apart in well-drained soil that's rich in organic matter. An ideal location will have morning sun and afternoon shade, but pansies do fine in full sun during winter (see page 45 for more details on planting annuals). Mix a pelleted slow-release fertilizer or a low-nitrogen organic fertilizer for flowering plants with the soil at planting time.

Growing Tips

Pansies require an inch of moisture a week. If the ground isn't frozen and rainfall is lacking, water deeply. To avoid disease, never water in the late afternoon or evening, and try to keep water off the leaves. Once plants are established, mulch to protect roots and prevent the plants from being heaved out of the ground. In spring, spread pelleted slow-release fertilizer, according to label directions, on top of the soil and under the mulch.

Care

Insects such as aphids and spider mites may appear in fall and spring. Keep old flowers trimmed off to extend the bloom season. Slugs can be a major pest when weather is mild and wet (see page 34 for ways to control them). Planting too closely, overwatering, and damp weather contribute to fungal diseases. Good air circulation and well-drained soil help prevent diseases. Consult the Extension service for help if problems appear.

Garden Design

Pansies look best when massed or used to edge beds. Grow them with Johnny-jump-ups in window boxes, or, in early spring, add snapdragons (which are cold-hardy) in complementary colors to beds and containers of pansies.

Try These

'Ultima Morpho' is covered with blue and yellow blooms patterned in a butterfly shape. Everyone will be talking about it. Matrix Yellow Pansy has excellent color that shows up well from a distance. It comes with or without a blotch.

During the times that I've temporarily moved away from our region and lived in cites with colder climates, one thing I really missed during winter were pansies. Oh, I tried some of the ones bred for cold regions, but if the ground is covered with snow most of the winter, you aren't going to see them. How fortunate gardeners in Tennessee and Kentucky are not to have that problem! As soon as fall arrives, pansies show up in garden centers and are quickly snapped up for planting in yards and commercial landscapes. And having gotten comfortable at growing pansies, more and more gardeners are also planting Johnny-jump-ups (Viola tricolor), which are taller and have smaller and more delicate flowers but are grown the same way.

Botanical Pronunciation
vy-OH-lah wit-rock-ee-AY-nuh

Bloom Period and Seasonal Color
Fall through early summer in red, yellow, orange, blue, violet, and white; single types and bicolors, many with "faces"

Mature Height × Spread
8 to 12 inches × 8 to 12 inches

Pentas

Pentas lanceolata

In April when you're at the garden center picking out annuals for your yard, it's hard to think about how they'll look several months hence—will they have wilted in high heat and humidity and need to be replaced, or kept their cool? But when late summer arrives, having heat-tolerant plants in the yard is suddenly a priority. This year, why not plan ahead and put pentas on your shopping list? They always shrug off the dog days of August, their brightly colored flowers continuing to bloom like crazy and attract butterflies from far and wide. Those round pink, red, white, or lavender flower clusters—consisting of dozens of tiny, star-shaped blossoms—are certainly attention-catching atop 3-foot plants, almost seeming to boast, "We're hot stuff."

Botanical Pronunciation
PEN-tas lan-cee-oh-LAY-tah

Bloom Period and Seasonal Color
Summer in pink, rose, purple, and white

Mature Height × Spread
14 to 24 inches × 10 to 14 inches

When, Where, and How to Plant

You'll find pentas available as a bedding plant in most garden centers in spring, ready to be placed in your yard when the soil has warmed up (about May). Or, you may sow seeds indoors in a cool (60 degrees Fahrenheit) environment ten weeks before the last frost, to plant outdoors about three weeks after the frost-free date. (See pages 37 and 45 for more about growing plants from seed.) Provide plenty of sun and well-drained, rich soil for successful pentas. Prepare clay or rocky soil by adding plenty of compost, ground bark, or rotted sawdust. Work in a pelleted slow-release fertilizer at planting time. Space plants 6 to 8 inches apart and mulch. (See page 45 for more details about planting annuals.)

Growing Tips

When the plants are young, water whenever rainfall is less than an inch. When mature, most cultivars of pentas are fairly drought-tolerant and need little additional moisture, except during prolonged dry spells. Overwatering pentas—especially in poorly drained soil—can result in root rot. Twice a month, fertilize with liquid seaweed or a water-soluble plant food made for flowering plants.

Care

Keep spent flowers picked off to encourage more blooms. Pinch back stems of young plants once to encourage bushy plants with multiple flower heads. As plants grow, pinch occasionally if needed to maintain shape; cuttings without flowers root easily in potting soil anytime during summer. Slugs sometimes make a meal of pentas (see page 34 for controls). Few other pests trouble healthy plants.

Garden Design

Grow pentas with *Euphorbia* 'Diamond Frost', pink or white petunias, and dwarf red fountain grass in a huge urn for a special patio centerpiece. Pentas are also nice paired with perennial salvia, which has blue flowers.

Try These

'Butterfly Sparkles Mix' combines pink and red star-shaped blooms. 'Northern Lights', which has lavender flowers, will bloom well in Zone 5 and in cooler summers.

Petunia
Petunia × hybrida

When, Where, and How to Plant

Start planting after all chance of frost has passed, and continue into midsummer, if desired. Petunias do fine in average garden soil that contains organic matter and is moist but well drained. If kept watered, petunias can grow in full sun, but they will appreciate a couple hours of afternoon shade. You may also place petunias where they're in the sun about half a day. Space regular petunias about 8 to 12 inches apart and Wave, or more spreading, plants 14 to 24 inches apart, slightly closer in containers. Mix pelleted slow-release fertilizer with the soil at planting time. (See page 45 for more details on planting annuals.)

Growing Tips

Because petunias like moist soil, water often enough to keep the bed or container from drying out, while avoiding constantly wet soil. Add liquid seaweed fertilizer to the water every other week.

Care

Pinch plants occasionally to encourage bushy growth and more blooms. If plants get leggy, shear back to rejuvenate. Do this before you go on vacation so you'll be greeted by newly flowering plants upon your return. On plants that don't automatically shed faded flowers, pinch them off. Overly dry conditions encourage whitefly infestations, while excessively damp conditions promote botrytis and pythium rots. Ask your local Extension service about controls, or remove diseased plants and replant.

Garden Design

You can grow a red, white, and blue flower garden with just petunias. For best appearance, grow trailing petunias in moss-lined hanging baskets. Or, place them at the front of window boxes or large containers, mixed with other plants, so they spill over the edge.

Try These

Easy Wave 'Burgundy Star' has eye-catching maroon and white flowers; it spreads about 3 feet. The flowers of Supertunia Pretty Much Picasso are mostly violet, with a purple throat and a showstopping chartreuse edge. Shock Wave Coral Crush has smaller blooms that are quite appealing.

When Wave petunias hit the gardening scene, many homeowners felt they'd found the perfect petunia and stopped searching for others. But you'll find some interesting new Wave developments. Cool Wave trailing petunias have flowers like pansies. The hallmarks of Double Wave are frilly flowers and a spreading habit. Easy Wave petunias are mounding and tolerate both hot and cool summers. Shock Wave has petite flowers; it's good for containers that are viewed close-up. Tidal Wave petunia plants are B-I-G—about 22 inches high and spreading up to 5 feet! And don't overlook the calibrachoas—Million Bells and Superbells—which look like mini petunias but don't need to have faded flowers removed. (See page 65.) You'll also find new cultivars of "regular" petunias, such as Supertunia. It's an exciting time for petunia lovers.

Botanical Pronunciation
peh-TUNE-ee-uh Hy-BRED-uh

Bloom Period and Seasonal Color
Spring until frost in white and every shade of red, pink, purple, yellow, and bicolors

Mature Height × Spread
4 to 22 inches × 12 to 60 inches

Scaveola
Scaveola hybrids

It's not hard to see why scaveola has become popular with homeowners. What's not to like about blue to purple flowers that are shaped like neat fans on a plant that's ideal for hanging baskets, window boxes, and even as a flowering groundcover? This Australian native continues to collect admirers with the introduction of new colors, including white and pink. If you're looking for a particular shade of blue—or just want blue instead of lavender—buy the plant locally when it's in flower to be sure of getting the shade you want. It thrives in hot, humid summers and requires little maintenance. When you head to the nursery for plants, ask for skuh-VOH-luh. Or just say "fan flower;" they'll know what you mean.

Botanical Pronunciation
skah-VOH-luh

Bloom Period and Seasonal Color
From late spring until frost in blue to violet, pink, or white flowers

Mature Height × Spread
4 to 12 inches × 12 inches to 3 feet

When, Where, and How to Plant
Start seeds indoors six to eight weeks before the last frost date (see pages 37 and 45 for more details on starting annuals from seed) or buy plants in spring, and plant in a sunny spot after the soil has warmed up. Space plants 12 to 18 inches apart in well-drained soil that's been enriched with organic matter, or place two to three plants in a hanging basket. Mix pelleted slow-release fertilizer with the soil at planting time. Mulch beds with pine straw. (See page 45 for more advice about planting annuals.)

Growing Tips
Water regularly, especially in containers, or growth and blooming will stop. In beds, don't let the soil dry out. Twice a month for in-ground plants and weekly for those growing in hanging baskets, fertilize with liquid seaweed or a water-soluble plant food for blooming plants.

Care
As soon as plants have produced 3 inches of new growth, pinch the tips of the stems lightly to promote bushiness. Continue pinching occasionally through midsummer. If you have a greenhouse or sunny indoor spot for plants, cut back scaveola in late summer and root the cuttings for growing indoors over winter. Next spring, take more cuttings and root them at 70 to 75 degrees Fahrenheit to plant outdoors in May.

Garden Design
Plant a true-blue scaveola with *Angelonia angustifolia* 'Serena White' or grow *Scaveola* 'Pink Topaz' with *Angelonia angustifolia* 'Serena Lavender'. Place pots of scaveola on top of a wall and let them cascade over, or pair blue varieties with your favorite red- or yellow-flowered annuals—petunia, salvia, celosia, or sunflower. It's also good by itself to fill large hanging baskets, trailing 3 or more feet. Most varieties can be used as a flowering annual groundcover, if desired.

Try These
'Pink Topaz' is a winner because not only are its flowers a lovely color, but it's an abundant bloomer. The Surdiva series has large flowers; I like the white-flowered cultivar.

Snapdragon
Antirrhinum majus

When, Where, and How to Plant
You don't have to wait until the chance of frost is past to plant snapdragons; since they can tolerate some cold, get them into the garden as soon as they're available. Amend average garden soil with compost and organic matter to enrich soil and improve drainage. Space plants 6 to 12 inches apart in sunny beds, although a bit of partial shade (especially in the afternoon) is okay. Or, plant in containers filled with a commercial potting mix. Mix a pelleted slow-release fertilizer with the soil in pots or beds.

Growing Tips
Water frequently until plants are established, then water enough that the plants don't dry out. Use a water-soluble fertilizer for blooming plants every two weeks until the flowers slow and eventually stop in summer. (In cooler summers, they'll keep blooming.) Then cut back the plants by one-third and keep them watered. When new growth resumes, start fertilizing again for fall flowers.

Care
Look for rust-resistant snapdragon varieties to avoid this common problem. Also, use soaker hoses to keep water off the foliage, and leave space between plants for air circulation. Deadhead (pick off faded flowers) regularly to keep the plants blooming. Stake tall varieties to keep flowers clean. If you want to cut them for arrangements, do it when one-third of the flowers are open on a stem. Don't be concerned when flowering slows or stops in summer.

Garden Design
For a cottage garden look, mix various shades of snapdragons. Otherwise, they look best massed in solid colors. Plant yellow snapdragons with cream-and-green variegated liriope or with purple-flowered perennial *Verbena bonariensis*.

Try These
'Twinny Peach' has the most unusual snapdragon flowers you've ever seen. They're double and peach, yellow, and light orange. Plus, the plant is heat-tolerant. 'Cascadia Mix', which comes in seven colors, is a trailing variety. 'Bronze Dragon' has burgundy foliage; it's best for spring and fall.

I'm always surprised at the number of people who don't know about the "snap" in snapdragon's name. I remember how much I loved as a kid to open the "jaws" of the flower by pinching the backs with my thumb and forefinger and letting them snap shut again. I enjoy these old-fashioned, very dependable plants, and I always introduce snapping them to young visitors, who seem to get as big a kick out of it as I did. In Zones 6 and 7, snapdragons are likely to come back year after year, becoming perennials in your garden. (They easily reseed, but not enough to be a pest, and are much more cold-hardy than you'd expect. I've had them survive 16 degree F weather.)

Botanical Pronunciation
an-tir-RHY-num MAY-jus

Bloom Period and Seasonal Color
Spring until frost in pink, red, purple, orange, yellow, and white; both solids and bicolors

Mature Height × Spread
6 inches to 3 feet × 1 foot

Sunflower

Helianthus annuus

I don't suppose we'll ever stop thinking of sunflowers as those tall, gangly plants with the "birdseed" in the center of the large yellow flowers. They still have their place in our gardens—especially to attract birds and to interest kids—but now there are so many other sunflowers available that fit better into typical flower beds. There's a color for every yard—creamy white, smoky red, orange, bronze, beige, and red. And flowers vary from 4 inches to more than a foot in diameter atop plants as diminutive as 24 inches high. Fortunately, growing these exciting new sunflowers, which make wonderful cut flowers, is still as simple as child's play. Kids and birds have always loved sunflowers; now the rest of us are catching on.

Botanical Pronunciation
hee-lee-AN-thuss AN-yew-us

Bloom Period and Seasonal Color
Summer to fall in yellow and brown, cream, red, bronze, beige, and orange

Mature Height × Spread
24 inches to 12 feet × 12 to 24 inches

When, Where, and How to Plant
Although every kindergartner has started sunflower seeds in a cup of potting soil, they don't always transplant well; success is more assured when you sow seeds outdoors where you want the plants to grow. Wait until the danger of frost is past, and give them a sunny location. If sunflowers are in too much shade, they will lean toward the light and need staking. Sunflowers can tolerate just about any kind of soil, but they grow better in soil that's been enriched with organic matter and a handful of 6-12-12 granular fertilizer. Keep soil moist until seeds sprout. Thin to 1 to 4 feet apart, depending on the ultimate size.

Growing Tips
Sunflowers are drought-tolerant, so they don't require a great deal of water. But regular watering when rainfall is lacking produces more consistent growth and flowers. In midseason, spread another handful of granular 6-12-12 fertilizer in a circle 6 to 12 inches away from the stem and water it in. Or use a balanced, water-soluble fertilizer, such as 20-20-20, several times when you water.

Care
Many of the new cultivars have multiple heads and bloom longer if deadheaded. Pest problems are few.

Garden Design
Place shorter varieties with butterfly weed, coreopsis, and gaillardia. Tall ones look best against a dark background, such as a fence or row of evergreens (watch out for too much shade, though). Many gardeners place shorter varieties of sunflowers, particularly those they're growing for cutting, among shrubs, although they're also excellent for a cottage garden.

Try These
'Cherry Rose' has 3- to 4-inch yellow and red flowers on a 5-foot plant. The 6-inch pale yellow flowers of 'Valentine' top 4-foot plants. 'Moulin Rouge' has deep red flowers and burgundy stems. 'Teddy Bear' has fluffy yellow flowers on 2-foot stems. Goldfinches love 'Italian White'.

Sweet Alyssum
Lobularia maritima

When, Where, and How to Plant
Buy bedding plants anytime in spring, or you can sow seed directly in the garden about three weeks before the last expected frost (and, if you like, in midsummer for an extended fall bloom). Amend clay or rocky soils with compost. Good drainage is a must. Work a pelleted slow-release fertilizer into the top few inches of the soil before planting. (See page 45 for more details on planting annuals.) When the plants are an inch tall, thin them 6 to 8 inches apart. Space purchased plants the same distance. Crowded seedlings won't bloom well.

Growing Tips
Water before the soil dries out completely, and add liquid seaweed or a water-soluble fertilizer, such as 20-20-20, every two or three weeks. Mulch when plants are established to moderate soil moisture.

Care
Alyssum will be more drought-tolerant in light to medium shade and may go dormant in the hottest part of the summer. Shear the plants to rejuvenate them if flowers stop forming in the heat of summer. There are few pests, except occasional caterpillars and slugs or snails (see pages 33 and 34 for control advice). Plants usually suffer little damage. Sweet alyssum reseeds but is not invasive; just pull extra seedlings out.

Garden Design
In early spring, plant purple-flowered alyssum with clear yellow pansies. This plant is also known as sweet Alison, so if anyone in your family is named Alison, be sure to grow it for her. Alyssum grows readily between cracks in sidewalks, in rock walls, and along flower bed edges. Plant alyssum beneath a rosebush with artemisia for a cheerful cottage-garden effect.

Try These
'Snow Princess' is vigorous and very heat-tolerant. Deep pink 'Rosie O'Day' is one of the most fragrant alyssums I've grown. For colors that are a little different, try 'Regal Violet', which has deep purple flowers and the Aphrodite series, which includes yellow, purple, and red cultivars.

This sweet little plant, covered with white, purple, or pink flower clusters that emit a delightful fragrance, has a wonderfully old-fashioned feel to it. It will remind you of your grandmother's garden, but will be right at home in yours—if you have a sunny spot that you don't, or can't, water. Low-growing, drought-tolerant, and producing a profusion of flowers that mix with everything, sweet alyssum brings the best of the past to the present. It can provide a neat edging to flower beds and containers (including hanging baskets) and combines nicely with many other kinds of annuals. Because it can tolerate a few light frosts, it's the perfect annual for early spring container gardens and it keeps going a long time in fall.

Botanical Pronunciation
lob-you-LAIR-ee-uh mah-RIT-ih-mah

Bloom Period and Seasonal Color
Spring to frost in white, purple, pink, and light salmon

Mature Height × Spread
3 to 6 inches × 8 to 18 inches

Wax Begonia
Begonia × semperflorens-cultorum

Sometimes you look for exciting plants for your yard. Other times, you prefer reliability; a plant that you know will perform well, look good, and not require much effort on your part. Wax begonia is one of those summer flowers you've probably known forever. But there's no annual that's more versatile or that you can count on more. Wax begonia will grow just about anywhere you put it—from full shade beneath a towering pine to blazing sun by the mailbox and in just about any size container. The neat, shiny leaves come in colors from bronze to bright green and provide an accent to red, pink, or white blossoms that bloom like crazy all summer, no matter what the weather.

Botanical Pronunciation
beh-GOAN-ee-uh sem-per-FLOR-ens cull-TORE-um

Bloom Period and Seasonal Color
Spring until fall with white, red, or pink flowers

Mature Height × Spread
6 to 14 inches × 6 to 18 inches

When, Where, and How to Plant
In spring, after the threat of frost has passed, plant wax begonias in soil that's rich in organic matter and will stay consistently moist. You may need to amend your soil with compost, rotted leaves, or finely shredded bark. Add a pelleted slow-release fertilizer at the time you plant. Mulch plantings to hold in moisture. (See page 45 for more details on planting annuals.) These annuals will do best in partial or full shade but can tolerate full sun, if watered abundantly. Those with bronze leaves are the most sun-tolerant. Space plants 8 to 12 inches apart.

Growing Tips
Keep the soil well watered. Twice a month, apply a water-soluble 20-20-20 fertilizer, or, twice a season, fertilize with an organic fertilizer for flowering plants.

Care
When plants reach 4 inches tall, pinch off the tips of the stems to encourage branching and a fuller appearance. Any time the plants grow leggy, pinch them back again. Wax begonias have few serious insect or disease problems. Slugs can attack seedlings; overwatering can promote root rot. Whiteflies and spider mites occur in very dry conditions; cut back the plants, mulch, and water more often to prevent. See pages 34 to 35 or call the Extension service for advice if problems crop up. It's easy to grow wax begonias indoors over winter. The simplest method is to bring a potted begonia in to a sunny windowsill; pinch the stems back regularly. Or take cuttings in August or early September and place in a jar of water till rooted. Pot-up rooted cuttings, and grow in a sunny spot indoors until spring.

Garden Design
Wax begonias are great in window boxes and for edging flower beds. They're often massed in flower borders. In shade, try them with coleus that has leaves in complementary or contrasting colors.

Try These
The BIG series (BIG Red With Bronze Leaf, BIG Rose With Green Leaf, and so forth) has been outstanding for me; the blooms are large and plentiful.

When, Where, and How to Plant

Zinnia elegans starts easily from seed sown directly in the garden once the soil has warmed up (May or later). Choose a sunny spot with average garden soil, amended only lightly with compost. Thin seedlings so they are spaced 6 to 18 inches apart, depending on the plant's mature size. Plant narrowleaf zinnias 8 to 10 inches apart or in containers. Mulch lightly, if at all; let the sun warm the soil. See pages 37 and 45 for more about starting plants from seed and about how to properly plant annuals.

Growing Tips

Use liquid seaweed or a water-soluble fertilizer made for flowering plants about every two to three weeks. Once plants are established, water enough to prevent wilting, but no more. Always keep the water off the leaves; soaker hoses are ideal for irrigating zinnias.

Care

Overwatering, overcrowding, and overcast weather promote leaf diseases that can plague zinnias; avoid these situations and choose varieties that are resistant. Ask the Extension service for advice about fungicides, but remember they're preventative not curative. Hot, dry conditions can promote spider mites; cut flowers from affected stems and remove those plants from the garden, or see page 34 for advice about controlling them. Use zinnias in flower arrangements; removing the blooms prompts the plants to produce more. Remove faded flowers from *Zinnia elegans* regularly; narrowleafs need no deadheading.

Garden Design

Common zinnias and narrowleaf zinnias are staples of cottage gardens and bring hot colors to tropical plantings. Make a sunny bed of *Zinnia elegans* with melampodium, marigolds, and globe amaranth.

Try These

'Old Mexico' has mahogany and gold blooms on a 2-foot plant. 'Liliput' has small flowers that are very attractive to several species of butterfly. The Profusion series offers compact plants covered with boldly colored blooms; it's resistant to mildew. 'Crystal White' and 'Star Gold' are my favorite narrowleaf zinnias.

We all recognize boldly colorful zinnias when we see them, and we know how easy they are to grow. We might also be leery that some zinnias mildew easily, not wanting to be bothered with that problem. But there's more to zinnias. Flowers on the common zinnia (Z. elegans) may be single, double, or resemble dahlias. And there's a neat little creeping or narrowleaf zinnia (Z. angustifolia), which has fernlike foliage, is resistant to mildew, and is particularly attractive when planted so it tumbles over the edges of containers. Zinnia tenuifolia 'Red Spider' has the unusual flowers you'd expect from a name like "red spider." All bloom nonstop through fall and are so simple to grow from seeds (or plants) that anyone can do it.

Botanical Pronunciation

ZIN-nee-uh

Bloom Period and Seasonal Color

Summer until fall in every color except blue

Mature Height × Spread

6 inches to 3 feet × 12 inches to 3½ feet

Bulbs, Corms, Rhizomes & Tubers

It's true that few of us would want to be without those colorful harbingers of spring we so commonly associate with the season: the tiny purple, golden, or white crocuses that announce that winter is on its way out; sunny yellow daffodils that brighten the landscape from February through April; and finally, the majestic tulips, in almost every shade of the rainbow, that remind us that summer will soon arrive.

But what about another joy of spring, irises? And summer's colorful cannas? You may not think of those plants as growing from bulbs.

*Daffodils (*Narcissus*)*

And it's true that, technically, they may not. But plants that grow from tubers, rhizomes, and corms are closely related to bulbs and are often grown in similar ways. That's why we've combined them in one chapter that includes such beauties as caladiums, dramatic elephant ears, Southern favorites like surprise lilies and crinums, as well as popular spring bulbs.

Technically Speaking

A true bulb, such as a tulip, is a complete plant wrapped in a skin. It has swollen leaf scales that protect the flower bud and store food during its rest period. Bulbs include almost all the food needed by the plant in order for it to grow and bloom. A *corm* is similar to a bulb in that it also stores food in fleshy, underground stems. It is somewhat flatter than a bulb and may be smaller. Gladiolus and crocus grow from corms. A *tuber* is another swollen, underground stem that has buds, or "eyes," which are the flower and growth buds. Caladiums and dahlias are examples of popular tubers. A *rhizome* is an underground stem that grows horizontally instead of vertically. Bearded iris is one example. All of these plants grow much the same way and use food stored in their underground storage units. Some are considered cold-hardy, and some are not. For simplicity's sake, we're going to refer to them all together as "bulbs." But in the plant profiles, we'll be more specific.

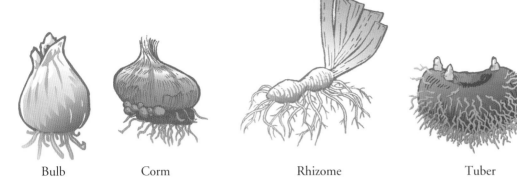

| Bulb | Corm | Rhizome | Tuber |

Advance Planning Required

One thing that all types of bulbs have in common is that enjoying them takes advance planning on the part of the gardener. In order to have bulbs blossoming in April, for instance, you must plant them six months earlier, in fall. Dahlia tubers set out in the garden at the end of April won't begin blooming until at least midsummer and often later. That's why patience and planning are the bywords with bulbs.

No, that isn't implying that bulbs are difficult; just the opposite is true. Spring-flowering bulbs are especially easy—dig a hole in autumn, drop a bulb in it, add some soil, and wait till spring for the beautiful flower to appear. But if you want your bulbs to last more than one season, you should prepare the soil for them, just as you would for any other flowering plants.

Good drainage is a must for all bulbs (including corms and tubers); in soil that stays wet, bulbs rot. To improve ordinary clay soil and rocky or sandy soil so they will be suitable for successful bulb growing, mix in ample amounts of compost, fine pine bark, or rotted leaves before you plant. In hard clay soil that stays wet for a day after rain, plant bulbs in raised beds.

Want to save some time when planting a hundred or more spring-flowering bulbs at once? Forget digging individual holes and placing a bulb in each one. It's easier to dig up an entire bed to the proper depth, piling the soil to the outside. Then space the bulbs evenly across the bottom of the bed, covering them with the soil that was removed from the hole.

If squirrels, chipmunks, and other vermin are a problem in your yard, you have several choices. Stick with daffodils, which rodents and deer leave alone because they're poisonous to them; plant bulbs in "baskets" of chicken wire; or use a liquid bulb protectant, available at garden centers and nurseries. Soak bulbs in the protectant solution before planting, and later, spray plant leaves with the product in spring to guard against deer damage.

How Low Should You Go?

The rule of thumb for spring-flowering bulbs such as crocus, daffodils, and tulips is to dig a hole three times as deep as the height of the bulb and to space bulbs three times their width apart. However, you'll be fine if you plant small bulbs, such as crocus and Spanish bluebells, 5 inches deep—measured from the bottom of the bulb—and larger bulbs, from tulips to giant alliums, 8 inches deep.

Plants that grow from corms and rhizomes may be exceptions to that depth rule, so check the plant profiles for each bulb to be sure. Bearded iris rhizomes are barely covered with soil, for instance.

In heavy clay soil, you may not be able to plant spring-flowering bulbs as deeply as recommended, but when possible it's worth making the effort, for two reasons: deeper planting discourages rodents from digging up and making a meal of your bulbs, and, in my experience, the deeper you've planted them in warm climates, the more likely the bulbs are to return in future years (provided the drainage is good). I've had tulips come back for more than seven years in a row when they were placed a foot deep in clay soil I'd mixed liberally with fine pine bark.

One thing I've discovered is that when people plant bulbs for the first time, they often puzzle over which end is considered the "top" for planting. Well, I'll be the first to admit that it isn't always easy to tell. But if you're one of those who've worried about this, I'll also relieve your mind a bit by letting you know that it usually doesn't matter. Look at the bulb, rhizome, or tuber carefully and see if you can find a pointed end, or little "eyes" (growth buds), both of which indicate "up"—and then don't give it another thought. Being upside down or even sideways rarely prevents spring-flowering bulbs from blooming and usually makes little difference to the others in this chapter either.

Plant bulbs with the pointed end or little "eyes" up.

Timing Is Important

When's the best time to plant your bulbs? Plant lilies and other summer-flowering bulbs as soon as you buy or receive them. With caladiums, wait until the soil is warm (sometime in May; you can even plant in June). The general rule with spring-flowering bulbs is that the smaller they are, the earlier they are planted. So you can plant crocuses in September (continuing until November); daffodils from October through December; and tulips beginning the first of November and continuing until the ground freezes. Because tulips need a chilling period, store them where the temperature is 50 degrees Fahrenheit or lower while waiting to plant. Keeping them in a refrigerator is fine, as long as you don't store them near apples or pears, which give off a gas that can harm tulip bulbs.

Starting in late November and continuing until after Christmas, the question I am asked most often about spring-flowering bulbs, is, "Is it too late to plant my bulbs?" The answer is, "No." As long as the ground is not frozen, you can still plant bulbs—even if it's January. Later than that, though, and they may or may not flower that spring. But if the bulbs are still in good condition, plant them, even during a late January or February thaw; they should bloom the following year.

The Scoop on Fertilizing

There are misconceptions floating around about fertilizing spring-flowering bulbs—and acting on some of that bad advice can mean a shorter lifetime or even failure for your plantings. Here are the dos and don'ts:

- Do use a special slow-release bulb fertilizer at planting time. Then mark your bulbs somehow (I often use inconspicuous stakes at the edges of bulb beds, or even a squirt or two of spray paint) so that you can spread the same fertilizer (organic and nonorganic brands are available) over the bed each fall. This gives your bulbs the nutrients they need when they need them. (You may also use a small amount of granular 5-10-10 fertilizer in fall, but then, because its effects aren't long-lasting, you'll need to use it again when about an inch of bulb foliage is peeking above the soil—and typically that's about February, when the weather is cold; not the time I want to be out fertilizing plants.)
- Don't fertilize when spring-flowering bulbs are in bloom or right afterward. Bulbs can take up food only when they're growing, and they grow from fall until just before blooming. Fertilizing when bulbs have finished flowering has been shown to cause them to rot.
- Don't use bonemeal. It encourages dogs and other animals to dig up the bulbs. Also, while bonemeal once contained the nutrients bulbs require, the way it's made has changed, and it no longer provides the ample food that bulbs need.
- Do fertilize summer-flowering bulbs with a slow-release plant food for flowering plants or a bulb booster fertilizer when foliage appears, and then use a water-soluble fertilizer once a month until the plants bloom.

Although this has nothing to do with fertilizing, another big "don't" for spring bulbs is never to braid their foliage (or fold it up with rubber bands) when it starts to turn yellow or brown. Everyone will admit that this practice improves the appearance of the flower bed. Browning foliage isn't pretty! But that foliage is actually performing a job: photosynthesis. That is, it's absorbing energy from the sun and storing it in the bulb. That keeps the bulb strong and enables it to bloom well next year. If you prevent it from absorbing as much sun as possible—and braided "packages" secured by rubber bands do—the bulb declines, and so do the future flowers. Always wait till foliage has browned and can be pulled off without tugging before you remove it. If it doesn't look good, plant annuals around the bulbs to hide the fading leaves.

Great for Beginners

For beginning gardeners—those who aren't yet sure of their abilities—bulbs are a grand place to start, because success is almost assured. More experienced gardeners know that lots of bulbs in a yard help you quickly build a reputation as a green-thumbed gardener—and you don't have to tell anyone how easy it was!

Caladium
Caladium bicolor

Colorful shade plants that shine in the shade all summer long aren't necessarily common (beyond impatiens, of course). But caladiums will easily add knock-your-socks-off color to beds containing more subdued ferns and hostas. From spring until fall, they perk up shady areas with their bold foliage in various shades of red, green, white, and pink, often complemented by contrasting veining and splotches. If you really want to make a splash, grow them en masse. As well as being stars of the woodland garden, caladiums grow well in containers and even as houseplants. And no matter how high summer temperatures climb, caladiums take the heat in stride. When you want something a little different, especially when planting in pots, look for miniature caladiums.

Botanical Pronunciation
kuh-LAY-dee-um BYE-cull-er

Bloom Period and Seasonal Color
Summer until frost; grown for heart-shaped leaves in green, red, white, pink, and bicolors

Mature Height × Spread
1 to 2½ feet × 1 to 2 feet

When, Where, and How to Plant
Caladiums will produce the best-looking leaves in a shady spot with average garden soil amended with compost. They'll rot in cold, wet, or heavy soils. Plant tubers indoors in April; bottom heat encourages faster sprouting. Or, in May and June, after the soil is warm, plant tubers and purchased plants outdoors in beds and pots. Space plants 12 to 16 inches apart. Work compost or a pelleted slow-release fertilizer into the soil at planting time.

Growing Tips
Water regularly. Apply a water-soluble fertilizer, such as 20-20-20, every other week to plants in containers, monthly to those in beds. To grow as a houseplant indoors, place potted caladiums in a warm spot (at least 75 degrees Fahrenheit) that receives at least four hours of direct sunlight daily (more for red-leaved cultivars, a bit less for those with green leaves). Keep the soil evenly moist, and fertilize once a month with any houseplant fertilizer.

Care
Slugs and snails may munch holes in tender new leaves. (See page 34 for controls.) One way to deter them is to wait until plants are up and growing before you apply mulch so you aren't providing early hiding places for the slimy mollusks. Caladiums are troubled by few other pests. The flowers that eventually develop are interesting but deplete the tubers; cut them off as soon as they appear. When the leaves die down in fall, dig up tubers and store in a dark, warm place in dry peat moss over winter.

Garden Design
Caladiums are excellent alone or with ferns, hostas, or white impatiens. In a container, intersperse with 'Diamond Frost' euphorbia and let 'Pink Frost' ornamental sweet potato spill over the edges.

Try These
'Scarlet Pimpernel', which grows from 20 to 30 inches tall, doesn't mind sun. Its leaves are light green with deep pink centers. 'White Christmas' has substantial white leaves boldly veined and edged in green.

Canna

Canna species and hybrids

When, Where, and How to Plant

Start rhizomes indoors in April in peat pots filled with potting soil; water just enough to keep soil moist but not soggy. After the soil warms outdoors, plant these starts or purchased plants in a sunny spot with average garden soil amended with compost, or in large containers filled with rich potting soil. Incorporate 10-10-10 fertilizer into the soil when planting. Mulch with 2 to 3 inches of organic matter.

Growing Tips

Keep soil evenly moist until plants are established, and then let it dry out slightly between waterings. Monthly, apply a water-soluble fertilizer formulated for flowering plants. Overfertilization with nitrogen will produce leaves but no flowers.

Care

Have some fun by letting seedpods remain on the plant until they turn brown and papery. Remove the seeds and store for six months; then nick them and soak overnight in warm water before planting them. Canna leaf rollers, slugs, and snails can be pests. Leaf rollers pupate inside newly emerging leaves and distort them. Cut the leaves off and sprinkle diatomaceous earth or insecticidal dust labeled to control these pests into the cut leaf area. For slug and snail control, see page 34. In Zone 7, cannas will usually survive most winters, if mulched well. But in the coldest parts of Zone 6—and in Zone 7 for special plants you don't want to lose—cut down clumps at the end of the season, dig up the rhizomes, and let them dry until the dirt falls off (do not wash or scrape). Store in a box filled with dry peat moss where temperatures will remain above freezing.

Garden Design

A combination of canna cultivars makes a bold bed. Or choose companions that can stand up to their drama—fountain grass, annual sunflower, and cleome.

Try These

'Intrigue' has orange flowers set against purplish leaves; it grows about 7 feet tall and has long, slender leaves.

I've always thought of cannas as plants my grandmother grew; old-fashioned and colorful, but not very exciting. I can't imagine what she'd say about the irresistible new canna cultivars being released every year. All I can say is, "Wow!" Cannas have turned into the glamour girls of summer bulbs with dramatic striped foliage that practically glows in the dark, making the plants beautiful even after the flowers fade. Just one leaf may feature red, pink, yellow, and gold, which sounds gaudy but somehow isn't. There's also a nice selection of dwarf cannas now, which are perfect for pots, since they stay small but have flowers up to 5 inches across. One thing remains the same: Butterflies and hummingbirds enjoy cannas as much as gardeners do.

Botanical Pronunciation

KAN-nuh

Bloom Period and Seasonal Color

Summer in red, yellow, salmon, white, and pink

Mature Height × Spread

20 inches to 7 feet × 12 inches to 3 feet

Crinum Lily
Crinum species and hybrids

Crinum lilies are old favorites in Southern gardens; you may know the striped ones as milk and wine lilies, but they come in white or pink solids too. The flowers are like those of amaryllis. Despite their charm, your question may be whether crinums, which came from Africa, are hardy in Tennessee and Kentucky? With mulch, most hybrid, or named, crinums ought to be hardy in Zone 7. Zone 6 gardeners should plant hybrid crinums in the warmest microclimate in their yards. You can also grow crinums in containers in summer and put them in a frost-free garage in winter. Crinum bulbispermum is the hardiest crinum. The least hardy are the spider lilies, which have flowers like spider daylilies, but I've grown them in Zone 7.

Botanical Pronunciation
CRY-num

Bloom Period and Seasonal Color
Summer in white, shades of pink and magenta

Mature Height x Spread
18 inches to 4 feet x 1 to 5 feet

When, Where, and How to Plant
In late spring or in summer, choose a spot in full sun that has well-drained soil rich in organic matter. An exception is *Crinum × moorei*, which tolerates a half day of shade and some wet soil. Place the bulb so the neck will be about 2 inches above the soil. Because the large bulb spends the first year in your garden putting down roots, it may not bloom the summer after you plant it. That's normal and nothing to worry about. To plant in a large container, mix 2 parts potting soil with 1 part compost or dehydrated manure. Wet the mixture thoroughly, and fill the container halfway. Place the bulb on top of the soil so that its neck will come to about the rim. Fill to within 2 inches of the rim with more moistened soil mix that's been combined with pelleted timed-release fertilizer. Water well and place the pot in a sunny spot. Water and use a liquid or water-soluble fertilizer weekly.

Growing Tips
Water when rainfall is less than an inch per week, but be aware that too much water can rot the bulbs. In the first year, fertilize once a month with a water-soluble fertilizer or liquid seaweed. Then, you'll need to fertilize only once in summer. Topdress the soil around crinums with compost in fall. Deer generally don't bother them.

Care
Pests are rarely a problem. Lift and divide crinums when clumps become crowded. Move container-grown crinum lilies to a frost-free garage or basement over the winter and allow them to go dormant. After warm weather returns, begin to water again, using a water-soluble fertilizer. When leaves appear, take the planter back outdoors.

Garden Design
Because of their boldness, plant crinums alone to make them a focal point.

Try These
'Sangria' has purple leaves and pink flowers. It's hardy in Zone 7 and grows about 4 feet tall.

Crocus
Crocus species and hybrids

When, Where, and How to Plant
In fall, plant spring-blooming crocus 3 to 4 inches deep and 3 inches apart in a sunny location. Plant fall bloomers, including saffron crocus (*Crocus sativus*), the same way, as soon as they become available. (Fall crocus will bloom several weeks after planting and will rebloom each fall.) Because they're small, crocus look best when grown in groups of 25 or more. Any average garden soil that drains well will sustain them. Add granular bulb fertilizer, according to package directions, to the soil at planting time and mulch the top of the planting area with shredded leaves.

Growing Tips
Each fall, spread a bulb fertilizer over the soil where crocuses are planted and water in. Root growth begins in fall, so it's important to water during dry spells from September until the ground freezes hard. Maintain a 2-inch mulch of organic material such as finely shredded bark or pine needles to keep the soil cool during summer and to prevent the corms from heaving out of the ground in winter when soil alternately freezes and thaws.

Care
Crocus require little maintenance. When the number of flowers diminishes, dig up and divide the clumps after flowering has finished. Replant immediately. Hungry rodents may dig up corms, but few other pests trouble crocus. Planting bulbs in a homemade chicken-wire basket or applying a repellent to them can deter field mice and chipmunks.

Garden Design
Plant crocus in groups in flower beds, at the base of evergreen shrubs, or in drifts across the lawn. Use a few dozen of each color for best effect, and place them where you can see them from inside the house or will go by them each day.

Try These
'Pickwick' has large flowers (for a crocus) that are violet striped with silver, an attractive look when planted with dark purple 'Purpurea Grandiflora'.

In Tennessee and Kentucky, we're fortunate that our winter weather doesn't begin to compare to the snows and blows of Minnesota or Vermont. But as winter progresses, we get just as tired of the cold as do folks in the North, and we eagerly look forward to spring. Just about the time you begin to wonder if winter is going on forever, crocus, heralds of spring, arrive. Tiny, cup-shaped flowers in white, as well as shades of purple and yellow, pop up—even if snow is on the ground—to remind us that yes, spring is on its warm way. You'll also enjoy fall-blooming true crocus, which provide a nice burst of color just a few weeks after being planted in early autumn.

Botanical Pronunciation
CROW-kus

Bloom Period and Seasonal Color
Late winter into spring, also autumn, in white, purple, yellow, and bicolors

Mature Height × Spread
4 to 6 inches × 1 to 3 inches

Daffodil

Narcissus species and hybrids

If I had to choose a favorite bulb, I'd probably pick the daffodils, which offer so much more variety than most people realize. There are white, pink-cupped, and fragrant ones, as well as a variety of yellows, that flower from late winter to late spring. It's easy to have an array of daffodils for a couple of months outside and also indoors, where they are nice in arrangements. Does it matter if you call it narcissus or daffodil? Not really. While Narcissus is the name for the entire genus, either daffodil or narcissus is fine as a common name. Southerners sometimes call all daffodils jonquils because English colonists brought this type of Narcissus with them, but jonquil really refers to a specific type of narcissus.

Botanical Pronunciation
nar-SIS-sus

Bloom Period and Seasonal Color
From February through April, yellow, white, orange, pink, or a combination of colors

Mature Height × Spread
4 inches to 2 feet × 2 to 6 inches

When, Where, and How to Plant
Plant small daffodil bulbs 3 to 5 inches deep and large bulbs 8 to 12 inches deep, both 2 to 6 inches apart, beginning in October and continuing until early January, if the ground isn't frozen. Just about any soil is suitable (as long as it's mostly in sun), but clay should be improved with organic matter. All bulbs need good drainage, or they'll rot. Mix a granular bulb fertilizer, according to label directions, with the soil in the hole.

Growing Tips
Every fall, spread granular bulb fertilizer according to package directions, on top of the soil where bulbs have previously been planted, and water well. Never fertilize when the bulb is blooming or just afterward, as this can cause bulbs to rot. Water occasionally during autumn dry spells when bulbs are growing underground. Add to the mulch on top of beds to keep it 2 inches deep.

Care
After the flowers fade, snap off the stalk, but leave the foliage to dry naturally. As the foliage browns over a period of about six weeks, it's producing and storing food in the bulb for next year. If you braid the foliage, you interfere with this process. When clumps have gotten crowded and aren't blooming much, dig up and divide the clumps after blooming is complete, and then replant right away. Daffodils are usually carefree, but possible pests include bulb mites (which suck the sap), botrytis (a disease characterized by reddish brown spots on the leaves), and fusarium wilt (which causes the plant to yellow and die). Call the Extension service for advice on how to deal with these problems.

Garden Design
Naturalize daffodils in meadows and on the edges of woodlands. I often plant yellow daffs near forsythia and kerria shrubs and intersperse them with purple grape hyacinths.

Try These
'Thalia' has beautiful white flowers that are fragrant. 'Canaliculatus' is an early bloomer that reaches 6 inches high.

Dahlia
Dahlia species and hybrids

When, Where, and How to Plant
Dahlia tubers come in clumps; don't divide them before planting. Work ample additions of organic matter into the soil of the planting area to a depth of 10 inches. (You want the same type of rich, loose soil you'd have in a vegetable garden.) In a sunny spot, dig a hole 1 foot wide and 6 inches deep. Work a pelleted slow-release fertilizer (or granular 10-10-10, or tomato fertilizer) into both the soil you leave in the hole and what you dig out. Next, lay tubers in a hand shape (horizontally) in the hole. Cover with 3 inches of soil; as the stems grow, add more soil gradually to cover them. Plant large dahlias 18 inches apart and smaller varieties 8 to 10 inches apart.

Growing Tips
Dahlias demand moist soil to perform. Use soaker hoses or water deeply by hand. This also helps keep flowers large. Fertilize with a water-soluble plant food for flowering plants or tomatoes every two weeks from planting until flower buds are set.

Care
Mulch with up to 3 inches of organic material. Dahlias may be troubled by various insects and diseases: slugs, snails, aphids, borers, beetles, mites, and powdery mildew. Check with the Extension service for recommended remedies. After frost kills the plants, dig up the tubers, hose them off, and let them dry in the sun. Store in layers in peat moss in a cool, dark place.

Garden Design
Little dahlias sold as bedding plants in spring can go in sunny beds that are home to annuals or perennials of complementary colors. Because taller dahlias need staking, put them in beds that aren't in prominent locations (on the side of the house, for instance, instead of the front). You may also want to group dahlias together in the border or fill one bed with them.

Try These
Bright red 'The Big Wow' is *exactly* that. It's larger than a dinnerplate.

As the gardening season begins to wind down in autumn, gardeners are often on the lookout for plants that produce colorful fall flowers. If you're ready to move beyond chrysanthemums, consider dahlias, which offer so much more—blooms no bigger than a button to larger than a dinner plate, and a variety of intriguing flower shapes, resembling waterlilies, zinnias, daisies, and cactus flowers. There's nothing dull about dahlias—they're sure to impress you as well as your neighbors. Some gardeners may hesitate to grow dahlias, since the tubers are planted differently from the mums picked up at the garden center. But don't hesitate. If you've ever raised tomatoes, you can be confident you'll be successful with dahlias—they like the same conditions.

Botanical Pronunciation
DAL-ya

Bloom Period and Seasonal Color
Summer to fall in white and shades of red, pink, yellow, and orange, as well as bicolors

Mature Height × Spread
1 to 7 feet × 8 inches to 2 feet

Elephant Ear
Colocasia species and hybrids

If you go for a dramatic look, elephant ears are for you. They're tropical plants with heart-shaped leaves that can grow 4 feet long or even bigger. And, unlike most tropicals, they're hardy in Zone 7, or, at least, Colocasia species are. But Alocasia, also sold as elephant ears, is not winter-hardy in our region and requires slightly different growing conditions. So it pays to buy bulbs labeled Colocasia. 'Black Magic', with purplish stems and leaves, is one of the most common hardy elephant ears passed along among gardeners. But even if you aren't in Zone 7, you can grow elephant ears much as you would dahlias, by digging them up each fall, storing in dry peat moss over winter, and replanting the next year.

Botanical Pronunciation
ko-low-KAY-see-uh

Bloom Period and Seasonal Color
Summer; grown for foliage

Mature Height x Spread
2 to 8 feet x 3 to 7 feet

When, Where, and How to Plant
In late spring, after weather and soil are warm, plant *Colocasia* tubers in rich, moist, but well-drained soil in full sun. *Alocasia* can tolerate wet soils and filtered sun (no more than half a day of shade). Mix timed-release fertilizer with the soil before planting. Both types will also grow in large pots. Plant the tuber so that 1 to 2 inches of soil cover its top. Space tubers 2 to 4 feet apart, depending on the eventual size of the cultivar.

Growing Tips
Elephant ears need plenty of water and fertilizer. Don't let their soil dry out. Once during June and July, and again in early August, feed with a granular fertilizer that's high in nitrogen, such as 10-0-0, according to label directions. Or, spray plants with a water-soluble or liquid plant food such as 20-20-20.

Care
When night temperatures fall to 50 degrees Fahrenheit, cut back on watering. When a frost kills the foliage, cut it off and mulch heavily if you're in Zone 7. In Zone 6, carefully dig up the tuber and let it dry in the sun for a few days before storing in a box of peat moss placed where temperatures are about 55 degrees Fahrenheit. Move plants growing in containers to a frost-free garage; remove foliage when it browns. Elephant ears may also be taken indoors and grown as houseplants, if you have a sunroom.

Garden Design
I like the contrast between large green (or dark) leaves of elephant ears and the smaller, colorful foliage of red sun-resistant coleus. Pair *Alocasia* with white- or red-flowered impatiens or red caladiums.

Try These
'Black Beauty' is one of the hardiest and most reliable. 'Hilo Beauty' looks just like a giant caladium, with cream markings in its leaves; it isn't hardy. *Colocasia esculenta* 'Mojito', which has leaves flecked with purple, is for warmer parts of Zone 7.

Giant Allium
Allium giganteum

When, Where, and How to Plant

Make sure the large bulbs are firm, not soft, and handle them carefully. In fall, set bulbs 4 to 6 inches deep (depending on the size of the bulb) and 12 to 18 inches apart in very well-drained soil. Like all bulbs, giant alliums will rot if their soil stays wet, especially over winter. It's best to plant giant alliums among other flowers to hide its unattractive fading foliage. Mix a granular bulb fertilizer, according to package directions, with the soil in the planting hole. In the coldest areas, you may want to spread 3 inches of organic mulch, such as pine needles, fine pine bark, or well-shredded pine bark, over the area after planting, although the bulb is generally hardy.

Growing Tips

Rainfall is generally sufficient so little watering will be needed. Spread a granular bulb fertilizer around the bulbs every fall.

Care

Remove dead foliage from the bed, for neatness and to help deter future insects and diseases; don't cut it off until it's completely brown. Thrips are a possible problem, as are a few diseases, but they're not common. Consult the Extension service for advice if problems appear. You may need to dig up and divide the clumps every two to three years just after flowering finishes, since giant alliums multiply quickly. Share extras with friends and neighbors.

Garden Design

Grow giant alliums with plants that bloom at the same time in yellow or white: coreopsis, early yellow-flowering daylilies such as 'Stella d'Oro' or 'Happy Returns', foxglove (white), *Kniphofia* (yellow cultivars), peony (white or yellow), and rhododendron. Place the alliums behind or among other perennials so that as their foliage yellows and dies, it will be hidden.

Try These

'Globemaster' reaches at least 4 feet tall; its flowers are long-lasting. The flowers of 'Mars' are spectacular and the size of softballs. 'Mount Everest' and 'White Giant' have white blooms.

If you've never seen a giant allium before, you'll be amazed, and so will people who see them in your late spring garden. The flowers form round balls (usually purplish) up to half a foot across atop hollow stems that are about 3 feet high, often taller. Once you start looking at these ornamental bulb-grown alliums (they're members of the onion family and are related to chives and garlic chives, which tells you how easy they are to grow), you'll find others you'll want to try: blue allium, Allium caeruleum, is similar to giant allium but has sky blue blooms and grows only 2 feet tall. Allium aflatunense 'Purple Sensation' has the deepest color I've seen. Allium moly looks more like a tulip, with yellow flowers.

Botanical Pronunciation
AL-e-um ji-gan-TEE-um

Bloom Period and Seasonal Color
Late spring to early summer in lavender, purple, white, and yellow

Mature Height x Spread
4 to 6 feet x 1 to 2 feet

Iris

Iris species and hybrids

Few other flowers have such a romantic image as irises. There are so many different kinds, it would take this whole page to list them all. So there's something that will appeal to everyone, including bulb-grown irises (such as delicate Dutch iris) and different species of rhizomatous irises from the familiar bearded irises to the low-growing native crested iris, which fits so nicely into woodland gardens. Siberian irises, with blooms that resemble butterflies, have become so popular because they're easy to grow, but don't overlook the dramatic Louisiana and Japanese irises, which prefer moist soil. The plant's name comes from the Greek word for rainbow, which gives you an idea of the colors available.

Botanical Pronunciation
EYE-ris

Bloom Period and Seasonal Color
Spring flowers in a rainbow of colors—all except true orange

Mature Height × Spread
4 inches to 4 feet × 4 inches to 2 feet

When, Where, and How to Plant

Plant rhizomatous irises in spring; fall, for those that grow from bulbs. Bearded irises need alkaline soil; Japanese, Louisiana, Siberian, and crested irises prefer acidic. Dutch irises aren't picky about soil pH. Choose a sunny site for bearded, Dutch, Louisiana, Siberian, and Japanese irises; shade for crested irises. All except bearded irises will bloom in light shade. Plant bearded iris rhizomes almost on top of the soil, half-exposed to the sun; other rhizomatous irises about 1 inch deep; Dutch irises, 5 inches deep. Space rhizomes by the mature size: 3 to 4 inches apart for crested iris to several feet for large bearded irises. Put Louisiana and Japanese irises in bogs; bearded, Dutch, and crested irises demand excellent drainage.

Growing Tips

Fertilize all but Dutch iris each spring with a slow-release fertilizer for flowering plants, according to package directions. (Fertilize Dutch irises in fall with a bulb fertilizer.) Keep soil moist around Japanese and Louisiana irises. For all others, water when less than an inch of rain falls weekly.

Care

Cut off faded flower stalks. Every three years, divide rhizomes in late July or August. If Dutch irises get crowded, divide and replant right away after blooming ends. The most common pest is the iris borer, which leaves tunnels in the leaves. Kill them by hand in the leaves. If they reach the rhizome, cut them out, discard the affected part, and replant the healthy section. Other potential problems include slugs and snails (see page 34 for control methods), root rot, leaf spot, thrips, and aphids. Ask the Extension service for control recommendations.

Garden Design

Siberian irises fit well in perennial borders. Japanese and Louisiana irises grow along the edges of water gardens. Bearded irises look best by themselves. Try them in front of a white picket fence.

Try These

An old favorite that's always reliable is purple-flowered *Iris siberica* 'Caesar's Brother'.

Lily

Lilium species and hybrids

When, Where, and How to Plant

Fall is the preferred planting time, although you can set out potted Easter lilies in spring after frost has passed. Don't let lily bulbs dry out before planting; that damages them. Pick a spot that's in sun for at least six hours daily and has well-drained soil. Amend clay and poor soils with organic matter such as compost or fine pine bark, and mix in pelleted slow-release fertilizer according to package directions. Plant bulbs 4 to 6 inches deep (measured from the bottom of the bulb to the top of the ground) and space them 14 to 18 inches apart. Place a stake next to taller varieties when you plant the bulb and before you cover it with soil so there's no chance to damage the bulb with the stake. Never plant Easter lilies with other lilies—they may transmit a virus that can kill the others.

Growing Tips

Lilies enjoy having lots of moisture up through the time they bloom. You don't need to water after flowering. If soil is poor, spread pelleted slow-release fertilizer on the ground around the stems when leaves sprout. Otherwise, topdress with an inch of compost. Mulch lightly with organic matter to conserve moisture.

Care

Deadhead flowers, removing as few leaves as possible. Dig and divide bulbs if necessary when stems are going dormant; cut stems down to 2 inches above ground in fall. Lily flowers last up to a week indoors; remove the anthers so the pollen won't stain whatever it touches. In the South, diseases are usually more of a problem than insects. Consult the Extension service for remedies.

Garden Design

Try *Coreopsis* 'Moonbeam' with yellow Asiatic lilies; pair 'Stargazer' with white-flowering hydrangeas and pink or red sun coleus.

Try These

Everyone stops to admire 'Arabian Knight', a martagon (turkscap) lily (*L. martagon*) that grows 2 to 3 feet tall, is fragrant, and has dramatic flowers.

Lilies have been grown around the world for more than 5,000 years and are the essence of elegance. No one could imagine calling lilies "cute" or "perky." They're graceful, beautiful, and versatile. Many gardeners grow them because they make excellent cut flowers, but they also add that touch of tasteful sophistication to any flower bed. When you can plant several different types of lilies, you can extend their flowering season. First to bloom are the Asiatics, then Aurelian hybrids, followed by the late Orientals. Lily flowers come in solids, stripes, dots, and bands, with and without fancy edges. Most grow face up, but some face out and others hang down. I always like to grow some of each and use as many as possible in arrangements.

Botanical Pronunciation

LIL-ee-um

Bloom Period and Seasonal Color

Summer to fall in orange, red, pink, yellow, cream, and white

Mature Height × Spread

2 to 8 feet × 1 to 3 feet

Lycoris
Lycoris species

What would you call a plant that suddenly pops up from bare ground and blooms without putting out any leaves? Well, common names for lycoris are naked ladies, magic lily, surprise lily, and resurrection lily. All are appropriate for a plant that's a lot of fun to grow. Actually, it's two plants that behave slightly differently. The straplike leaves of Lycoris squamigera *appear in spring and grow until summer, then wither and disappear. A month later, leafless stems pop up, with pink flowers radiating from the top. Red-flowered Lycoris radiata (for Zone 7 only, unless grown in containers) puts up its flower stalk in August or September, and then leaves appear. These are great plants for gardening with kids, who are fascinated by their unusual habits.*

Botanical Pronunciation
lie-KORR-is

Bloom Period and Seasonal Color
Summer or early fall in red, pink, cream, golden, or pale yellow

Mature Height × Spread
12 to 36 inches × 6 to 12 inches

Zones
7 for *Lycoris radiata*; all for *Lycoris squamigera*

When, Where, and How to Plant
Lycoris prefers rich, well-drained garden soil amended with compost and in full or partial sun, but is very adaptable. When bulbs are available, dig holes about 8 inches deep. Mix a slight handful of granular 10-10-10 fertilizer with the soil, and plant bulbs 4 to 6 inches deep and 6 to 12 inches apart. In the cooler parts of Zone 6, you may want to grow lycoris in containers.

Growing Tips
L. squamigera is dormant in summer and so doesn't require much watering, just enough to keep the plant from wilting. Let the soil dry out between waterings in summer. Fertilize with pelleted slow-release fertilizer or cottonseed meal, according to package directions, when the leaves sprout.

Care
Mark the location of the bulbs so you don't accidentally dig them up or damage them when the foliage goes dormant. Don't mow or cut down the clumps of faded foliage. After crowded clumps stop blooming—probably every 3 to 5 years—divide them in late spring. Replant immediately. They don't like being moved though, and may take a couple of years to begin blooming again. Few pests bother lycoris, but bulbs will rot in wet soils.

Garden Design
Lycoris looks great with blue flowers. I like *L. radiata* with anise sage (*Salvia guaranitica*) or anise hyssop (*Agastache foeniculum*). They're nice with white Madagascar periwinkle, too.

Try These
After I tried growing both kinds of common lycoris bulbs, I decided to experiment with some that grew and bloomed the same but weren't pink or red: *L. albiflora* has cream-colored flowers, and *L. aurea* produces pale yellow blooms. They're not winter-hardy, so I dig mine up before winter and replant the next spring. Especially hardy are Chinese surprise lily (*L. chinensis*), which has golden flowers, and *L. sprengeri*, known as tie-dye surprise lily because each flower petal starts out pink and then turns blue toward the tip.

Montbretia
Crocosmia species and hybrids

When, Where, and How to Plant

Plant in spring or fall in humus-rich soil (add compost or other organic materials to clay). Avoid areas that stay wet during winter. Full sun is best, but the plant prefers some afternoon shade in Zone 7. In the coldest areas, choose the warmest spot in your yard (near a south-facing wall, for example). Plant the corms 4 to 5 inches deep and space about 5 or 6 inches apart. After the plants are growing, mulch well with 3 inches of organic material. Fertilizer isn't needed at planting time in good soils, but you should toss a handful of granular 10-10-10 into the planting hole in marginal or poor soils. Incorporate pelleted timed-release fertilizer into the potting mix when planting in containers, or just use a potting soil that already contains timed-release fertilizer and a water-holding polymer.

Growing Tips

Keep the soil moist. Fertilize in early spring with an organic fertilizer made for flowers.

Care

You should experience few insect or pest problems, but watch out for spider mites. (See page 34 for controls.) Leaving the seed capsules on the plant will attract fall birds. Cut down foliage after it's killed by frost and remove from the garden. In Zone 6, renew the mulch to 3 inches deep each fall, for winter protection.

Garden Design

Because montbretia comes in such fiery colors, it's usually best combined with perennials that bloom in similar colors at the same time—black-eyed Susans, short annual sunflowers, *Helenium*, goldenrod—or with plants that have silver leaves or purplish flowers ('Silver King' artemesia, for instance, or a perennial blue salvia). It's an ideal plant for a cottage garden.

Try These

You can't beat the old favorite 'Lucifer'; it's the largest plant, as well as the hardiest and fastest growing. 'Jackanapes' has orange and yellow flowers that last a long time. 'Emily McKenzie' has large orange flowers with contrasting throats.

You may know this plant just as Crocosmia *or you may have admired 'Lucifer', the best-known cultivar, which has scarlet flowers on graceful stems above swordlike foliage that resemble gladiolus leaves. (That foliage is an effective design element even when the plant isn't blooming.) Montbretia is popular with gardeners who plant perennials and certainly deserves wider distribution because of its bright colors—orange and yellow as well as red—and easy care. It's always nice to have bold blooms in mid to later summer too. Give montbretia a good winter mulch and it will be winter-hardy in Zone 6; 'Lucifer' and some other cultivars can tolerate even colder weather. They're easy to grow from corms in any sunny or mostly sunny spot.*

Botanical Pronunciation
Crow-COZ-me-uh

Bloom Period and Seasonal Color
Mid to late summer in red, yellow, orange, and bicolors

Mature Height x Spread
18 inches to 3 feet x 1 to 3 feet

Spanish Bluebell
Hyacinthoides hispanica

Many gardeners share my fondness for blue flowers and hunt for plants that bloom in various shades of blue. Spanish bluebell is definitely a blue gem. Actually you can find it in several different shades of blue, which look good together in one planting or combined with pink or white varieties. Of course color isn't the only reason to grow Spanish bluebell, which produces loose spikes of attractive bell-shaped flowers in mid-spring. Unlike Virginia bluebells, which are strictly a woodland plant, Spanish bluebells don't mind adapting to varied soil and light conditions. They bloom nicely in mostly sunny spots or in partial shade, and they're no trouble. They even make nice cut flowers, which combine beautifully in arrangements with daffodils and stems of forsythia.

Botanical Pronunciation
hy-ah-sin-THOY-deez his-PAN-ih-kuh

Bloom Period and Seasonal Color
Spring in blue, pink, or white

Mature Height × Spread
6 to 18 inches × 6 to 12 inches

When, Where, and How to Plant
Grow Spanish bluebells in average garden soil. Locations with winter sun and summer shade under deciduous trees are ideal for naturalizing. They'll grow in full sun, but some shade is recommended for success in the South. Plant the bulbs in fall before the ground freezes, about 4 to 6 inches deep and at least 6 inches apart; clumps will be loose and stems sprawl attractively when not crowded. Mix a granular bulb fertilizer, according to label directions, with the soil when planting.

Growing Tips
For best flowering, keep the soil evenly moist during the growing season (fall to early spring), but allow plantings to dry out when the bulbs go dormant in summer. Spread granular fertilizer made for bulbs annually in fall. Mulch lightly with an inch or two of pine needles or other organic matter to keep the soil moist and the temperature even.

Care
Snap off flower stalks as they fade. Remove dying leaves only after they turn brown. Spanish bluebell bulbs multiply rapidly and may need dividing every few years. Dig, divide, and replant clumps of bulbs after the leaves have begun turning brown. Seedlings and offsets can be left in place until large enough to transplant. Few pests trouble the plant, but bulbs can rot when weather is wet and drainage is poor. If there are insect or disease problems, consult your local Extension service for advice about controlling them.

Garden Design
Spanish bluebells are excellent in deciduous woodland gardens with wild ginger and dwarf evergreen shrubs such as white azaleas. Because Spanish bluebells make good cut flowers, you may want to plant a row or two in a cutting garden.

Try These
'Excelsior' (an heirloom with deep violet-blue flowers) blooms later than most other Spanish bluebells and thereby extends the season nicely. 'Danube' has dark blue blooms, and 'Rose Queen' is an appealing pink with a slightly different appearance.

Tulip
Tulipa species and hybrids

When, Where, and How to Plant

Tulips thrive and naturalize best in a sunny spot that has deep, rich, well-drained soil amended with organic matter. Plant bulbs in mid to late fall—as late as December (even January) if the ground isn't frozen. Keep tulip bulbs refrigerated (in a paper bag and away from fruit such as apples and pears) or in a cool basement or frost-free garage until time to plant. Space hybrid tulips 6 inches apart and 6 to 10 inches deep. Plant species tulips at a depth twice the height of the bulbs and a similar distance apart. Add bulb fertilizer to the soil in the planting bed according to package directions, and then cover the bed with 2 inches of mulch. Hungry deer and rodents are fond of tulip bulbs, so if your neighborhood often has visits from these four-footed gourmands, you will need to protect the bulbs by planting them in a chicken-wire basket or spraying or soaking bulbs with a protectant before planting.

Growing Tips

If autumn rainfall is lacking, water tulips. Spread granular bulb fertilizer according to package directions on top of the soil of previously planted bulb beds each year in September or October.

Care

Be sure to let the leaves die down naturally; this help tulips come back year after year. Species tulips seldom have pests. Rodents and deer may dig up hybrids. To deter rodents, line the planting area with close mesh wire or spray bulbs with a repellent. The only sure control for deer is a very tall fence.

Garden Design

Place pansies or violas in complementary colors in front of tulips in beds or surrounding them in containers. Plant tulips in clumps, rather than in rows.

Try These

'Fusilier' is a multiflowered tulip with vivid red-orange blooms that returns well. 'Montreux' has to be the most romantic-looking tulip ever. Its soft primrose-colored flowers resemble peonies.

Even though tulips aren't ideal in our climate, just about everyone thinks of them as the quintessential spring flower. That's why we continue to plant them even though they don't come back for as many years as daffodils do. (Darwins and early tulips perennialize best.) But what else blooms in April in so many different colors, shapes, and sizes? Even if I had to replant tulips every year, I'm sure I would do it. It's hard to match the drama of a lush, burgundy-colored parrot tulip with fringed flowers or the delicate charm of early-blooming lily-flowered tulips. By choosing different types of tulips that flower at different times, it's possible to have various tulips in bloom easily for six weeks or more.

Botanical Pronunciation
TOO-lih-pa

Bloom Period and Seasonal Color
Spring in every color except true blue

Mature Height × Spread
6 to 18 inches × 4 to 6 inches

Groundcovers & Vines

When you're thinking about selecting a vine or groundcover for your yard, you may initially decide that an attractive appearance is the most important consideration. But look a little deeper. Sure, looks matter—a lot—but groundcovers and vines combine usefulness with beauty. They can eliminate yard chores and make your landscaping more practical.

Among groundcovers' many attributes, for instance, is their ability to thrive in dense shade beneath trees where grass won't grow. Once you've planted a groundcover, you won't have to worry about sowing grass seed beneath trees every fall and watching it struggle to grow.

Groundcovers are also excellent for edging pathways and for preventing erosion on slopes and hills that are too steep to mow. Want more? Think of a groundcover as a green carpet that unites different parts of your yard and as a living mulch, keeping the soil beneath it moist and weed-free.

Vines are also landscape problem solvers—by quickly screening off an unsightly view, for example. And they can have quite an impact on your energy bills, as well as on outdoor comfort. Studies have shown that a deciduous vine that's planted so it shades the west or south side of a house cuts cooling costs considerably, and an evergreen vine can block cold winter winds, saving you money on your heating bills. If you move into a new home with little landscaping, vines can be trained on a lattice frame to create an area with cooling shade while you're waiting for young trees to grow. In addition, vines attract desirable backyard wildlife, such as shelter-seeking birds.

Walkway with creeping juniper (Juniperus) *and pachysandra* (Pachysandra)

Beware the Bullies

Groundcovers and vines share another important characteristic you need to be aware of: they are usually vigorous (sometimes aggressive or invasive) spreaders. In moderation, energetic spreading is a good thing in a vine or groundcover; it's actually what you want them to do. A groundcover or vine that didn't expand wouldn't serve its purpose.

The problem comes when aggressive plants try to take over the yard. English ivy and Japanese honeysuckle are two good examples; almost everyone who's ever planted them lives to regret it. And nearby woodlands often suffer too, since these two plants, and some other common groundcovers and vines, are on the invasive species lists of both Kentucky and Tennessee. (See page 39 for more information about invasive plants.) They may spread by underground runners or through seeds that are spread far and wide by birds and the wind.

Frequently, when friends or neighbors give you a start of a groundcover or vine from their yard, it's one of which they have an oversupply, which may mean it's a plant that's quite aggressive. Beware! Before you buy a vine or groundcover, or even accept a free one, check the profiles in this chapter for recommendations of those that are considered mild-mannered. A pretty plant such as *Houttuynia* (chameleon plant) may look innocent, but you'll spend many frustrating hours trying to banish it from your yard and may never succeed. Don't let that deter you from planting vines and groundcovers, just be certain to avoid those that are bullies.

Groundcovers

After you've decided what purpose you want a groundcover to serve—grass replacement, erosion prevention, and so forth—then match the sun and soil conditions in the spot where it will grow to the conditions preferred by various groundcovers. That helps you choose the ones that will be successful in your yard. In addition, you may want to consider groundcovers with small leaves—creeping thyme, for example—for small areas, and those with a more assertive appearance—such as creeping juniper—for large areas, although this isn't a hard and fast rule.

Other considerations include whether you want a groundcover that also flowers (a nice bonus), and whether you prefer evergreen plants that look good all year or a deciduous species that will lose its leaves in fall. (For the most visible places in the yard, evergreen usually is best.)

Junipers (Juniperus) in the landscape

How Many Plants Do I Need?

One of the most puzzling things for the gardener installing a groundcover is how many plants will be needed. Here is a handy guide to help you figure how much ground 100 plants will eventually cover, according to how they're spaced. As you'll see, if you place creeping thyme 6 inches apart, 100 plants will cover 25 square feet. If you place them 12 inches apart, they'll cover 100 square feet, which will be a considerable cost savings to you, but complete coverage will be much slower.

Space Covered by 100 Groundcover Plants

Planting Distance Apart (in inches)	6	12	18	24	30	36	48	60
Area Covered (in square feet)	25	100	225	400	625	900	1,600	2,500

To avoid future maintenance problems, it's a good idea to plant a groundcover growing along a walkway so that it's no closer to the walk than half its projected spread. That is, if the plants are supposed to spread 2 feet, plant them 1 foot from the walk. Yes, it may look a bit odd in the beginning, but it will save you much shearing over the life of the groundcover, and prevent the ugly edge that develops from constant cutting back at the same spot (you'll notice this especially with junipers).

Prepare the Soil First

It's important to prepare the soil before installing a groundcover because it will be a permanent planting. On steep slopes, you may not be able to do much amending of the soil; if so, it's important to match the type of soil in the spot with a groundcover that will grow well in that type of soil.

Take a soil sample six weeks before planting and have the agricultural Extension service office in your county send it off to be tested. That will tell you how much and what type of fertilizer you'll need. Dig or till the soil about 8 inches deep. Spread 2 inches of organic matter (compost, peat moss, finely shredded bark, or well-rotted leaves) over the area and till it in. Depending on the results of the soil test, you may want to place some pelleted slow-release fertilizer in the individual planting holes, or spread granular fertilizer over the entire area and till it in. (If you didn't have a soil test, use 20-20-20 pelleted fertilizer or 10-10-10 granular according to label directions.)

See "When, Where, and How to Plant" in each plant profile for the spacing needs of individual groundcovers. After planting, water well with a sprinkler and mulch with 2 to 3 inches of organic matter (use pine needles on hills and slopes). On hills you may need to cover the entire area with special netting under the mulch to keep the soil and plants from washing away in hard rains. You should be able to find this type of netting at a nursery or garden center.

Yes! Groundcovers Must Be Weeded

One of your most important chores the first year or two after planting a groundcover will be weeding. If you keep a 3-inch mulch in place, it will probably be just a matter of yanking up a few stray weeds here and there. But it's important to pull weeds out when they're young—once they've matured, it's much harder to kill them. Not only are weeds unsightly, they compete with your groundcover plants for moisture and nutrients, lessening the chances of success.

Everyone who plants a groundcover gets impatient after it goes in. We all want those little plants to instantly cover the space and look full and lush. That isn't going to happen. But I'll share a little secret about how to make your groundcover grow faster: Water and fertilize it frequently. Instead of watering weekly when rainfall has been less than an inch, water deeply twice a week with a sprinkler. Then mix liquid seaweed, fish emulsion, or 20-20-20 water-soluble fertilizer in a hose-end sprayer, and spray a new groundcover once a week (maybe every Saturday morning, so you'll remember) until the middle of August (no later). It will really take off!

Vines

Southerners have two opinions of vines: We love them, and we hate them. We've seen how quickly Japanese honeysuckle can take over a wooded area, and how kudzu devours everything in its path. Yet, that's still not enough to erase the nostalgic memories of sweetly scented moonflower blossoms unfurling on warm summer evenings.

With the renewed popularity and availability of attractive pergolas, arches, and trellises, vines are once again growing in favor. Gardeners dream about ivy-covered cottages, romantic roses rambling over arbors, and vines such as trumpet creeper to lure acrobatic hummingbirds to our yards.

How Vines Climb

Vines have four different methods of climbing. It's important to know which method a particular vine uses, because that determines the type of support on which you should place it.

Twining vines wrap themselves around a structure or object. They'll weave in and out of a chain-link fence or lattice, scurry to the top of a lamppost, and be right at home on a trellis. A good example of a twining vine is moonflower.

Clinging vines cover large expanses of territory, such as blank walls or vacant hillsides. These vines produce aerial rootlets—called holdfasts—that attach themselves to a structure. Think twice—

| Twining | Wrapping tendrils | Holdfasts | Aerial roots |

Vines cling to supports in one of four ways: twining around, wrapping tendrils, or clinging with holdfasts or aerial roots. Be sure to know what type of method a vine needs before you bring it home from the nursery.

maybe three times—before planting a vine that climbs this way to be sure that the spot you've chosen will be the plant's permanent home. Holdfasts are tough to remove and leave behind a residue that's almost impossible to scrape off. Examples are English ivy and climbing hydrangea.

Vines that produce *tendrils* reach out and cling to whatever's near—a chain-link fence, netting, lattice, shrubs, or a wire. Passionflower is a vine that produces tendrils.

Climbers aren't vines in the strictest sense, although we use them that way. They don't really "climb." Instead they depend on the gardener to tie their arching canes to a support as they grow. Examples of climbers include climbing and rambling roses.

Pick Your Vine

Consider which type of vine will work best in each situation—evergreen or deciduous, perennial or annual. Annual vines grow fastest and are inexpensive; usually they're started from seed. Perennial vines generally take longer to grow, but you plant them only once. Evergreen vines look good all year and are perfect for prominent spots in the yard. Deciduous perennial vines are cold-hardy, and they can block the heat of the sun in summer, but let warming rays shine through in winter.

Should Vines Be Grown on Houses or Trees?

Experts generally agree that vines should not be grown on wood-frame homes. That's because vines can cause moisture damage when placed directly on wood, and some vines can work themselves under siding or roof shingles. Then, too, there's the problem of what to do with the vine when the house needs painting. If you're interested in having vines on a wooden building, consider training the vine on a hinged trellis that's placed six inches away from the house.

Vines generally don't harm masonry and brick that are in good condition. However when a surface is completely covered by an evergreen vine, it's difficult to know when mortar is beginning to crumble or cracks have developed. Vines often attach themselves to these cracks, making them larger. If you have ivy growing on a brick house or

English ivy (Hedera) *growing up a tree*

wall, occasionally check under the leaves to make sure the brick and mortar are in good shape.

Do a little research before growing vines on trees. A strong vine (such as wisteria) can eventually strangle a tree, but non-aggressive clinging types may beautify a bare trunk.

Putting Vines to Work

When selecting vines for any purpose, it's important to check the plant listings in this book and match the size and growth habit of the vine to the space where you want to put it. The majority of the time, when a homeowner becomes disenchanted with a vine, it's because the vine grows too large or too aggressively for its location, or because several vines were planted too closely in an attempt to get faster coverage of a fence or other structure.

Put a vine to work in your yard by letting it

- hide an ugly fence or climb a trellis that's used to set apart sections of your landscape.
- bring beauty to a smaller spot; most vines don't take up much horizontal space but their climbing and spreading top parts can make quite an impact. (A few can be grown in containers.)

Vines

- create shade when trained to an arbor and add height and structure to the garden.
- add interest to the garden by attracting birds, butterflies, and other beneficial insects to the vine's flowers, berries, or fruits. Another bonus may be fall color.
- Or, create a living screen for privacy or to obscure an unsightly view.

Vines are more likely to require a little maintenance—regular pruning and keeping the vine confined to its support—than some other plants. Still, because of their benefits and beauty, I believe they're definitely worth the time and energy you put into them. The same is true of groundcovers, which are a big planting project, although they save hours of maintenance later on. Because of their combination of beauty, utility, and intrigue, you're sure to find a vine or groundcover that's perfect for every location and every need.

Climbing rose (Rosa) *against a stone wall*

Creeping Juniper
Juniperus species and hybrids

Creeping junipers are often used to cover a huge section of yard that slopes down to the street. If you want a very low-growing juniper, it's possible to find cultivars that reach no higher than 4 or 5 inches. The needles of some prostrate junipers, such as 'Bar Harbor', 'Prince of Wales', and blue rug (Juniperus horizontalis 'Wiltonii'), turn a brownish plum color in fall, which some people like and others (including me) don't care for. Avoid the brown look by choosing cultivars such as 'Blue Pacific' and 'Blue Star' that remain green or bluish green. But select another groundcover if your site doesn't receive full sun for at least eight hours. All junipers slowly decline in partial shade.

Botanical Pronunciation
jew-NIP-er-us

Bloom Period and Seasonal Color
Evergreen

Mature Height x Spread
4 inches to 3 feet x 18 inches to 8 feet

When, Where, and How to Plant
Creeping juniper has three requirements for success: full sun, well-drained soil, and plenty of space to spread. If junipers are placed in too much shade, they will die, but that often takes several years, so homeowners may be left wondering what went wrong. Plant in average, well-drained soil from spring until fall, spacing the plants 2 to 5 feet apart, according to the mature spread of the juniper cultivar you bought (read the label). Planting too closely can sometimes lead to plant dieback after the plants have matured. Mix ½ cup of granular 10-10-10 fertilizer or the fertilizer recommended by your soil test into the dirt in the planting hole. It's important to mulch well between the junipers to hold down weeds.

Growing Tips
For the first year or two, water weekly if rainfall is less than an inch. Water mature plants during dry spells. Make sure the plants are well watered going into winter. In April or May, fertilize lightly with a product for acid-loving shrubs.

Care
Add to the mulch as needed to keep it about 3 inches deep. Remove any weeds that pop up. Trim trees whose branches produce too much shade on the shrubs. Junipers are subject to a number of insects and diseases, including bagworms, which may be picked off by hand in the evening. For other problems, often indicated by tips or entire branches browning and dying, check with the Extension service for help in deciding on the proper controls.

Garden Design
Creeping junipers are usually planted alone. They're especially popular for difficult hillsides but need to be placed at least several feet from the road so they won't need constant trimming that leaves bare wood showing.

Try These
Juniperus procumbens 'Greenmound' stays about 6 to 8 inches high but spreads 4 to 6 feet. The needles are light green.

Creeping Phlox
Phlox species and hybrids

When, Where, and How to Plant

Purchase plants in spring when they are in bloom to match the flower color to that of plants that will be growing nearby, making sure they don't clash. *Phlox subulata* prefers well-drained, alkaline soil and a sunny to partially sunny location. *Phlox divaricata* grows in shady, well-drained soil that has been amended with organic matter. *Phlox stolonifera* likes a shady to partially shady location with average, well-drained soil. If creeping phlox is planted in spots that stay wet over winter, it will probably die. Mix fertilizer recommended by your soil test with the soil when planting. Space plants 12 to 18 inches apart.

Growing Tips

In hot summer months, when weekly rain totals less than an inch, water young plants regularly so the soil doesn't dry out. Otherwise, creeping phlox manages nicely on average rainfall. Fertilizer generally isn't needed, but if a stand looks thin, spray with water-soluble fertilizer according to package directions in spring.

Care

Shear lightly after blooming to ensure better growth (creeping phlox generally grows slowly). Spider mites may be a problem in dry weather. Prevent or help control them by occasionally spraying the foliage with water, or ask the Extension service for advice. Watch out for rabbits and woodchucks. Deer may also be a problem (despite the fact that phlox may be advertised as deer-resistant). If needed, divide plants in spring, right after blooming is finished.

Garden Design

Combine shade-tolerant types of creeping phlox with Spanish bluebells, columbine, and white-flowering evergreen azaleas. Creeping phlox is attractive when planted so it spills over the edge of a wall. It's a good choice for rock gardens too.

Try These

Phlox divaricata 'Montrose Tricolor' has variegated foliage and fragrant violet flowers. *Phlox pilosa* 'Moody Blue' (often sold as 'Chattahoochee') has blue flowers with a reddish eye. I love the blue of *Phlox subulata* 'Emerald Blue'.

Most of the year, Phlox subulata (you may know it as "thrift") isn't very noticeable, but in mid-spring, it creates sheets of shocking pink on hillsides and banks across our region. They're so attention-grabbing that it's impossible not to be impressed. If you like the look but not necessarily that vivid shade of pink, choose plants that have white or lavender-blue blooms, which are more subdued. Or consider planting other spreading phloxes: wild blue phlox, P. divaricata (which has pale blue blooms); trailing phlox, P. nivalis (white and pink); and downy phlox, P. pilosa (pink, lavender, or white). All are excellent performers. Besides being a groundcover, creeping phlox is also a good choice for growing in the cracks of rock walls.

Botanical Pronunciation
FLOCKS

Bloom Period and Seasonal Color
Spring blooms in pink, white, blue, and lavender

Mature Height x Spread
4 to 10 inches x 1 to 3 feet

Creeping Thyme
Thymus praecox

Isn't thyme an herb? Yes, but that doesn't mean that it can't also do double duty in your yard as a groundcover. Creeping thyme forms a low-growing, aromatic mat that's often covered with flowers in spring and summer. Another advantage of creeping thyme is that you can walk on it—and when you do, it gives off that characteristic thyme scent. When you go to the nursery to buy plants, you may find cultivars that smell like lemons or oranges—run your hands lightly over the foliage and sniff your fingers. Then choose the ones that have a scent you especially like. Place them between steppingstones and along walkways to take advantage of the fragrance, which is more pronounced in hot weather.

Botanical Pronunciation
TIME-us PRE-cox

Bloom Period and Seasonal Color
Late spring or early summer blooms in red, pink, lavender, or white

Mature Height x Spread
2 to 4 inches x 1 to 2 feet

When, Where, and How to Plant
From spring through summer, plant creeping thyme in a sunny spot that has extremely well-drained soil. This isn't a plant for clay; if it gets too wet, it dies. Rocky or sandy soils are fine. A good solution is to use raised beds where soil doesn't drain well. In Zone 6, place creeping thyme in sun most of the day. In Zone 7, it welcomes three or four hours of afternoon shade in the hottest part of summer. Mix fertilizer recommended by your soil test with the soil at planting time. Space plants 6 to 12 inches apart.

Growing Tips
The first six weeks, water enough to keep the plants growing. After they're established, they usually manage on their own, although you may want to water plants in prominent spots during prolonged drought. Fertilize yearly in spring with liquid seaweed or a 20-20-20 water-soluble fertilizer, according to package directions.

Care
After plants finish flowering, mow them lightly with the lawn mower blade at its highest setting, or shear with a hedge trimmer. This encourages bushy new growth. If creeping thyme "melts" (becomes thin and anemic looking) in hot, humid summer weather, cut it back or shear lightly. If plants become woody, rejuvenate by cutting back to 1 or 2 inches tall and letting them regrow. Creeping thyme has few pest problems. Unfortunately, the thymes that are most suitable for groundcovers aren't suitable for culinary use, so you won't have to cut them regularly during the growing season.

Garden Design
Plant creeping thyme in rock gardens, along pathways, or on the top of a wall, so it can cascade over; or pair it with lamb's ear. Even though creeping thyme isn't edible, it makes a nice edging in a formal herb garden.

Try These
'Coccineus' has brilliant scarlet blooms. 'Albus' is a white-flowered cultivar. *Thymus serphyllum* 'Minor' stays less than an inch high and has lavender blooms.

Epimedium
Epimedium hybrids

When, Where, and How to Plant

Epimediums tolerate just about any conditions—deep shade, sun, poor soil, dry ground—but what they prefer—and what will cause them to thrive—is partial shade (morning sun, afternoon shade is ideal) and rich, evenly moist soil that's acid to neutral. (A soil test will tell you the pH.) Plant from spring until late summer in soil that's been amended with organic material. Space plants about a foot apart. Water thoroughly and mulch with pine needles.

Growing Tips

Epimedium's only fault is slow growth, especially until they're two or three years old, but you can help the plants along by watering them regularly (enough to keep the soil moist to the touch) and also fertilizing them. Use a pelleted slow-release fertilizer according to label directions at planting time and again each spring, or feed monthly from spring until early August with a water-soluble plant food.

Care

Cut back damaged evergreen foliage in spring before flowers appear. This makes the groundcover look better and lets you see the flowers more easily too. Epimediums have almost no pest or disease problems.

Garden Design

Any of the epimediums make excellent groundcovers beneath trees because they aren't bothered by, and don't interfere with, tree roots. Plant them near taller, shade-loving perennials such as astilbe and ferns.

Try These

Red barrenwort (*Epimedium* × *rubrum*) has reddish foliage in spring and fall, and sometimes into winter; depending on the temperatures, it may be semi-evergreen. It has bicolor flowers and is one of the fastest-growing epimediums. Look also for Young's barrenwort (*E.* × *youngianum*), which has white flowers in spring, red leaves in spring and fall, and is easy to grow but isn't evergreen. Bicolor barrenwort (*E.* × *versicolor*) is generally evergreen, with red or yellow flowers and young foliage that's mottled red. Longspur barrenwort (*E. grandiflorum*) has large flowers and is deciduous.

Epimedium, also known as barrenwort, is versatile plant, adapting itself to whatever conditions it finds itself in, rather than expecting the gardener to cater to its whims. Besides being easygoing, it offers other advantages: It thrives in shady spots, isn't fussy about soil and watering, and requires almost no maintenance. Even pesky deer leave these plants alone! One feature you'll really enjoy is the ever-changing look of the leaves. They're often chartreuse in spring, green in summer, and red in fall, but some varieties have red or silvery leaves during summer. The flowers will remind you of columbines. Not all epimediums are evergreen though, so choose carefully if you need an evergreen groundcover.

Botanical Pronunciation
ep-uh-MEE-dee-um

Bloom Period and Seasonal Color
For two to six weeks in mid to late spring, pink, red, violet, white, or yellow flowers; colorful foliage in several seasons

Mature Height × Spread
6 to 16 inches × 12 to 18 inches

Foamflower

Tiarella species and hybrids

Foamflower proves that old adage about not judging a book by its cover. This native plant looks so sweet and dainty with velvety foliage, pink buds, and airy white (or pink) flowers. But there's no need to handle it carefully. Beneath that charming exterior is a rugged plant that's evergreen and doesn't just survive but thrives in those deeply shaded spots where little else seems to grow. An added benefit is that the interesting-looking leaves turn reddish or yellow in fall. (Many gardeners think that foamflower is worth planting for the foliage alone.) Nicest of all, it's simple to create a carefree carpet of foamflowers that will make that "difficult" wooded area into the centerpiece of your landscape each spring.

Botanical Pronunciation
tee-a-REL-a

Bloom Period and Seasonal Color
Spring blooms of white or pink

Mature Height x Spread
6 to 18 inches x 6 to 22 inches

When, Where, and How to Plant
Set out plants in spring or until midsummer. While you can place foamflower in dappled or partial shade, it grows nicely in deep shade where many plants won't. Its main requirement is moist, but well-drained, acidic soil. If soil is dry, plants will become scrawny. Avoid planting in areas where water stands during winter; that causes the roots to rot. Mix fertilizer recommended by the soil test with the soil when planting. *Tiarella cordifolia* spreads by stolons; space plants 12 to 15 inches apart. Wherry's foamflower (*Tiarella cordifolia*, var. *collina*) is slower growing and develops into clumps; space plants 1 foot apart.

Growing Tips
To keep foamflower thick and spreading, water when rainfall is less than normal. Regular moisture is essential. At the end of March, April, and May, fertilize by spraying the plants and the ground around them with a water-soluble fertilizer made for acid-loving plants.

Care
First thing in spring, and after thunderstorm season, remove any tree debris that has fallen on this groundcover. If the planting isn't too large, and you'd like to keep it looking neat, cut down flower stalks after they fade. For repeat bloom, remove faded flowers promptly. The next blossoms won't be as prolific as the first flowering, but it's still nice to have a second show. Because Wherry's foamflower is shallow rooted, it may be heaved out of the ground by alternate freezing and thawing of the soil in winter. Recover the roots with soil when you notice this has happened. Foamflower pests are few. If a plant dies over winter, the cause is usually poor drainage.

Garden Design
Let foamflower wander in woodland flowerbeds among Lenten roses, spring-flowering bulbs, evergreen azaleas, ferns, Solomon's seal, and rhododendrons.

Try These
Tiarella cordifolia 'Spring Symphony' produces masses of white flower spikes above dark-veined leaves. It grows about 10 inches tall.

Pachysandra
Pachysandra species and hybrids

When, Where, and How to Plant
Plant after the chance of frost is past in spring and until August in slightly acidic soil. Pachysandra likes partial to deep shade; too much sun turns the leaves yellow. This dependable groundcover prefers loose, well-drained soil that's been amended with organic matter, such as sphagnum peat or fine bark. Place plants 6 to 12 inches apart (slower-growing cultivars and *Pachysandra procumbens* at the closer spacing, if you want faster coverage; *P. terminalis* farther apart). Mix a 20-20-20 pelleted slow-release fertilizer with the soil when planting.

Growing Tips
Water when less than an inch of rainfall has fallen during a week; the soil shouldn't be allowed to dry out completely, especially during the plants' first two years. Fertilize annually. You may spread a pelleted slow-release fertilizer over the bed in late spring, or spray leaves and ground with liquid seaweed, 20-20-20 water-soluble fertilizer, or a liquid fertilizer made for acid-loving plants at the end of March, April, or May.

Care
Keep leaves and other tree debris picked up from the bed, not just for neatness, but because it helps prevent diseases that affect the plants. Remove any weeds that appear. Pachysandra is subject to several diseases, a leaf blight, and a virus. If leaves turn brown, ask the Extension service to help you identify the problem and recommend a control. To increase your supply of pachysandra, take cuttings in summer and root them in equal parts rich soil and sand. They root so easily that they'll be ready to be planted in their new beds by early fall. You may also cut off runners that have rooted naturally and replant them. Set them 8 inches apart for quick coverage.

Garden Design
Compatible companions include bleeding heart, astilbe, and caladiums. Spring-flowering bulbs grow nicely through pachysandra.

Try These
'Silver Edge' has light green foliage edged in silvery white that complements hostas that have white-and-green leaves.

Some groundcovers are little more than a splash of green among the more exciting plants in your yard. Not pachysandra. When viewed up close, its swirls of evergreen foliage add elegant texture and interest to areas that are in partial to full shade. The pachysandra that you're most likely to see in garden centers (Pachysandra terminalis) is Japanese and forms a mat that prevents erosion and crowds out weeds. But it's worthwhile searching for native Allegheny spurge (Pachysandra procumbens), which is a nice choice for a wildflower garden. Its leaves are wider—a flat green color and often mottled. It also spreads somewhat more slowly than Japanese pachysandra. Both are very hardy and ideal for growing under trees (even pines), where grass hasn't been successful.

Botanical Pronunciation
pack-ih-SAN-dra

Bloom Period and Seasonal Color
Spring flowers are white or pinkish

Mature Height x Spread
6 to 12 inches x 18 inches

Stonecrop
Sedum species and hybrids

Not all sedums are low-growing, spreading plants suitable for a groundcover, but it's worth hunting for the sedums that are because they're evergreen, drought-tolerant, often deer-resistant, and grow well in poor, dry soil. Unfortunately, they don't do well in clay soil, which holds too much moisture. (Sedum acre, which doesn't mind clay, is very aggressive and not recommended.) Some to look for are Sedum selskianum 'Spirit', which grows 4 inches high and has brilliant yellow blooms; Sedum rupestre 'Angelina', which is a vigorous grower that has needlelike foliage that's golden in summer and turns reddish in winter; Sedum spurium 'Voodoo' which has rose-red foliage and red flowers, grows about 6 inches tall and spreads 18 inches; and Sedum tetractinum 'Coral Reef', which has attractive succulent foliage.

Botanical Pronunciation
SEE-dum

Bloom Period and Seasonal Color
Summer blooms in red, pink, white, or yellow

Mature Height x Spread
2 to 8 inches x 1 to 3 feet

When, Where, and How to Plant
Plant in full sun once reliably warm weather has arrived in late spring. (If you don't get around to it earlier, summer planting is okay too.) Sedum prefers fast-draining soil and doesn't mind poor, rocky soil. Plant growth will usually be better if you mix compost with the soil in the planting hole. Place plants about 12 inches apart at the same level they grew at in their pots. Water soil thoroughly and mulch lightly, keeping the mulch off the plants themselves.

Growing Tips
Once the plants are established (about a year), they rarely require watering, but they'll appreciate water during extended dry spells. You'll rarely need to fertilize. To encourage slow growers, you can apply a slow-release fertilizer for flowering plants at half the recommended amount in springtime, if desired, but this is a low-maintenance groundcover that tolerates mild neglect.

Care
Apply a 2-inch layer of compost in spring, and renew the mulch so that it's at least 2 inches deep but isn't touching the plants. The groundcover will look neater if spent blooms are cut off in summer, but it isn't strictly necessary. If the plant grows out of bounds, it's easily dug up and placed elsewhere. You may also want to remove fallen leaves and tree litter, which can shade parts of the plant and eventually kill them. Divide plants if needed every four years or so.

Garden Design
All of the groundcover sedums work well in rock gardens and in sunny island beds throughout the landscape. They're excellent choices for butterfly gardens.

Try These
Sedum album 'Coral Carpet' has coral new growth (it turns green in summer but reddish in cold weather), as well as a multitude of white, starlike blooms in early summer. It grows only 4 inches high and spreads about 18 inches.

Sweet Box
Sarcococca hookeriana var. *humilis*

When, Where, and How to Plant
Set out plants from spring until early fall, spacing them several feet apart and mulching well between them. Mix a pelleted slow-release fertilizer with the soil in the planting hole. Sweet box grows best in shady areas where the soil is amended with plenty of organic matter, is slightly acidic, and drains well. Don't give it too much sun, or the leaves won't be very green. Get more enjoyment from sweet box by planting it in an area that people frequent in early spring, so they'll smell the intensely fragrant flowers.

Growing Tips
For the first two years, water weekly if rainfall is less than an inch. After sweet box is established, it is drought-tolerant. Each March, fertilize with a water-soluble fertilizer made for acid-loving plants.

Care
Keep tree debris removed from the planting to keep it looking neat. About the only pest problem sweet box experiences is occasional scale, which appears as brown dots on the stems and undersides of the leaves. There are several effective organic controls for scale; which one is best depends on the time of year, so call the Extension service for advice. Sweet box is sometimes called Christmas box because its foliage is available for December wreaths and holiday decorations. So keep it in mind if you're cutting greenery for the holidays.

Garden Design
Sweet box, a member of the boxwood family, creates a wonderful foil to spring-flowering bulbs growing beneath deciduous trees. It also goes well with lycoris, which flowers in later summer or early fall, as well as with caladiums and coleus.

Try These
I've never found named cultivars of sweet box at nurseries, but I did see *Sarcococca hookeriana* var. *digyna* 'Purple Stem' growing in a Georgia garden. It was about 2 feet high and had purplish new growth. I was impressed, but am not sure it would be hardy in our region's Zone 5 gardens.

You may never have heard of sweet box. I often get blank looks when I recommend this neat little evergreen plant. But it's well worth knowing about and hunting for. It has dark green, lustrous foliage and fragrant flowers, as well as blue-black berrylike fruit that birds enjoy. It grows in partial to full shade, slowly spreading to 8 feet or more. If you live in an urban area or near a highway, sweet box is handy because it's resistant to air pollution. You would think a plant like that would be snapped up by everyone with a shady yard, especially since sweet box is an easy plant to grow. But so far, it's a well-kept secret. Here's hoping that will change.

Botanical Pronunciation
sar-koh-KOH-uh hook-er-ih-A-nuh hum-uh-lis

Bloom Period and Seasonal Color
Very early spring blooms of white flowers

Mature Height x Spread
8 to 18 inches x 6 to 8 feet

Wild Ginger
Asarum species and hybrids

It's easy to fall in love with wild ginger's glossy, heart-shaped leaves veined in silver. But the hidden bonus is this delightful groundcover plant's charming "little brown jug" blooms. Wherever I've lived, I've added wild ginger to the wooded sections of my yard and have always gotten compliments on it. It's surprising how few people are familiar with wild ginger anymore. For an extensive groundcover, you may want to stick with European wild ginger (Asarum europaeum), which has glossy ever-green leaves. But for an interesting accent in a shady wildflower garden, the deciduous, native—and extremely hardy—Canadian ginger (Asarum canadense) is an excellent choice, and, as a nice extra, it's a food source for the pipevine swallowtail butterfly.

Botanical Pronunciation
a-SAIR-um

Bloom Period and Seasonal Color
Spring blooms of reddish brown

Mature Height x Spread
4 to 9 inches x 14 inches

When, Where, and How to Plant
You can plant wild ginger—so named for the gingery fragrance of its roots—in the garden almost anytime the ground isn't frozen, but spring to summer is best. Choose a spot that has plenty of shade and moist soil that's been enriched with lots of organic matter (well-rotted manure, compost, fine pine bark, and so forth). Mix into the planting hole the type and amount of fertilizer recommended by your soil test. Space plants 6 to 10 inches apart (12 inches for *Asarum canadense*, which spreads more quickly). Mulch with up to 3 inches of pine needles or fine bark.

Growing Tips
Wild ginger welcomes watering when weather is drier than normal. For best growth, aim to keep the soil moist, especially when the plants are young. I have never fertilized my plants; decaying mulch and an occasional dressing with compost (spread on top of the soil around the plant) have always kept them growing well. However, if they're growing in poor soil, consider a spring application of organic fertilizer, used according to label directions.

Care
When European wild ginger is growing beneath deciduous trees, remove fall leaves so they don't completely cover and kill the groundcover's evergreen foliage. Although this plant spreads, it isn't invasive or even aggressive. If it outgrows its bounds, just pull up the extra plants. Occasionally slugs—which may pollinate the inconspicuous little flowers—will eat holes in the leaves. If the damage becomes serious, see page 34 for advice on controlling slugs and snails.

Garden Design
Wild ginger provides a lovely green foil for a host of blooming wildflowers, as well as ferns, azaleas, rhododendrons, and dogwoods.

Try These
Asarum shuttleworthii 'Callaway' has rounded evergreen leaves that are extensively mottled with silver. It's relatively slow growing.

Carolina Jessamine

Gelsemium sempervirens

When, Where, and How to Plant

Plant container-grown vines anytime from spring until fall. Although Carolina jessamine will grow in most well-drained soils, it performs best in moist, fertile soil. Similarly, while tolerating some shade, it grows most vigorously and flowers heaviest when in full sun. Carolina jessamine climbs by twining, so it is ideal for posts, chain-link fences, and trellises. Note that all parts of the plant are said to be poisonous if swallowed, so don't place it where small children will come into contact with it.

Growing Tips

Water regularly when rainfall is less than an inch per week or temperatures remain over 90 degrees Fahrenheit. If the vine isn't growing as well as you'd like, fertilize in spring with a pelleted slow-release fertilizer for flowering plants.

Care

Pinch off ends of stems in late spring to encourage bushy growth. After severe winters, wait for the vine to leaf out before removing damaged growth. When Carolina jessamine gets top-heavy, with sparse growth at the base, cut it back to 2 feet high just after blooming ends. Then apply a slow-release fertilizer at half the rate recommended on the label; water well. You may also choose to prune by cutting one-third of the stems back to the ground each year for three years. Insects and diseases shouldn't be troublesome.

Garden Design

This is a vine for trellises, arbors, lampposts, and mailboxes. It can also be used as a groundcover. Use the vine's evergreen foliage as a backdrop for a variety of annuals and summer-flowering perennials, which will hide legginess at the plant's base. This attractive vine, which is *not* a jasmine, can be grown in a large container (to trail over the edges) or even up a trellis indoors, if you have a Florida room that receives lots of sun.

Try These

'Pride of Augusta' has double, nonfragrant flowers and often blooms in fall as well as spring.

One of the pleasures of my yearly drive down to St. Simons, Jekyll, or Sea Island in late February or early March is seeing the golden blooms of Carolina jessamine as the vines scamper up power poles, climb fences, and decorate mailboxes. One year I bought three of these cheerful evergreen vines at a nursery on Sea Island, took them back home, and planted them along my back fence. What a joy—bright yellow blooms in very early spring definitely lift the spirits. When temperatures dip into the low teens, the foliage becomes semievergreen, but the flowers are usually reliable. Carolina jessamine isn't ideal for the coldest sections of our region, but for gardeners in Zone 7 and warmer, it's a true deer-resistant delight.

Botanical Pronunciation

jell-SEE-mee-um sem-per-VIE-renz

Bloom Period and Seasonal Color

Late winter and very early spring blooms in yellow

Mature Length × Spread

20 feet × 3 to 4 feet

Zones

7 and 8

Clematis
Clematis species and hybrids

Clematis can be hard to resist. One homeowner plants a clematis vine on his mailbox, and, as soon as the big blooms appear, many of the neighbors rush to plant clematis on their mailboxes and fences too. It offers much beauty for very little care, displaying a profusion of spectacular flowers against dark green foliage. After the blooms fade, the fluffy seedpods add interest to the vine or they may be cut off to use in flower arrangements. The only clematis you want to avoid planting in your Kentucky or Tennessee yard is the fall-blooming sweet autumn clematis (Clematis terniflora), which produces cloudlike masses of small, white flowers and, unfortunately, sows its seeds everywhere, making it a huge (although pretty) pest in our region.

Botanical Pronunciation
KLEM-a-tis

Bloom Period and Seasonal Color
Summer to fall in white, pink, red, blue-violet, purple, and bicolors

Mature Length × Spread
6 to 10 feet × 2 feet

When, Where, and How to Plant
The common planting advice is that clematis likes its "head in the sun, feet in the shade." That means the roots should stay cool, while the top of the vine requires sunshine, so plant in a sunny spot, but use a thick layer of mulch at the base. In spring, plant in light, well-drained soil, mixing fertilizer recommended on the soil test into the planting hole. Place the stem 2 inches deeper than it grew in the container. Young stems are fragile; protect them from being bumped.

Growing Tips
Water regularly when rainfall is below normal. Don't let the roots dry out. In April, apply a slow-release fertilizer made for flowering plants.

Care
Without pruning, clematis becomes a tangled mess and won't bloom well. When and how you prune depends on the type you have. This is easy to figure out by observing your vine. If it blooms in spring or summer on stems that grew last year, prune lightly right after flowering to keep it in shape. If flowers appear in late summer on stems that have grown since spring, cut young plants to 14 inches tall and mature plants to 2 feet in early spring. If the vine flowers twice, cut out weak growth or dead stems in spring; after flowering, shorten stems that bloomed.

Garden Design
Let clematis scamper across shrubs and up trees, or let it cover a decorative trellis. For months of enjoyment, plant a row of clematis vines of varying colors and bloom times across a wooden rail fence.

Try These
British plant breeder Raymond Evison has hybridized a number of clematis vines that are ideal for growing in containers. They have short vines but lots of flowers. 'Bourbon', which has red blooms, freely flowers all summer. An interesting native, *Clematis ochroleuca* (known as ochre clematis), is a bush clematis for Zones 6 to 8.

Climbing Hydrangea
Hydrangea anomala petiolaris

When, Where, and How to Plant

This is a very large vine, so give it plenty of space when you choose its site. Plant in spring or, if you can water frequently, in summer. Climbing hydrangea likes a shady or partially shady spot with rich, moist, well-drained soil. If your soil doesn't match that description, mix it liberally with compost, peat moss, or finely shredded bark. The vine's aerial roots may damage wooden supports, so it's a better choice for brick walls than wood. Climbing hydrangea is a vine that provides four seasons of interest in the garden, so plant it where you can make the most of its spring greenery, summer flowers, exfoliating (shedding) bark on older vines in the winter garden, and brilliant yellow fall color.

Growing Tips

The main concern for those with a young climbing hydrangea is that it doesn't seem to be growing much. Don't worry that you've done something wrong—it's perfectly normal. Climbing hydrangea vine grows very slowly during its first few years. To help encourage more growth, water regularly to keep the soil moist. Fertilize each spring with a shrub fertilizer applied according to label directions.

Care

The more sun the vine receives, the more likely that Japanese beetles may be a pest. Pick them off by hand or consult the Extension service about controls. Little pruning is necessary if you gave it room to roam. If you inherit an overgrown vine, cut it back by one-fourth each year for four years. You may also cut severely overgrown vines to 3 feet tall, but they won't bloom for several years afterward.

Garden Design

Plant evergreen shrubs, such as white-flowered azaleas and rhododendrons, at the base of this deciduous vine. Also attractive with it are hostas and liriope that have green and white leaves.

Try These

If you don't have much room, try 'Brookside Littleleaf', which grows 5 to 20 feet long.

There's something intriguing about seeing white lacecap hydrangea flowers—6 to 10 inches across—on a vine instead of a shrub. Climbing hydrangea is a big vine—ideal for covering the side of a building or an entire fence. It also grows well in shade or partial shade where most vines don't. This vine has two downsides, both of which are easily overcome. It isn't suitable for planting in a crowded spot; to keep it small, you have to prune constantly, which isn't fun and means the vine never looks as good as it should. Also, you may have to hunt for a local source, although availability is constantly improving. Even if it takes effort to locate climbing hydrangea, you'll be glad you did.

Botanical Pronunciation

hy-DRAN-gee-uh uh-NOM-uh-luh pet-ee-oh-LAY-ris

Bloom Period and Seasonal Color

Late spring to early summer in white

Mature Length × Spread

50 to 60 feet × 10 to 20 feet

Climbing Rose
Rosa species and hybrids

A fragrant pink rose scampering up a trellis or across a picket fence is such a romantic image, and one many of us have thought about transforming into reality. Maybe you hesitated because you thought roses were hard to grow or too disease-prone. But today's easy-care roses aren't difficult at all. Climbing roses love to grow up and over any structure and even beyond, if you don't pull out your pruners occasionally. Why not plant a climber on each side of a decorative wooden archway and use it as a sweet-smelling entrance to your back or side yard? You might also enjoy miniature climbing roses, which aren't well known but are perfect for training up mailboxes or gracing the proverbial white picket fence.

Botanical Pronunciation
ROW-suh

Bloom Period and Seasonal Color
May until frost in red, pink, orange, yellow, white, and bicolors

Mature Length × Spread
8 to 30 feet × 4 to 10 feet

When, Where, and How to Plant
The key to success with climbing roses is to choose the best ones. The American Rose Society publishes a yearly Handbook for Selecting Roses, in which members rank the roses they've grown. I always choose the top ones. (See the ARS website for details about ordering the booklet.) Some of the best-ranked climbing roses recently have been 'Casa Blanca', 'Demokracie', 'Royal Sunset', 'Clair Matin', and 'Sombreuil'. Plant bare-root roses in early spring when forsythia blooms. Set out container-grown roses in late spring or early summer, after roots have almost completely filled the pot. Roses prefer full sun and soil that's been liberally enriched with organic matter.

Growing Tips
Unless an inch of rain has fallen, soak the soil around your roses once—or in very hot, dry weather, twice—a week. (Poke a stick into the ground to make sure soil is moist to a depth of 14 inches deep.) Don't splash water on the leaves. Use a granular rose fertilizer monthly around climbing roses that flower repeatedly. For more blooms, spray twice a month with water-soluble fertilizer for blooming plants. For plants that flower once, feeding in April or May is enough.

Care
Remove flowers after they fade. Keep canes tied to supports. Rose canes growing horizontally will bloom better than ones growing vertically. Roses attract many pests, from aphids to blackspot. Avoid many problems by choosing disease-resistant types.

Garden Design
Let climbing roses wrap around pillars and posts, scramble up a stone wall, soften the lines of a split-rail fence, and cover arbors and pergolas. The David Austin climbing English roses are charming in herb gardens.

Try These
'Orange Crush' has double flowers the color you'd expect—great for fans of the University of Tennessee Volunteers—and the color doesn't fade in summer's heat. Leaves are glossy and deep green. (University of Kentucky fans don't have to plant this one. . . .)

Crossvine
Bignonia capreolata

When, Where, and How to Plant
Plant container-grown vines anytime from spring through early autumn in a sunny or partially sunny place. To encourage vigorous new growth, cut the vine back by one-third to one-half when planting. Although crossvine will tolerate some shade, it blooms best in full sun. It prefers moisture-holding but well-drained soil that contains plenty of organic matter, so you may need to mix compost, peat moss, or well-rotted leaves with poorer soil when you plant. In the wild, crossvine is often found growing at the edge of a pond or river, so it's good next to a water garden or in a boggy spot.

Growing Tips
Crossvine is a vigorous grower that doesn't usually require a boost from fertilizer. Do water regularly during the vine's first two years and during dry spells.

Care
To keep the plant in good shape, prune out weak or winter-damaged growth in spring. Once the vine has reached the length you want, cut back one-half to two-thirds of the previous year's growth each spring. This encourages the vine to flower more profusely, as well as keeping growth in check. Crossvine has no serious insect or disease problems.

Garden Design
The vine produces tendrils that are backed by holdfasts, so it readily climbs walls but is also suitable for chain-link fences. It's an excellent choice for growing horizontally—across the top of a split-rail fence, for instance—and in a wildlife-attracting garden. Good companions are potentilla, butterfly weed, Shasta daisies, and goldenrod, which bloom at different times in complementary colors. Leaves are often reddish in winter, adding interest to the landscape in cold weather, so you may want to plant crossvine where the foliage can be seen and enjoyed from indoors.

Try These
'Jekyll' blooms sporadically throughout the summer. Its flowers are orange on the outside with yellow inside, but aren't fragrant. 'Tangerine Beauty' produces large quantities of spectacular flowers on a fast-growing vine.

Crossvine's trumpet-shaped flowers, which are often orange, yellow, and red and really stand out against the vine's glossy evergreen foliage, have great appeal for hummingbirds. If you're looking for a vine to ramble across a rustic rail fence, this fast-growing evergreen is ideal because it looks nice in all seasons but needs almost no care except being cut back when it grows too far. You'll find yourself answering questions, though, about the identity of this nice native vine. Non-gardeners don't seem to know it at all, and gardeners sometimes confuse it with trumpet creeper, which also has orange blooms but is deciduous. Crossvine's big advantage is that it doesn't try to take over, as trumpet creeper so often does.

Botanical Pronunciation
big-KNOWN-ee-uh cap-ree-o-LA-tuh

Bloom Period and Seasonal Color
From late April into summer in shades of orange, yellow, and red

Mature Length × Spread
20 to 40 feet × 5 to 15 feet

Gold Flame Honeysuckle

Lonicera × heckrottii

Because of Japanese honeysuckle (Lonicera japonica), which smells sweet but runs rampant over everything in its path, many people are reluctant to even consider planting any vine with honeysuckle in its name. No need to hesitate—gold flame honeysuckle is a well-behaved member of the family. It's so nonaggressive that it's mostly used to decorate suburban mailboxes, although it's an excellent choice for growing up lampposts too. You'll want to grow this twining deciduous vine in a well-traveled location so you—and everyone else—can sniff its fragrance and enjoy the flowers, which bloom from late spring through summer and even intermittently into fall. Red or orange berries generally appear on the vine in autumn. They're quite popular with birds.

Botanical Pronunciation
lon-ISS-er-a hek-ROT-ti-eye

Bloom Period and Seasonal Color
Late spring until frost in coral or maroon (and creamy yellow interior)

Mature Length × Spread
10 to 20 feet × 3 to 4 feet

When, Where, and How to Plant

Plant container-grown vines from spring, after chance of frost has passed, until late summer in a sunny or mostly sunny spot. This vine will grow fine in any average soil. However, since it will be in the same place for many years, it's smart to mix ample organic matter—compost, finely shredded bark, rotted leaves, and so forth—with the soil in the hole before planting. Also incorporate into the planting hole the type and amount of fertilizer recommended by your soil test.

Growing Tips

To encourage more vigorous growth, fertilize in April with a pelleted slow-release fertilizer, or use half the recommended amount of a granular fertilizer made for flowering shrubs (an organic fertilizer would be an excellent choice). Water regularly when weekly rainfall totals less than an inch.

Care

Aphids may cause misshapen leaves or blossoms. If that happens, stop fertilizing, to slow the rapid plant growth that attracts aphids. Knock off aphids with a strong stream of water from the hose, or spray with insecticidal soap. (Both treatments may have to be repeated; see page 33.) Gold flame honeysuckle isn't usually bothered by any other pests. Do any necessary pruning or pinching back right after the main flush of blooms fades. To keep the plant inbounds, cut the longest stems back by one-fourth. To renovate an overgrown vine, cut all stems back by one-fourth each year for four years.

Garden Design

Gold flame honeysuckle is a good vine to espalier. Make a design out of heavy wire, place it up against a fence or building, and train the vine along it. The leaves' new growth is often purplish, adding a nice touch of color to the garden, so you may want to complement that with white-flowered annual vinca at the base.

Try These

I like 'Mardi Gras', which has deep maroon flowers, and 'Pink Lemonade', which is a lighter color. 'Goldflame' is popular and easy to find.

Hardy Kiwi Vine
Actinidia kolomikta

When, Where, and How to Plant

Plant anytime from spring through early summer in full to partial sun in Zones 5 and 6; in partial to full shade in Zone 7. (The vine will grow well in shade in all zones, but the foliage variegation—which is an important feature—will vary with the light intensity, so it needs more sunlight in the cooler zones.) Hardy kiwi vine needs moist soil that's well drained, since roots will rot if they're too wet. Improve the drainage abilities of clay soil by adding organic matter, such as compost, peat, or fine pine bark. Mix fertilizer according to soil test recommendations into the planting hole. Spread a 2-inch mulch of organic material—fine pine bark is good—on top of the soil around (but not touching) the vine to keep down weeds.

Growing Tips

Spread slow-release fertilizer or an organic fertilizer for shrubs, according to package directions, around the plant's base each spring when the vine leafs out. Unless growth is slow or you want the vine to fruit, that's all that's needed. For fruiting vines, spread 2 pounds of 10-10-10 granular fertilizer around the base right after flowering. Keep the vine watered well its first year. Fruiting vines will need regular watering—at least an inch per week if rainfall doesn't provide that much—to avoid leaves falling off prematurely and the fruits dropping before ripening (which is messy).

Care

Cut back hardy kiwi vine in early spring to control size and spread if needed. You should experience few pest problems.

Garden Design

Plant anywhere you need a charming deciduous vine for screening, to clamber across a rock pile, or to grow on a fence.

Try These

'Red Beauty' produces leaves that are reddish in summer and develop wonderful fall color. (Avoid planting near a male hardy kiwi vine because it's a female that will develop fruit.)

Like a romantic look? Want something a little different? Then you'll love hardy kiwi vine. Its heart-shaped leaves and unusual variegation—pink, cream, and green—are perfect for a cottage garden, but also eye-catching whenever you need something out of the ordinary. Its only fault is that cats may like it too much and claw the foliage. Vines are sold as male (which has the best variegation) and female. Should you plant male and female vines near each other, clusters of fruit may appear in late summer or early fall. The fruits won't be like kiwis at the grocery store, but they're quite sweet. For a troublefree ornamental vine though, it's best to grow one or more male plants.

Botanical Pronunciation

ak-ti-NID-ee-uh koe-low-MIK-tuh

Bloom Period and Seasonal Color

Spring brings small white flowers; grown for variegated leaves spring to fall.

Mature Height × Spread

10 to 15 feet × 3 to 5 feet

Hyacinth Bean
Dolichos lablab

I'll never forget my first sighting of hyacinth bean years ago when I was visiting the Antique Rose Emporium in Texas. I was admiring the roses and snapping photographs when I noticed purple bean pods up in the air. The glowing pods and pinkish purple blossoms silhouetted against a clear blue sky made a memorable photo, and the vine made a real impression on me since I love to grow plants that aren't all that common. Maybe you do too. Hyacinth bean is an annual vine that can easily and inexpensively be started from seed, will quickly grow up to 20 feet high, and doesn't mind hot, humid summer weather. And it won't get out of control, as some vines can.

Botanical Pronunciation
DOL-li-kos LAB-lab

Bloom Period and Seasonal Color
All summer long purple-tinged blooms followed by shiny purple fruits

Mature Length × Spread
6 to 20 feet × 5 to 8 feet

When, Where, and How to Plant
In late spring, after the soil has warmed up, plant seeds 1 foot apart in a sunny spot with average, well-drained soil. Mix the type and amount of fertilizer recommended by your soil test into the planting hole, or use 10-10-10 in amounts according to label directions, if you didn't have a soil test. After plants are 3 inches tall, mulch the soil around the plants to hold in moisture. The vines, which climb by twining, will grow up strings, as pole beans do, but they look best rambling over a decorative trellis. You can still sow seeds as late as midsummer if you need a replacement for a plant that didn't make it. Some sources say that the mature beans inside the pods are poisonous, so you may want to plant the vine in a spot where young children won't be tempted to pick any of the pods.

Growing Tips
Ample moisture is necessary to sustain the fast growth of hyacinth bean vine, so water regularly, especially in hot weather, just as you do plants in your vegetable garden. Fertilize monthly during summer with liquid seaweed or a water-soluble plant food for flowering plants.

Care
Pruning is generally not required, but if the plant gets out of bounds, trim it to the length you want. This vine rarely attracts pests. In fall, when the pods dry and begin to shrivel—indicating that the beans inside are purple and mature—save and dry some of the seeds to plant next year and to share. (Seeds left on the vine will often reseed naturally.)

Garden Design
Hyacinth bean complements silver- or gray-foliaged plants, such as Russian sage, artemisia, dianthus, lamb's ears, gray-leaved sedum, and dusty miller. You may also enjoy the contrast that orange plants provide. If so, try butterfly weed, *Rudbeckia hirta* 'Marmalade', or short, orange sunflowers.

Try These
'Ruby Moon' produces intensely purple pods.

Mandevilla

Mandevilla × amoena

When, Where, and How to Plant

Mandevilla can be grown in a sunny spot that has well-drained soil or in a large pot. Plant in late spring, after the weather has turned reliably warm. In the ground, mix a slow-release fertilizer and a tiny amount of a water-holding polymer (see page 21) with the soil in the hole. When growing in a container, choose a pot about the size of a half-barrel. The best potting mix for mandevilla will contain a slow-release fertilizer and a water-holding polymer. Moisten it thoroughly before pouring it into the container. Set the vine at the same depth it was growing before. Water well and place next to a support.

Growing Tips

Mandevilla likes plenty of water and fertilizer, as well as heat. Don't let its soil dry out. Beginning in July, use liquid seaweed or a water-soluble fertilizer for flowering plants twice a week. Take containers indoors in autumn when temperatures fall near 50 degrees. If you take a container-grown vine indoors over winter, keep the soil on the dry side and don't fertilize.

Care

In spring, prune back all stems of overwintered vines when you take the container outdoors. In summer, remove faded flowers. Pinch the tips of the stems monthly throughout the growing season to encourage dense growth.

Garden Design

Mandevilla is the star of the show when planted by itself along a fence, in the middle of a shrub border, or among foundation plantings, trained on a trellis set up against the house. Or plant white-flowered Madagascar periwinkle around the base of the vine, especially in a large container.

Try These

The Vogue series of mandevilla ('Ginger'—pink flowers; 'Audrey'—deep red; 'Rita'—reddish pink) grow between 18 and 36 inches tall (48 inches for 'Rita'), spread 12 to 24 inches wide, and work well as houseplants when given enough sun indoors. The faded flowers fall off naturally, so deadheading isn't needed.

Mandevilla is riding high in the current boom of heat-tolerant tropical plants. Not only is it pretty, but it's a vine that anyone has room for—even a condo dweller with a small patio or porch. While most vines act like Superman, mandevilla behaves more like mild-mannered Clark Kent, growing only 10 feet or so a season but producing plenty of pretty pink or red flowers. Put this vine next to your mailbox or on the deck, and everyone will take notice when it starts to bloom—and continues all summer. It's an excellent choice for containers, which can be taken indoors over winter and then brought outside again when temperatures rise, saving you the cost of a new vine. It also attracts hummingbirds.

Botanical Pronunciation
man-dee-VIL-uh a-MEE-na

Bloom Period and Seasonal Color
From spring until fall, large flowers in shades of pink or red

Mature Length × Spread
10 to 20 feet × 2 to 3 feet

Zones
Not hardy; grow as an annual or winter indoors

Moonflower

Ipomoea alba

It's easy to see by the flowers that moonflower is related to morning glory. Each bloom opens in the evening and lasts only until the next morning, but since the vine produces an abundance of blossoms, there's never a shortage. Years ago, it was common for people to sit out on their front porch each evening and enjoy the spectacle of the moonflowers opening. For kids, the way these large white blossoms swirled open and filled the air with sweet perfume seemed almost magical—even more so if you noticed one of the unusual-looking hawk moths that pollinate the beautiful blooms. This annual vine with heart-shaped leaves is easily grown from seed but needs summer heat to really reach its full potential.

Botanical Pronunciation
ip-poe-MEE-uh AL-ba

Bloom Period and Seasonal Color
Summer in white blossoms at night

Mature Length × Spread
8 to 12 feet × 5 feet

When, Where, and How to Plant
Start seeds indoors in pots in April, or sow them outdoors in May or after the weather is reliably warm day and night. Because the seeds have a hard covering, you'll need to nick them with a knife to speed germination, or place them in warm water and soak overnight before planting. Incorporate the type and amount of fertilizer recommended by your soil test into the planting hole. Or, if you didn't have the soil tested, use granular fertilizer made for flowering plants. Plant in a sunny spot by an arbor, fence, or trellis that's near a deck or porch so you can enjoy the nightly show. If necessary, help this twining vine get started up the support by attaching it to the lowest level of the support by hand.

Growing Tips
Water regularly if rainfall is less than an inch per week. To keep the vine growing and blooming well, mix liquid seaweed or a water-soluble fertilizer for flowering plants in a hose-end sprayer and spray on the vine every two weeks during summer.

Care
Since moonflower is an annual vine, it needs little pruning. Pinch it back to shape it or to keep it in bounds as necessary. Few pests bother the plant. You can save some of the seeds for next year, but will find that the vine may self-seed—although those volunteers will begin blooming rather late in the summer. Pull up unwanted volunteers.

Garden Design
For a night-and-day combination that's hard to beat, interplant moonflower with a morning glory, such as 'Crimson Rambler', 'Heavenly Blue', or 'Flying Saucers' (which has blue and white blooms). (Warning: morning glory may be invasive.) Or, surround the base of the vine with colorful nasturtiums.

Try These
Few cultivars are available. When you find a vine you particularly like, save the seeds to plant the next year.

Ornamental Sweet Potato
Ipomoea batatas

When, Where, and How to Plant
Once weather is consistently warm in spring (which is sometimes not until mid-May), plant in a sunny spot that has soil rich in organic matter. Water well.

Growing Tips
Don't let the plants wilt, if possible (although, if it happens, they usually perk back up if watered thoroughly as soon as you notice). On the other hand, don't let the soil stay wet all the time; let it dry out slightly between waterings. Fertilize with 20-10-20 water-soluble fertilizer every other week for plants in containers and monthly for those in the garden.

Care
If the vine grows too long or spreads too wide, pinch or cut it back. Slugs or snails may occasionally be a problem (see page 34 for control advice). Identify any chewing insects—usually beetles—and ask the Extension service for recommendations. Early in the summer, you can easily root cuttings of the vine in water to produce more plants. In fall, when you dig up the plants, you'll find little tubers. These can be dried and saved to plant again the next year.

Garden Design
In a hanging basket, plant a purple-leaved ornamental sweet potato vine with Purple Wave petunia or Grape Punch Superbells (*Calibrachoa*) for a colorful monochromatic look, or one that has chartreuse leaves with scaveola. In a large container, plant *Pennisetum purpureum* in the center, 'Diamond Frost' euphorbia around it, and purple-leaved ornamental sweet potato vines along the edges. 'Blackie' looks nice with red geraniums. But these twining plants can be planted in a container (or the ground) next to a trellis to be a true vine. I like them grown at the top of a wall, to tumble downward, but they can also serve as an annual groundcover.

Try These
'Sweet Caroline Red' is a bit of a change from the chartreuse and purple foliage of other ornamental sweet potatoes. It's a trailer, with deep red (or maroon), palmate leaves.

Surprisingly for a foliage plant, ornamental sweet potato (or sweet potato vine, as it's often called) has become a prized annual in the past few years. And you're going to see even more different kinds before long, not just the trailing vines but plants that have a more compact and bushy habit and some different colors (chartreuse is currently the most popular). Even now we're seeing varying leaf shapes (heart-shaped, palmate, and broad with serrated edges). All are heat-tolerant and perform best in high temperatures. The older types are the most vigorous and are better as vines than their usual use in containers, where they need trimming to shorten them during the season. Varieties such as the Sweet Caroline series stay shorter.

Botanical Pronunciation
ip-poe-MEE-uh bah-TAH-tass

Bloom Period and Seasonal Color
Colorful foliage from spring until fall frost

Mature Length x Spread
4 to 12 feet x 10 to 24 inches

Passionflower
Passiflora species and hybrids

Passiflora incarnata is an attractive vine that's Tennessee's official wildflower. It's a native plant with appealing violet (occasionally pink) flowers, although other species and new hybrids are now available in red, reddish purple, blue, white, and glowing deep purple, which make the vine even more appealing to gardeners. Passionflower's appeal isn't just to people, though—it's an important host plant for fritillary butterflies. Wildflower folklore relates each part of passionflower to the crucifixion of Christ Jesus. The fringed crown symbolizes the crown of thorns, the three stigmas represent the nails, and the stamens symbolize the wounds. Maypop, another common name for this plant, refers to the little orange-yellow fruits that the vine produces, from which generations of kids have sipped sweet juice.

Botanical Pronunciation
pas-ih-FLOOR-uh

Bloom Period and Seasonal Color
From mid-June until October, pale lavender, white, or pink flowers; yellow fruits appear in late summer

Mature Length × Spread
15 to 25 feet × 5 to 8 feet

When, Where, and How to Plant
In fall or mid-spring, thickly sow seeds of *Passiflora incarnata* ½ inch deep in any rich, well-drained, soil. Knick seeds or soak overnight in warm water first. Germination is generally spotty, so plant more seeds than you think you'll need. Mix compost or other organic matter with the soil in the planting hole. Plant containers of *Passiflora caerulea*, blue passionflower, in spring after chance of frost has passed. Although both types of passionflower prefer full sun, some afternoon shade will be acceptable.

Growing Tips
Water deeply whenever an inch of rain doesn't fall during the week. At the end of April, fertilize older vines with two handfuls of 10-10-10 fertilizer spread in a circle at the base of the plant; water it in well. Then spread 2 to 3 inches of mulch on the ground around—but not touching—the vine.

Care
In Zone 6 and when winter has been very cold, *Passiflora incarnata* may die back to the ground. If so, cut back stems by two-thirds in late winter. Since the vine is root-hardy to at least minus 10 degrees Fahrenheit, the top usually grows back. Once that has started happening, remove the rest of the dead stems. *Passiflora caerulea* may be an annual in the colder parts of our region, so it may not survive bad winters and will need to be replanted. Dig up and dispose of suckers anytime. When you see caterpillars on the vine, don't remove them; they're the larvae of the fritillary butterfly, for which passionflower vine is an important food source.

Garden Design
Place passionflower in front of a solid wall or shrubs with dark green foliage so its unusual blossoms are displayed to greatest advantage.

Try These
Although it's not hardy, I sometimes grow *Passiflora coccinea*, red passionflower, a tropical plant that likes hot weather.

Trumpet Honeysuckle
Lonicera sempervirens

When, Where, and How to Plant
Plant in any moist, well-drained soil from spring until late summer, improving the soil in the planting area with organic matter such as compost or fine bark. Trumpet honeysuckle will tolerate shade, but it won't bloom well in it, so a sunny spot is best. Because the vine is such a favorite with hummingbirds, you'll want to place it in a spot where you can observe the antics of these tiny winged acrobats. An ideal location is where the vine's blooms can be seen from inside the house or from a porch, deck, or patio. A twining vine, trumpet honeysuckle will grow on trellises, chain-link fences, lattice, or netting.

Growing Tips
You usually won't need to fertilize this fast-growing, deciduous vine. Should you think it looks as though it needs extra nourishment, spread well-rotted compost around the base of the vine and water it in, or give it one application of a liquid plant food made for flowering plants. Water during prolonged dry spells.

Care
Aphids are the major pests, particularly in spring. Hose them off or spray with insecticidal soap (see page 33 for ways to control aphids). Because the vine blooms mostly on old wood (last year's growth), it is important to prune it after the main flush of flowering—not in winter, when pruning will prevent flowering. An exception is an overgrown vine, which can be cut back to the ground in early spring if necessary.

Garden Design
Grow next to a fence, with annuals and perennials at the base to hide its lower stems. Coordinate the color of the flowers in the bed to the blooms on the vine.

Try These
'John Clayton' has fragrant, pale yellow flowers and is one of the most reliable repeat bloomers. It grows about 12 feet long. The best red I've tried is 'Alabama Crimson'. The tips of its flowers are yellow and fall berries are large and longlasting.

Trumpet honeysuckle, also called coral honeysuckle for the color of the long, tubular flowers, is guaranteed to attract birds to your yard. Throughout summer, it's a hummingbird magnet. In autumn, it produces abundant red berries appreciated by a variety of birds. Some even build nests in the vine. It's covered with clusters of flowers all summer and continues blooming sporadically until frost. Once I had a trumpet honeysuckle vine growing on a solid wood fence, and when it reached the top, instead of falling to the other side, it puffed out and became rounded and almost shrublike—an interesting look that I liked. Don't confuse this mild-mannered native vine with trumpet creeper (sometimes called trumpet vine), which can be very aggressive.

Botanical Pronunciation
lon-ISS-er-a sem-per-VI-renz

Bloom Period and Seasonal Color
From spring until fall in red, orange-red, or yellow

Mature Length × Spread
3 to 30 feet × 10 to 20 feet

Lawngrasses

Many people love the look of a lush green lawn surrounding their home. They don't mind spending hours mowing it and making sure it's fed, weeded, and watered when necessary. But these days, love of lawns can be controversial. Some gardening professionals suggest that a lawn is too much work, and that the chemicals homeowners may douse it with aren't good for the environment. Expending a natural resource such as water on grass isn't environmentally friendly either, they say, suggesting that homeowners get rid of their lawns and replace them with groundcovers or other types of plants, such as ornamental grasses.

Many people love the appearance of a well-tended lawn to set off beds and borders.

You may have already made up your mind on this issue. You wonder what the fuss is about since you think that a wide expanse of green grass sets off your landscape as nothing else can. On the other hand, maybe you can't imagine spending all that time taking care of a lawn when you hate to mow, and no matter how hard you try, it never seems to look as good as those photos on the bags of fertilizer. I'm in the middle. There's no way kids can play an impromptu game of touch football in a bed of groundcover. And I prefer soft grass beneath a swing set rather than mulch.

But I fertilize my lawn no more than twice a year (preferably with an organic fertilizer) and rarely water unless I've planted new grasses. I try to keep my lawn small enough to cut it easily with an old-fashioned (non-motorized) reel mower. (Yes, they still make them; more lightweight than before.). I also know that lawns do have some environmental benefits (among them: they clean the air, absorb pollutants, cool temperatures, and reduce noise).

So the choice is yours—be a lawn ranger, get rid of your grass, or grow a low-maintenance lawn (one that's less than perfect). But if you want to be successful at growing lawngrass, read on to find out what you need to know.

*Cross-section of Kentucky bluegrass (*Poa pratensis*)*

Tennessee and Kentucky Are in Transitional Zones

Our region is in a transition zone when it comes to lawngrasses. Both warm- and cool-season grasses grow here, but cool-season grasses don't look as good as they would farther north, and warm-season species won't perform as well as they do farther south. That unfortunately means you have to work a little harder if you want great-looking grass.

Cool-season grasses—fescues, perennial ryegrass, and Kentucky bluegrass—grow best when temperatures range from 60 to 75 degrees Fahrenheit. Cool-season grasses do best in spring and fall and often grow some in mild spells during winter. In the hottest part of summer—especially if rainfall is lacking—they go dormant, greening up again when temperatures moderate and rain returns.

Grass	Bermuda	Centipede	Fine Fescue*	Kentucky Bluegrass	Tall Fescue	Zoysia
Type	Warm Season	Warm Season	Cool Season	Cool Season	Cool Season	Warm Season
Zone	6-8	7b, 8	5, 6	5, 6	6-8	6-8
Method of Planting	Sod, sprigs	Sprigs, sod	Seed	Seed	Seed, sod	Sprigs, plugs, or seed
Heat Tolerance	Good	Good	Poor	Poor	Fair	Good
Cold Tolerance	Fair	Poor	Good	Good	Good	Good
Drought Tolerance	Good	Fair	Fair	Fair	Fair	Good
Shade Tolerance	Poor	Fair	Good	Fair	Good	Fair
Traffic (wear) Tolerance	Good	Poor	Varies	Fair	Fair	Good
Mowing Height (Inches)	½ to 1½	1 to 2	1½ to 2½	½ to 2½	2 to 3	½ to 1½

*Fine fescue = chewings, hard, and creeping red fescue

Cross-section of zoysiagrass (Zoysia spp.)

Warm-season grasses—mostly Bermuda (*Cynodon dactylon*) and zoysia, although some areas in Chattanooga and Memphis can grow centipede—thrive at temperatures above 80 degrees Fahrenheit. They stay green in the heat of summer, but turn brown when frost arrives in fall and don't green up until temperatures are consistently warm in mid to late spring. Warm-season grasses are also not as winter-hardy as cool-season grasses, and they generally don't do well in shade. When temperatures fall below 15 degrees Fahrenheit—and especially zero and below—they may be damaged or killed. (Meyer or Z-52 zoysia is considered the hardiest.) One reason that people are willing to put up with those drawbacks of warm-season grasses is that they grow shorter and thicker than fescue, making a thick "carpet" of grass that looks and feels so great. Many people fall in love with the look of the warm-season grasses they see on golf courses but forget how many workers it takes to maintain them.

Cool-season grasses are usually started inexpensively from seed, although more and more, gardeners are turning to sod for its ease of installation and instant effect. Warm-season grasses are almost always sodded, although zoysia may be started from small sprigs or plugs. Sprigging is less expensive than sod, but it can take a very long time for it to grow into a thick lawn.

If you have a new home, or you've decided to replant your existing lawn, start by choosing the type of grass you prefer. Tall fescue (*Festuca arundinacea*) and *Zoysia* spp. are the most versatile, but look at the chart on page 125 to see which grasses excel at qualities that mean the most to you (drought or shade tolerance, for instance, or how hard-wearing they are).

Advantages and Disadvanages of Grass Types

Bermudagrass

Cynodon dactylon

- *Advantages*: Beautiful, thick grass; good in heat; survives some drought; tolerates heavy traffic.
- *Disadvantages*: Needs lots of care; can become a pest by spreading into flower beds; not good in shade; subject to several insects; brown from fall until spring; not always winter-hardy.

Centipedegrass

Eremochloa ophiuroides

- *Advantages*: Low-maintenance; few insects and diseases; tolerates poor soil; needs less mowing because it grows slowly.

- *Disadvantages*: Not cold-hardy in most of the region; doesn't tolerate heavy traffic; needs more water than most; brown from fall to spring.

Fine Fescues

Chewings fescue (*Festuca rubra* var. *commutata*), creeping red fescue (*Festuca rubra* var. *rubra*), and hard fescue (*Festuca longifolia*)

- *Advantages*: Shade tolerant, fine leaf texture; low-maintenance; tolerates poor soil.
- *Disadvantages*: Doesn't tolerate heat well.

Kentucky Bluegrass

Poa pratensis

- *Advantages*: Hardy, adaptable, nice color and texture, withstands traffic, good for cooler areas.
- *Disadvantages*: Needs more watering and fertilizing than tall fescue; subject to insects and diseases; not very heat-tolerant.

Annual and Perennial Ryegrass

Lolium multiflorum and *Lolium perenne*

- *Advantages*: Good for overseeding warm-season lawns in winter so they'll be green; seed is relatively inexpensive and germinates quickly; not heat-tolerant so it dies out about the time overseeded warm-season grasses begin to grow again; tolerant of partial shade.
- *Disadvantages*: Not a good choice as a long-term lawngrass; it isn't heat-tolerant; may need mowing in winter; overseeding a warm-season lawn with it every year can restrict permanent grass growth.

Tall Fescue

Festuca arundinacea

- *Advantages*: Doesn't mind partial shade; low maintenance; cold-tolerant; versatile.
- *Disadvantages*: Coarse texture; older cultivars may clump rather than spread; goes dormant during drought and when temperatures are higher than 90 degrees Fahrenheit.

Zoysiagrass

Zoysiagrass (*Zoysia* hybrids such as Meyer, Emerald, Belaire, and El Toro)

- *Advantages*: Beautiful appearance; heat- and drought-tolerant; slow growing; resists weeds and insects.
- *Disadvantages*: Some cultivars aren't cold-hardy in all areas of Kentucky or Tennessee; must be dethatched regularly; some are susceptible to diseases.

Whichever type of grass you decide on, the first step will be to decide on a cultivar. Check with your local Extension service office for current recommendations. You'll find that these up-to-date varieties will look better and far outperform old standards such as Kentucky 31.

Avoid Seed Mixes

When you go to buy seed, instead of finding just the cultivar you want, you may see bags of mixed seeds of different types of grasses. Avoid them. It's fine to grow a blend of three cultivars of tall fescue—because they all need the same conditions and care. But not a mix that contains Kentucky bluegrass, creeping fescue, and tall fescue. Each of those grasses has different watering, mowing, and fertilizing requirements. Eventually one of those grasses will "win out" and take over; and the survivor may not be the one that's best for your yard.

The mixes of several species of cool-season grass seed are usually for shade, because there's not one outstanding grass for shade in our area. It can be tough to grow grass in shade, because most types of grass are sun-loving. Chewings fescue is a good shade grass, but usually goes dormant in summer heat. Tall fescue is generally the best selection for shade, but even it may need to be overseeded (at half the recommended amount of seed for new grass) each fall. If tall fescue doesn't grow well, your shade may be too deep for grass; consider trying a shade-tolerant groundcover instead.

Getting Started

When preparing to plant grass seed or have sod installed, the first thing you need to do is have your soil tested. Among other things, a soil test tells you whether you need to lime your soil (something that's best done several months ahead, as lime takes some time to become effective).

The best and—if you really want to do it right—the *only* time to start a new fescue or bluegrass lawn or renovate an old one is fall. It's okay to patch bare spots in these lawns in spring or install pieces of their sod, but September is the month to start from seed.

On the other hand, you should wait until May—when temperatures have warmed up—to install or patch a zoysia or Bermuda lawn.

Whether you're planting seed or sod, begin by getting rid of weeds. Don't use a selective herbicide (one that kills only the weeds and not the grass) because that stays in the soil for some time and will prevent germination of new seed or harm roots in new sod. Instead, water the bare soil daily for a week, and then kill the weeds that appear by hoeing, hand, or, if necessary, with a nonselective herbicide that doesn't remain in the soil. Then repeat the process. That gets rid of most of the weed seeds that would come up among your grass.

Decide whether you want to sow seed or install sod. More cultivars of grass are available in seed than sod, and seed is much less expensive than sod. But seeding takes longer to establish a lawn than sod, which looks good almost instantly. High-quality sod is generally more weed-free than a lawn grown from seed, and it's easier to use on hills and slopes.

Soil testing kit

(Top left) Begin by using a hard rake to spread compost, topsoil, or garden soil in a one-half-inch layer covering the bald spot. (Top center) Using a hand spreader, spread grass seed thickly over the entire area, slightly overlapping the edges of the grass not covered with soil. (Top right) Sprinkle wheat straw (available at garden centers and home-improvement stores) over the newly seeded area, helping to keep the seeds moist until they sprout. (Bottom right) Water the newly seeded area twice a day for ten minutes until the grass is 1 inch tall; then water three times a week for ten minutes.

Sowing Grass Seed

Prepare the soil by removing rocks and debris and tilling 2 to 4 inches deep, adding topsoil if your soil is extremely poor. Mix in a slow-release lawn fertilizer. Then rake the area, afterwards rolling it with a lawn roller (from an equipment rental store), if you're establishing an entire lawn.

Use a drop-type fertilizer spreader for large areas; a broadcast spreader for small ones. Follow the directions on the bag of seed for the amount to use. Rake to cover the seeded area with ⅛ to ¼ inch of soil. Mulch lightly to help keep the soil from drying out. Most homeowners spread too much mulch—you should still be able to see the ground beneath the straw or other mulch.

Watering a newly seeded lawn is the critical part of the operation. Once the seeds have become wet, they can't be allowed to dry out or they won't germinate. This means at least daily watering (or twice daily in hot weather) until the new grass has grown to 2 inches tall; then water every other day until it has reached 4 inches tall. The water doesn't have to penetrate deeply, because there aren't any roots yet. So count on setting up the lawn sprinkler and turning it on each morning for seven to twelve days. Do the first mowing when the grass reaches 4 inches tall, cutting it to 3 inches high.

Installing Sod

The initial work of soil preparation is the same as with seeding. Calculate how much sod you'll need by multiplying the width of a strip of sod by its length. Arrange delivery of large amounts of sod so that it arrives just as you're ready to install it. If you plan to pick up a few strips of sod at a nursery, be sure you get it shortly after it has been delivered to the garden center; sod dries out quickly. Hose it down before you use it.

To start, lay the first piece of sod in a spot with a straight edge, such as along a driveway or sidewalk. After placing the first piece, unroll the second and put it as close as possible to the first one—without overlapping, but avoiding gaps. Be sure that each piece is in close contact with the soil. Try to stagger the seams. It's not a bad idea to sprinkle each strip lightly with water after you get it in place, especially if you're working on a large area. Use a heavy-duty knife to cut apart strips so you can piece them into odd-shaped areas. Use a lawn roller on a large expanse of sod, then water deeply.

Just as you would a newly seeded lawn, stay off sod for at least two weeks. Walking on it when it's beginning to grow will harm it. Turn the sprinkler on and water daily for the first twelve to fourteen days, until the grass begins growing. Then you can cut back to twice-weekly watering and finally to once a week. Mow when zoysia and Bermuda reach 2 to 2½ inches high and when fescue reaches 4 inches high.

Lawn Care and Mowing Tips

The most important thing you can do for a fescue lawn is never to mow it shorter than 3 inches high. Taller grass shades out weeds and keeps the soil moist and cooler. Switching from "scalping" the lawn to letting it grow taller will make a world of difference in its appearance.

Scalping happens when the mower blade is set so low that it cuts the top of the grass, or rips the grass plant out of the lawn so that the plant stops growing.

When to Fertilize a High-Maintenance Lawn

Cool-Season Grasses (Fescues, Perennial Ryegrass, Kentucky Bluegrass)

Application Dates	Amount of Fertilizer per 1,000 Square Feet
March 15 (Tennessee only)	4 to 5 pounds of high-nitrogen fertilizer (such as 24-4-12; may be a pre-emergent crabgrass control formula) or 17 pounds of Milorganite (organic sewage sludge)
May	Same as March
September 1	10 to 15 pounds of granular 6-12-12 (for healthy root growth going into winter)
October 15	Same as March and May

Warm-Season Grasses (Bermuda and Zoysia)

Application Dates	Amount of Fertilizer per 1,000 Square Feet
April 15	4 to 5 pounds of high-nitrogen fertilizer (24-4-8 for Tennessee only example) or 17 pounds of Milorganite
May to June	Same as April
July 15	Same as April and June
September 1 (Tennessee only)	10 to 15 pounds of granular 6-12-12 (for healthy root growth going into winter)

The dates noted above are Extension Service recommendations for a high-maintenance lawn that's watered in summer. If you prefer low-maintenance, which also means lower amounts of fertilizer entering the watershed, you can fertilize once a year (October for cool-season lawns and May to June for warm-season grasses); twice (September and October for cool-season grasses; May and June for warm-season grasses); or three times (May, September and October, cool-season grasses; April, June and July for warm-season grasses).

In spring many gardeners like to use lawn fertilizer that contains a pre-emergent crabgrass control. But they don't always understand that it works by spreading a chemical that prevents seed germination. Not just crabgrass seed, but *any* seed. So you won't get any grass seed to grow for several months in areas that have been treated with pre-emergent crabgrass control (including corn gluten).

Never use a lawn fertilizer that contains weedkiller when you have trees and shrubs in or near the lawn. It can do unexpected damage. (Actually, experts never recommend fertilizers than contain weedkiller. If you have weeds in portions of your lawn, kill them separately rather than spreading herbicide on areas where it isn't needed.)

Don't collect or rake up your grass clippings, unless the grass was so tall that the clippings are in big clumps. Regular glass clippings provide fertilizer to your lawn—and they're free.

Perennials & Ornamental Grasses

Often I hear people gripe about having to set out bedding plants every spring in order to have a colorful yard all summer. If that's your complaint, then this is the chapter for you. Plant any of the perennial flowers or ornamental grasses listed here and they'll return year after year. They'll require some maintenance that annuals don't, but spring won't be consumed with planting.

Perennials

Perennial plants come in such a tremendous variety of shapes, sizes, colors, types, and blooming times that you will never tire of them. Spring-flowering candytuft creeps along the edges of flowerbeds, white and pristine, welcoming a new growing season. At 6 feet tall, Joe-Pye weed towers over the fall garden in pinkish purple majesty. And in between, a succession of perennial flowers—from pinks to goldenrods and daylilies to sedum—bursts into bloom and then fades into the background.

*Chrysanthemum (*Dendranthemum*)*

Unlike summer annuals, such as petunias and impatiens, which usually bloom constantly from spring planting until fall frost, most perennials are in flower for a much shorter time, occasionally for as little as two weeks. Rather than seeing this as a limitation, however, gardeners use the fact that irises, daylilies, and mums bloom at different times to plan a flower bed that features a varying progression of bloom that lasts from early spring to late autumn. A particular perennial may flower for two weeks in May, half of July, or all of fall. Often catalogs or books will say that a certain perennial "blooms from spring until frost." Well, take that with the proverbial grain of salt. It may flower that long in Minnesota or New England, but here very few perennials bloom all summer because of our heat and humidity.

Designing a Perennial Garden

If you want to plan your perennial gardens so that something is blooming constantly from spring until fall, then you'll need to learn the bloom times of different species—through reading, observation, asking other gardeners, and trial and error. The first time you plant a perennial bed, you may find that all your flowers have finished blooming by the end of June. Oops! Back to the drawing board to extend your seasonal palette to include plants that flower in midsummer and those that bloom in fall. Especially valuable in this quest are rebloomers—many daylilies flower in June and again later in the season—and repeat bloomers (gaillardia, for instance, and also some daylilies, such as 'Stella

*Joe-Pye weed (*Eupatorium*)*

d'Oro'). You'll also figure out that many perennials will rebloom if the first flowers are deadheaded. The idea may surprise you at first, but a valuable ally in having a perennial flower bed that looks good all during the growing season are plants that are grown for their foliage instead of flowers. Good examples include hostas and ferns in the shade; *Artemisia* 'Powis Castle' and ornamental grasses in the sun. And don't overlook heucheras.

In addition to timing your perennials' blooming, you'll want to coordinate flower colors so the plants that are in bloom at the same time complement one another. Some other considerations for selecting perennials that you need to think about (and are included in the plant profiles) are how long the plant stays in bloom, the plant's height, spread, and habit, any feature the plant will add to the garden once its flowers have faded (interesting leaves, showy seedpods), growing conditions, such as sun or shade, and the plant's soil preferences, and winter hardiness.

Although a *perennial* is defined as a plant that returns to the garden year after year, perennial doesn't necessarily mean "permanent." Some perennial flowers live long lives (peonies do), while others, such as gaillardia, may return for two to three years and then have to be replanted. Still, some perennials that are short-lived do reseed themselves so you always have plants of them.

Colors are usually divided into cool (green, blue, violet) or warm (orange, red, yellow). Warm or hot colors are more exciting and make the garden look "closer" to the viewer. Cool colors are more peaceful and seem to recede—to appear to be farther away from the viewer. Light colors tend to illuminate dark areas and also tend to stand out more at dusk. Gardeners often separate blocks of color, but if you do plant cool and warm colors together (and there's no reason not to—it's your garden), put the warm colors in the foreground so the cool flowers don't get "lost." Also avoid planting so many plants with variegated leaves.

Give some thought to a plant's form and texture after blooming. Perennials are usually planted in groups of three, five, or seven in informal gardens. In more formal settings, it's fine to use even-numbered groupings of plants—four, six, and so forth. In both cases, these spread to form blocks or patches of color, which make quite an impact in the perennial border. Except for massive plants, rarely should perennials be planted singly.

For the best aesthetic effect, also vary flower and foliage forms. Although perennials with daisy-type blossoms are among the easiest to grow, an entire garden of plants with round flowers is rather dull.

Don't be afraid to experiment. A perennial garden should contain plants that you like. After all, you're the one who will be out there to enjoy it.

Preparing the Soil and Planting

It's always a good idea to have your soil tested anytime you're planting a new flower bed. For a small fee, your local agricultural Extension service office will send samples off to be tested in a laboratory. The results not only will tell you the pH of your soil (whether it's acidic, alkaline, or somewhere in between), but they will also give fertilizer recommendations.

Because perennials stay in the same place for at least several years, it's important to prepare the soil carefully before planting. Till or dig the soil at least 12 inches deep and mix it with organic matter—peat moss, well-rotted mushroom compost, fine bark, compost, and so forth. This will improve drainage, which is essential to almost all perennials. Unless noted in the plant profile in this chapter, perennials are planted much as annuals are. So if you aren't an experienced gardener, or you'd like to refresh your memory with a few tips, see page 45 for planting advice.

A slightly different situation is when mail-order companies send you bare-root perennials. These may scare you a bit; they don't look like much, but if handled correctly, will grow just fine.

Remove the sawdust or other packaging material. Soak a bare-root perennial plant in water (or in water mixed with a transplant solution) for an hour before planting. Dig a hole wide and deep enough to hold the dormant plant when the roots are spread out. Build a cone of soil in the middle of the hole and place the plant on top with the roots fanning out over it. You'll want the top of the roots of the plant to be at ground level. Cover the roots with soil and press down firmly so the roots and soil are in good contact. Water well and mulch with an inch of compost, fine bark, or pine needles. Watch out for unseasonable frosts, and protect young plants if necessary with more mulch or a fabric covering.

The No. 1 reason perennials don't return in spring is poor drainage—the plant roots stood in too much water over winter. If your soil doesn't drain well, and you don't want to spend the time or energy to amend flower beds with drainage-improving organic matter, you can avoid this problem by planting perennials in raised beds.

Caring for Perennials

Some perennials need to be staked to look their best. Double-flowered peonies, for example, often end up facedown in the mud when it rains while they're in bloom. Placing a support around the plant as soon as it begins growing in spring can prevent this. Look through catalogs and at garden centers for a variety of long-lasting supports made for various kinds of perennials. These go way beyond the old green-stained bamboo sticks. But if staking is a chore you'd prefer to avoid, choose shorter and strong-stemmed species and cultivars that don't need to be supported.

Staking perennials

Sometimes perennials flop over instead of standing straight because they've been overfertilized, especially with too much nitrogen. I rarely feed my perennials unless a plant looks a bit peaked or isn't growing as well as it should. Then I may spray it once or twice with liquid seaweed or a water-soluble plant food. This regimen assumes that the soil has been improved before planting takes place and that organic mulches are allowed to rot and provide a constant, gentle dose of nutrients. In average soil, perennials need less fertilizer than just about any of the other plants in your garden.

Pinching back mums

Other care is pretty easy—weeding, watering, pinching off flowers after they've faded. In fall, after a hard frost, cut down the flower stalks and plant stems and compost them. (Be sure that you don't include any seeds, or new plants will pop up everywhere you apply the compost the next year!)

Eventually, most perennials get crowded and stop blooming as profusely as they did in the past, and the center of large ornamental grasses may die out. Those are signs to the gardener that these plants need to be separated: dug up, divided, and then replanted farther apart (or elsewhere in the yard). To put this chore off for as long as possible, avoid crowding your perennials and ornamental grasses when you plant—space them so that they have elbow room. This is especially important with plants such as hostas, which don't like to be divided and take a year or so to recover from it.

Dividing a perennial varies somewhat with the type of plant. But the basic procedure is to wait for a relatively cool, overcast day and carefully dig up the entire clump. Division may be done in spring or fall. I prefer spring, but if you choose to wait until autumn, don't put it off too long. New plants need to establish roots before cold weather; otherwise, they may be killed by low temperatures.

After you've dug up the clump, shake and wash the soil off so you can see what you're doing. Work the roots apart—discarding old sections that no longer bloom—and then replant the newer sections. This is easier and faster if two people work together and if you—or rainfall—have soaked the soil first. If the plant's root system is large, tease it into sections using two spading forks (this is where a partner comes in handy). With smaller sections of roots, you may be able to do the separating with a sharp knife. The pieces along the outside of the root system are generally the youngest and most vigorous. Excessively woody sections in the middle should be discarded (this applies particularly to chrysanthemums); no new growth will come from those old root sections.

Place the new divisions in a pail of water to soak while you finish dividing other plants; then replant immediately. That's all there is to it. Once you're finished, you have a number of new plants for other spots in the garden or to share with friends and neighbors.

Ornamental Grasses

Ornamental grasses fit right into the gardeners' goal of having plants in the yard that are interesting and attractive to look at over a long period of time—early spring to late fall, and maybe even beyond. It's the "beyond" where decorative perennial grasses excel—although they're usually light tan during cold weather, it's an attractive color, especially if the graceful plumes are a different shade. And as the wind blows, big grasses add a sense of movement and sound to the landscape.

Grass or grasslike plants bordering lawn

American homeowners have embraced various kinds of ornamental grasses. Instead of planting another deciduous shrub, many gardeners are now adding a tall fountain grass. Or rather then using a dwarf annual or perennial to edge a flower bed, they might plant shade-loving carex or colorful hakone grass.

But these grasses have many excellent qualities to recommend them: low maintenance, affected by almost no insects or diseases, tolerant of a wide range of soils, mostly deer-resistant, attractive in the fall, provide seeds and shelter for birds and small wildlife, and they give you dried material for winter flower arrangements. Ornamental grasses, which come in an array of sizes to fit any garden, add pizzazz to the landscape. The larger grasses have an imposing presence year-round; the smaller ones make nice accents. And I love the sound they make when they rustle in the breeze.

Grasses and Grasslike Plants

Not all the "grasses" listed in this chapter are true grasses; some are classified as "grasslike plants." That shouldn't matter to gardeners; they're used the same way. Something you may want to know about real ornamental grasses is that they're divided into "cool-season" or "warm-season" species. A cool-season grass begins growing very early in spring; it may even be evergreen or semievergreen.

It flowers in early to midsummer and then stops growing. It looks best in spring and the first half of summer. Feather reed, purple moor, stipa, and tufted hair grasses are cool-season species. A warm-season ornamental grass is very slow to start growing in the spring and flowers later in summer than cool-season grasses, often into fall. That's when they look their best. These grasses generally handle heat and humidity well. Examples of warm-season ornamental grasses are fountain grass, miscanthus, pink muhly, and switchgrass.

Plant and Grow Ornamental Grasses

Plant ornamental grasses as you do perennials and annuals (see pages 45 and 134). The main difference is that spring is usually the best time to set out ornamental grasses; in fall, they may not have enough time before cold weather to develop a good root system. It's also important not to plant them too deeply. The crown of the plant—where the roots and leaves join—should be at ground level.

One other thing you want to be very aware of with grasses is their potential to spread aggressively. Some (such as northern sea oats) reseed prolifically and others (like Japanese blood grass) have running roots that quickly extend the planting quite a distance. I've tried to include grasses that don't present problems, but you may want to talk with gardening friends about their experiences with specific grasses in your area.

Pruning and Rejuvenating Ornamental Grasses

There's nothing difficult about growing ornamental grasses. The simple directions you need are given with each entry in this chapter. The only thing you'll find different is that all ornamental grasses need to be cut back each year; about the beginning of March in Kentucky and Tennessee.

With smaller grasslike plants, such as mondo and liriope, the process is simple. Using handpruners, loppers, hedge clippers, or a string trimmer (depending on how large a stand of grass you need to cut back), cut off most of the old foliage (leave about 1 inch so you don't damage the plant's crown) and remove the brown foliage from the garden. Then, when the plants begin growing in a few weeks, you won't have any ugly mixture of brown and green strap-like leaves.

The annual pruning is somewhat more difficult with larger ornamental grasses, simply because of their size. The first year or two, a string trimmer will do the job, although most of the time you'll need to leave a base of leaves 9 to 12 inches high. In following years, as the grasses grow thicker, you may have to use a chainsaw. Don't avoid this chore. It makes all the difference in the appearance of your grasses, as well as how they grow.

You'll need to divide ornamental grass about every three or four years. If you don't, the grass will die out in the center or become thin. It's best not to put it off too long, because division is harder if the plant is greatly overgrown. Dividing ornamental grasses is the same as dividing perennial plants, except that spring is usually the best time to divide all grasses. See page 135 for directions.

If you haven't tried grasses yet, select one from the following pages and give it a try. You may discover a new, low-maintenance plant that's just right for your yard.

Anemone
Anemone × hybrida

When you plant a perennial garden, you naturally want to have something in flower from spring until fall. But as you're planning which plants to include, you'll discover that the most difficult to find are the ones that bloom in late summer and early fall. Enter hybrid anemone. No, not the spring bulbs called anemones (and sometimes windflowers). Japanese anemone A. hupehensis var. japonica and Anemone tomentosa (grape-leaf anemone) are perennials that bloom in autumn with delicate, pastel blossoms. The pink, white, or red flowers sway in the slightest breeze on slender stems. For me, grape-leaf anemone spreads too aggressively. I've heard similar complaints about Japanese anemone, but just as many say that's not their experience; it's usually a true delight in shady or partly shady gardens.

Botanical Pronunciation
uh-NEM-o-nee high-BRED-duh

Bloom Period and Seasonal Color
Late summer and fall in white, rose, and pink

Mature Height × Spread
2 to 5 feet × 2 to 3 feet

When, Where, and How to Plant
Plant container-grown anemones in early spring or early fall, preferably in a partially shady spot. You may need to experiment to find the ideal soil. It should be moist (or kept moist by watering), but very well drained. Standing water over winter will kill anemones. Amend poor or average soil with organic matter, especially compost, to improve drainage. Space clumps 1 to 2 feet apart, out of the wind, and mulched. Hybrid anemones are less likely to spread aggressively when grown in dry soil.

Growing Tips
In Zone 7, which is the southern limit for these plants, keep the soil evenly moist at all time, but never standing in water. The plants can't tolerate drought, so water enough to keep the soil evenly moist at all times. As with most perennials, anemones require little if any fertilizer if growing in good soil. Too much nitrogen causes fast, floppy growth. Renew mulch as needed so that it stays about 2 inches thick.

Care
If anemones spread too aggressively, pull up runners (getting all roots, if possible) and remove them from the garden. Divide clumps every three years. Tall stems may need staking; do this early in the season so the plants aren't flattened by thunderstorms. You should encounter few insects or diseases, although Japanese beetles like them (see page 34 for control advice).

Garden Design
In partial shade, grow anemones with hostas, ferns, and carex. Turtlehead (*Chelone*) is another perennial that has similar flower colors, likes about the same conditions, and blooms near the same time.

Try These
'Richard Ahrens' has double, pink-and-white flowers; it often starts blooming in midsummer and continues through September. 'Margarete' has very large, semi-double flowers late in the season. The blooms are a medium pink. 'Honorine Jobert' is a very old cultivar that bears an abundant crop of white flowers filled with contrasting yellow stamens.

Arkansas Blue Star
Amsonia hubrichtii

When, Where, and How to Plant
In spring, after the chance of frost has passed, set out plants in full sun, or a mostly sunny spot, in average soil that's well drained. If it's slightly acidic to just neutral, so much the better (a soil test will tell you the pH of your soil). Don't apply any fertilizer when planting. Arkansas blue star will tolerate other situations, but if placed in too much shade or in soil that's too rich and moist, the plants will grow floppy (see page 137 for more about how to plant perennials). You can also grow this plant from seed sown in spring indoors (see page 37 for directions for starting seeds). When the plant needs dividing, do it in spring.

Growing Tips
This is a very low-maintenance perennial. It needs no fertilizer and is drought-tolerant once it's mature. Young plants, however, need to be kept watered when rainfall is less than an inch per week, until they're established.

Care
Arkansas blue star resists insects and diseases, as well as deer and rabbits. It doesn't need deadheading or pruning either. Should you need to do any pruning, wear gloves, as some people have skin that can be irritated by the sap.

Garden Design
Plant a row of *Amsonia* behind *Sedum* 'Purple Emperor', 'Purple Dome' New England aster (which is compact and has a nice deep color), and chrysanthemums. You may want to add a couple of plants to the cutting garden, since they're good in arrangements. In winter, *Amsonia* looks good with ornamental grasses and plants, such as black-eyed Susans, that retain their seedheads.

Try These
Amsonia ciliata 'Spring Sky' is drought-tolerant and grows about 18 to 24 inches tall. 'Blue Ice' is a pretty interspecific hybrid (combining two different species) that forms a compact plant 12 to 16 inches high and has more vivid color than many others. 'Short Stack' grows 10 inches tall and 18 inches wide.

Here's a native plant that's grown as much for its striking fall appearance as for its late-spring flowers. The tiny pale to medium blue blooms, which grow in clusters, are star-shaped. In autumn the plant will remind you of a shorter, bright yellow smoke bush. The airy foliage is like a bottlebrush, but very soft. The plant is also easy-care and adaptable as to sun and soil, as well as being heat- and cold-tolerant, making it perfect for a beginning gardener or someone starting to grow perennials. Although it's a wonderful plant, it never got much publicity—which limited its popularity—until the Perennial Plant Association named it Plant of the Year. Now it's easy to find, and I recommend that you do.

Botanical Pronunciation
am-SO-nee-uh hugh-BRICK-tee-eye

Bloom Period and Seasonal Color
Blue flowers in late spring; yellow billowy foliage in fall

Mature Height x Spread
2 to 3 feet x 3 to 4 feet

Artemisia
Artemisia 'Powis Castle'

Plants with gray or silver foliage are useful in the garden because of their softening effect and the way they complement many colors of flowers. But gray-leaved plants don't like the summer heat—and especially the humidity—of our area. Gardeners often call this typical midsummer decline "melting." But 'Powis Castle' is one artemisia that won't melt in the dog days of August, and it also won't take over, as some aggressive species of Artemisia may. Like all artemisias, 'Powis Castle' is drought-tolerant too. All that plus it's good-looking and has fragrant foliage. It fits well into a bed of perennial flowers and looks right at home in an herb garden. Gardeners who enjoy crafts find artemisia to be very useful when dried.

Botanical Pronunciation
ar-te-MEEZ-ee-uh

Bloom Period and Seasonal Color
Grown for lace-cut, silvery-gray leaves from summer to fall

Mature Height × Spread
3 feet × 3 feet

When, Where, and How to Plant
In spring, after chance of frost has passed, set out purchased plants (or your own cuttings that you took the previous summer; see Care below) in any average garden soil that drains well. Artemesia won't tolerate wet or poorly drained soil. Set the plants at the same depth they were growing at in their pots. Space the plants about 3 feet apart on all sides. Artemisias prefer full sun, but won't object to an hour or two—no more—of afternoon shade. Don't add fertilizer to the soil at planting time—this causes rampant growth and floppy stems. Also, to avoid keeping the soil too moist, do not mulch.

Growing Tips
Once 'Powis Castle' has started growing, it shouldn't need watering. No fertilizer is necessary either.

Care
Prune 'Powis Castle' in spring, when needed. If the plants should flop over in summer, cut them back to 2 inches tall and let them regrow. Pinching the tips of the stems throughout the season keeps artemisia compact and provides cuttings for new plants, which root easily in a mixture of one part sand to one part packaged potting soil. If you notice yellow spots on the plants' lower leaves, this is a sign of rust, a fungal disease that can develop in humid conditions. Cut the plant back to the ground, removing all leaves from the garden and destroying them. Ask the Extension service for help if the problem persists or others develop.

Garden Design
Artemisia is an excellent filler plant with antique or English roses, asters, purple coneflowers, and flowering shrubs. In a perennial bed, combine it with perennials that have colorful flowers. Use it to edge herb gardens or beds. *Artemisia schmidtiana* 'Silverado', a mounded form of artemisia, is often used to create knot gardens.

Try These
Artemisia ludoviciana 'Valerie Finnis' is also tolerant of our region's humidity.

Baptisia
Baptisia species and hybrids

When, Where, and How to Plant
Baptisia prefers rich soil that drains well, but it tolerates average soil. Give plants with blue flowers full sun, but the white ones can manage some shade. Set out plants anytime in spring, or sow freshly collected seed in late summer. Space plants 3 feet apart where they are to grow; transplanting is difficult because of a deep taproot. Mulch with organic matter to keep the soil cool. To grow baptisia from seed, soak the seeds overnight in warm water, nick them with a knife, and plant them outdoors in fall.

Growing Tips
Water young plants regularly—so that the plants don't wilt—until they are established. Mature baptisia plants are drought-tolerant. Be patient with baptisia. Plants are slow to begin blooming—a few flowers the second year and then it can take some time (up to five years for seed-grown plants) to form a nice clump. You can encourage the growth of young plants by spreading a slow-release fertilizer around the plants in spring, although mature plants need no fertilizer and actually add nitrogen to the soil. If leaves turn yellow prematurely during summer, use chelated iron or a water-soluble fertilizer for flowering plants that contains iron, according to label directions.

Care
Plants in partial shade may need staking. Keep plants deadheaded to promote continuing bloom. Let the last flowers go to seed, if you like; the graceful seedpods may be cut off while they still rattle to dry for arrangements. Watch out for voles.

Garden Design
Grow baptisia with bearded iris, black-eyed Susans, Shasta daisies, and cleome which appreciate similar conditions. Carolina lupine (*Thermopsis caroliniana*) looks a lot like baptisia, but with yellow flowers instead of blue. Grow the two together.

Try These
'Blueberry Sundae' has deep indigo flowers and grows vigorously. 'Purple Smoke' has lavender flowers and is especially heat-tolerant. 'Solar Flare' has yellow blooms that change to orange.

Although it's a drought-tolerant native plant and has blue flowers, which are coveted by many perennial gardeners, easy-to-grow baptisia isn't as well known as you'd expect. That doesn't mean it has a number of hidden faults, though; Baptisia australis was named a Perennial Plant of the Year by the Perennial Plant Association. Both it and white false indigo (Baptisia alba) have stalks of attractive pealike blooms that later produce black seedpods, which are popular with flower arrangers. If left on the plant, the dried pods make a rattling sound in the wind—a pleasant garden sound effect. White baptisia is shorter than blue baptisia and blooms a few weeks later. You'll probably want both; they make a fine combination.

Botanical Pronunciation
bap-TIZ-ee-uh

Bloom Period and Seasonal Color
Spring in blue or white

Mature Height × Spread
3 to 4 feet × 4 to 5 feet

Black-Eyed Susan
Rudbeckia species and hybrids

It's sometimes easy to get confused when shopping for new Rudbeckia, because there are 23 species and some are annuals, others biennials or perennials, some are more like coneflowers than black-eyed Susans, and still others have orange flowers rather than yellow blooms. And pay attention to mature sizes—they range from 1 foot tall to a towering 7 feet! Almost all of the perennial species have yellow or gold petals around a brown or black center, and they bloom a long time. That and their versatility—plus drought-tolerance—make black-eyed Susans excellent plants. Because of their attraction for butterflies and the popularity of their fall seeds with birds such as goldfinches, they're also good in a garden that's planted to attract wildlife.

Botanical Pronunciation
rood-BEK-ee-uh

Bloom Period and Seasonal Color
Summer to fall in gold, red, maroon, and yellow

Mature Height × Spread
8 inches to 3 feet × 18 inches

When, Where, and How to Plant
In spring, plant black-eyed Susans in any soil that drains well and is in full or partial sun. It tolerates clay as long as it drains reasonably well and doesn't stay wet over winter. Space plants of *Rudbeckia fulgida* and hybrids such as 'Goldsturm' 18 inches apart, cutleaf coneflower (*Rudbeckia laciniata*) 1 foot apart, and *Rudbeckia nitida* 2 feet apart. Mulch lightly.

Growing Tips
Water frequently to keep the root zone moist until the plants are established; mature plants are drought-tolerant. Fertilizer isn't usually necessary except in very poor soil; in that case, spread a pelleted slow-release formula for flowers once in spring. Or use a water-soluble flower fertilizer monthly during the growing season. Leave the flower stalks standing in fall to provide seeds for the birds, or you may cut the seedheads when dry in fall and save the seeds to plant in flats in late winter for spring transplanting.

Care
Divide *Rudbeckia* every three years in spring or early fall, but lift offsets and new seedlings anytime during the growing season. Replant them immediately, or pot them up and place in the garden later. This isn't a demanding plant—no pinching or pruning and few pests. Spider mites may occur in very dry sites at midsummer; spray with water once a week to prevent. Mildew may appear in late fall but it is inconsequential.

Garden Design
Grow black-eyed sussans with compatible sun lovers such as butterfly weed, gaillardia, and small- to medium-sized ornamental grasses (or grow it in front of or between taller ornamental grasses).

Try These
Rudbeckia fulgida var. *speciosa* 'Viette's Little Suzy' is a delightful yellow-flowered cultivar; it grows 18 to 24 inches high. *Rudbeckia hirta* 'Cherry Brandy' is covered with 3- to 4-inch red and maroon flowers with black centers on plants that reach 2 feet tall. It isn't a perennial, but is a good-looking and long-blooming plant that readily self-sows so that it comes back each year.

When, Where, and How to Plant

Prepare the soil by adding organic matter to produce humus-rich soil that will drain quickly. *Dicentra* doesn't do well in clay soil that stays wet in winter. Plant dormant roots or purchased plants in spring, following the directions on pages 45 and 134. Space plants or roots 18 inches to 2 feet apart in shade or part shade. Mulch lightly.

Growing Tips

Let the soil dry out slightly before watering; bleeding hearts don't like wet feet. *Dicentra eximia* rarely needs watering. Fertilize with a slow-release fertilizer—granular or pelleted—according to package instructions, when leaves appear every year.

Care

If aphids, slugs, or snails appear, see pages 33 and 34 for advice about getting rid of them. Consult the Extension service if plants mildew. When foliage dies in early summer, toss it on the compost pile. Pull up new plants that result from self-sown seed; their flowers won't look like the parent plant. Crowded clumps can be divided in spring or fall. Cut pieces of the rhizome with two to four buds (or eyes) each and replant. But avoid dividing unless the plant is overcrowded; it takes several years for it to recover. The best time to divide is just after flowering is complete. But if you don't mind forgoing flowers, you may divide overgrown plants in very early spring, soon after they come up.

Garden Design

This is an excellent woodland plant combined with ferns, pulmonaria, coral bells, and foamflower. Use rose-colored impatiens planted around bleeding hearts to hide the clumps of yellowing leaves as they're going dormant. Or, plant bleeding heart in a bed of groundcover that will mask its dying foliage.

Try These

'King of Hearts' has very large rose-pink blooms topping lovely foliage; it makes a good cut flower. *Dicentra scandens* 'Athens Yellow' is a different color, but isn't hardy in Zone 6. The red stems on 'Valentine' complement the red flowers.

Have you noticed that some of the prettiest plants have some of the most unfortunate names? This charming perennial is a good example. It's hard to resist the dangling heart-shaped flowers—pink, white, crimson, bicolor—that arch over deeply cut leaves in shades of green, grayish, and blue-green. If you have a shade garden, overlook the gory name (or call it Dicentra) and grow this plant; it's a must for spring. You'll find several other species besides—I especially like the fernlike leaves of fringed bleeding heart (Dicentra eximia), which is native and reblooms in summer. New hybrids may flower in summer and fall. Don't be surprised when this plant "disappears" by midsummer. That's normal; it will reappear on schedule in spring.

Botanical Pronunciation
die-SEN-tra spek-TAH-bil-iss

Bloom Period and Seasonal Color
Spring with pink, white, or red flowers

Mature Height × Spread
8 to 30 inches × 12 to 36 inches

Boltonia

Boltonia asteroides

I'm not sure why I'm so attracted to plants that have daisylike flowers. I know that others don't always agree with me about them. I recall a man who asked me to design a perennial border, and his only request was that it contain no "daisies." I think he was missing out on a good thing. Daisy-type flowers always look cheerful, their colors mix nicely with other plants, and they're oh-so-easy to grow. That describes boltonia perfectly, but this plant has another valuable trait: It's completely covered with flowers in late summer and early fall when few other perennials are putting on a performance. You'll find a pink cultivar, if you're not fond of white with yellow centers; there's even a native with purple flowers.

Botanical Pronunciation
bowl-TONE-ee-uh as-ter-OY-deez

Bloom Period and Seasonal Color
Late summer and early fall in white, purple, or pink

Mature Height × Spread
4 to 6 feet × 4 feet

When, Where, and How to Plant
Boltonia must be grown in full sun; otherwise, the plants will sprawl all over. Excellent drainage is another essential. Though this plant prefers moist but well-drained soil, it will tolerate dry to average soils, although they may reduce the height of the plant somewhat (which isn't a bad thing for some gardeners). Plant in spring after chance of frost has passed. Set plants at least 2 to 3 feet apart, or more, on all sides (see page 134 for tips on planting perennials). Mulch with 2 inches of organic matter, but keep it from touching the stems of the plants.

Growing Tips
Apply a balanced slow-release fertilizer to the soil around the plants each spring. Established plants are drought-tolerant, but plants and flowers will be smaller if plants aren't watered in dry spells.

Care
If you like, boltonia can be cut down to 2 feet high in late June to create a denser clump that will be shorter, bloom a little later, and have better-looking lower leaves in early fall. Few pests or diseases bother boltonia. As a favor to goldfinches and other birds, leave the plants standing for a while after they've been killed by frost. You'll find that the birds quickly eat up the seeds.

Garden Design
Boltonia is a good candidate for the back of the flower border (because of its height), but due to its airy appearance, it isn't useful for screening, as many taller perennials are. Boltonia is ideal for naturalized plantings and to add fine texture and light colors to bolder, fall-blooming perennial borders. Grow with asters, chrysanthemums, *Sedum* 'Autumn Joy', and goldenrod. It's often called false aster and is nice planted with asters.

Try These
Boltonia asteroides var. *latisquama* 'Jim Crockett' has lavender flowers with yellow centers on a compact plant that grows about 2 feet tall and 2 feet wide. 'Pink Beauty' has pale pink blooms on a large plant.

Butterfly Weed
Asclepias tuberosa

When, Where, and How to Plant

Plant in spring, after chance of frost has passed, in a sunny spot that has average, well-drained soil. Too little sun and the plants will flop over. Too much moisture, especially over winter, and the plants won't return. Plant butterfly weed in its permanent location, since full-grown plants are difficult to transplant because of a deep taproot. Space seeds 10 to 12 inches apart (see page 134 for more about planting perennials). Mulching isn't necessary.

Growing Tips

Established plants are drought-tolerant and rarely need watering. Unless the plants aren't growing well, they won't need fertilizer.

Care

Remove faded flowers to encourage a longer blooming time. Few pests bother butterfly weed, except for aphids. Dislodge them with a blast of water from a garden hose and spray with insecticidal soap. Caterpillars found munching the plants will be the larvae of the monarch butterfly; don't kill them. If they do too much damage, see if you can transfer them to butterfly weed or milkweed plants in the wild. Instead of dividing clumps, cut back plants to rejuvenate them. If you deadheaded the first flowers, leave the second ones on the stems so that the purple pods—great for dried arrangements—will open in late fall. The plant often reseeds; remove any extra plants that you don't want while they're small and can be moved.

Garden Design

Butterfly weed is ideal for a wildflower meadow. This member of the milkweed family looks nice paired with Shasta daisies, black-eyed Susans, and dwarf red hot pokers (*Kniphofia uvaria*). Or make it part of a butterfly garden that includes cardinal flowers, columbines, coreopsis, coneflowers, goldenrod, coral bells, Joe-Pye weed, and sedum.

Try These

'Gay Butterflies' is easily grown from seed sown where the plants will grow. It has a mixture of orange, yellow, and red flowers. 'Hello Yellow' has blooms exactly the color you would expect. Swamp milkweed (*Asclepias incarnata*) is ideal for those always-damp spots in your yard.

If you like the idea of enticing butterflies to visit your yard, this is the perennial flower for you, even if you aren't sure about the "weed" part of the name—which just indicates that this native plant can often be found growing wild along roadsides, without any care. And that tells you how carefree it will be for you, as long as you plant it in sunshine. Butterfly weed attracts "winged jewels" by the dozens, especially the beautiful monarch butterflies. It also provides nectar for moths at night. Butterfly weed will add color to your landscape, too, with bright orange flower clusters sitting atop shiny green leaves. Some new hybrids feature red or yellow blooms, and you can occasionally find white or pink flowers, but orange is still the most popular choice.

Botanical Pronunciation
as-KLEE-pee-us too-buh-RO-suh

Bloom Period and Seasonal Color
Summer in orange, red, yellow, white, or pink

Mature Height × Spread
1 to 3 feet × 12 to 18 inches

Candytuft

Iberis sempervirens

Gardeners who want their yards to look neat and tidy appreciate the pure white flowers and glossy evergreen foliage of candytuft, which spreads to form a compact mound. It seems to shine like glossy snow on sunny early spring days. If temperatures stay cool, candytuft blooms a long time, accenting a variety of spring-flowering plants. Several cultivars flower in fall as well as spring—provided you keep them well watered over summer and temperatures don't get too hot. When you're shopping, be sure to get perennial candytuft; there are annual candy-tufts too. If you like plants that are different, as I do, try a new candytuft with purple flowers, instead of the traditional white; it has performed well in my garden.

Botanical Pronunciation
eye-BEER-is sem-per-VIE-renz

Bloom Period and Seasonal Color
Early spring (and sometimes fall) in white; late spring in purple

Mature Height × Spread
4 to 12 inches × 6 to 18 inches

When, Where, and How to Plant

Well-drained soil is necessary for candytuft. Amend average soil with organic matter to improve drainage. In clay soils, plant in a raised bed. Full sun is recommended; flowering will be less in partial shade. Set out plants anytime in spring, following the directions on page 134. Space plants about 8 inches apart and mulch with pine straw or finely shredded bark. You may also grow candytuft from seed that's started indoors about 8 weeks before the average last frost or sown in the garden in late spring (see page 37 for directions).

Growing Tips

When rainfall is below an inch a week, water deeply, then let soil dry out slightly before watering again. If you're growing varieties that flower in fall as well as spring, these need to be watered weekly during summer if rainfall is lacking, particularly if temperatures are high. Fertilizer isn't usually necessary, but you may want to apply a slow-release fertilizer after you cut back the plants when they've finished blooming.

Care

Cut candytuft back by half after flowering to rejuvenate the plants and promote some flowering again in late spring and sometimes in fall. Never prune candytuft in fall; you'll be removing the following spring's flowers. Insect and disease problems should be few. Both deer and slugs usually avoid candytuft. If plants rot, the drainage was poor; try the plant in another location.

Garden Design

Plant candytuft around evergreen azaleas with red, pink, or coral flowers. It looks nice when allowed to spill over the edges of a rock wall. Use as edging around spring bulb plantings. Many gardeners like to plant spring-flowering bulbs so they come up through a bed of candytuft.

Try These

'Absolutely Amethyst' is the first candytuft in a color other than white. This free-flowering purple hybrid blooms much later than white varieties. 'Little Gem' grows well in rock gardens and containers. 'Autumn Snow' an excellent fall-blooming candytuft.

Cardinal Flower

Lobelia cardinalis

When, Where, and How to Plant

In spring, after the chance of frost has passed, set out plants in good soil that has been amended with compost or other organic material so it retains moisture (see page 134 for instructions on planting perennials). Space plants 18 to 24 inches apart in part shade or part sun. Mix a granular or pelleted slow-release fertilizer with the soil before planting.

Growing Tips

Water often enough to keep the soil moist; otherwise, blooms are fewer and the plants don't return the next year. If you have a group of cardinal flowers in an area of dry soil, it's worthwhile installing a soaker hose or drip irrigation to keep them gently watered. Fertilizer usually isn't needed, but if lower leaves turn yellow, spray with an iron-containing, water-soluble fertilizer made for flowering plants.

Care

Pruning, pinching, and dividing are seldom needed. Cardinal flowers don't like deep mulch. If you use mulch in summer, make sure it doesn't touch the stems of the plants. In winter, it's often best—especially in heavy soils, such as clay—to remove the mulch altogether. The exception is if you plant cardinal flowers in early fall, when you can apply a light mulch, such as pine needles, for winter protection. Cardinal flower should have few insects or diseases. Aphids and spider mites may be a problem in dry sites (see pages 33 and 34 for control advice). Cardinal flower can be short-lived; to always have plants, pull back the mulch around plants after flowering to enable them to reseed.

Garden Design

Plant cardinal flower near a water garden, or use it in a shady corner near the house to bring hummingbirds into viewing range from a window.

Try These

'Fan Blue' has blue-violet flowers instead of the traditional red; it grows 1 to 2 feet tall. 'Rose Beacon' has rosy pink flowers on 40-inch stems.

I like to grow cardinal flower for many reasons, including its brilliant red blooms, which are hummingbird and butterfly magnets. Those colorful flowers also appear in late summer, when few other perennials are blooming, and stay in bloom as long as three weeks, which is nice for gardeners as well as hungry hummers. If you have clay soil, or spots in your yard that stay damp in spring or summer, cardinal flower is an excellent perennial choice for those sites. I especially appreciate cardinal flower's versatility when it comes to light; it's easily grown in part sun or part shade. It's true that the plant is short-lived, but it makes up for it by reseeding, so in moist soil, you should always have plants.

Botanical Pronunciation

lo-BEE-lee-a kar-di-NAH-lis

Bloom Period and Seasonal Color

Late summer in red or pink, also in blue-violet

Mature Height × Spread

2 to 4 feet × 2 feet

Chrysanthemum

Dendranthema × grandiflorum

Every fall, I read complaints in garden blogs and magazines that mums are "overplanted." It's true that we see them everywhere in autumn, but they're colorful, easy, and readily available in full bloom, so they're a perfect impulse purchase to brighten your yard after summer annuals begin to fade. Consider buying small mum plants in spring and letting them grow to blooming size in fall; it's fun and gives you a nice sense of accomplishment. Also those spring mums often have names, so you can plant one named after your best friend, your granddaughter, or even yourself. A tip: Many people don't know that if a dusk-to-dawn light shines on mums with partially opened flowers, the flowers will not open. Instead, plant mums away from artificial light.

Botanical Pronunciation
Den-DRAN-thuh-muh gran-dih-FLOOR-um

Bloom Period and Seasonal Color
Fall in white, yellow, pink, bronze, and shades of red, orange, and purple

Mature Height × Spread
10 to 48 inches × 10 to 30 inches

When, Where, and How to Plant
Anytime the weather is frost-free, you can plant potted mums that you bought in full bloom to grow indoors. In spring, after the change of frost has passed, set out bedding plant mums in a sunny spot that has average well-drained soil that's been amended with organic matter (follow directions on page 134 for planting perennials). Mix a pelleted or granular slow-release fertilizer with the soil before planting. Plant fall-purchased plants that are in bloom in full sun and well-drained soil. Avoid areas where lights will shine on the plants at night; chrysanthemums won't bloom without nighttime darkness. Don't fertilize fall-planted mums.

Growing Tips
Mums need regular watering to ensure that the soil doesn't dry out. Beginning in June, use a water-soluble fertilizer for flowering plants every other week until buds form. Don't fertilize after buds open.

Care
From late spring until July 15, occasionally pinch 2 inches off the tips of the stems. If you don't, the mums will bloom in summer, not fall, when you really need the color. Pinching will also cause the plant to form a more compact shape that's less likely to require staking (commercial mum plants are kept compact by a growth regulator; in future years, they will be taller in your yard). If aphids or spider mites appear, see page XX about controls. After plants are killed by frost, wait until spring to cut them back. Every other spring, dig up and divide the plant, discarding the woody center portion.

Garden Design
Garden mums make a show *en masse* in drifts where annuals might otherwise be used—between the sidewalk and driveway or street. Use them in perennial beds near other fall bloomers, such as asters.

Try These
Dendranthema zawadskii (also sold as *Chrysanthemum rubellum*) 'Clara Curtis' is easy to grow and has deep pink, daisylike blooms on a 2-foot plant. It readily returns each year.

Columbine
Aquilegia species and hybrids

When, Where, and How to Plant

Ideally, you'll plant columbines in mid-spring in a location with partial shade and moist but well-drained soil. But the plant is adaptable and can be set out in part sun or even full shade (for some cultivars) anytime during the growing season. But avoid afternoon sun. Place plants at the same depth they grew in their containers; never deeper (see page 134 for more about planting perennials). Space plants about 1 foot apart. Mulch to hold moisture in the soil, but don't cover the plant's crown (where the roots meet the stem), especially in winter.

Growing Tips

Water so that the soil stays barely moist. Fertilizer is rarely required; rotting mulch usually provides enough nutrients. Add to the mulch each spring so it stays about 2 inches deep. Columbines are usually short-lived, so if the plants don't return one spring, it's probably not your fault.

Care

If you don't want the plants to reseed, remove the flowers as they fade. Or, you can also deadhead the first flowers to encourage more blooms, and then allow the second blooms to reseed. Columbine is subject to several diseases, including powdery mildew, and a large number of insects, from caterpillars to leaf miners (which leave little "trails" in the foliage). Ask the Extension service about controls. One way to avoid pest problems is to cut most of the plants back to the ground after flowering.

Garden Design

Grow several different colors of columbines in a partly shady wildflower garden. Or, plant columbines at the front of a perennial border or along a walk where the delicate nature of their flowers can be appreciated. Or, interplant with perennials that flower later in the year—maybe asters in sun or heucheras in shade.

Try These

Aquilegia chrysantha 'Denver Gold' has clear yellow blooms. *Aquilegia canadensis* 'Little Lanterns' grows only a foot tall and does well in containers and in full shade.

Certified wildlife gardens have become all the rage over the past decade. If you have one or are considering planting one, this is a plant you'll want to include for its ethereal spring beauty as well as for its ability to attract hummingbirds and butterflies. Practically everyone recognizes the distinctive—often two-toned—nodding flowers and fan-shaped leaves that are columbine's best-known characteristic. You'll encounter several different types of columbine. If you haven't seen columbine recently, you'll be surprised at the new flower colors and appealing variegated leaves. If breeders improve disease-resistance, it could become the almost perfect plant. There are two predominant types of columbine. Wild columbine (Aquilegia canadensis), my favorite, has yellow and red blooms, and a large group of hybrids in many colors, shapes, and sizes. Wild columbine seems more resistant to leaf miners than most; however, Aquilegia chrysantha is very attractive to leaf miners. Columbines are also generally deer-resistant.

Botanical Pronunciation

ack-wi-LEE-gee-uh

Bloom Period and Seasonal Color

Spring in red, yellow, white, blue, purple, or pink

Mature Height × Spread

9 inches to 3 feet × 1 foot

Coneflower

Echinacea purpurea

Once upon a time, gardeners called this wonderful plant "purple coneflower." That was a bit of a misnomer since the most commonly grown varieties had pinkish flowers, not purple (and some were white). But nowadays, the name purple coneflower really doesn't fit since the Chicago Botanic Garden (and other breeders) began creating coneflowers in colors as varied as red, orange, and mango. I'm a gardener who's always anxious to try the latest and the most unusual plants, but I confess that after growing a number of the new coneflowers—and having many of them die during the first winter—I've become more cautious, waiting for the best of the bunch to become obvious. If you're new to coneflowers, try an older pink cultivar first.

Botanical Pronunciation

ek-ih-NAY-see-uh pur-pu-RE-uh

Bloom Period and Seasonal Color

Summer to fall in dusty pink, magenta, white, orange, yellow

Mature Height × Spread

2 to 4 feet × 1 to 2 feet

When, Where, and How to Plant

Any type of soil that drains well can sustain coneflowers. But the plants are more likely to develop weak stems that flop over when grown in rich organic soil. Plant in a sunny spot anytime from mid-spring (after chance of frost is gone) through summer (see page 134 for more about planting perennials). Space clumps 18 to 24 inches apart, placing the plants at the same depth they grew at in their containers, never deeper. Keep mulch away from the stem, so the crown isn't covered.

Growing Tips

When weekly rainfall is less than an inch, water coneflowers deeply but infrequently to encourage deep rooting and drought tolerance. Do not fertilize except for a light dressing of compost in spring. Too much fertilizer, especially when the plant is grown in partial sun, will lead to tall, weak stems. The plants will produce fewer flowers when crowded. When that happens, divide the clumps in spring or early fall and replant immediately.

Care

Keep faded flowers picked off to encourage more blooms, but leave the last ones intact. They will reseed, and over winter their attractive seedheads will attract hungry birds. Japanese beetles can be a problem; pick them off by hand and drop into a jar of water or oil to drown them. Remove and discard mulch around affected plants. Caterpillars may be a problem since the plant attracts many butterflies, which lay eggs on them. It's best to recognize that this may happen and grow enough plants for you and the butterfly larvae. If plants are being completely stripped, you can pick caterpillars off.

Garden Design

Grow in a cottage garden or in butterfly gardens planted with ornamental grasses, gaillardia, black-eyed Susans, and yarrow.

Try These

One of the interesting new cultivars is 'Burgundy Fireworks', which has sturdy burgundy-colored stems as well as attractive quilled petals. Old favorites include 'Bright Star', 'Magnus', 'Kim's Knee High', and 'White Swan.'

Coral Bells
Heuchera species and hybrids

When, Where, and How to Plant

Too much sun on dark-leaved coral bells will "bleach" the foliage, so shade or partial shade is a must. Avoiding sun also helps keep the soil moist, another requirement for this group of plants, which produces new leaves throughout the growing season. But soil should also drain well; add compost or other organic materials, if necessary, to lighten soil. The best time to set out coral bells is spring, but you may plant them until late summer (see page 134 for more about planting perennials). Space plants 8 to 12 inches apart, and mulch with organic matter to keep moisture in the soil.

Growing Tips

Keep soil moist during the growing season, but never saturated. Fertilize in early spring with half an inch of compost or with a slow-release plant food at half the amount recommended on the label.

Care

Cut faded flowers with their stems to keep plants neat and encourage reblooming. Renew the mulch each year so that it's at least 2 inches deep around plants, but not touching them. Divide clumps in early spring every third year and replant immediately. Take care when dividing— break the clump apart; don't cut straight through the crown. Older plants may develop woody stems and sprawl over. Dig them up and replant a bit deeper. Coral bells have few insect or disease problems.

Garden Design

Because of their colorful foliage, coral bells are perfect for edging flower beds, but be careful about the leaf and flower colors of companion plants, so they don't clash. They usually go well with foamflower, creeping phlox, bleeding heart, ferns, and hosta. Show off the interesting foliage by planting near the house or a walkway, so they can be seen easily. Purple-leaved varieties shine near flagstone patios.

Try These

'Marvelous Marble' has variegated foliage that changes colors throughout the growing season; its flowers are white and bloom early. 'Creme Brulee' has bronze foliage.

We often think that flowers are what make a plant stand out. But you'll change your mind when you see coral bells. True, the common name relates to the flower spikes, which are attractive but not showy; you appreciate them mostly close-up, but I've grown coral bells with green leaves with red veins and silver blotches, deep purple foliage with silver markings, and silver foliage with purple veins. After that, the flowers are just a bonus. Of the two most common species, the one with the best blooms is Heuchera sanguinea *and related hybrids.* Heuchera americana, *a native called alumroot, has the most spectacular foliage. But most of what are available to gardeners are spectacular evergreen cultivars—and more of these are being introduced every year.*

Botanical Pronunciation
HEW-ker-uh

Bloom Period and Seasonal Color
Spring in shades of white, pink, and red

Mature Height × Spread
1 to 2 feet × 12 to 18 inches

Coreopsis
Coreopsis species and hybrids

Threadleaf coreopsis (Coreopsis verticillata) is the most popular type in perennial gardens; it produces hundreds of tiny pale yellow, starlike blooms on an airy, delicate-looking ball of plant that's 12 to 18 inches tall and 2 feet wide. It combines beautifully with other perennials without calling much attention to itself. But if, like me, you want a showstopper of a plant, try Coreopsis grandi-flora (which grows up to 3 feet tall and has bright yellow daisylike flowers). It's the sort of plant that, when grown en masse, turns a flower bed into a sunshiny sea of yellow in May, causing passersby to stop and ask what it is. It's also one of the easiest perennials to grow and attracts butterflies lavishly.

Botanical Pronunciation
ko-ree-OP-sis gran-di-FLOOR-uh

Bloom Period and Seasonal Color
May and June, occasional summer rebloom, in yellow to gold

Mature Height × Spread
1 to 3 feet × 6 inches to 3 feet

When, Where, and How to Plant
Set out coreopsis plants in spring after the chance of frost has passed, and continue, if desired, until early September. Plant 12 to 18 inches apart in a sunny spot that has average, well-drained soil (see page 134 for more details on planting perennials). Coreopsis is easily grown from seed; but be careful that you don't accidentally buy seeds of *annual* coreopsis. (See page 37 for guidelines on growing plants from seed indoors.)

Growing Tips
Coreopsis is one of the easiest perennials to grow. It needs no fertilizer, and, although you should water regularly when the plants are young, mature ones are generally drought-tolerant. Because taller cultivars tend to get beaten down by thunderstorms, you may want to stake them or provide some support.

Care
If you have many coreopsis plants, pinching faded flowers off by hand can be time-consuming. The simplest way to do it is to make a broad swath with handpruners or loppers. Don't skip it, though. Removing spent flowers encourages the plant to rebloom, prevents it from aggressively reseeding, and makes the flower bed look neater. But if you leave the seedpods on the plants, they'll entice large numbers of goldfinches. I wouldn't trade any amount of tidiness for the entertainment provided by these acrobatic birds standing upside down on stems waving in the breeze to get at the seeds. Divide coreopsis every three years to keep it blooming well. Knock aphids off with a stream of water or spray with insecticidal soap.

Garden Design
Coreopsis grandiflora is excellent for massing. In a flower bed, plant it near early-flowering yellow daylilies or beside Shasta daisies. Place threadleaf coreopsis near annuals or perennials with pastel pink or blue flowers.

Try These
'Sunray' has semidouble to double flowers. 'Early Sunrise' stays less than 2 feet tall and blooms the longest. Pink coreopsis (*C. rosea*) does better in Zone 6 than Zone 7.

Daylily
Hemerocallis hybrids

When, Where, and How to Plant

Daylilies will survive in almost any soil, but for best growth and flowering, amend average soils with organic matter. Plant the tuberous roots in spring after frosts have passed, and purchased plants anytime from spring through summer. Space them 1 to 2 feet apart in full to partial sun. Mix a slow-release fertilizer, according to package directions, with the soil before planting.

Growing Tips

Keep new plantings moist until growth appears. During the first year, water plants when rainfall is less than usual. A second crop of flowers on rebloomers depends on their receiving an inch of water weekly from the end of the first flowering period until new buds form. Daylilies are drought-tolerant once they're established but deliver fewer flowers if they're neglected. Fertilize with a slow-release plant food each spring after leaves appear, or use 20-20-20 water-soluble fertilizer once or twice a month during the growing season. If daylilies aren't blooming well, the reason may be too much shade, too much fertilizer, lime (maybe drifting from an application to the lawn), too little water, planting too deeply, or a crowded clump that needs dividing.

Care

Keep faded flowers removed and don't let seedpods form. Cut down stalks after flowering, but let leaves stand until killed by frost. Divide overgrown clumps in spring. Daylilies experience few pests, but watch out for rust. Check with the Extension service about controls.

Garden Design

Daylilies can fill a bed of their own and are nice interplanted with other perennials. Their grasslike foliage is attractive after they bloom.

Try These

'Primal Scream' produces a profusion of vibrant orange flowers. 'Red Volunteer' grows about 30 inches tall and has brilliant red blooms about 6 inches across. 'Eenie Weenie' is an extra-early bloomer that grows about 10 inches high; its flowers are bright yellow. 'Happy Returns' is a good repeat-bloomer. And naturally I love the pink eyed daylily (shown here) that Lee Pickles named for me, 'Judy Lowe'.

If I were limited to only one flowering perennial in my yard (awful thought!), there's no contest as to what it would be—a daylily—or, I would hope, dozens of daylilies. I really began learning all about how impressive daylilies can be by going on tours of daylily gardens, sponsored by a local daylily society (there are three societies in Kentucky and six in Tennessee, plus 25 official daylily display gardens in our two states). What a revelation for anyone who tends to think of daylilies only in terms of those gangly orange ones that bloom along roadsides or 'Stella d'Oro'. (Although sometimes derisively called "ditch lilies," those orange ones are real survivors.) 'Stella' has the wonderful trait of blooming numerous times through the season, but don't stop with just one. Attend a daylily show or visit a local grower (they're located throughout our area), and you'll find spidery flowers in colors that appear to be dusted with gold or silver (or maybe fairy dust!). The curved and ruffled blossoms are what I love. Today's daylilies are really something to look at—and they're as carefree as ever.

Botanical Pronunciation
hem-er-oh-KAL-iss

Bloom Period and Seasonal Color
Late spring to fall in all colors except true white and blue

Mature Height × Spread
6 inches to 6 feet × 18 inches to 3 feet

Deciduous Ferns
Many genera, species, and varieties

There are so many deciduous ferns that you'll probably choose your first ones because you like how the fronds look. A few are particularly distinctive: Cinnamon fern (Osmunda cinnamomea) has impressive cinnamon-colored fronds that are nice in arrangements. Japanese painted fern (Athyrium nipponicum 'Pictum') has grayish leaves that sometimes take on a blue or red cast. Royal fern (Osmunda regalis) grows 6 feet tall and 4 feet wide. But the plainer species are also valuable for their grace and charm. Some—such as hay-scented fern, marsh fern, and New York fern—aggressively spread, and these are often the ones passed along by other gardeners who have an overabundance, so be careful in accepting a gift of one of them if you have little space.

Bloom Period and Seasonal Color
Grown for foliage

Mature Height × Spread
1 to 6 feet × 1 to 4 feet

When, Where, and How to Plant
Ferns need a rich, organic soil to thrive, preferably one that stays moist. Shade or part shade is ideal for most deciduous ferns, but read the plant's label to be sure; some ferns (such as maidenhair, royal, and sword ferns) tolerate quite a bit of sun. Plant from spring through summer, spacing plants 2 to 3 feet apart, depending on their mature size. Mix an organic slow-release fertilizer with the soil in the planting hole, according to package directions. Mulch with leaf mold or other organic matter to conserve moisture.

Growing Tips
Consistent moisture is critical to success. The easiest way to keep the soil cool and moist is to use soaker hoses or sprinklers on timers. No fertilizer is needed if you're planting in woodsy soil rich in organic matter. In poor soil, you may apply a small amount of an organic fertilizer in spring.

Care
Plants ferns in the shade, give them ample moisture, and few pests should bother them. Gardeners also don't need to prune or pinch them, just remove the occasional browned frond. Some ferns have a habit that's known as self-shedding; their leaves will fall off in autumn. After they do, rake them up. But if the foliage withers in place, leave it as-is over winter to protect the plant's crown; remove the dead fronds in early spring before new growth starts.

Garden Design
Much more than woodland plants, ferns are excellent for containers and provide a jungle effect when grown near tropicals. Some (such as *Dryopteris affinis* 'Crispa Gracilis') do nicely in rock gardens and some (like cinnamon fern, ostrich fern, and royal fern) grow well in wet spots. Enjoy cinnamon fern for excellent fall color, then trim off the bronze fronds and use them indoors in arrangements.

Try These
Osmunda regalis 'Purpurascens' is a royal fern with reddish purple fronds in spring. Lady fern (*Athyrium felix-femina*) is lacy and delicate.

When, Where, and How to Plant

All dianthus species like full sun and any soil that's slightly alkaline and drains well. If your soil is acidic, you may need to lime it in fall before planting in spring. (A soil test will tell you the pH of your soil.) Space the plants according to type: sweet Williams at 10 to 12 inches apart, and mat-forming pinks at least 15 inches apart. Mulch upright-growing sweet William lightly, but don't mulch the ground-huggers (see page 134 for more about planting perennials). You can also grow dianthus from seed, either indoors or out (see page 37 for more information on growing plants from seed).

Growing Tips

Avoid overwatering, which can lead to leaf diseases, but dianthus will need to be watered some during drought or long dry spells. If plants are growing in poor soil, fertilize in spring, before buds form, with a slow-release organic fertilizer, applied according to package directions. Sweet William may do better if fertilized once in early spring and again a month later.

Care

Remove faded flowers to promote reblooming and keep the plants looking neat. Cut sweet William's flower stalks to the ground after each flowering, but shear pinks to keep the plants compact. Divide sweet William every three years or so; cut stems will root easily in summer. Dig up spreading pinks after the third year and cut into several chunks for replanting. You'll encounter few pest problems, except that sweet William is attractive to rabbits.

Garden Design

Grow low, spreading types of dianthus at the front of a border or in rock gardens. Or combine them with tulips or coral bells.

Try These

Dianthus Scent First Passion has beautiful red blooms that reach up to a foot tall. The color of the double flowers of 'Candy Floss' reminds me of cotton candy. Both will spread about a foot. 'Bath's Pink' is considered the best performer in southern heat and humidity.

The common name for this group of plant is pinks, and you'll find different species: Allwood pinks (Dianthus × allwoodii), cheddar pinks (D. gratianopolitanus), cottage pinks (D. plumarius), and maiden pinks (D. deltoides). Even sweet William (D. barbatus) can be considered part of the group—although officially a biennial, it generally acts like a perennial in this region. All have spicily fragrant flowers that are long-lasting in arrangements. These are cool-weather plants that bloom in spring and have ground-hugging green or grayish foliage the rest of the year. Dianthus is ideal for a cottage garden and as an edging plant. If you buy annual dianthus bedding plants in spring, you'll often find that they become perennial in your garden, especially in Zone 7.

Botanical Pronunciation
die-AN-thus

Bloom Period and Seasonal Color
Late spring to early summer in pink, white, or red

Mature Height × Spread
2 inches to 2 feet × 1 to 2 feet

Evergreen Ferns
Many genera, species, and varieties

Ferns that are deciduous in cold-winter climates have been the most popular of the approximate 12,000 species of ferns, but in states such as Tennessee and Kentucky, where the yard is used almost year-round and snow rarely covers the ground for very long, choosing evergreens makes a great deal of sense. A touch of green amid a sea of brown in a woodland garden is very welcomed in winter. Here are some good evergreen ferns to look for: autumn fern (Dryopteris erythrosora), Christmas fern (Polystichum acrostichoides), deer fern (Blechnum spicant), evergreen wood fern (Dryopteris intermedia), Hart's tongue fern (Phyllitis scolopendrium), soft shield fern (Polystichum setiferum), and Korean rock fern (Polystichum tsussimense). In Zone 7, Japanese holly fern (Cyrtomium falcatum) is another choice.

Bloom Period and Seasonal Color
Evergreen foliage

Mature Height × Spread
18 inches to 2 feet × 24 to 30 inches

When, Where, and How to Plant
Most evergreen ferns appreciate shade and moist soil that contains lots of organic matter. They will usually grow all right—but won't reach their full potential—in average soil. *Polystichum* ferns are exceptions; they don't mind average, well-drained soil and adapt to part sun and part shade. (Several *Polystichum* species are drought-tolerant: licorice fern, Braun's holly fern, and sword fern. Lady fern is also drought-tolerant.) Plant ferns from spring until late summer. Space them 2 to 3 feet apart, according to mature size. Fertilize at planting time with a slow-release organic fertilizer applied at half the recommended rate (see page 134 for more about planting perennials). Mulch the soil. Ferns may also be grown from spores (those little brown or black "dots" on the undersides of the fronds). Remove the spores from the plant and let dry two days. Refrigerate in a plastic bag until ready to plant (up to a year). See page 37 for advice on sowing seed indoors.

Growing Tips
Water as needed the ferns that need moisture, especially in dry weather. You don't usually need to fertilize evergreen ferns. With organic-rich soil and mulch, ferns should get all the nutrients they need naturally. But if leaves become pale, spray with a water-soluble fertilizer that contains iron.

Care
A few of the oldest leaves will die each year and be replaced by new ones. As with deciduous ferns, evergreens may be self-shedding or wither in place. Groom as necessary to keep the plants looking neat. Add more mulch as it decomposes. Pest problems should be few.

Garden Design
Because of their stiff texture and evergreen leaves, ferns add to naturalized landscapes, formal beds, and containers. Some ferns work well as a groundcover, including oak fern, sword fern, and deer fern.

Try These
Alaskan fern (*Polystichum setiferum*) is perfectly happy in our heat and is ideal for shady and constantly wet spots.

Foxglove
Digitalis species and hybrids

When, Where, and How to Plant
Set out plants in early spring in an area of partial shade and moist soil that's rich in organic matter. Avoid windy sites. If growing from seed, you may start in summer and transplant seedlings in early fall where you want them to grow. Or, sow seeds indoors about 10 weeks before the last spring frost (see page 37 for more information on starting seeds). Space plants 12 inches apart in the garden. Add an organic slow-release fertilizer to the soil before planting and mulch well afterward.

Growing Tips
Foxgloves require consistent moisture to flower, so water deeply and frequently. Fertilize with slow-release fertilizer in early spring. If leaves yellow, spray with an iron-containing, water-soluble fertilizer for acid-loving plants.

Care
Stake individual stems if needed. Cut down the flower spikes right after blooming, and most plants will rebloom, although the new spikes will be shorter. Don't remove the second flowers, so they can reseed. (Foxglove is a short-lived perennial that may die out in about three years if not allowed to reseed.) If mulch is thick, pull it back to allow seeds to come into contact with the soil. Lift out crowded seedlings in very early spring and replant. Pests are few, except for slugs (see page 34 for advice on controlling snails and slugs).

Garden Design
Don't plant in yards frequented by young children; foxglove is considered poisonous. Foxgloves are perfect for adding height to shady borders and cottage gardens. They grow well with ferns, bleeding heart, and cardinal flower. They also are excellent cut flowers, so do place a few foxgloves in your cutting garden.

Try These
'Camelot Rose' is tall with dramatic flowers. The 'Polkdot' series is perennial, and the flowers are large and long-blooming because they don't set seed. *Digitalis purpurea* 'Pam's Split' (sold as Pantaloons) has white and maroon flowers in an unusual and attractive form.

The most beautiful foxgloves I ever saw were in the sculpture garden on the grounds of the Kröller-Müller Museum in the Netherlands. The foxgloves were large and lush, and the thousands of flowers, planted on a rise, were at eye level, all the better to enjoy them. Spectacular! Shopping for foxglove plants can get confusing. Some are annuals, and the most common kind (Digitalis purpurea) is a biennial, which grows one year and flowers the next. But there are attractive perennial foxgloves, such as Digitalis grandiflora and Digitalis × mertonensis. The good news is that once you've planted foxglove in the right conditions, you should have plants from then on, since they reseed prolifically. Among their nicest traits are that they attract hummingbirds and resist deer.

Botanical Pronunciation
di-ji-TAL-liss

Bloom Period and Seasonal Color
Spring and summer in lavender, yellow, white, pink, and purple

Mature Height × Spread
2 to 5 feet × 18 inches

Gaillardia

Gaillardia × grandiflora

If you have one of those difficult spots in your yard with full sun and dry soil, gaillardia is for you. Plants with daisylike flowers are always the simplest to grow, and gaillardia—also called blanketflower—is among the easiest of the easy. If you're just getting started with perennials, it should be among your first choices. I've planted these heat- and drought-tolerant plants in all sorts of situations from hard clay to steep hillsides and, as long as they were in full sun, they bloomed for months. The blossoms of most gaillardias have dark red centers and two-toned red or orange and yellow petals that butterflies find appealing. But you can also find gaillardias with all-yellow or all-red flowers, which I find appealing.

Botanical Pronunciation
gay-LAR-dee-uh gran-di-FLOOR-uh

Bloom Period and Seasonal Color
Summer to fall in red and yellow

Mature Height × Spread
6 inches to 2 feet × 1 to 2 feet

When, Where, and How to Plant

Set out gaillardia plants anytime from spring until midsummer, placing them 12 to 16 inches apart in a sunny spot with average soil that drains well (see page 134 for more about planting perennials). Mulch lightly to deter weeds. You may also start gaillardia from seed, sown in the garden in early fall or in spring.

Growing Tips

Keep soil moist until young plants begin growing, and then water only to keep plants alive during prolonged dry spells. Fertilizer isn't necessary, but if blooming has slowed in midsummer and you feel the plants need a boost, use a water-soluble plant food formulated for flowers.

Care

Deadhead fading flowers to promote a long blooming season in hottest weather. Because individual plants rarely last more than three years, you may want to root stem cuttings in a mixture of sand and potting soil. Or, you can divide a few plants each spring to prolong the planting. Good drainage is essential—root rot, crown rot, and mildew can be troublesome in wet or heavy soils. Gaillardia experiences few pests in appropriate sites. If leaves look mottled, suspect leafhoppers; shear off the affected leaves and remove them from the garden, and then spray plants with insecticidal soap. If the entire plant turns yellow, suspect a disease called "yellows," and remove the plants from the garden. Because the disease is spread by aphids and leafhoppers, controlling these insects will prevent it (see page 33.)

Garden Design

Mass them alone or with medium-height sunflowers and other bold textured, brightly colored flowers, such as coreopsis, black-eyed Susans, red-flowered daylilies, and goldenrod.

Try These

The 'Gayla' series is uniformly excellent. The flowers on 'Oranges and Lemons' change color throughout the summer. I've fallen in love with *Gaillardia × grandiflora* Commotion® 'Moxie', a mouthful of a name but an exciting plant with eye-catching yellow flowers that have unusual fluted petals and a bright orange center.

Gaura

Gaura lindheimeri

When, Where, and How to Plant

In spring, after weather has warmed reliably, plant gaura in a sunny or mostly sunny spot that has well-drained soil. It doesn't do well in clay. Space plants 3 feet apart (see page 134 for tips on planting perennials). Mulching at planting time isn't necessary, but a light mulch to keep down weeds is okay. In spring, around the time of the last frost, you may sow gaura seeds outside where you want them to grow.

Growing Tips

Watering isn't usually needed after the first year. In spring, before new growth starts, cut the plant back about half; at the same time, spread a slow-release fertilizer, according to package directions, over the soil and water in. Too much fertilizer results in lanky growth.

Care

In Zone 6, mulch gaura in fall for winter protection. Cutting the plant back as flowering lessens in midsummer encourages fall rebloom. Insects or diseases aren't usually a problem, but leaf spots may appear. If they become serious, ask the Extension service for advice. Root rot is usually caused by poor drainage so plant in well-drained soil. Gaura doesn't usually need dividing but may be divided in spring to provide more plants. If the top is killed back in a very cold winter, the plant should regrow from the roots.

Garden Design

Place gaura in the back of a perennial border, not far from daylilies with pink flowers or coneflowers with pink blooms. Gaura also looks nice in front of ornamental grasses.

Try These

'Passionate Pink' has reddish foliage and deep-pink flowers; it's a compact, upright-growing plant that's drought-tolerant and grows about 30 inches tall and 24 inches wide. 'Siskiyou Pink' is similar, but flowers are a lighter pink and the plant is slightly taller. 'Crimson Butterflies' has hot-pink blooms on a plant that grows only 18 inches tall. 'Corrie's Gold' has green and gold variegated leaves and whitish pink flowers. It tops out at 3 feet high.

Not so long ago, gaura was a white-flowered native of the Deep South that didn't get much attention, because it was large for a perennial garden (some plants grew up to 5 or 6 feet) and often rangy. Then a new gaura with pink flowers on a compact plant was introduced. As it became wildly popular, suddenly plant breeders sat up and took notice of gaura. In the years since, a number of gaura cultivars have been introduced, with both white and pink flowers on compact and shorter plants, and with better winter hardiness. All are tolerant of heat and humidity and, once established, drought-tolerant too. In Zone 6, buy locally to be sure you get a cultivar that is winter-hardy.

Botanical Pronunciation
GAR-uh lind-HYE-mur-eye

Bloom Period and Seasonal Color
White or pink in late spring and summer

Mature Height x Spread
3 to 5 feet x 4 feet

Goldenrod
Solidago species and hybrids

Why in the world would anyone pay good money for goldenrod plants to grow in the garden, even if it is Kentucky's official state flower? That's a good question if you're still thinking of goldenrod as a weed that grows too tall, spreads like crazy, and causes hay fever. But the first objections have been remedied by plant breeders and the last was never true. (The real culprit for all that sneezing, experts say, is ragweed, which blooms at the same time.) Today's goldenrod cultivars are shorter than the species and more manageable, but still undemanding and attractive. Goldenrod is a reliable performer in almost any soil condition from soggy to bone-dry and is a great choice to really brighten the landscape in fall.

Botanical Pronunciation
sol-ih-DAY-go

Bloom Period and Seasonal Color
Late summer to fall in shades of yellow

Mature Height × Spread
1 to 5 feet × 1 to 3 feet

When, Where, and How to Plant
Although it's adaptable, goldenrod grows best in full sun and average to poor soil that's well drained. (An exception is Canada goldenrod, *Solidago canadensis*, which grows wild in Tennessee and Kentucky. It thrives in wet places, but will also tolerate drier soils.) Avoid partial shade, if possible, because it results in fewer flowers and floppy stems. Overly rich soil also causes rampant growth, with the plants becoming floppy and falling over. Set out plants anytime from spring until fall, spacing them 12 to 18 inches apart (see page 134 to learn more about planting perennials).

Growing Tips
Once established, goldenrod is drought-tolerant, but water enough the first growing season so that the plant develops good roots. The first two years, fertilize once in early spring with a pelleted or granular slow-release formula used at half the label recommendation. After that, you shouldn't need to fertilize again.

Care
Clip off spent flowers to promote repeat flowering and prevent reseeding of hybrids; offspring will not grow true. If new plants pop up, dig them up if they're in the wrong spot and replant elsewhere. If powdery mildew appears, thin stands to increase air circulation. If the center of the clump dies out, dig it up and divide it in spring, discarding the center.

Garden Design
Goldenrod is the perfect plant to naturalize in meadows. It looks nice with asters, boltonia, ornamental grasses, and chrysanthemums, all of which will be flowering at the same time. It also pairs well with black-eyed Susans, purple coneflowers, and coreopsis, which flower earlier but like the same conditions.

Try These
Solidago rugosa 'Fireworks' really puts on a show; it tolerates wet soil. *S. canadensis* 'Baby Gold' is a nice dwarf. *S. sphacelata* 'Golden Fleece' is a creeping goldenrod that grows 1 foot tall (remove its faded flowers, because it may reseed profusely). The flower panicles on 'Goldenmosa' look almost like yellow feathers.

Hardy Begonia
Begonia grandis

When, Where, and How to Plant

Prepare a rich garden soil that drains well by adding compost, sphagnum peat, or finely shredded bark to average soil. Any shady spot is fine—from dappled light to deep shade. Plant in mid to late spring, after the chance of frost has past. Space the plants at least 18 inches apart. Be careful not to bury the crown. Plant shallowly, and cover the soil with shredded leaves or other organic mulch.

Growing Tips

Hardy begonias require consistent moisture to thrive, but cannot tolerate wet feet. When new growth emerges in spring, fertilize with a slow-release fertilizer or spread half an inch of compost around plants growing in fertile soils. Use a water-soluble fertilizer for flowering plants anytime during the growing season if lower leaves turn yellow.

Care

Pinch off stem tips anytime during the growing season if plants are leggy. Then remove the flowers and root those cuttings in water to increase your supply of plants. You may also let the little bulbils in the leaf axils drop to the ground and create new plants. Or you may cut the bulbils off and plant them in a flat of rich potting soil to root. Cut plants back to the ground after the first fall frost, and make sure the mulch is 3 inches deep, for winter protection; this is especially important in Zone 6, where unmulched plants may not survive especially cold winters. Hardy begonia has no serious insect or disease problems.

Garden Design

Grow in woodland gardens with ferns, hostas, and caladiums, heuchera, or columbine.

Try These

'Heron's Pirouette' is a showstopper with an abundance of large, deep pink blooms on a plant that grows 15 inches tall. 'Barbara Rogers' reaches 3 to 4 feet high and 3 feet wide; its nicest feature is large white flowers. Both readily attract hummingbirds. (Something related but different is 'Kalen'; although a wax begonia, it's *perennial* and cold-hardy to 0 degrees Fahrenheit.)

You're familiar with wax begonias, but did you know that there's a perennial begonia that grows well in Tennessee and Kentucky? The plant is about the size of an angel wing begonia and has the begonia-style blooms you know and like on wax begonias. The leaves are attractive— the same shape as angel wing, but with attractive red veining on the undersides. Best of all for anyone with lots of trees in the yard, hardy begonia is carefree in light or deep shade. Plant it once, and it will expand to a nice clump that returns each year. I can't count the times someone has admired one of these plants in my yard and wanted to know where in the world they could find one for themselves.

Botanical Pronunciation
beh-GOAN-ee-a GRAN-dis

Bloom Period and Seasonal Color
Summer to fall in pink, white, or red

Mature Height × Spread
10 inches × 2 feet

Hardy Hibiscus
Hibiscus species and hybrids

To me, the true test of a plant is how it looks in August, in the heat, the high humidity, and, often, receiving less water than it would prefer. That's why I like hardy, or perennial, hibiscus. When other plants droop at the end of summer, this hibiscus is going strong, producing enormous flowers in clear, bold colors. The way to tell the difference between tropical hibiscus, which is grown as an annual in our area, and perennial hibiscus, which returns, is that the leaves of tropical hibiscus are shiny and those of the perennials aren't. (Hibiscus syriacus, rose of Sharon, is a shrub.) Hardy hibiscus looks somewhat shrubby, but the stems die over winter and grow back the next spring.

Botanical Pronunciation
high-BIS-cuss

Bloom Period and Seasonal Color
Summer in red, pink, or white

Mature Height × Spread
2 to 7 feet × 3 to 4 feet

When, Where, and How to Plant
Late spring and early summer are the best times to plant. Sun is essential; so is moist, well-drained soil that's been enriched with organic matter. Space the plants 3 feet apart.

Growing Tips
Water deeply and often throughout the first two growing seasons if rainfall isn't regular. In later years, the plant can tolerate drier conditions. Although perennial hibiscus doesn't require as much fertilizer as a tropical hibiscus, it does like to be fed several times a year. Spread a pelleted or granular slow-release fertilizer, according to package directions, around the base of the plant at the end of April. Follow up with liquid seaweed or water-soluble fertilizer for flowering plants at the beginning of July and the first of August.

Care
The plants don't reappear until late in spring, after the soil has warmed up. After new stems are up and growing, cut down old ones. In Zone 6, a 3-inch mulch of shredded leaves around the base of the plant in fall will provide winter protection. Japanese beetles may be a problem on all but *Hibiscus coccineus* (see page 34 for information on controlling them). You may want to leave seedpods on swamp hibiscus over winter to add interest to your garden.

Garden Design
For best effect, group several hibiscus plants together. Put the taller cultivars toward the back of a flower border.

Try These
'Plum Crazy' has deeply cut purplish foliage and pink flowers on a 3- to 4-foot plant. 'Summer Storm' has pink flowers and purple, almost black, foliage. Grow 'Lady Baltimore' for its 6- to 9-inch ruffled blooms, which are deep pink with red "eyes" (centers). The 'Disco Belle' series (in red, pink, or white) and 'Southern Belle' offer big blooms on compact plants and are good patio plants. Swamp hibiscus (for Zone 7 and warmer) is a native that likes wet soils and doesn't attract Japanese beetles.

Hosta

Hosta species and hybrids

When, Where, and How to Plant

Plant in spring or early summer in a shady or partially shady bed with rich, organic soil that drains well. Since hostas don't like to be moved, space them to accommodate mature spread, at least 1 to 3 feet apart. Overcrowding will slow the plants' growth and will mean the plants will need dividing sooner, which they usually take a year or two to recover from. Fertilize at planting time with a pelleted or granular slow-release fertilizer worked into each hole. Mulch unless slugs are usually a problem.

Growing Tips

Hostas grow better when they receive consistent moisture but will tolerate soil that dries out between waterings. Water when rainfall is less than an inch per week. Apply a slow-release fertilizer around each plant when leaves appear in spring.

Care

Keep mulch about 2 inches deep, except where slugs are rampant. Cut down flower stalks as blooms fade so seeds don't form and sap the plant's energy. Holes in leaves are usually caused by slugs. Look for telltale slime trails to be sure (see page 34 for controls). If homemade traps don't work, ask at a garden center about organic controls. Hostas may need dividing when they're three or four years old. The best time to do it is in spring (see page 135 for how to divide perennials).

Garden Design

Group miniature hostas together in a bed. Mass other hostas in shady beds or use as accents with ferns, coleus, and caladiums.

Try These

Who can resist a hosta named 'Wheee'? Not me. It has ruffled leaves with irregular cream edges. 'Francee' is an old favorite with deep green leaves edged in crisp white. 'Patriot' is similar but with a wider white margin. Although they may not be easy to find except by mail order, I like the Lakeside hybrids, bred by Mary Chastain of East Tennessee. Special favorites include 'Lakeside Parsley Print', 'Lakeside Shore Master', and 'Lakeside Cupcake'.

There are now so many hostas that it almost takes an expert to tell them apart. What that means for gardeners is that you can find all sizes, miniatures (such as 'Pandora's Box' at 8 inches tall) as well as old giants like 'Sum and Substance'. Interesting new color combinations appear each year ('Fruit Punch', for example, has yellow leaves in spring, chartreuse in fall, and red petioles all season). Even more noticeable is the variety of leaf shapes and forms—cupped, ruffled, corrugated, and so on. It's a far cry from when gardeners decided between green-leaved hostas and those that were variegated. Hostas are even being bred for interesting flowers, many with fragrance. For homeowners with shady yards, this is all good news.

Botanical Pronunciation
HOSS-tuh

Bloom Period and Seasonal Color
Late spring to fall in white, lavender, and purple; mostly grown for foliage

Mature Height × Spread
6 inches to 3 feet × 1 to 5 feet

Joe-Pye Weed

Eupatorium purpureum

When you see plants growing wild in fields, it may not occur to you that they could be just as good in your garden too—especially if plant breeders have created hybrids that fit better into home gardens by giving us plants that are a more manageable size, bloom better, and aren't aggressive. Joe-Pye weed is a good example. You know that fall is on its way when you see the tall plants with their reddish flower clusters appear along roadsides. But the Brits noticed something in Joe-Pye that we Americans hadn't. They took it across the pond, began breeding it, and are now selling wonderful new cultivars of this native plant back to us! Look for shorter varieties and those with white flowers.

Botanical Pronunciation
u-pa-TOE-ree-um pur-pu-REE-um

Bloom Period and Seasonal Color
Late summer to fall in pink, shades of purple, and white

Mature Height × Spread
3 to 7 feet × 2 to 4 feet

When, Where, and How to Plant
As its locations in the wild testify, Joe-Pye is an adaptable plant. Although it will grow and bloom best in wet spots, it will tolerate almost any kind of soil. Full sun is also preferred, but the plant will manage with a couple of hours of daily shade, especially in the afternoon. Plant it from spring until fall. Many of these are big plants, so space them 30 to 36 inches apart and place at the back of a border. If growing in average or dry soil, mulch with 2 to 3 inches of organic material such as shredded leaves, to retain soil moisture.

Growing Tips
Keep the soil moist at all times. Standing water is all right for a short period, and boggy conditions are ideal. Use fertilizer sparingly. If Joe-Pye weed isn't growing or blooming well, spread a slow-release fertilizer for flowering plants on the ground around it, or spray plants and soil with a water-soluble fertilizer.

Care
Control height by pinching Joe-Pye weed once or twice after growth starts in spring and before May 15. This is a plant that rarely suffers from insects or diseases. Cut stems to the ground after flowering is finished. Clumps of the species spread to form good-sized groupings that may need dividing in early spring every two to three years. Hybrids are less likely to spread and may not need dividing as often if given adequate space at planting time.

Garden Design
Joe-Pye weed is just right for a butterfly garden and a wildflower meadow. Plant it with black-eyed Susans, coneflowers, perennial phlox, and Shasta daisies. Use it also in bogs with water cannas.

Try These
'Little Red' grows only 4 feet tall and begins blooming in summer. 'Bartered Bride' has white flowers. 'Baby Joe' offers purple flowers on 4-foot stems. Spotted Joe-Pye weed (*Eupatorium maculatum*) has stems with purple mottling and fragrant flowers.

When, Where, and How to Plant

Lenten rose shines in shade, but be careful about placing it beneath deciduous trees, because winter sun can burn the leaves and stunt the flowers. Dig average soil 12 inches deep and add compost, peat moss, and finely shredded bark to create a deep, fertile planting area. Unfortunately for those with clay soil, Lenten rose can't tolerate "wet feet" (water standing at the roots), especially in winter. Plant container-grown hellebores in early spring (see page 134 for more about planting perennials). Transplant seedlings from around mature plants when they're 4 inches tall. Space plants 18 to 24 inches apart. Mulch with 2 inches of organic matter, such as pine straw.

Growing Tips

Although Lenten roses prefer constantly moist soil, they're surprisingly tolerant of dry weather—once they're established and if they're planted in moisture-retaining soil that's mulched. But you'll want to water enough to keep the soil moist when plants are young and during droughts. Use fertilizer sparingly, if at all; the decaying mulch will usually be sufficient to supply needed nutrients.

Care

The plant's evergreen leaves can sometimes suffer winter damage. As the flowers appear, clip off torn leaves so the blooms can take center stage. The plant grows slowly, so it seldom needs dividing. But if it becomes crowded, divide plants in spring, after flowering is finished (see page 135 to learn more about dividing perennials). Lenten roses reseed enough to increase the clump if the mulch is pulled away as the seeds mature. These plants aren't usually bothered by pests (including deer—a big plus).

Garden Design

Place Lenten rose in shaded areas near the house, where the flowers can be seen in winter.

Try These

'Pink Frost' has lovely flowers that open pale pink and darken to rose. 'Amber Gem' has double peach-colored flowers. The Sunshine strain, bred by Barry Glick of Sunshine Farms and Gardens in West Virginia, are some of the best bloomers.

I love the idea of flowers blooming in my yard in winter, and everyone else must, too, because the past few years have seen a huge surge in breeding Lenten roses. This evergreen perennial with oh-so-romantic flowers is a standout in shade. Once you've planted Lenten rose, you'll have it in your garden forever because it reseeds (but not aggressively). Look for the new strains and hybrids hitting the market—they've been selected for intriguing colors. More difficult to grow in the U.S is the Christmas rose (Helleborus niger). It dislikes too much heat in summer or cold in winter and may be unhappy with too much—or too little—water. If you try it, get an early-blooming cultivar.

Botanical Pronunciation

hell-e-BORE-us or-ih-en-TAL-iss

Bloom Period and Seasonal Color

Late winter to spring in pink, burgundy, white, lime, and rose

Mature Height × Spread

14 to 18 inches × 12 to 18 inches

Peony
Paeonia lactiflora

Your grandmother or mother or a maiden aunt may have grown gorgeous peonies. Why not you too? Peonies take time to get established, but once they are, they practically live forever. In our warmest areas, gardeners have more success with peonies that have single flowers and bloom early. Also be aware that in Zone 7 and warmer, tree peonies bloom only fleetingly. To avoid the problem of the flowers ending up facedown in the mud after hard rain, grow single-flowered peonies instead of doubles, and support the plants as soon as they begin to grow in spring (I use a little wire cage). Those who like something different may want to look for fernleaf peony (Paeonia tenuifolia), which has single red flowers and blooms early.

Botanical Pronunciation
pee-OH-nee-uh lac-ti-FLOOR-uh

Bloom Period and Seasonal Color
May in pink, red, purple, yellow, and white

Mature Height × Spread
12 to 30 inches × 12 to 30 inches

When, Where, and How to Plant
Till or dig soil at least 12 inches deep, and work in organic matter. Soil preparation matters more with peonies than most plants because they stay in one place for a long time. Full sun is recommended, but a couple of hours of afternoon shade are often welcomed. The best time to plant peonies is in the fall; however, the plants may be available only in spring; if so, plant then. Do not plant peonies too deeply; set container plants at the same level or slightly higher than they grew before transplanting. If you obtain dormant roots, plant them with no more than 2 inches of soil covering the "eyes" (see page 134 for more information on planting bare-root perennials). Do not crowd them; plant peonies 20 to 24 inches apart, depending on their mature size. There's no need to fertilize at planting time. Mulch with an organic material.

Growing Tips
Consistent moisture is essential; use soaker hoses or trickle irrigation for best results. Fertilize by placing ½ inch of compost on top of the soil in spring and summer and applying a pelleted or granular slow-release fertilizer in mid-spring.

Care
Set up peony supports as soon as the plants begin growing. Plants seldom need dividing and recover from it poorly. But if the plant becomes so crowded as to almost stop flowering, divide it in fall after it comes dormant (see page 135 for how to divide perennials). New peonies may take two years to bloom well. If fungus problems or insects strike, consult the Extension service. Contrary to folk myth, ants aren't a pest on peonies; they help the flowers open.

Garden Design
Peony plants tend to look best when grouped together. Or, place them on the sunny edge of a groundcover bed.

Try These
The pink single flowers of 'Seashell' bloom a long time. 'Early Bird' has red flowers and fernleaf foliage. 'Festiva Maxima' is an old peony variety that still can't be beat.

When, Where, and How to Plant

Perennial salvias thrive in sunshine and average soil that drains well. Amend heavy soils with organic matter to improve drainage. Wet soil in winter causes the plants to rot. Plant salvias any time after the last frost of spring through summer. Space plants 10 inches to 2 feet apart, depending on the type. Mix a pelleted or granular slow-release fertilizer with the soil before planting and mulch lightly afterward (see page 134 for more about planting perennials).

Growing Tips

Salvia is relatively drought-tolerant once it's established in your yard but blooms better when it receives regular moisture. If possible, water if rainfall is less than an inch a week during the plant's first year in your yard. Apply an organic slow-release fertilizer to the soil in early spring, and feed once in early summer with liquid seaweed.

Care

Pinch the stem tips when plants grow to 4 and 8 inches tall to promote bushy new growth and more flowers. Remove faded flowers to encourage reblooming and prevent seeds from forming. Perennial salvias may become woody at their crown and need dividing every four years or so in spring. There should be few pest problems.

Garden Design

Use in beds and borders with Russian sage, dusty miller, *Artemisia* 'Powis Castle', and pink-flowered daylilies.

Try These

'Marcus' is a dwarf with dark purple flowers; at a foot tall, it's good for edging. The stems and reblooming flowers of 'Caradonna' are vibrant purple. 'May Night' reblooms heavily; its flowers are dark purple. Texas sage (*Salvia greggii*) is the most heat-tolerant of the perennial salvias, although it may not be perennial in Zone 6. It has attractive red flowers and will often bloom from midsummer until fall. *Salvia × sylvestris* (often seen written as *Salvia × superba*) is the group of hybrids that does best throughout our region, although they prefer the slightly cooler summers of Zone 6.

Many call this perennial "blue salvia," because that's the color of the flowers of the most popular varieties, but blooms may also be purple and—sometimes—red, pink, or white. All have tubular flowers borne on spikes and are excellent butterfly-attracting plants that don't need much attention. You'll want to be careful as you look for the right perennial salvia for your landscape and ask questions as you shop at the local nursery or garden center. You'll probably find salvias that are biennials, annuals, and some that are grown as annuals because they're not always winter hardy for us. All are good garden plants, but for plants that will return, be sure the ones you choose are perennial in your part of Kentucky or Tennessee.

Botanical Pronunciation
SAL-vee-uh

Bloom Period and Seasonal Color
Late spring to fall in blue, purple, red, pink, or white

Mature Height × Spread
1 to 2 feet × 1 to 3 feet

Phlox
Phlox species and hybrids

Phlox is another of those plants that can confuse gardeners not familiar with it. Several creeping phloxes are listed in the "Groundcovers & Vines" chapter on page 103, and some phloxes are annuals. But two other species provide outstanding perennial selections that every gardener should try. Phlox paniculata (garden phlox or summer phlox) produces large, long-lasting flower clusters on 3- to 5-foot stalks. It has a nice variety of colors, with many cultivars sporting contrasting eyes. Phlox maculata—sometimes referred to as Carolina phlox—has mildew-resistant foliage. Both stay in flower for a long time, impressing all who see them. There's a phlox flower to complement almost any color scheme: red, pink/salmon, orange/salmon, purple/lavender, and white. Many have attractive darker "eyes" (centers). A few cultivars even have variegated foliage.

Botanical Pronunciation
FLOCKS

Bloom Period and Seasonal Color
Summer in pink, red, white, orange, and violet

Mature Height × Spread
2 to 5 feet × 1 to 3 feet

When, Where, and How to Plant
In mid to late spring, set out plants in average soil that stays moist or can be kept watered. Add peat moss to rocky or sandy soils to improve their water-holding capacity. Plant cultivars with deep-colored flowers where they will receive two to three hours of afternoon shade, if possible. All others will do fine in full sun. (Too much shade leads to floppy stems that need staking.) Space plants 18 inches apart and mulch well.

Growing Tips
Water deeply if weekly rainfall is less than an inch. Keep the water off the foliage. Fertilizer may not be necessary, but if plants aren't growing or blooming well, use a water-soluble fertilizer for flowering plants.

Care
Deadhead flowers so plants will bloom longer. Don't let phlox go to seed; self-seeded plants will have magenta flowers and be so vigorous that they crowd out the good plants. Mildew is phlox's Achilles' heel. Avoid the problem by buying mildew-resistant cultivars, spacing the plants farther apart than recommended so they have good air circulation, and avoid splashing water on the leaves. You can also consult the Extension service for a solution. In dry weather, spider mites may also appear (see page 34 for controls). Divide plants about every three to five years, as needed, in spring (page 135 explains how to divide perennials).

Garden Design
Plant phlox in informal drifts, or place it at the back of a flower bed with other summer-flowering perennials in complementary colors.

Try These
The pink and lavender flowers of 'John Fanick' are striking; the plant grows about 3 feet tall and is tolerant of mildew and other fungal diseases. The Peacock series is shorter and has good heat- and disease-resistance. Bold colors include 'Neon Purple' and 'Purple Bicolor'. I can't imagine not having *Phlox maculata* 'Miss Lingard' in my garden; it doesn't mildew. 'Peppermint Twist' has pink and white flowers on a compact plant.

Pulmonaria
Pulmonaria species and hybrids

When, Where, and How to Plant

Plant pulmonaria in spring, spacing 18 to 24 inches apart in a spot that gets morning sun. Good air circulation may help keep mildew—pulmonaria's biggest enemy—at bay. Moist soil is essential, but just as important is excellent drainage. (Poor winter drainage kills the plants quickly.) Enrich all soils—especially clay—with organic matter (see page 134 for more about planting perennials). Mulch with pine needles.

Growing Tips

When pulmonaria lacks water, leaves turn brown and dry up. Water often enough to keep the soil moist but not soggy. Use a soaker hose to keep water off the leaves. If the plants grew well the year before, no fertilizer is needed. Otherwise, spread a slow-release organic fertilizer around the plants, and water well.

Care

In spring remove last year's leaves before flowers appear. Slugs and mildew are the biggest problems when growing pulmonarias (see page 34 for a discussion of slug controls). Consult the Extension service about mildew. (Use commercial organic fungicides only in the cooler weather of spring and fall; many can "burn" leaves when temperatures are high.) You may avoid mildew by planting pulmonaria where it receives morning sun and by picking off mildewed leaves and removing them from the garden. Divide in early spring when needed (see page 135 for information about dividing perennials).

Garden Design

Beneath deciduous trees, pair pulmonaria with spring bulbs and Lenten roses in harmonizing colors. In shady beds, grow *en masse* or near hostas, ferns, or bleeding hearts. Place pulmonaria at the edge of a bed, so you can admire its spotted foliage.

Try These

'Benediction' has silver-spotted leaves and deep blue flowers that stay in bloom a long time. 'Roy Davidson' produces a lot of pale blue flowers that open pink; the leaves have white spots. 'Bubble Gum' has good mildew-resistance. Heat-tolerant 'Excalibur' has silver leaves with a green border. 'Mrs. Moon' is an old favorite.

You may not be familiar with pulmonaria, but when you see the plants with silver or white spots or freckles on green leaves or cool silvery foliage, you'll understand their growing popularity for wooded gardens and flower beds in shady yards. The flowers (blue, pink, violet, white) can also be fun—in most cases, they appear before the leaves do and often they open as one color and change to another color. Not all pulmonarias adapt well to summer heat that's typical in this part of the country. Many are better in Zone 6 than Zone 7, but with so many new hybrids being introduced, more heat-tolerant cultivars are appearing. I've found that, generally, pulmonarias with silver leaves are the most heat-tolerant.

Botanical Pronunciation
pull-mon-AIR-ee-uh

Bloom Period and Seasonal Color
Spring in pink (usually fading to blue), coral, red, and violet

Mature Height × Spread
9 to 24 inches × 24 to 30 inches

Red Valerian

Centranthus ruber

I discovered red valerian—which isn't a true valerian at all and also comes in pink and white—by accident when I was planning a perennial border at a new house and leafing through a catalog to find a few plants I hadn't grown before. And I've found that most friends who like this plant—also known as Jupiter's beard—have had similar experiences. We didn't expect much but now can't live without red valerian in our flower beds. It's unassuming but so dependable, producing a nice array of airy reddish blooms in late spring. But from then until frost, you'll always find a couple of perky valerian flower spikes on the plants, which is perfect for flower arrangers.

Botanical Pronunciation
ken-TRAN-thus ROO-ber

Bloom Period and Seasonal Color
Late spring and summer in red, pink, and white

Mature Height × Spread
1 to 3 feet × 2 to 3 feet

When, Where, and How to Plant

Red valerian will grow in almost any soil but prefers one that's well drained and neutral to slightly alkaline (a soil test will tell you if your soil is acid or alkaline). In spring, after the average last date of frost, set out plants about 30 inches apart in full sun, although red valerian will readily tolerate a few hours of afternoon shade. (See page 134 for directions on how to plant perennials.) Unless soil is extremely poor, don't fertilize at planting time. Red valerian may be grown from seed you've collected from the plants, but seed-grown plants are not usually like the parent plant.

Growing Tips

Water regularly until the plant is established—then it will seldom need watering except in prolonged droughts. When the plants are growing in poor soil, fertilize once a year in spring with an organic slow-release fertilizer. Too much fertilizer causes red valerian to get leggy and flop over instead of growing straight and tall.

Care

Deadhead flowers to encourage reblooming. Cut plants back to 6 inches tall if they get leggy or to encourage a large crop of fall flowers. Red valerian reseeds freely, but the flowers won't necessarily be the color of the original plants; pull up those that you don't like. Divide when necessary in spring or early fall. Aphids and mealybugs may be occasional visitors (see page 33 or check with the Extension service for help combating them).

Garden Design

Red valerian is a good plant for a cottage garden, a butterfly garden, and to attract wildlife. Grow it in groups of at least three plants so it will make more of an impact. This is an *excellent* plant for tough, dry sites. Combine it with perennial salvia, verbena, and white-flowering garden phlox.

Try These

Cultivars aren't usually available. Buy plants when they're in bloom to get the flower color you prefer (some are more red than others).

Russian Sage
Perovskia atriplicifolia

When, Where, and How to Plant
In spring space plants 2 feet apart in a sunny spot that has very well-drained soil. Close spacing helps keep the plants more upright. Although growth will be all right in light shade, anything less than full sun will cause stems to flop over and need staking. Russian sage does well in dry, rocky soil that's alkaline, but tolerates other soils as long as they're well drained. It will even grow in clay soil as long as it doesn't stay wet. It's also salt-tolerant. (See page 134 for more about planting perennials.)

Growing Tips
You don't need to fertilize this plant. In fact, fertilizer can cause floppy growth. But if the plant should need a boost, use an organic slow-release fertilizer, applied according to label directions, in spring just before the plant starts growing. Russian sage is drought-tolerant once it's established; it rarely needs additional watering beyond rainfall.

Care
Because flowering occurs on new growth, you must cut last year's stems almost to ground level just before new growth begins in spring. Few pests bother Russian sage, which is also generally disease-free. If problems arise, contact your local Extension service. Russian sage can spread, so dig up unwanted plants to place elsewhere or share with friends.

Garden Design
Russian sage really stands out when it's massed with at least three plants grown together. Good companions include rudbeckia, pink varieties of coneflower, feather reed grass, white garden phlox, butterfly weed, and 'Autumn Joy' sedum. Russian sage is also outstanding planted with roses, if you have an area of drier soil near the rose bed. It's also a nice plant for a cottage garden.

Try These
Cultivars may be hard to find except by mail order. 'Little Spire' stays about 2 feet tall and wide and doesn't flop over. 'Filagren' has fern-like foliage. 'Blue Spire' has deeper-colored flowers. 'Longin' is more upright.

You wouldn't think that a plant with "Russian" in its name would be known for its ability to stand up to heat and humidity (especially when it has silvery foliage, which rarely tolerates humidity). But Russian sage may surprise you on several levels. This is a fairly large plant—it may get as big as 4 feet by 4 feet—but it's very airy and it's also deer resistant, thanks to leaves that smell like sage. It likes to be placed in full sun, doesn't mind poor soil, doesn't need watering or fertilizer, and is easy for anyone to grow. A welcome feature is its long blooming time: The lavender-blue flowers appear in midsummer and continue into early autumn, making this perennial a joy.

Botanical Pronunciation
Per-OFF-ski-uh at-rih-plih-see-FOAL-ee-uh

Bloom Period and Seasonal Color
Midsummer to early fall in lavender-blue

Mature Height x Spread
3 to 5 feet x 2½ to 4 feet

Sedum

Hylotelephium species and hybrids

You probably know 'Autumn Joy' sedum, because it's highly recommended for its fall color in the perennial garden. But if you have a sunny spot with well-drained soil, do look at some of the less-planted (so far) sedums because of the fascinating texture they bring to the landscape throughout the growing season. The fleshy foliage—which may be purple, burgundy, or silver, as well as green—is quite a contrast to that of most other perennials. For example, 'Autumn Joy' (as well as related hybrids) offers large, dense flower heads that change color as they mature and attract hoards of butterflies. These plants are also simple to grow and use very little water. They're also pretty much carefree year after year.

Botanical Pronunciation
high-low-te-LEE-fe-um

Bloom Period and Seasonal Color
Late summer to fall in pink or reddish shades

Mature Height × Spread
18 inches to 2 feet × 18 inches to 2 feet

When, Where, and How to Plant
Amend heavy soils with organic matter to improve drainage. Excellent drainage is especially important in lightly shaded sites, as sedums will die in wet soils. Plant in a sunny or mostly sunny spot anytime from late spring until early fall (see page 134 for more about planting perennials). There's no need to fertilize when planting. You may mulch to keep down weeds, but it isn't necessary.

Growing Tips
Water regularly but moderately if rainfall is less than an inch per week. Sedums prefer to dry out between waterings and have shallow root systems that cannot take huge amounts of water when they are small. Don't fertilize.

Care
Pinch 'Autumn Joy' sedum once in late spring and again in early summer to encourage bushiness and to keep it compact (these cuttings root easily if you'd like more plants). If plants growing in part sun tend to flop over, cut them back by half toward the end of June, and move them into more sun the following year. Few insects or diseases bother sedum. If spaced correctly when planted, they won't need dividing for many years. When division is necessary, do it in spring.

Garden Design
The common name stonecrop tells you this is a great plant for rock gardens. Sedums are interesting massed in a bed where they can spread freely. Upright sedums also make a contribution to the perennial border when planted with dusty miller and *Artemisia* 'Powis Castle', as well as with small ornamental grasses.

Try These
If you'd like plants similar to 'Autumn Joy', but a bit different, look for 'Mohrchen', which has burgundy leaves and pink flowers on a 2-foot-tall plant. 'Vera Jameson' is less than a foot tall. I especially like 'Purple Emperor', which has purple leaves and pink flower clusters, and 'Raspberry Truffle', which has purple foliage, burgundy stems, and raspberry pink flowers. 'Neon' and 'Brilliant' are real showoffs.

When, Where, and How to Plant

Shasta daisies would rather grow in rich, moist soil, but will tolerate just about any kind as long as it drains well. Amend clay with finely shredded bark or compost to improve drainage. Plant Shasta daisies in spring or early summer in a spot that's in full or mostly sun. Space plants 18 to 24 inches apart (see page 134 for planting how-to information). Mulch new plants lightly, but do not cover the crowns (the point where the roots meet the stem).

Growing Tips

Although Shasta daisies can tolerate some dry weather, they perform better and produce more blooms if watered regularly so that the soil stays moist but not saturated. Water deeply each time you water, then let the soil dry an inch or two deep before watering again. You should not have to fertilize in average soil; too much fertilizer causes tall, floppy stems.

Care

Keep flowers deadheaded or cut for arrangements. As flowers fade, cut down to the next visible bud to encourage reblooming. Stake tall varieties with flower rings, if necessary. Insects and disease problems are few. Clumps of Shasta daisies will die out unless you divide them occasionally. Every third year, divide in spring or early fall and replant. Self-sown volunteers may pop up; you may want to let them grow to blooming size before deciding if you want to keep them, but don't let the bed become too crowded.

Garden Design

Fill a bed with Shasta daisies, bearded iris, and antique roses for a great cottage garden look.

Try These

'Becky' is the best Shasta daisy I've ever grown. It's more vigorous, blooms later than other cultivars, and produces large flowers for a long time. 'Alaska' is a close second. I love the look of the frilly double flowers of 'Aglaia'. It's also long-blooming and makes a wonderful cut flower. 'Banana Cream' has large, all-yellow flowers.

It's no secret to any reader of this book that I love daisies—all daisies—but even if you don't share my enthusiasm, you really must grow Shasta daisy, whether you're an experienced perennial gardener or just getting started. The cheerful flowers are impressively large, bloom prolifically over a long period of time, and go well with many other perennials. Beginners will be pleased to find the plants couldn't be simpler to grow, producing armloads of blooms in return for little effort. The attractive hybrids of Shasta daisy are just as adaptable as their cousins (Leucanthemum vulgare) that grow naturally in fields and along roadsides, but are much more suited to home flower gardens, where they're attractive outdoors and inside, in flower arrangements.

Botanical Pronunciation
loo-KAN-thuh-mum sue-PER-bum

Bloom Period and Seasonal Color
Spring to summer in white and yellow

Mature Height × Spread
1 to 3 feet × 18 to 24 inches

Sundrops
Oenothera fruticosa

I used to wonder why I rarely saw sundrops growing in the public or private flower gardens I visited. A neat little plant—usually about 18 inches high, it's covered from May into June with 1- to 2-inch buttercup-shaped flowers the color of melted butter. But it doesn't seem to be very well known, although it isn't hard to find plants. I finally decided that sundrops have probably been overshadowed by showy evening primrose (Oenothera speciosa). That night-blooming relative can often be seen clambering over undisturbed sites. It has large pink or white flowers and can become a real weed, spreading by underground runners. Not so with day-flowering sundrops, which are mild-mannered (although they may reseed some).

Botanical Pronunciation
ee-NOTH-er-a fru-ti-CO-suh

Bloom Period and Seasonal Color
Late spring to early summer in yellow

Mature Height × Spread
1 to 2 feet × 1 to 2 feet

When, Where, and How to Plant
You can plant sundrops in rocky to average soils that drain well and amend heavy soils with finely shredded bark to improve drainage. But the plants will perform much better if grown in moist but well-drained soil. Wet conditions, especially in winter, cause sundrops to rot. Full sun produces the best plants and most abundant blooms, although an hour or two of afternoon shade is usually tolerated. Set out plants 18 inches to 2 feet apart in spring (see page 134 for more about planting perennials). There's no need to mix fertilizer with the planting soil unless the soil is poor. Sundrops may also be grown from collected seed sown in the garden in fall.

Growing Tips
Water young plants occasionally the first year. Once established, sundrops tolerate dry soil. You probably won't have to water mature plants, except during prolonged droughts. Fertilizer is rarely required. In fact, while this plant doesn't spread as much as its relatives, too much fertilizer can cause quite a bit of spreading.

Care
Trim back leggy stems anytime during summer. Cut sundrops down after the first frost, and pull up unwanted volunteers. Sundrops have few pests except spittlebugs, which leave gobs of foam on stems. Control them with a blast of water from the hose. Divide crowded clumps in spring or early fall. If plants fail to appear in spring, it's usually due to poor drainage.

Garden Design
Sundrops are perfect for informal beds with blue flowers, such as perennial salvia, stokesia, and baptisia, as well as pink perennial phlox. I also like to grow them near catmint (*Nepeta*). Because of sundrops' tolerance of less-than-ideal conditions, they're also good for sunny, dry beds around a mailbox or lamppost.

Try These
'Fireworks' (also sold as 'Fyrverkeri') has red stems and lots of large yellow flowers. 'Summer Solstice' blooms about a month later than other cultivars.

When, Where, and How to Plant

Grow verbenas in any garden soil that drains well; amend clay soils with organic matter to improve drainage. These plants grow well in rocky or sandy soils and, once established, will tolerate drought and keep blooming. Plant seeds or plants in spring; both will bloom the first year. Space plants 2 feet apart in a sunny spot (see page 134 for more on how to plant perennials). Mulch lightly.

Growing Tips

Keep soil moist until plants are established, then water infrequently but deeply to encourage drought tolerance. Fertilize in spring, after plants are a few inches tall, with an organic slow-release fertilizer, according to package instructions. Too much fertilizer causes the plants to flop over so they must be pruned back.

Care

Pinch new plants when they are 6 inches tall and again at 10 inches to encourage branching that contributes to their airy effect. In mass plantings, cut back lightly after each flush of blooms. To promote reblooming, deadhead flower clusters as they fade. Verbena experiences few pests except powdery mildew, which may appear in late summer. Talk with the Extension service about a possible control.

Garden Design

Verbenas are excellent butterfly plants, attracting many species to seek its nectar all summer. Plant a group with *Artemisia* 'Powis Castle', coreopsis, Joe-Pye weed, and Shasta daisies. Because of its trailing habit, plant the trailing verbenas so they will spill over a wall. They will also be nice edging flower beds and as an informal groundcover.

Try These

'Homestead Carpet Red' isn't as hardy as 'Homestead Purple', but it has eye-catching red flowers that bloom a long time. Even in Zone 7a you'll want to plant it in a protected place and see how it does. 'Pink Sunrise', another creeping *Verbena canadensis*, has fragrant rose-colored flowers on stems that rarely get higher than 6 inches. 'Snowflurry' (also sold as *Verbena canadensis* 'White') blooms a long time.

After Drs. Michael Dirr and Allan Armitage of the University of Georgia discovered a low-spreading Verbena canadensis *that they named 'Homestead Purple' (because they found it growing outside an abandoned homestead), it became very popular. A vigorous grower covered in purple flower clusters, 'Homestead Purple' was said to be hardy only in Zone 8 and warmer, but gardeners soon discovered that it survives well in Zone 7, too. In Zone 6 winters, it may or may not survive, but there's little chance of losing it, since it reseeds prolifically. A nice result of the popularity of 'Homestead Purple' is that other rose verbenas—in pink, reddish shades, white, and lavender—are getting new attention and finding homes in gardens around our region.*

Botanical Pronunciation
ver-BEE-nuh kan-uh-DEN-sis

Bloom Period and Seasonal Color
Spring to fall in purple, violet, white, and pink

Mature Height × Spread
6 inches to 3 feet × 3 feet

Virginia Bluebell

Mertensia virginica

There's no nicer welcome to spring than the pretty pink buds of the native Virginia bluebell, which are quickly followed by soft blue, bell-shaped blooms contrasted against light green foliage. Not only do the flowers look dainty and pretty, they provide a source of nectar for early butterflies and hummingbirds, a wonderful advantage if you have a wildlife garden or a butterfly garden. Be prepared for the plants to spread and form small colonies in wooded areas. It's also important to know that these are ephemerals—they die back and disappear when summer and hot weather arrive and pop up again the next spring. This may convince gardeners that the plant has died and they should dig it up, but the process is perfectly normal.

Botanical Pronunciation
mer-TEN-see-uh vir-GIN-ih-kuh

Bloom Period and Seasonal Color
In spring pink buds open to pale blue flowers

Mature Height x Spread
18 to 24 inches x 12 to 18 inches

When, Where, and How to Plant

In spring, plant potted Virginia bluebells in a partially shady place that has average, well-drained soil that's slightly acid, or in typical humus-rich woodland soil. Plant tubers (usually available by mail order) anytime in fall. (Since this is a wildflower, make sure they're nursery-propagated, not dug from the wild.) Place Virginia bluebells where you want them to stay, because mature plants don't like to be moved. Space them about 2 feet apart and the same distance, or even more, from other plants, because they will spread and form small colonies. There's no need to fertilize at planting time as long as the soil contains organic matter. If you like, you can mix some compost into average soil to provide gentle nutrients.

Growing Tips

If soil is poor, you may want to spread an organic bulb fertilizer on top of the ground in very early spring just as growth starts. Otherwise, the plants usually don't require fertilizer when growing in good soil. When the plants are in flower, water enough that the soil stays moist but not wet. Stop watering when they begin to go dormant. Avoid overwatering.

Care

These plants are typically insect- and disease-free. Bloom will probably be sparse the first year after planting but will improve the year after as the plants settle into their new home. In spring, just as new growth starts, divide plants that have become crowded. To avoid reseeding, remove as many flowers as possible as they fade.

Garden Design

Because Virginia bluebells go dormant in summer, it's important to plant them with other shade-loving perennials that will look good when the bluebells have faded; for me, this is often foamflower, pulmonaria, or wild ginger, but hostas will do the job too.

Try These

'Alba' is a white-flowering cultivar that mixes nicely with the traditional blue flowers, but it may be hard to find.

Yarrow
Achillea species and hybrids

When, Where, and How to Plant

As long as it has sun and well-drained soil, yarrow is happy. If soil is too rich or moist, stems will be weak and flop over. Amend clay soil enough to improve drainage, but not so much that it becomes humus-rich. Plant yarrow in spring, spacing plants 2 feet apart. Don't mulch, because it may keep the soil too wet.

Growing Tips

Water sparingly until the plants are established, then only in prolonged droughts if they appear to be suffering. Avoid fertilizer unless plants aren't growing well. Shade, too much soil moisture, and too much fertilizer cause stems to fall over instead of growing sturdy and tall. Fertilizer also causes rampant leaf growth at the expense of flowers.

Care

No pruning or pinching is needed except deadheading faded flowers. If desired, dig up small plants around established clumps in spring and summer and replant right away, watering with a transplant solution. Fungal diseases are occasional problems and are more prevalent when plants aren't in full sun or dry (well-drained) soil. They include mildew, rust (spots on leaves), and rot. The first two are cosmetic; cut back the plants if they bother you. If clumps die out in the center, divide in spring or early fall (see page 135 for tips on how to divide perennials). When nighttime temperatures stay about 70 degrees Fahrenheit, the stems of common yarrow (*Achillea millefolium*) weaken and are likely to topple over. In Zone 7, 'Moonshine' often "melts" in high humidity. Cut the plants back.

Garden Design

Plant yellow-blossomed yarrow with blue- or purple-flowered annuals or perennials that don't mind dry soil. Or, grow with purple coneflowers, sunflowers, black-eyed Susans, and boltonia.

Try These

'Peachy Seduction' has sturdy stems and blooms a long time in midsummer; it's very heat-tolerant. 'Coronation Gold' is a yellow-flowered hybrid that never flops over or needs staking. It's completely trouble-free. 'Terra Cotta' has three colors on the same plant.

As I've moved to various places, I often end up with an area in my yard that's in full sun, has poor, dry soil, and is far from a water faucet. After trial and error, I finally could make a list of the perennials that worked in such spots. I wanted plants that didn't mind the difficult conditions, of course, but also that were colorful and completely carefree. Topping that list is yarrow. It doesn't mind sun, rocky soil, hillsides and slopes, lack of water, or almost no attention. It's also colorful—yellow, pink, red, white, and cream. Some plants have gray leaves, some green. Yarrow's flowers bloom for a long time, make excellent cut flowers, and are easily dried for winter arrangements.

Botanical Pronunciation

a-kil-LEE-uh

Bloom Period and Seasonal Color

Summer to fall in yellow, white, and pink

Mature Height × Spread

6 inches to 4 feet × 1 to 4 feet

Carex

Carex

As decorative and useful as ornamental grasses are, many have two potential drawbacks for some gardeners: they need full sun and they usually take up a good chunk of space in the landscape. Carex is an exception. It's a small sedge (most are under 2 feet tall) that does well in shady or partly shady locations. All like moist soil and some, such as Carex frankii (Frank's sedge), thrive in wet areas. At least one (Carex muskingumensis) is native to Kentucky and Tennessee. You'll be able to find carex with green foliage, various forms of green-and-cream or gold variegation, and with yellow or golden leaves. Some are evergreen; all are deer-resistant. The only one to avoid is Carex riparia 'Variegata', which spreads aggressively.

Botanical Pronunciation
CARE-ex

Bloom Period and Seasonal Color
Flowers are insignificant; grown for its leaves

Mature Height × Spread
4 inches to 3 feet × 6 inches to 3 feet

When, Where, and How to Plant
Plant during spring in partial to full shade. Most do fine in sun if given copious amounts of water. Carex tolerates average soil but prefers rich, moist soil; amend clay and poor soil with organic matter. Space plants about a foot apart if massing, 18 inches for individual plants. Mix organic granular fertilizer, according to package instructions, into the planting hole (see page 134 for more about planting perennials). Mulch with 2 inches of pine straw or fine pine bark.

Growing Tips
Water when weekly rainfall is less than 1 inch, especially if temperatures are over 90 degrees Fahrenheit. Carex needs moist soil in order to thrive. Fertilizer isn't usually necessary.

Care
Carex isn't bothered much by insects or diseases. If problems crop up, check with the Extension service. To keep the plants looking nice, trim back ratty-looking foliage in late winter or early spring (no later than the end of the first week of March). When plantings become crowded, dig up and divide plants in spring, replanting immediately. Remove unwanted self-sown plants anytime.

Garden Design
More and more, I include a plant or two of carex in my large container gardens. Any carex will grow well in containers, but those that stand out when mixed with other plants include *Carex elata* 'Aurea', *Carex oshimensis* 'Evergold', and 'Toffee Twist' (for Zone 7 and sun sites). In the garden, combine black-flowering sedge (*Carex nigra*) with pale pink astilbes. Use *Carex morrowii* 'Aurea-variegata' to form a graceful, low-growing edge to a woodland flower border. *Carex elata* 'Bowles Golden' will be at home along the boggy edge of a water garden. Most make nice accents in a perennial bed or to edge a border. The natives spread, rather than clump, and can be used as groundcovers.

Try These
Carex caryophyllea 'Beatlemania' produces a cute mophead of green-and-yellow variegated foliage. 'Banana Boat' has broad yellow leaves edged in green.

Feather Reed Grass

Calamagrostis × acutiflora

When, Where, and How to Plant

Plant in early spring or early fall in a sunny or mostly sunny spot, spacing the plants 4 feet apart. Feather reed grass prefers soil that stays slightly moist, but generally adapts to almost any kind of soil, including rocky soil, and it does well in clay. Plant so that the grass's crown (where the top and roots join) is at ground level.

Growing Tips

You'll rarely need to fertilize; too much encourages fast, weak growth. But if you think the grass isn't growing as well as it should, spread composted manure around the base of the plant in spring. Keep the soil moist the first year after transplanting, or until the grass is established.

Care

Using handpruners, loppers, a string trimmer, or a saw, cut the plant back in early spring to 12 to 24 inches from the ground. If the plant needs dividing, dig it up in spring and cut it into several sections with an ax or saw. Replant immediately and keep the soil around the plants moist until they start to grow, then water regularly for a few weeks. You shouldn't encounter insect or disease problems. If rust appears, cut the plant back and remove the foliage from the garden; if it persists, consult the Extension service.

Garden Design

Feather reed grass can be used as an informal hedge. Grow it in a perennial border surrounded by perennials with daisy-type flowers—Shasta daisies, black-eyed Susans, and gaillardia—as well as yarrow and spiky lavender *Liatris*, or group several *Pennisetum* hybrids together.

Try These

'Overdam' has green-and-cream striped foliage that turns pinkish in cool weather. It likes partial shade and grows no more than 3 feet tall and about as wide. 'Eldorado' has gold-variegated leaves; it reaches 4 to 5 feet high. 'Karl Foerster' is the best known cultivar of feather reed grass; it has sterile seeds and won't self-seed.

Have you ever admired an ornamental grass in someone's yard and thought you'd like to grow it, too, but didn't have any idea which grass it is? Often so many of the large grasses look a lot alike, and the increasing numbers of new hybrids being introduced make identification even more difficult. Feather reed grass makes it easy—instead of forming a fountain shape, it grows upright. And rather than developing plumes in late summer or early fall, its tall flower stalks spike up through the center of the grass in late spring or early summer and then turn golden in midsummer. Most are adaptable to various kinds of soils but do well in clay, a plus in this part of the country.

Botanical Pronunciation

kal-a-ma-GROS-tiss ah-ku-ti-FLOOR-uh

Bloom Period and Seasonal Color

Late spring or early summer, greenish purple flowering stems; the airy plumes gradually turn golden yellow and become light tan by fall

Mature Height × Spread

1½ to 4 feet × 2 feet

Fountain Grass
Pennisetum species and hybrids

I love the "foxtails" produced by these plants in late spring or early summer, and any child who sees them will too. Clump-forming fountain grass is aptly named. Its graceful stems and fuzzy flower spikes arch outward, resembling a fountain of grass. With a size more moderate than some ornamental grasses, this is a good choice for containers and small spaces. But beware: Several species—including the very popular Pennisetum setaceum *'Rubrum' (known as purple fountain grass) —are not perennial in Kentucky and Tennessee. When people have lamented to me that they can't grow ornamental grasses, that theirs didn't return in spring, the problem was almost always that they had planted an annual* Pennisetum. *Avoid 'Moudry' (black fountain grass), which aggressively self-seeds.*

Botanical Pronunciation
pen-ni-SEE-tum

Bloom Period and Seasonal Color
Summer, abundant cream to pink flower plumes

Mature Height × Spread
1 to 5 feet × 2 to 5 feet, depending on species

When, Where, and How to Plant
Plant in late spring or early summer, after the soil has warmed. The best soil for fountain grass is moist but well-drained, with *well-drained* being the key. It's important to amend clay with organic matter such as rotted compost, peat moss, or fine bark. Choose a spot in full sun to plant container-grown fountain grass, or those that you've just divided, but a little afternoon shade shouldn't be a problem. All of the smaller fountain grasses grow and bloom well in large containers.

Growing Tips
Water weekly until the plants develop a good root system and are thriving; then water deeply whenever rainfall is less than normal. Fertilizer isn't often needed.

Care
Cut back perennial varieties in spring to about a foot tall. That's also the time to dig up and divide the plants, if they've become crowded. At the same time, remove and replace those that are annuals. You won't find many pest problems with fountain grass. Its biggest fault is that it can self-sow, becoming a weed that has to be pulled out. (This isn't a problem in all areas or with many of the newer cultivars, but be cautious.) If that happens to you, clip off the flower heads before they fade.

Garden Design
Pair perennial fountain grass with black-eyed Susans and daylilies of all colors. Plant annual varieties that have purple foliage or pink blooms with gray-foliaged lamb's ear or artemisia and near pink-flowered English roses.

Try These
I like the little fountain grasses: 'Piglet', which has whitish pink flowers, often stays under a foot high. 'Hameln' grows about 18 to 30 inches tall. 'Cassian's Choice' has greenish white blooms and stays under 30 inches high. 'Little Bunny', a true dwarf, is nice in rock gardens. *Pennisetum orientale* 'Karley Rose' is slightly taller at 3 feet but has eye-catching purple-rose blooms over a very long period; mine always garner lots of favorable comments.

Hakone Grass
Hakonechloa macra 'Aureola'

When, Where, and How to Plant
In mid to late spring, find a partially shady spot in which to plant golden hakone grass. Place it in too much sun and the bright color fades; too much shade, and the foliage turns greenish (the plant tolerates more sun in Zone 6 than Zone 7). Space the plants 2 feet apart in moist but well-drained soil that you've enriched with ample amounts of organic matter (fine bark or shredded compost).

Growing Tips
Don't let the soil dry out, especially the first year; moist soil is important. In spring, after new growth has begun, spread an organic or pelleted slow-release fertilizer, according to label directions, on the ground around the plants; water well. Fertilize plants in containers monthly with a water-soluble plant food until late July and then stop. In fall, after a few hard frosts, mulch around the plants (especially in Zone 6) to protect the grass from the soil's alternate freezing and thawing. Poor drainage over winter is usually a death knell.

Care
In March, before new growth begins, cut plants back to 3 inches tall and remove the old foliage from the garden. Hakone grass experiences virtually no pest problems. Division won't be necessary except maybe once every five years.

Garden Design
Hakone grass is a must for Japanese or Oriental-style gardens. It's great for a rock garden and makes a charming accent with green-leaved hostas and ferns and yellow-green coleus, all of which share the same growing conditions, or with purple-flowered perennials. It's also attractive at the base of a clump of river birch and will grow well in containers. Think of it as a colorful and usual edging plant for flower beds or borders.

Try These
Hakonechloa macra 'All Gold' is another excellent hybrid; its leaves are all yellow, not variegated, and it grows slightly taller and faster than 'Aureola'. It also has a more upright form, instead of cascading.

Hakone grass is becoming deservedly popular among gardeners as the most attractive and distinguished of the small ornamental grasses, which, as a group, don't usually call attention to themselves. It's hard not to notice hakone grass, though. Its shape is different—masses of arching stems about 14 inches long—and its brilliant, mostly gold color certainly makes any shady spot shine. Hakone, also known as Japanese forest grass or sometimes just as golden grass (although there are also varieties that have green or green-and-white foliage), is deer-resistant, noninvasive (it spreads very slowly), and its foliage often turns pinkish in fall. This delightful little grass tolerates both light shade and those wet spots in the yard and attracts almost no insects or diseases.

Botanical Pronunciation
hah-koh-neh-KLOH-uh MACK-rah

Bloom Period and Seasonal Color
Grown for colorful foliage: gold with green streaks; turns pinkish red or orangish in autumn

Mature Height × Spread
14 to 24 inches × 16 to 30 inches

Liriope

Liriope muscari

The reason you see liriope planted everywhere is that it's nearly impossible to kill. It survives—yea, thrives—in sun or shade, moist soil or dry, even when neglected. This is a tough plant that doesn't mind being grown right up against curbs or sidewalks. It doesn't need fertilizer, and it grows so thickly that weeds don't penetrate the planting. Its lavender blooms attract butterflies, and birds enjoy its black fruits. But you may want to avoid Liriope spicata, which spreads aggressively. When people ask me if the name of this plant is pronounced leer-ee-O-pee or la-RYE-oh-pee, I laughingly suggest that they call it by its common names, monkey grass or lilyturf. But if you want to be botanical, say li-RYE-oh-pee.

Botanical Pronunciation
li-RYE-oh-pee mus-CARE-eye

Bloom Period and Seasonal Color
Early summer flowers in violet, purple, or white, followed by stalks of black fruits

Mature Height × Spread
8 to 18 inches × 12 to 18 inches

When, Where, and How to Plant
Plant in ordinary soil anytime from just after the last frost of spring until early autumn. Mix a pelleted slow-release fertilizer with the soil in the planting hole if planting before July; in July and after, don't mix fertilizer in the planting hole. Mulch new plantings lightly with an inch or two of pine straw or fine pine bark. While most liriope prefers to live in light shade or partially shady areas, a few cultivars ('John Burch' and 'Silvery Sunproof', for example) like full sun, so check the plant label to be sure before you choose a location.

Growing Tips
Water young plants weekly if rainfall is below normal; this is particularly important if the plants receive half a day or more of sun. Once it's mature, liriope is drought-tolerant and needs little watering. Gardeners rarely fertilize mature plants, or even young ones, but if small plants aren't growing as quickly or robustly as you would like, spread a pelleted slow-release fertilizer around the plants under the mulch in spring, after you have trimmed back the foliage. Or, if you're fertilizing the lawn, let some of that fertilizer get close to liriope (but not on its foliage). Water and replace the mulch.

Care
With a string trimmer, loppers, or pruners, cut liriope's foliage back to 1 to 2 inches high in early March each year before new growth starts. This prevents the plants from being an unsightly mixture of old brown and new green foliage. Insects and diseases are rarely a problem on liriope.

Garden Design
While the most common uses of liriope are as a groundcover and around the edges of a border, consider placing individual plants (especially showy cultivars) in rock gardens, at the bases of trees or shrubs, around ponds, or in containers.

Try These
'Monroe's White' produces large clusters of white flowers on a 1-foot plant with green foliage.

Miscanthus
Miscanthus sinensis

When, Where, and How to Plant
Although miscanthus prefers soil enriched with organic matter, it tolerates just about any kind of soil. Give it as much sun as possible, since the grass becomes floppy in too much shade. Plant in spring, spacing plants about 3 feet apart.

Growing Tips
There's no need to fertilize unless the plant isn't growing well; if needed, spread organic slow-release fertilizer on the ground around the base of the plant in early spring and water in. The first year the grass is in your yard, water when weekly rainfall is less than an inch; in following years, additional moisture is rarely required. Slow growth the first year is normal and not a concern.

Care
Cut the grass back at the beginning of March. In early years, it can be done with loppers, then you'll need a string trimmer, and finally you may have to get out the ax. But it's a job that must be done—new green growth popping up through old brown leaves is unsightly. But that's about your only chore, since miscanthus is trouble-free—it's rarely bothered by pests.

Garden Design
Because miscanthus grows tall and wide, one or more makes an excellent privacy screen. You can also use this grass as an informal hedge. Planted singly as specimens, miscanthus adds a sense of height beside a water garden and also serves as a background for colorful perennials, such as black-eyed Susans, purple coneflowers, and daylilies.

Try These
'Andante' is really tall—about 7 feet—and its green-and-white leaves tend to weep. The white plumes are very prominent. This plant has not reseeded at all in my garden. 'Gold Bar' has heavily banded green-and-gold leaves, an upright habit, and is very slow growing. 'Cosmopolitan' (from the National Arboretum) has attractive green-and-white leaves and impressive plumes; it grows 6 to 8 feet high.

I had to think long and hard about including miscanthus in this book. After all, it's on the invasive species lists of Tennessee and Kentucky. But I talked with a number of experts who said that as long as homeowners stick with hybrids (those that have names) and not the straight species, they didn't think there would be a problem. The University of Minnesota even declared of miscanthus cultivars, "These ornamental forms are not the same as the species or wild type that have become invasive in the Middle Atlantic States." So if you want miscanthus, buy only named cultivars, and watch the plants carefully to see that they don't reseed. This is a wonderful grass, but none of us wants to harm the environment.

Botanical Pronunciation
mis-KAN-thus si-NEN-sis

Bloom Period and Seasonal Color
Late summer and early fall in showy plumes that fluff out and last until cut off the next spring

Mature Height × Spread
3 to 12 feet × 2 to 6 feet

Mondo Grass
Ophiopogon japonicus

Do you know the differences between mondo grass and liriope, or do they seem much the same to you? It's true that the plants are similar—both are short grasses that grow well in shade, make good groundcovers, and bear lavender or white blooms. But mondo grass is shorter and has thinner leaves than liriope and its flowers are hidden down in the foliage rather than being above it, as with liriope. Mondo grass also spreads by underground stems and prefers shade to sun. It isn't always as hardy as liriope, so—especially in Zone 6—you may want to plant it in a protected place. But when you need a tiny, grasslike plant, especially one with dark or black foliage, this is your plant.

Botanical Pronunciation
oh-fee-oh-PO-gon ja-PON-ih-cus

Bloom Period and Seasonal Color
Early summer flowers in lilac or white, followed by blue seed stalks but grown for foliage

Mature Height × Spread
6 to 8 inches × 1 foot

When, Where, and How to Plant
Buy container-grown plants and set out anytime from mid-spring until early summer in Zone 6 and mid-spring to late summer in Zone 7. The best location is a shady or mostly shady spot with average to good soil. Mondo grass will tolerate dry soil but grows much better when it has regular moisture. Space the plants 5 to 12 inches apart depending on how quickly you want coverage. Mix a slow-release fertilizer, according to package directions, with the soil in the planting hole. Mulch with light organic material, such as pine needles or shredded leaves, to keep down weeds and retain soil moisture.

Growing Tips
Water weekly when rainfall is less than an inch during the growing season. Each spring, spread granular or pelleted slow-release fertilizer, according to label directions, around established plants, and water well.

Care
Cut back to a few inches high in early March each year to keep the planting looking neat. Snails and slugs may nibble leaves, especially when the plants are in shade and when the soil is moist or the mulch is thick (see page 34 for control advice). Divide plants as needed every three years or so in early spring.

Garden Design
Mondo grass, much like liriope, is used as a groundcover and path edging. But it also adds an arching, grasslike note to container plantings. It looks nice with astilbes, coral bells, and other shade-loving flowers, and it grows well under trees. It's traditionally used in Japanese gardens.

Try These
'Nanus' is a cute dwarf that forms a 4- to 6-inch-tall mound; its flowers are purple and leaves are solid green.

Pink Muhly
Muhlenbergia capillaris

When, Where, and How to Plant

Plant in late spring after the temperature and soil are reliably warm. Pink muhly grass prefers full sun but won't mind some afternoon shade. Full sun is best for Zone 6, though, to make sure the grass blooms well before frost. Ideal soil is moist but well drained, although it easily adapts to just about any other kind of soil, including damp clay and dry soils. Space plants 3 to 4 feet apart; mulch dry soil.

Growing Tips

Especially when it's growing in dry soil, pink muhly grass needs regular watering its first year if weekly rainfall is less than an inch to give it ideal conditions for becoming established. After that, this warm-season grass shouldn't need extra water and is usually drought-tolerant. Fertilizer is rarely needed, but if you need to give the grass a boost, spread pelleted or organic slow-release fertilizer, according to package directions, on the ground around the plant in spring, just as growth is apparent, and water well.

Care

Zone 6 is the northern limit for pink muhly grass, so you'll need to mulch in fall to provide winter protection, especially in Zone 6a. The plant has few problems with insects and diseases, but often attracts beneficial insects such as ladybugs to your garden. Divide in spring, if needed. Cut down old stalks in spring before new growth begins.

Garden Design

This grass—either individually or grouped—is usually a focal point in the garden, because when it shows off in fall, it's the automatic center of attention. It's a good choice for a meadow garden or a naturalistic garden created to attract wildlife.

Try These

Hybrids of pink muhly grass may be difficult to find except by mail order. The ones I've seen and admired are 'White Cloud' (yes, white flowers instead of pink) and 'Pink Flamingos', which produces pink plumes rather than an airy cloud of pink.

This was the plant that most impressed me as I walked around my new neighborhood in autumn. "Wow!" I thought, "A cloud of pinkish purple." Not a haze of wimpy pink but a glowing, almost fluorescent, pink impossible to ignore. Sometimes this plant is called hair grass, but you've never seen hair like this except on troll dolls. And actually, if you look closer, you'll see that those are tiny pink flowers. The pink eventually fades to tan, but during its long bloom time, this native grass is quite a showstopper. It's a moderate size and easy to grow too— doesn't mind heat and humidity, adapts to poor soil, and is drought-tolerant once it's mature. I was enchanted and immediately ordered some for spring planting.

Botanical Pronunciation

muh-len-BERG-ee-uh kap-ill-AIR-us

Bloom Period and Seasonal Color

Fall in bright pink "clouds"

Mature Height x Spread

2 to 4 feet x 2 to 4 feet

Purple Moor Grass
Molinia caerulea

The most interesting thing about purple moor grass is that the grass itself is relatively short—less than 3 feet—but the flower plumes are tall, making them quite noticeable in fall and winter. This habit makes this grass a good choice for those who want some height but don't have room for an ornamental grass that takes up a lot of space. Moor grass is also known for outstanding fall color, which can range from clear yellow and gold to orange and red (the "purple" in its name is for the flowers—purple and yellow—not the foliage, which is actually bright green, variegated green-and-white, or bluish.) Unusual among grasses, the flower stalks break off by themselves; they don't need cutting back.

Botanical Pronunciation
moe-LIN-ee-uh sir-U-lee-uh

Bloom Period and Seasonal Color
Late summer through winter with showy flower stalks; excellent fall color

Mature Height x Spread
1 to 3 feet x 1 to 3 feet

When, Where, and How to Plant
Plant this cool-season grass anytime from mid to late spring and into summer. It prefers moist, fertile, acid soil (a soil test will tell you if your soil is acid or alkaline). It grows especially well in wet soils. Place purple moor grass in full sun in Zone 6; in Zone 7, in afternoon shade. Space plants 1 to 2 feet apart and group several together for best appearance. To grow it in drier soil, give it some shade and water regularly (see page 137 for more about planting ornamental grasses). Don't fertilize at planting time, but mulch to retain moisture in the soil.

Growing Tips
The more sun and heat that purple moor grass experiences, the more water it will need. When weekly rainfall is less than an inch during the growing season, check the soil to see if it's moist, and water if isn't. The plant typically grows well without fertilizer, but if you feel that it's occasionally needed, spread an organic slow-release product, according to package directions, in very early spring.

Care
Purple moor grass won't need dividing often. When it becomes necessary, do it in early spring just after new growth starts. Don't be concerned if the grass doesn't bloom for the first few years it's in your yard; it's slow to become established, and flower stalks may take three or four years to appear.

Garden Design
This ornamental grass looks nice when paired with cannas, dahlias, sedum, and *Achillea* 'Coronation Gold'. The smaller hybrids look nice and grow well in containers.

Try These
The foliage of *Molinia caerulea* ssp. *arundinacea* 'Sky Racer' grows about 3 feet tall and as wide, but the flower plumes rise about 6 to 7 feet in late August or early September. Fall color is an excellent yellow. 'Variegata' has gold-and-green variegated leaves and grows about 2 to 2½ feet tall. 'Rotschopf' has red foliage.

Stipa
Stipa species and hybrids

When, Where, and How to Plant
In mid-spring to early summer, plant in a sunny to partially shady spot that has slightly moist but well-drained soil. The plant will tolerate most types of soil though, as long as they drain well. A soil that's too rich in organic matter will cause the plant to flop over. Although Mexican feather grass is usually rated hardy to Zone 6, it may not always return after the coldest winters, so try a relatively protected spot the first time you plant in Zone 6 or 7a. Space plants about 2 feet apart. Fertilizer isn't needed at planting time, but if soil is poor you may mix an organic slow-release fertilizer, according to label directions, into the planting hole. Mulch isn't necessary unless it's to prevent weeds.

Growing Tips
Although it's drought-tolerant once it's mature, stipa will need watering regularly its first year if weekly rainfall is less than an inch during the growing seasons, and you will want to water some during dry spells when the plant is young. Like most ornamental grasses, it needs little to no fertilizer. An organic slow-release fertilizer is best if you use a fertilizer; apply in spring.

Care
Mexican feather grass does reseed, although this is more likely to happen in climates warmer than those in Tennessee and Kentucky. If new plants appear, pull them up. Cut back foliage in spring. If the plant needs dividing, do this in late spring, after growth has started, or in early summer.

Garden Design
Stipa is attractive when massed, and it adds interest when grown among flowers and foliage plants in a large container. Pair with *Crocosmia* 'Lucifer'.

Try These
'Pony Tails' forms an eye-catching clump.

Although several species of Stipa *are nice ornamental grasses (with names like needle grass, spear grass, and Korean feather grass) and there is some botanical confusion— plants that used to be called* Stipa *are now categorized as* Achnatherum *and* Nassella*—it's worth persisting to find these attractive grasses with thin, wispy foliage for hot and dry garden spots. My favorite—and the easiest to find at a local nursery—is Mexican feather grass (*Stipa tenuissima *or* Nasella tenuissima*). It grows 1 to 2 feet high and 20 to 24 inches wide, producing billows of airy whitish plumes in late summer that love to dance in the wind. The foliage grows upward in a vase shape and then gracefully spills over.*

Botanical Pronunciation
STY-puh

Bloom Period and Seasonal Color
Late summer to fall, white to beige plumes

Mature Height x Spread
12 to 24 inches x 20 to 24 inches

Switchgrass
Panicum virgatum

Switchgrass is native to American prairies, as well as to Kentucky and Tennessee, and tolerates just about any kind of soil, from dense and soggy to sandy and dry. That's good news for gardeners who have one of those difficult spots in their yards or are suffering through one of those growing seasons that can range from too much rain in April to drought conditions in August. This warm-season grass is most impressive in autumn, when its long-lasting fall color makes it stand out. Switchgrass has a more erect form than some other grasses and isn't bothered by being planted near black walnut trees (whose roots adversely affect many other plants). Switchgrass is considered noninvasive; most cultivars are very slow spreaders.

Botanical Pronunciation
PAN-i-kum ver-GAY-tum

Bloom Period and Seasonal Color
Midsummer blossoms of purplish pink fading to white and then tan; in summer and/or fall, some hybrids have colorful foliage

Mature Height × Spread
3 to 8 feet × 2 to 4 feet

When, Where, and How to Plant
Wait until soil is warm in late spring before planting container-grown plants. Set out bare-root grasses in mid- to late May. Space plants about 3 to 4 feet apart, according to mature size. You probably don't have an area in your yard that isn't acceptable to switchgrass; it's one of the most adaptable plants around. Give it at least half a day of sun (although full sun is preferable), and it won't mind what the soil is like—be it wet or dry, clay or rocky. You don't need to add fertilizer to the soil when planting.

Growing Tips
Water weekly the first year if weekly rainfall is less than an inch; after that, water during dry spells. In very poor soils, fertilize lightly with a granular organic fertilizer, following package instructions, but usually switchgrass doesn't need fertilizing.

Care
To encourage quick new growth in spring, cut switchgrass back before new growth begins; dispose of old foliage. Few insects or diseases bother this grass. Divide the plant, as needed, in spring just after new growth has started.

Garden Design
You can use the various cultivars of switchgrass in many ways. Because it likes wet soil, switchgrass is a natural choice for areas beside ponds and water gardens. It also is right at home with perennials of all types—from creeping phlox in spring to Mexican sunflower (*Tithonia rotundifolia*) in summer and asters, sedum, and boltonia in fall. It's a good grass to use as a screen or in masses. It also looks nice in groupings with other grasses and right at home in naturalized areas.

Try These
The foliage on 'Shenandoah' starts out bluish green and quickly develops the best red-burgundy color I've seen in switchgrass; it has pink blooms (maturing to silver) on a plant that reaches approximately 3 feet high and about the same width.

Tufted Hair Grass

Deschampsia caespitosa

When, Where, and How to Plant

Plant in spring in a spot that's lightly shaded or that's in sun for only a few hours each day. Too much sun will bleach out the leaves. The appearance of the flowers and seeds is more impressive if the sun shines on the plant from the back. Tufted hair grass grows best if placed in moist, rich soil, especially in Zone 7. It doesn't like hot, dry locations. There's no need to fertilize at planting time. Mulch the soil after planting, to help hold moisture in the soil.

Growing Tips

Unless the grass is planted in naturally moist soil, you'll need to water regularly when weekly rainfall is less than an inch during spring and summer. Tufted hair grass rarely needs fertilizer.

Care

Cut down old plants in early spring before new growth starts. This grass may reseed; if so, pull out unwanted new plants as they appear. Divide plants as needed in spring after the plant has begun growing. The grass is rarely affected by insects or diseases, but rabbits may be a problem.

Garden Design

Plant a row of one of the colorful hybrids of tufted hair grass along the driveway or a sidewalk. In a perennial bed, grow with coral bells and carex. It's a nice choice to plant along the lightly shaded banks of a water garden.

Try These

'Goldtau' produces a cloud of golden flowers in midsummer on a plant that's 1 to 2 feet high. Both flowers and foliage of 'Northern Lights' change colors as the season progresses; it grows 1 to 3 feet tall and 1 foot wide. 'Pixie Fountain' is a dwarf (10 to 15 inches high) that's great for Zone 6, although the heat of Zone 7 may be too much for it. 'Bronzeschleier' (Bronze Veil) and 'Goldgehaenge' (Golden Pendant) are among the best in Zone 7; they don't mind heat.

Not too many of the medium-sized grasses—especially those with showy flowers—will perform well if grown in much shade, but tufted hair grass will. This is not full shade, but in those spots that are shaded part of the day. It's a deer-resistant grass that attracts birds to eat its interesting seeds that appear after the multicolored— gold, silver, light purple, and so forth—flowers fade. Seeds and flowers are more impressive when the plant is placed so it's backlit by the morning or evening sun. In our area, this cool-season grass may be evergreen or semievergreen, although sometimes the foliage freezes and the plant goes dormant over winter, much like other ornamental grasses. The species is usually more tolerant of heat than the hybrids, which have been bred in Europe.

Botanical Pronunciation

des-CAMP-see-uh cess-pi-TOE-suh

Bloom Period and Seasonal Color

Summer multicolored blooms; fall and winter with yellow flower panicles

Mature Height x Spread

1 to 3 feet x 1 to 3 feet

Shrubs

A shrub can deliver season-spanning interest to your landscape without much effort on your part beyond initial planting and watering (sometimes only when the plant is young). That's a good deal for those who want their yards to look great but don't consider themselves to be avid gardeners.

The Versatile Nature of Shrubs

Banks of red, pink, and white evergreen azaleas create a springtime paradise whose beauty returns year after year. Shrubs such as camellia and witch hazel may bloom in the cold winter months when the sight of flower blossoms is a rare and welcome treat. But shrubs aren't grown just for their beauty—they're also useful. Hollies and other berried shrubs entice scores of birds to visit your property (helping rid it of insects while they're there). Hedges separate your land from your neighbor's, and shrubs planted as a screen ensure privacy and block unsightly views.

Shrubs come in many forms—from pyramidal to rounded to columnar—and have varied textures that can be mixed and matched for a pleasing effect. Small-leafed shrubs have a neat appearance and fit nicely into little landscapes. Shrubs with big leaves are bolder looking and are ideal for larger areas, especially where they will be seen from a distance.

Shrubs can be colorful too—and not just those that flower. If you like a large splash of color, look for shrubs with gold, purple, or red foliage or those with variegated leaves. But don't overdo it; use these shrubs as accents in a sea of green for the best effect.

Shrubs may be evergreen—either broadleafed, such as boxwood, or needled, like false cypress. Or they may be deciduous and lose their leaves in fall. Usually, evergreens are placed in the most prominent spots for year-round effect and deciduous shrubs fade into the background except when they're flowering.

Whichever type of shrub you choose, always check the root system before buying to make sure it's in good shape. Don't buy a shrub that's rootbound—one whose roots wind round and round the ball of soil. It's hard to get such a plant to grow well.

Mature Size Is Important

If you want to be happy with the shrubs you buy, pay attention to the eventual height and width given with each

*Crape myrtle (*Lagerstroemia*) with foxglove (*Digitalis*) and hosta (*Hosta*)*

Beautyberry (Callicarpa)

plant in this book and often on plant labels. When you're planting a 1-gallon azalea, it's hard to imagine that it might grow to be 4 feet tall and at least as wide. So you plant a half-dozen of them, spacing them maybe a foot apart—and then in a couple of years, they're crowded together and you have to dig up every other one. Digging up good-sized shrubs and transplanting them is a lot of work! Avoid it by spacing them right the first time. If newly planted shrubs look too far apart, fill in between them with annual or perennial flowers until the shrubs reach their mature sizes. Sure, it's possible to plant a big shrub instead of a little one, to have a more finished look from the start, but you'll find that large shrubs cost more, they don't grow as fast as small ones, and they tend to have more problems after transplanting. Not to mention that they require more attention—especially watering—the first year or two they're in your yard.

Planting a Shrub

Some experts advise using just the soil removed from the hole, as you would to plant a tree. Others suggest that if your soil is poor, it's all right to mix the soil in which a shrub will grow with some organic material. Since I rarely have gardened anywhere that my soil would be classified as "good," here's how I plant: Dig a hole that's twice as wide as the rootball and not quite as deep (this is to prevent the newly planted shrub from sinking into the hole and ending up lower than it was in its container, which can lead to root rot). Mix the soil removed from the hole with 15 to 20 percent compost, peat moss, fine bark, or other organic matter. (I usually use fine bark, which is excellent for clay soil.) Carefully remove the well-watered shrub from the pot, and place it on firm soil at the bottom of the hole. Replace the amended soil firmly around the shrub's roots, leaving a shallow indented circle around the shrub to hold water. Spread 2 to 3 inches of mulch around the shrub to hold moisture in the soil and to keep down weeds. Water slowly and thoroughly, and continue watering weekly the first year if rainfall totals less than an inch. Water deeply during dry spells the second year, to allow the shrub's roots to become established. Don't fertilize a shrub at planting time; wait until the next spring.

The shrubs on the next pages include those that flower; have berries; provide several seasons of interest; attract birds, butterflies, and other small wildlife; serve as screens or hedges; and look great in your yard. You'll find several that are ideal for any landscape.

Aucuba

Aucuba japonica

The most common cultivar of aucuba is often referred to as gold dust plant because its glossy evergreen leaves seem to be dusted with bright yellow or gold dots of varying sizes and shapes. As you might imagine, this shrub can really brighten a dark corner of the yard. The same is true of all the other variegated aucubas. They're great shade-loving evergreen shrubs that are mostly for Zone 7, although more cultivars are being introduced that will survive in Zone 6. This is a shrub that's becoming more popular as gardeners continue to search for good shade plants. You'll find cultivars with leaves edged in chartreuse and boldly splashed with yellow, as well as the more common gold spots. I love it!

Botanical Pronunciation
ah-Q-bah juh-PON-ik-uh

Bloom Period and Seasonal Color
Early spring, insignificant maroon to purple flowers; red berries in fall and winter; grown for foliage

Mature Height × Spread
6 to 10 feet × 4 to 9 feet

When, Where, and How to Plant

To ensure a good crop of berries, a male and a female cultivar are needed, but since the berries are often hidden by the leaves, you may not care. Place aucuba where it will be in shade, or mostly shade, year-round. Winter protection from wind and sun is especially important in Zone 6, so look for a protected place that has moist, well-drained soil with plenty of organic matter. Spring planting is best, but you can set out container-grown shrubs from May until the end of August if you water well during summer. Use a transplanting solution at planting time, and mulch with pine straw or fine bark.

Growing Tips

Adequate moisture is a must for aucuba. Water well to keep the soil slightly damp when the plant is young. After it becomes established, water deeply when weekly rainfall is less than an inch per week. Spread a slow-release shrub fertilizer around the base at the end of April, if desired.

Care

If necessary, prune to keep aucuba's shape neat and rounded. Don't do this with a hedge trimmer or shears; that will damage many of the leaves and the plant won't look good for some time. Instead use handpruners to cut stems back to just above a bud. This shrub has few insect or disease problems.

Landscape Design

I love aucuba planted with hakone grass, which has graceful yellow- or gold-striped leaves and is shade tolerant (see page 181). Aucuba is excellent for foundation plantings on the north side of the house and beneath tall trees. It's also nice grouped with other shade-loving shrubs in woodland beds.

Try These

'Variegata' is the most common cultivar; its leaves are heavily speckled with gold. 'Rozannie' does *not* have variegated foliage, but it's a compact plant that grows to 3 feet by 3 feet and produces large, showy red berries in fall and winter without the need for a male plant.

Beautyberry
Callicarpa species and hybrids

When, Where, and How to Plant

Plant beautyberry anytime from spring through fall. While it will grow nicely in part sun—especially in dappled shade—the production of berries is greater when the shrub is placed in full sun. Beautyberry isn't particular about soil type and, in fact, probably does better in poor or average soil than where soil is rich. It's okay for clay sites that don't stay wet all the time. See page 191 for shrub-planting instructions. Apply 2 to 3 inches of organic mulch after planting to keep down weeds and to lessen reseeding.

Growing Tips

Ample watering causes an abundance of fruits, so if spring and summer rainfall is low, soak the soil around the shrub weekly. Avoid fertilizing, which leads to lanky growth and fewer berries.

Care

In early spring, cut the shrub back to 1 foot high to encourage lots of new growth—and therefore an abundance of flowers and berries, which are produced only on new growth. In severe winters, if the top of the plant is killed, cut it back, and it will generally grow from the roots. Beautyberry has no serious insects or diseases. It can reseed itself (and sometimes the birds help), so remove the extra plants or transplant them elsewhere so the clump doesn't grow too large.

Landscape Design

Naturalize American beautyberry under tall pine trees whose lowest limbs are at least 10 to 12 feet from the ground. All beautyberries are stunning in fall when massed in groups. They're ideal for gardens that are designed to be wildlife-friendly.

Try These

Callicarpa dichotoma 'Early Amethyst' grows quickly. 'Duet' has variegated leaves and white berries on a very showy, hardy shrub (grow it in light shade in Zone 7, in full sun in Zone 6). *C. japonica* 'Luxurians' is a large shrub with correspondingly large fruit clusters. *C. bodinieri* 'Profusion' begins berry production when the shrub is young and lives up to its name in developing bountiful crops of berries.

Purple *berries? Yes, this shrub is really covered with purple berries. The first time you see a beautyberry in late summer or fall, you may do a double take. You've seen shrubs with red, orange, yellow, or black berries, maybe even white, but this color is amazing. And you can grow different types of beautyberries, from a native, the American beautyberry* (Callicarpa americana), *to several Asian species, such as Japanese beautyberry (C. japonica). Fruit color may also be lavender or white. On the native beautyberry, the fruits are in fat, round clusters up and down the stems. Japanese beautyberry has smaller fruits on a hardier shrub. C. dichotoma is slightly smaller and has a more graceful arching form. All are easy to grow.*

Botanical Pronunciation
kal-i-CAR-puh

Bloom Period and Seasonal Color
Summer flowers in pink or lavender, followed by purple or white fruits

Mature Height × Spread
3 to 10 feet × 4 to 8 feet

Blue Mist Shrub

Caryopteris species and hybrids

When a plant has a number of common names, they usually give you an idea of what you can expect. For Caryopteris *species, they all include the word "blue" —blue spirea, blue mist shrub, and bluebeard. Yes, blue flowers are why you grow it, but it has other nice traits, including fragrant flowers, foliage, and stems; drought-tolerance; and low maintenance. It's reportedly deer-tolerant too. Even if it weren't so easygoing, you'd want blue mist shrub in your yard, because it blooms in July and August, when few other shrubs do. Occasionally in bad winters, it may die back to the ground (and then grow back from the roots) in Zone 6, but if that's a problem, you can find cultivars that are very hardy.*

Botanical Pronunciation
kar-ee-OP-ter-iss in-can-a

Bloom Period and Seasonal Color
Mid to late summer flowers in blue

Mature Height × Spread
2 to 4 feet × 3 to 4 feet

When, Where, and How to Plant
Plant blue mist shrub in spring. Although a sunny spot with well-drained soil is ideal, it will tolerate a little afternoon shade. Improve all hard soils, such as clay, with organic matter—compost, peat, finely shredded bark—before planting. Good drainage is vital for blue mist shrub. See page 191 for directions on how best to plant shrubs.

Growing Tips
When the shrub is young, water it regularly if weekly rainfall is less than an inch. After it becomes established, usually after a year or two, it will generally need watering only in severe droughts. Avoid fertilizer because it causes lanky growth.

Care
Blue mist shrub has few disease or insect problems. If the shrub dies back to the ground during a particularly cold winter, prune all dead wood back to live wood in early to mid-spring. It should grow back just fine. Actually, it's important in all zones to prune this shrub back to about 8 inches high in early to mid-March (early March in Zone 7; later for Zones 6 and 5) just as you do butterfly bush. Its masses of flowers are borne on new growth, and cutting back severely causes the plant to put on plenty of new stems to produce blooms. Pruning also keeps the plant compact and more attractive.

Landscape Design
A star in a butterfly garden, blue mist shrub is also at home in the perennial border. It looks nice with yellow-flowered perennials, including daylilies that bloom at the same time. Its mounded growth habit of blue "mist" means that it can be planted as an attractive low hedge or edging along a sunny path.

Try These
'Grand Bleu' has dark blue flowers that stay in bloom for weeks and is hardy. 'Blue Balloon' has showy blooms on a bush about 2 feet tall. 'Longwood Blue' grows to 4 feet high and flowers profusely.

Boxwood
Buxus species and hybrids

When, Where, and How to Plant
In spring, plant boxwoods in full to partial sun. Moist, well-drained soil is ideal; enrich it with organic matter if your soil is poor. The most favorable pH is 6.5 to 7, which means that acid soils may need to be limed. A soil test will tell you the pH of your soil; lime needs to be applied some time before planting since it takes time for it to become effective. (See page 191 for directions on planting shrubs.) Avoid planting boxwoods where they're subject to drying winds or in clay soil, which can contribute to root rot.

Growing Tips
Water deeply once a week when rainfall is lacking. Fertilize each spring with a slow-release fertilizer for evergreen shrubs, used according to package directions.

Care
Maintain a year-round mulch to protect its shallow roots. Prune in early spring; winter damage can occur if boxwood is pruned or trimmed after July. Plants that are pruned with handpruners are better able to withstand snow and cold than those trimmed with hedge shears. Boxwood is subject to many insects and diseases. If foliage develops an off color in spring or summer, the plant may be suffering from root rot. Nematodes will stunt roots. Check with the Extension service about remedies. To prevent male dogs from constantly wetting on the same spot, which damages the foliage, you may need to place a barrier around the boxwood or spray a commercial product that discourages pets from coming close.

Landscape Design
Boxwoods are generally used as hedges and foundation plantings; they're perfect for formal or Colonial-style gardens and make an excellent green background for other plants. Dwarfs are nice in perennial gardens, as topiaries, and as herb garden edging.

Try These
Buxus microphylla doesn't have the odor that some find objectionable in other boxwoods. Gardeners in the coldest areas will like 'Winter Gem'. 'Little Gem' rarely needs pruning; give it partial shade.

I love visiting historic properties that have boxwood gardens—some are little hedges surrounding formal herb gardens and some shrubs are much bigger than many of us imagined that boxwood grew. Today, most of us are most familiar with boxwoods as foundation shrubs and as hedges, but these handsome, broad-leaved evergreens have plenty of other uses, including adding a touch of green to a perennial border in winter. Not everyone likes the smell of the leaves, and you may have to discourage male dogs from wetting on them and damaging the foliage. But if you prefer the classic look and want a touch of elegance in your landscape, boxwood delivers. It tolerates heavy pruning (making boxwood good for topiary) and always looks neat. It can even be grown in big containers.

Botanical Pronunciation
BUCKS-us

Bloom Period and Seasonal Color
Evergreen foliage

Mature Height × Spread
2 to 20 feet × 3 to 25 feet

Buckeye
Aesculus species and hybrids

Although not as well-known as, say, forsythia, these showy native shrubs have become very popular with gardeners and are well worth growing. Bottlebrush buckeye (Aesculus parviflora) has white flowers that look like the brushes you wash baby bottles with, only softer and larger. The blooms are a foot tall and 2 to 4 inches around. (They're just as intriguing as they sound, and loved by butterflies.) Its leaves turn yellow in fall. Red buckeye (Aesculus pavia has 6- to 8-inch red (or, occasionally, yellow) flower panicles in mid- to late spring, which are quite popular with hummingbirds. Both grow to be big bushes, so you need only one to really make an impact in your yard. They're also considered deer-resistant.

Botanical Pronunciation
ESS-ku-lus

Bloom Period and Seasonal Color
White in midsummer (bottlebrush buckeye), or red in April or May (red buckeye)

Mature Height × Spread
8 to 20 feet × 8 to 25 feet

When, Where, and How to Plant
Bottlebrush buckeye will grow in any almost light; so will red buckeye, but it's less likely to lose its leaves early in fall if it's placed in part shade. Plant in moist, well-drained soil, preferably acidic, to which you've added compost, finely shredded bark, or peat moss, if your soil is poor. Be sure to give these buckeyes plenty of room to grow—they spread considerably and produce suckers, so they shouldn't be crowded. Plant in early spring before growth starts (see page 191 for directions on how to plant a shrub). Mulch with 2 to 3 inches of organic material such as pine needles or fine bark.

Growing Tips
Water young plants regularly to keep the soil moist. In future years, water mature plants deeply when weekly rainfall is less than an inch. Fertilizer probably won't be needed, but if growth isn't fast enough, use a slow-release shrub fertilizer, according to package directions, at the end of March.

Care
Most buckeye shrubs are troubled by leaf spots and diseases, but not bottlebrush buckeye. Occasionally red buckeye will develop spots, but it's rarely serious. Prune in winter if needed to keep them within bounds. Overgrown specimens may be cut back to ground level. Dig up or cut down unwanted suckers anytime during the year. Red buckeye begins dropping its leaves in August and early September, and they're usually gone by the end of September. This is normal.

Landscape Design
Plant buckeye shrubs beneath limbed-up tall trees or in a shrub border. They're also nice as specimen shrubs (a focal point) and as part of a garden planted to attract wildlife.

Try These
Buckeye cultivars aren't easy to find, but *Aesculus parviflora* var. *serotina* 'Rogers' has the largest flowers I've seen on a bottlebrush buckeye (about 30 inches long), and it usually blooms a couple of weeks later than the native species.

Butterfly Bush
Buddleia davidii

When, Where, and How to Plant
In spring, plant in a sunny spot that has slightly acid soil (6.0-7.0 pH; a soil test will tell you the pH of your soil); soil should be well drained and fertile. Partial shade cuts down on the shrub's growth and on the number of flowers.

Growing Tips
Butterfly bush will survive some dryness, but it won't produce lots of blooms all summer unless it receives ample moisture. That means you'll need to water when weather is dry. The usual rule is an inch of water per week, from rainfall or that is applied by the gardener. Spread a slow-release shrub fertilizer at the base of the shrub after you've pruned the bush back in early spring or, if necessary, you can wait to fertilize in April. Either time, water in well. If your soil is very acid, a light application of lime every other fall can be beneficial. Watch out for plants that pop up from reseeding and remove them. In the coldest parts of Zone 6, a winter mulch will help protect plants from cold.

Care
Because butterfly bush produces its flowers on new growth, you'll need to cut the bush back to about a foot tall in early spring. That encourages an abundance of new growth and, consequently, flowers. In summer, cut off flower clusters as they fade so the shrub will continue to bloom for a longer period of time. Insects and diseases are not usually troublesome. Avoid insecticides, as they can harm butterflies. Consult the Extension service about other controls of any problems

Landscape Design
Make butterfly bush the centerpiece of a perennial flower border, or place one in a butterfly garden or an area of your yard that's planted to attract wildlife.

Try These
'Butterfly Heaven' has big, fragrant flowers that attract large numbers of butterflies. *Buddleia* × *weyeriana* 'Honeycomb' has yellow blossoms. 'Blue Chip' (sometimes called Low and Behold) is heat- and drought-tolerant, has fragrant flowers, and stays under 3 feet tall.

Many plants in this book attract butterflies (look for the little symbol at the bottom of the plant profiles). But one is simply foolproof. The flowers of a butterfly bush are like a magnet to these winged jewels. The grayish foliage is attractive too, as is the shape of the shrub. The graceful plumes of fragrant flowers (8 to 10 inches long) come in shades of purple, lavender, blue, magenta, pink, rose, orange-yellow, and white to match any flower bed color scheme. All that and it also resists deer! However, the shrub is on the "alert" list of the Tennessee Exotic Pest Council list, meaning that it's invasive in other states with similar conditions, so proceed with caution.

Botanical Pronunciation
BUD-lee-uh day-VID-ee-eye

Bloom Period and Seasonal Color
Midsummer to frost in shades of purple, lavender, blue, magenta, pink, rose, orange-yellow, and white

Mature Height × Spread
2 to 15 feet × 4 to 10 feet

Camellia

Camellia species and hybrids

The first time my family and I lived in Chattanooga, Tennessee—many years ago—I loved to see the large camellia shrubs grown by gardeners in the older parts of town. Pink flowers outdoors in winter! It seemed wonderful to someone like me who had moved from farther north where camellias grew mostly in greenhouses. I wanted to plant some of my own, but then an exceptionally cold winter killed most of them back to the ground. Many of the camellias resprouted, but the owners had to start over with plants that were now much smaller. Now I was less enthusiastic. But I found my solution in a group of cold-hardy camellias, developed by Dr. William Ackerman of the National Arboretum, which extends the range of these beautiful flowering shrubs.

Botanical Pronunciation
ka-MEAL-yuh

Bloom Period and Seasonal Color
Fall through spring blooms in pink, white, red, or variegated

Mature Height × Spread
10 to 15 feet × 5 to 10 feet

When, Where, and How to Plant
Although many people recommend planting camellias in fall, I prefer spring planting. The reason is that an extra-cold winter can kill or severely damage fall-planted shrubs that haven't had time to develop root systems. And often the choice of camellias is much greater in spring, but the decision is yours. Camellias need moist, well-drained, acidic soil that's been amended with lots of fine pine bark or peat moss (with clay, plant on a mound of soil slightly above ground level). Place camellias on the west side of your house or where evergreens block the morning sun in winter, preventing it from "scorching" frozen leaves (see page 191 for shrub planting instructions). Always mulch camellias.

Growing Tips
Camellias have shallow root systems and need regular watering when weekly rainfall is less than an inch. Wait a year after planting before fertilizing; then you may spread 1 pound of cottonseed meal per inch of trunk diameter around the bases of the plants in March or April, or spray with a water-soluble fertilizer for acid-loving plants after blooming ends.

Care
During cold spells, don't cover plants with plastic to protect them—that causes foliage to burn when the sun shines through it; use a blanket, mattress pad, or quilt instead. Although flowers may be damaged by temperatures below 32 degrees Fahrenheit, unopened buds aren't harmed. Do any necessary pruning after blooming stops. Potential insect and disease problems are legion, but you may never experience any.

Landscape Design
Camellias look lovely planted beneath tall pines whose lowest limbs are 20 feet high.

Try These
Of the cold-hardy camellias, I like 'Winter's Interlude', which has pretty pink flowers on a shrub that reaches about 8 to 10 feet tall and is hardy to minus 15 Fahrenheit. 'Winter's Beauty', which has double, pink blossoms, often blooms in December and January. *Camellia japonica* 'Debutante' is an old pink favorite that's relatively hardy.

Crape Myrtle
Lagerstroemia species and hybrids

When, Where, and How to Plant

If you're planting your crape myrtle near a tree or another shrub, be sure you know its eventual width so you can give it plenty of room. If you don't have a spot with full sun, I have bad news—forget about crape myrtle. It simply doesn't bloom well in partial shade. Plant in spring in moist, well-drained soil that has been amended with organic matter (see page 191 for shrub-planting instructions).

Growing Tips

Water deeply when weekly rainfall is less than an inch. Spread a slow-release fertilizer for flowering shrubs at the base of a plant when leaves appear, or spray it with a water-soluble fertilizer in April and in May.

Care

Remove spent flowers (dead or dying ones) to increase the duration of bloom time. After an especially cold winter, wait until crape myrtle has leafed out before assessing damage and pruning out dead wood. Don't be concerned when the shrubs produce leaves late—that's typical. After a normal winter, prune in early spring. Crape myrtles look best when lower branches are gradually removed to expose its beautiful bark. Although other pests are possible, Japanese beetles are the worst. Pick them off by hand, or check with the Extension service about the latest controls. Do not place traps nearby—they attract more beetles to your yard.

Landscape Design

For maximum impact, place several crape myrtles together and underplant with a groundcover.

Try These

Lagerstroemia fauriei 'Fantasy' is a white-flowered crape myrtle bred in North Carolina that's hardy from minus 10 to minus 15 degrees Fahrenheit. It gets to medium tree height. Of the National Arboretum introductions, I like 'Tuskegee', which grows 20 feet tall and as wide. It's cold-hardy, has beautiful red blooms for more than three months, doesn't develop mildew, and has colorful orange-red fall foliage. 'Hopi' is a nice rounded shrub with pink flowers.

Are crape myrtles trees or shrubs? Certainly some grow as tall as small trees, but they aren't in the category of shade trees, even though their fall leaves are colorful. Besides, most of us have more space in our yards for medium-sized shrubs than for trees with flowers way up at the top. Fortunately plant breeders, especially at the National Arboretum, have made huge strides breeding new crape myrtles, which now come in an array of sizes and are more cold-hardy while retaining great heat tolerance. Most of the new cultivars won't mildew, and all of them bloom a long time—often from June into September. Look for crape myrtles with the names of Indian tribes; they're among the best.

Botanical Pronunciation
lay-gear-STRO-me-uh

Bloom Period and Seasonal Color
Summer flowers in red, white, pink, or lavender flowers

Mature Height × Spread
2 to 30 feet × 2 to 25 feet

Deciduous Azalea
Rhododendron species and hybrids

It's hard to imagine that an easygoing shrub with intriguing, often fragrant flowers was once mostly overlooked. But it's true—few homeowners knew there were deciduous azaleas, although everyone was aware of the evergreen ones. The bushes grow more upright than the evergreens, are taller, and most develop fiery fall foliage. They also tolerate more sun. Native plant enthusiasts will find over a dozen species that grow well in many parts of our area. Look for names like sweet azalea (Rhododendron arborescens; white flowers and glossy foliage in summer), pinkshell azalea (R. vaseyi; large pink blooms in May), and flame azalea (R. calendulaceum; yellow-gold to orange flowers in late spring or early summer). Exbury azaleas, bred in England, typically don't stand up well to heat and humidity.

Botanical Pronunciation
row-doe-DEN-dron

Bloom Period and Seasonal Color
Spring to August, depending on species, in bloom colors of yellow, cream, white, red, orange, or violet

Mature Height × Spread
3 to 20 feet × 4 to 15 feet

When, Where, and How to Plant
Don't dig azaleas from the wild to transplant into your yard; buy them from a reputable nursery that specializes in native plants. Deciduous azaleas prefer more sun than their evergreen cousins. Filtered light, beneath tall trees with the lowest limbs at least 20 feet above the ground, is ideal, but half a day of sun is okay for most. Except for swamp azalea, which grows in wet ground, deciduous azaleas appreciate the same soil as the evergreens—moist, acidic, and containing plenty of organic matter. Excellent drainage is important. See page 191 for planting instructions.

Growing Tips
Water during the growing season when weekly rainfall is less than an inch. Most deciduous azaleas aren't sensitive to occasional dry spells once they're mature. But watering *is* important during the shrub's first few years in your yard, while it's getting established. Also, growth and blooming will be better if you water regularly when rainfall is lacking. Fertilizer usually isn't necessary. If you need to fertilize, use an organic fertilizer formulated for shrubs or a pelleted timed-release fertilizer, according to directions, in mid-spring.

Care
Don't shear deciduous azaleas with hedge trimmers. Instead, as soon as the plants have finished blooming, use handpruners to thin any out-of-control growth. These shrubs usually have few pest problems. Cuttings of deciduous azaleas aren't as easy to root as cuttings of evergreen azaleas. If you want to try, take cuttings of new growth as soon as it appears in spring.

Landscape Design
Plant deciduous azaleas as part of a wildflower garden. To extend the season from spring through summer, plant as many of the various species as you can find at the edge of woodlands or beneath tall pines.

Try These
I like swamp azalea (*Rhododendron viscosum*) because I can grow it in wet places; it's hardy to minus 25 degrees Fahrenheit. Its flowers are white or pink.

When, Where, and How to Plant

Plant from spring until early fall, making sure that each group of female cultivars has at least one male (such as 'Raritan Chief' or 'Jim Dandy') to pollinate it. Full sun is best, although most can tolerate a few hours of shade (a few hybrids don't mind more shade; read the label or catalog description to be sure). Winterberries prefer moist, acidic soil and don't mind wet soils. Possumhaw will grow in moderately alkaline soil. Give them plenty of room.

Growing Tips

Although mature plants can usually manage during dry weather, winterberry and the deciduous holly hybrids produce greater crops of berries if they're watered when weekly rainfall is less than an inch. Fertilize with an organic fertilizer for holly shrubs, in March or April.

Care

Cut berry-covered branches in fall and take them indoors to a tall vase (no need to put water in the bottom); they'll last quite well. If deciduous hollies get too large, wait until early spring to cut one-third of the stems back to ground level each year for three years. No serious insect or disease problems affect hollies.

Landscape Design

Deciduous hollies are excellent for massing, as natural hedges, and for attracting wildlife to your yard. If you plant them against a background of needled evergreens, the red berries really stand out.

Try These

I never met a deciduous holly I didn't like, but if you want to start with just a plant or two, I recommend 'Sparkleberry', which is an all-around winner. (Try pairing it with 'Apollo', a male that "blooms" (produces pollen) at the same time; that will ensure a large crop of berries.) *Ilex verticillata* 'Aurantiaca' has orange berries, grows 6 to 8 feet tall, and tolerates wet soil. Give 'Bonfire' plenty of room to spread and stand back to enjoy the visiting birds. It will grow in shade. 'Red Sprite' stays about 5 feet tall.

Deciduous hollies aren't nearly as well known among homeowners as they should be. Maybe that's because they aren't impressive in spring, when most plants are sold. But they more than make up for that in fall when their long stems are completely covered in red or orange (occasionally yellow) fall berries. They really knock your socks off. Birds love them too. Another advantage, for those who don't like the sometimes prickly leaves of evergreen holly, is that deciduous hollies have soft, non-spiny foliage. There are two native species, winterberry (Ilex verticillata) and possumhaw (Ilex decidua), plus Japanese winterberry (Ilex serrata) and lots of hybrids from crosses between native and Japanese winterberries. All are very hardy, large shrubs that are excellent for a naturalized landscape.

Botanical Pronunciation

EYE-lex

Bloom Period and Seasonal Color

Inconspicuous white blooms in spring, followed by fall berries in red, orange, or yellow

Mature Height × Spread

2 to 18 feet × 4 to 10 feet

Evergreen Azalea
Rhododendron species and hybrids

The name azalea comes from the Greek word azaleas, which means "dry." Any gardener familiar with how quickly an evergreen azalea dies when its soil becomes completely dry may wonder why. The name could refer the plants' heat tolerance, which has made them a hit in Southern states for generations, although they originated in various parts of Asia. Some gardening professionals think that evergreen azaleas are overplanted, and I agree. But I nevertheless love the way they brighten up spring. And for those who can't get enough, there are now a number of Encore azaleas—in all the familiar colors—that flower in fall as well as in spring. (Many of them do well in normal Zone 6 winters but can be killed by unusually low temperatures.)

Botanical Pronunciation
row-doe-DEN-dron

Bloom Period and Seasonal Color
Spring in shades of red, pink, white, lavender, orange, and variegated

Mature Height × Spread
1 to 10 feet × 3 to 10 feet

Zones
6 (some hybrids), 7

When, Where, and How to Plant
Plant in spring in a partially shady to shady spot that has rich, moist, well-drained, and acidic soil that contains ample organic matter (add fine pine bark to poor soil). Encore azaleas usually do better in sites with more sun; don't plant them in full shade (see page 191 for shrub planting advice).

Growing Tips
Water when weekly rainfall is less than an inch. In hot, dry summers, it's important to keep the soil moist, because that's when the shrubs are producing their flower buds for next spring. If they don't get enough water, future blooms will be sparse. Mature azaleas won't need fertilizing, but you can encourage young plants to grow and flower by spreading a slow-release organic fertilizer around them in spring or fall.

Care
Pine needle mulch will hold moisture in the soil and protect shallow roots from the cold. Do any necessary pruning right after plants stop blooming. Also prune Encore azaleas, if needed, in spring, after they've finished flowering. Galls may be a problem in wet years and spider mites in dry ones. Pick off galls by hand and remove them from the garden. For spider mite control, see page 34. It may take a year for some Encore azaleas to hit their stride in the garden, so give them time.

Landscape Design
Evergreen azaleas pair beautifully with dogwood trees and make nice foundation shrubs if a house faces north. Surround them with wildflowers in a woodland garden. I like white tulips planted near red azaleas.

Try These
'Glacier' is my favorite white azalea; it produces 3-inch blooms on a 6-foot plant and is hardy in Zone 6. 'Girard Hot Shot', a hardy cultivar that has showy orange-red blooms, draws lots of compliments. It blooms in midseason, so the flowers—which almost cover the plant—rarely get nipped by frost, as early bloomers often do.

Evergreen Holly
Ilex species and hybrids

When, Where, and How to Plant
First learn the eventual height and width of the plant you're buying. Then you won't have to spend hours pruning overgrown hollies that cover up the view from the living room windows or that crowd other shrubs in your yard. In spring plant evergreen hollies in a sunny or mostly sunny spot in well-drained, slightly acidic soil. *Ilex crenata* does fine in partial sun or even partial shade, although it won't grow very fast in shade.

Growing Tips
For the first two years after planting, keep evergreen hollies watered regularly when weekly rainfall is less than an inch. This is especially important in hot weather. (Chinese holly can withstand drought and heat once it's established.) Fertilize yearly in spring, before blooming, with a slow-release shrub fertilizer made for hollies, applied according to package instructions.

Care
Prune in December to take advantage of the shrub's usefulness for holiday decoration. Inkberry has few pests. Spider mites may trouble Japanese holly; Chinese holly may be bothered by scale. See page 34 for control advice or consult the Extension service.

Landscape Design
Depending on the type, evergreen holly shrubs make excellent hedges and barriers, borders along walkways, foundation plantings, and topiaries.

Try These
If you need a nice-looking evergreen for a narrow spot, I highly recommend *Ilex crenata* 'Sky Pencil', which I've had the opportunity to grow since before it was introduced by the National Arboretum. It grows 10 feet tall and no more than 3 feet wide, and doesn't have to be pruned to maintain its shape. It will grow in sun or shade, but needs acid soil. However, it's hardy only in Zone 7 and warmer areas. *Ilex crenata* 'Beehive' is a compact, mounded plant that's hardy; I like it in large containers and use it for winter color in a perennial border. *Ilex cornuta* 'September Gem' fruits very early.

Evergreen holly shrubs take several different forms. The smooth, round leaves of Japanese holly (Ilex crenata) will remind you of boxwood, but it's hardier and more disease-resistant. (It has also earned an "alert" status on the Tennessee Exotic Pest Council's list of invasive plants, which means that it's invasive in regions with similar habitats, so be careful.) An excellent substitute is inkberry (Ilex glabra), a native that's very similar; both have inconspicuous black fruits. Chinese holly (Ilex cornuta) is known for red berries and prickly, glossy leaves, but it isn't always hardy during extra-cold winters. Consider some of the versatile hybrids. A good example is the long-time favorite 'Foster', which has attractive, small leaves and can be kept pruned to size.

Botanical Pronunciation
EYE-lex

Bloom Period and Seasonal Color
Inconspicuous white blooms in spring, followed by red or black berries in fall

Mature Height × Spread
1 to 8 feet × 4 to 15 feet

False Cypress

Chamaecyparis species and hybrids

Until this needled evergreen shrub began to be called false cypress, it was stuck with only its botanical name, which few homeowners could pronounce. It also had another problem, which still lingers today: It almost seems as though no two Chamaecyparis plants look the same—they may be upright or drooping, remain dwarf or grow to 50 feet, have green needles or gold. They've been planted everywhere, but even now many people don't know what they are. The main landscape species are Hinoki false cypress (Chamaecyparis obtusa) and Sawara false cypress (Chamaecyparis pisifera). Just be sure to read the plant's label to understand the eventual size, because some become enormous trees.

Botanical Pronunciation
kam-uh-SIP-a-ris

Bloom Period and Seasonal Color
Evergreen needles; some cultivars have gold needles

Mature Height × Spread
4 to 20 feet × 6 to 8 feet

When, Where, and How to Plant
Plant in spring or early autumn in a sunny spot that has moist, well-drained, slightly acid to neutral soil (a soil test can determine the pH of your soil). If your soil is poor, mix it with some organic matter such as fine pine bark, peat moss, compost, or rotted leaves to fill the planting hole. Otherwise just use the soil that's there (see page 191 for more details about shrub planting).

Growing Tips
Water when weekly rainfall is less than an inch, especially when temperatures are high. Soak the soil thoroughly each time you water. Fertilize with a fertilizer for evergreens at the end of November or with a slow-release shrub fertilizer at the end of March.

Care
In late winter or early spring, remove dead stems and needles from the interior of the shrubs. Pinch the tips of branches in late spring or early summer to shape false cypress. When pruning, don't cut into older sections of the branches that have no needles; the shrub will not regrow from such areas. Insects and diseases should not be a problem, but snow or deer damage may.

Landscape Design
Match the type of *Chamaecyparis* to the spot where you need an evergreen shrub; some dwarfs are ideal for rock gardens and taller cultivars make good screens or hedges. Many are excellent as foundation plantings or in shrub groupings. Those with an unusual appearance make nice specimen shrubs, noteworthy on its own.

Try These
Chamaecyparis obtusa 'Juniperoides' grows 1 foot tall and as wide; it's a nice choice in rock gardens. The native *Chamaecyparis thyoides* (called Atlantic white cedar) grows well in wet areas throughout our region; 'Top Point' is an attractive dwarf form. *Chamaecyparis pisifera* 'Golden Mop' is a dwarf with a threadleaf form (corded branchlets) that can only be described as "cute" (and I don't usually like yellow shrubs).

Flowering Quince
Chaenomeles species and hybrids

When, Where, and How to Plant
Flowering quince is an adaptable shrub, although its leaves may yellow in very alkaline soil. It prefers to be planted in moist, well-drained, slightly acid soil but will readily tolerate dry spots and ordinary clay and doesn't mind being planted in a windy area. Flowering will be best in full sun, but a little afternoon shade generally won't hurt. Plant anytime from spring to early fall (see page 191 for details about the best way to plant shrubs).

Growing Tips
Although flowering quince can be drought-tolerant once it's mature, you'll want to water young plants whenever weekly rainfall is less than an inch. That will help them develop a good root system that enables them to tolerate dryness. Fertilize in early spring with a slow-release shrub fertilizer, according to package instructions.

Care
A number of insects and fungal diseases are common on flowering quince. If you have problems, check with the Extension service about causes and controls. The shrub will live for years without ever needing pruning, but if it does need shaping or cutting back, the best time to do it is just after the flowers have faded. The fruits are said to make good jelly. They're very sour by themselves but good with apples and a sweetener.

Landscape Design
Flowering quince is attractive in a border, and those with thorns make good barriers to keep kids and dogs from crossing the yard at a particular place. They're also good candidates for espalier.

Try These
'Cameo' has double apricot or coral flowers on a bush that reaches about 4 to 5 feet tall. It's ideal for those who prefer soft, pastel color schemes in the garden. Of the Double Take series, 'Scarlet Storm' has large, velvety red double flowers; 'Pink Storm' is coral colored; and the form of the flowers on 'Orange Storm' (my favorite so far) reminds me of a camellia bloom.

This is another shrub that's been getting a new look by breeders. Also called Japanese quince, it's an old-fashioned favorite that provides bright color very early in spring. It requires little effort on the part of the home-owner beyond raking up fallen fruits (if the birds didn't get them). Among its traditional drawbacks are thorns, and the flowers on your shrub look just like your neighbor's and anyone else's in the neighborhood; there's not much variety for those who want something different. But now there's a new group of flowering quinces (called Double Take). They have no thorns but are covered to the tips of the stems with double flowers—in pink, red, and orange—that occasionally rebloom. Suddenly, I'm interested in flowering quince again.

Botanical Pronunciation
key-NOM-uh-leez

Bloom Period and Seasonal Color
Early spring flowers in red, pink, white, and orange followed by berries in fall and winter

Mature Height x Spread
6 to 10 feet x 6 to 10 feet

Forsythia

Forsythia species and hybrids

I realize that my fondness for forsythia, which is often called yellow bells, might put me in the minority. But I'm not going to apologize; I love the bright yellow flowers and the fact that they appear very early in spring. They cheer up my whole world when they bloom. People who don't like this exuberant shrub have usually planted it in a place where it quickly became crowded, or they tried to keep it pruned into short, boxy hedges or little round balls (that removes most of the flowers, the main reason to grow it). But if you give forsythia's arching stems room to grow, and prune the shrub correctly, you'll have a harbinger of spring of which to be proud.

Botanical Pronunciation
for-SITH-ee-uh

Bloom Period and Seasonal Color
Early spring blooms in bright yellow

Mature Height × Spread
2 to 10 feet × 4 to 12 feet

When, Where, and How to Plant
Forsythia is quite an adaptable shrub, although it blooms best in full sun or in a mostly sunny spot. Any average soil—even clay—is fine, either acidic or alkaline, but moist, well-drained soil that contains organic matter is preferred. Plant anytime from early spring until fall, being careful to give forsythia plenty of room to spread (even the dwarfs usually grow wider than they do tall).

Growing Tips
Forsythia is a tough shrub, but it prefers soil that doesn't dry out. When the plant is young, water often enough to keep the soil moist. Once it's older, water when weekly rainfall is less than an inch, if possible, to ensure better blooming. Spread a slow-release shrub fertilizer in spring if growth is slower than desired or if flowering has been sparse (unless you sheared off the flower buds by pruning in summer).

Care
There's more poor pruning done to forsythia than almost any other shrub. It should not be trimmed into a round ball or given a "haircut" (its top lopped off). The correct way is to wait until flowering is finished, then cut one-third of the stems back to the ground each year for three years. That retains the natural, gently weeping habit of the shrub while reducing its size. Forsythia generally experiences few pest problems except (in some areas) deer.

Landscape Design
Since temperatures are likely to still be nippy when forsythia blooms, plant it where the flowers can be seen from inside the house or from the street. Plant large-cupped, gold-flowered daffodils nearby to echo the color of the blooms. Forsythia is a good choice for planting on banks.

Try These
For a small forsythia, try 'Little Renee', which gets 2 feet tall and 4 feet wide. The flowers of *Forsythia* × *intermedia* 'Show Off' cover every inch of the 5-foot-tall, 6-foot-wide shrub. 'Spring Glory' is said to be deer-resistant.

Fothergilla
Fothergilla species and cultivars

When, Where, and How to Plant

Fothergilla likes to be planted in moist, acidic, well-drained soil that contains organic matter. In poor soil, you'll get the best performance if you mix in peat moss, compost, or very fine bark before planting. Avoid alkaline soil and soil that stays wet. Even though this shrub will grow in a spot with a bit of shade, it blooms, and the leaves turn color better in fall, if it's given full sun. Spring is the best time of year to plant (see page 191 for advice about planting shrubs).

Growing Tips

Fothergilla needs regular moisture all its life. Follow the usual rule: Water deeply whenever weekly rainfall is less than 1 inch per week. Fertilize in spring with a slow-release shrub fertilizer spread in a circle on the ground around the shrub, beginning an inch from the trunk and continuing to a foot beyond the tips of the branches.

Care

This is an easy-care shrub. To keep moisture in the soil, maintain a 3-inch mulch of organic matter (pine needles make a good mulch for fothergilla) around the base of a shrub. *Fothergilla gardenia* tends to sucker; dig up unwanted suckers at any time of year (if you do it in spring, you can replant them elsewhere or share them with gardening friends). Pruning is rarely needed on either species. Insects or diseases are almost never a problem.

Landscape Design

Place it along the sunny edges of a woodland flower garden with azaleas and rhododendrons, as well as perennial flowers. Because *Fothergilla gardenia* generally stays lower than 3 or 4 feet high, it's excellent for small spaces and is a good choice for a perennial bed.

Try These

Fothergilla major 'Mt. Airy' has blue-green foliage and *spectacular* yellow-orange-red fall foliage. The leaves of 'Blue Shadow' are even bluer, so it's especially striking when paired with plants that have yellow foliage or flowers. 'Arkansas Beauty' is a taller bush.

When you want a yard that looks great year-round with a minimum of work on your part, it's a good idea to look for shrubs that will do double duty. That is, they have traits that make them standouts in the landscape for two or more seasons. If that's your benchmark, as it is mine, fothergilla, a hardy native of the Southeast, is a triple threat. It has spikes of white, honey-scented flowers in spring (appearing before the leaves on the dwarf species Fothergilla gardenia and with the foliage on Fothergilla major). In summer, nice green or bluish pest-resistant leaves add interest to the shrub border. Then, in autumn, the plant produces some of the most colorful fall foliage around.

Botanical Pronunciation
father-GILL-uh

Bloom Period and Seasonal Color
White flowers in April and May; colorful fall foliage

Mature Height × Spread
2 to 10 feet × 2 to 9 feet

Gardenia
Gardenia jasminoides

A few years ago, I couldn't have imagined recommending growing gardenia as an outdoor shrub in Kentucky or Tennessee. But boy, have things changed! You may still think of gardenia as a super-finicky houseplant, but don't let that image deter you from trying the new, hardier cultivars now available. These charming evergreen shrubs covered with beautiful, wonderfully fragrant flowers during summer aren't always reliable in Zone 6, but I've had them survive to 10 degrees, and each year sees the introduction of hardier cultivars. And they're not fussy at all, in my experience. I love their intriguing variety (and I think that's going to continue). The flowers have different forms—like roses, a pinwheel, or single blooms—and varying fragrances, from light to potent.

Botanical Pronunciation
gar-DEE-nee-uh jazz-min-OY-dees

Bloom Period and Seasonal Color
White flowers in summer

Mature Height x Spread
2 to 6 feet x 3 to 6 feet

When, Where and How to Plant
In spring, plant container-grown gardenias in a protected place, if possible, with moist, well-drained, acid soil that contains plenty of organic matter (acidic soil is a must; have your soil tested if you don't know if it's acidic). Avoid a windy location. Full sun is best, but a spot that's in sun most of the day is fine. Partial shade cuts down on the number of flowers. See page 191 for shrub-planting instructions.

Growing Tips
Gardenias will need watering anytime weekly rainfall is less than an inch. Soaker hoses or trickle irrigation is a good idea if you have more than one of these shrubs. Fertilize every spring with a fertilizer for acid-loving plants; if you use a water-soluble fertilizer instead of a granular one, repeat the application in April and May.

Care
Yellow leaves usually occur because watering hasn't been sufficient or the soil isn't acidic enough. To help correct the latter, spray the plant with a water-soluble fertilizer for acid-loving plants that contains iron, or with chelated iron, according to label instructions. Gardenias are subject to a number of pests. See page 35 for advice on whitefly control. Spray mealybugs with insecticidal soap. Consult the Extension service for advice about other problems that appear. Mulch with 3 inches of shredded leaves or other organic material in fall to protect it from winter's cold. If pruning is needed, do it after flowering. Protect flower buds from late spring frosts.

Landscape Design
Put gardenias near the front door, by the deck, or in a location that you pass by frequently in summertime so you can enjoy their fragrance.

Try These
'Frost Proof' produces very fragrant, velvety white blooms over and over during summer. (It's rated for Zone 7, although I grew it successfully for two winters when living in Zone 6. But your experience may not be the same.) 'August Beauty' has grown quickly and been adaptable for me in Zone 7b. 'Hardy Daisy' (Zone 7) has pinwheel flowers with yellow centers.

Glossy Abelia

Abelia × grandiflora

When, Where, and How to Plant

Glossy abelia prefers moist but well-drained acidic soil, although it will tolerate dry soil and clay that doesn't stay too wet. The shrub also will grow well in either sun or partial shade. Plant in spring or early summer, if possible (see page 191 for directions on how to plant shrubs).

Growing Tips

Fertilize in spring with a slow-release fertilizer for shrubs, applied according to label instructions. Glossy abelia may be semievergreen or even evergreen in Zone 7, depending on the winter; in the coldest parts of Zone 6, it may die back to its roots some years. You should water young plants from spring till frost whenever weekly rainfall is less than an inch. This helps them develop strong roots and become established. Mature plants don't usually need watering, except possibly in prolonged drought.

Care

Glossy abelia flowers on new growth, so prune in late winter or early spring before new growth begins. If the shrub gets lanky, it may be pruned back hard, or you may remove one-third of the stems back to ground level each spring for three years.

Landscape Design

Compact cultivars with variegated leaves make a splash in a perennial border. Abelia stands out in a shrub border.

Try These

If you like your shrubs to have bold, long-lasting color, especially on leaves, 'Kaleidoscope' has impressive variegated foliage that's different from season to season—lime green and yellow in spring and summer (non-fading in the heat), orange and red in fall, and persistent leaves in early winter (plus bright red stems). It grows 2 to 3 feet high and a bit wider. The flowers are white. Silver Anniversary (*Abelia* × 'Panache') is also a compact grower with green-and-silver leaves on red stems with tiny white blooms. 'Edward Goucher', which grows about 5 feet tall and as wide, has large pink flowers and leaves with a reddish cast. 'Pinky Bells' has large flowers all summer.

I've taken a new look at glossy abelia the past few years. There was nothing wrong with it in the past—semievergreen most years, depending on the winter, with (usually) variegated leaves, and small flowers that attracted lots of butterflies and hummingbirds. The flowers are sometimes lightly fragrant. But for some reason, I didn't usually grow abelia. Then some cultivars began to catch my attention. They were compact without pruning, had interesting variegated foliage, and still attracted tons of butterflies. As so often seems to happen with these things, I bought one, and then I saw another that I liked even better, and before long I had abelias in several sections of my yard. I've become a big glossy abelia fan. I bet you will be too.

Botanical Pronunciation
uh-BEE-lee-uh gran-duh-FLOW-ruh

Bloom Period and Seasonal Color
Early summer through fall flowers of pink or white

Mature Height x Spread
3 to 6 feet x 3 to 6 feet

Hydrangea
Hydrangea species and hybrids

I always enjoyed the pink or blue flowers of mophead hydrangeas (Hydrangea macrophylla) and the white blooms of peegee hydrangea (Hydrangea paniculata 'Grandiflora') in others' yards but rarely planted them in my own. Instead I fell in love with the enormous cone-shaped, white blooms of the shade-loving native oakleaf hydrangea (Hydrangea quercifolia). And I became a big fan of 'Annabelle', a cultivar of smooth hydrangea (Hydrangea arborescens), which has impressive 1-foot blooms on a 4- to 6-foot bush. Gradually I warmed up to graceful lacecap hydrangeas, which have more delicate and subtle flowers than the mopheads. But finally I returned to the mopheads, after the introduction of reblooming hydrangeas such as 'Endless Summer', which flower not just once a summer but over and over.

Botanical Pronunciation
high-DRAN-gee-uh

Bloom Period and Seasonal Color
Summer blooms in pink, blue, red, or white

Mature Height × Spread
3 to 10 feet × 3 to 10 feet

When, Where, and How to Plant
Most hydrangeas will grow in sun or shade—although if in sun, they prefer some afternoon shade in the heat of summer. But oakleaf hydrangea needs full to partial shade all day, and lacecaps like to live in the dappled shade beneath trees. Because more exposure to sun means more watering, I plant most hydrangeas in partial shade. Give them moist, well-drained soil that you've enriched with organic matter and a location you can reach with a hose. Plant hydrangeas in spring; see page 191 for directions.

Growing Tips
Regular watering is essential—hydrangeas wilt to let you know they're thirsty. Typically, you can water them deeply after they've drooped, and they'll perk right up. In the hot summer months, you may need to water twice a week if rainfall isn't adequate. Fertilize in spring with an organic shrub fertilizer, according to package directions.

Care
Always mulch to keep moisture in the soil. Hydrangeas don't necessarily need much pruning, but if they do, the best time for most is right after they bloom. Exceptions are smooth hydrangea and peegee hydrangea, which are pruned in late winter or very early spring. Reblooming hydrangeas are pruned in the spring. Rejuvenate any hydrangea by removing one-third of the stems each year for three years. Cut flower heads from the plant just after they've faded for use in dried arrangements. If the shrub didn't bloom, it's often because the buds were killed by a late-spring cold snap (or it was pruned at the wrong time). Insects and diseases aren't usually serious.

Landscape Design
Surround pink-flowered hydrangeas with blue-flowered perennials. Oakleaf hydrangeas are nice with ferns and variegated hostas.

Try These
Hydrangea arborescens 'Invincibelle' resembles 'Annabelle' but has pink flowers instead of white. 'Snowflake' is an oakleaf hydrangea with double blossoms. *Hydrangea quercifolia* 'Snow Queen' grows 4 to 6 feet high; its leaves turn red in fall.

Kerria

Kerria japonica

When, Where, and How to Plant

Give kerria some space to grow since it suckers freely (especially in loose or rich soil) and eventually forms large colonies, if you let it. If you have a woodland spot, that's ideal. But even if you plan to control its spread, this is a shrub that's likely to reach from 6 to 10 feet wide. Because the shrub's leaves will burn in the afternoon sun, it needs to be planted in shade or partial shade. Plant it anytime from late winter until August. Kerria adapts to almost any soil, but prefers it moist and well-drained. See page 191 for shrub planting directions.

Growing Tips

Keep the soil moist in early years, until the plant becomes established. Later, if you can water during dry spells, you'll see less stem dieback, and the shrub will flower more. Occasional watering will probably be necessary in rocky soil. Don't fertilize; that encourages excessive stem growth at the expense of flowers.

Care

Kerria must be pruned each spring after it flowers to remove dead stems and tips of stems that have died back, as well as to control size. To rejuvenate an overgrown shrub, cut one-third of the stems back to the ground each year for three years. Dig or pull up unwanted suckers at any time of year. Insects and diseases are not usually a problem with kerria.

Landscape Design

I always put kerria not too far from my front door so I can glimpse the green stems in winter and enjoy the flowers in spring. The single-flowering species is an excellent companion for woodland wildflowers. I like to plant daffodils nearby to echo its cheerful color.

Try These

'Golden Guinea' produces 2-inch single flowers that stay in bloom a long time. 'Shannon' has been trouble-free in my garden; it grows 5 to 6 feet tall and produces good-sized single blossoms.

Why don't many people know about kerria? It has much to recommend it: It blooms in spring, right about the time forsythia finishes, extending the flowering season. And you can find kerrias that have two different forms of flowers. The one that's most common ('Pleniflora', above) has small, double blooms in a bright gold color. They look like little gold balls. (I've heard gardeners call this plant Yellow Rose of Texas.) But my favorite cultivars have single, clear yellow blossoms shaped like buttercups. In winter, the shrub's stems—which have a graceful arching habit in the species and some cultivars—are bright green, adding an interesting touch to the landscape. As well as being attractive, this shrub is easy to grow. Now you know about kerria too, so plant some in your garden!

Botanical Pronunciation
KER-ee-uh ja-PON-ick-uh

Bloom Period and Seasonal Color
Yellow or gold in mid-spring

Mature Height × Spread
3 to 8 feet × 6 to 10 feet

Leucothoe
Leucothoe species and hybrids

If you're looking for something different in a flowering evergreen shrub for a shady or partially shady area, look at leucothoe. You'll find several species, including some natives. What the various species and cultivars of leucothoe have in common is broad, evergreen leaves on graceful arching branches. This almost weeping effect is especially welcome in a shrub. Leucothoe fontanesiana grows 3 to 6 feet tall, and about as wide, in Zones 6 and 7a. Leucothoe axillaris (hardy throughout Kentucky and Tennessee) stays about 2 to 4 feet high. Florida leucothoe (Agarista populifolia, also sold as Leucothoe populifolia) may reach 15 feet tall, although it can be kept pruned much shorter. It's good in Zone 7 gardens and is probably hardy in Zone 6.

Botanical Pronunciation
loo-KOTH-oh-ee

Bloom Period and Seasonal Color
Spring blooms in white

Mature Height × Spread
2 to 6 feet × 3 to 7 feet

When, Where, and How to Plant
Plant in moist, well-drained, acidic soil in a shady or partially shaded spot (full shade may be better in Zone 7). If you're interested in plants that have reddish coloration on the new leaves, buy the shrub in spring to make sure you get one that has this characteristic. Leucothoe doesn't do well in rocky soils that dry out or where it can be whipped by the wind. In colder climates, placing it in a protected location will help protect it from winter damage. Improve the soil with organic matter, if your soil doesn't contain ample humus. You may plant from spring until early fall, but spring is best, because it lessens the possibility of winter damage the first year. See page 191 for advice about how to plant shrubs.

Growing Tips
This is a shrub that must be kept watered; it may develop problems if it's stressed. Water often enough to keep the soil moist. Fertilize in early spring with an organic fertilizer made for shrubs, applied according to package directions.

Care
Keep a mulch of organic material, such as pine needles or fine pine bark, around the plant year-round to hold moisture in the soil. Prune, if needed, right after flowering. If the plant becomes overgrown, it may be cut back to 18 inches high and allowed to regrow. Leaf spots, caused by fungi, are fairly prevalent. Check with the Extension service about possible controls.

Landscape Design
Plant leucothoe with rhododendrons, or put it on a hill where its drooping form can be admired. I like to place it so it hides the leggy base of Carolina jessamine.

Try These
Leucothoe axillaris 'Sarah's Choice' is about 3 feet tall and produces more flowers than any other leucothoe I've grown. *Leucothoe fontanesiana* 'Girard's Rainbow' has pinkish coppery new foliage.

When, Where, and How to Plant

Plant in moist, well-drained, acidic soil (alkaline soil causes yellowish leaves). Enrich the planting hole with organic matter to hold moisture. Loropetalum tolerates many light intensities, from full sun to full shade, but part sun and part shade seem to be best. (In full shade, flowering is less and leaf color may not be as intense.) You can plant anytime from spring until early fall, but I prefer spring to avoid potential problems with cold damage on fall-planted shrubs.

Growing Tips

Water to keep the soil moist around young plants. Mature shrubs can tolerate some dryness, but all grow and bloom better (and are better able to withstand extra cold winters) if regularly watered whenever weekly rainfall is less than an inch. The color of the leaves is often brighter if you fertilize each spring with a slow-release fertilizer made for shrubs.

Care

Damage to stems and defoliation may occur when temperatures drop to 0 to 5 degrees Fahrenheit (although those planted in protected places are less likely to be harmed). If damage occurs, wait to see if leaves and stems regrow, and then prune dead wood out as necessary. Try to maintain the graceful shape, rather than lopping off the top of the plant. Every time you trim this shrub in summer, it will bloom. Loropetalum doesn't usually suffer from insect or disease infestations. Maintain a year-round mulch of pine needles to hold moisture in the soil.

Landscape Design

Use loropetalum as a screen, hedge, or foundation plant, or group several together for maximum impact.

Try These

'Sizzling Pink' has deep purple foliage and hot pink flowers. 'Purple Diamond' has leaves that are purple on top and bottom. In Zone 6, look for 'Zhuzhou Fuchsia'; it has deep burgundy leaves and fuchsia flowers on a 3- to 6-foot shrub. 'Purple Pixie' is a groundcover loropetalum that grows about 18 inches high and 3 feet wide.

My friend Steve Bender, senior writer at Southern Living *magazine, says that most homeowners call this "that purple plant." Well, with a name like loropetalum, you can understand why. Although practically unknown about 10 years ago, it has grown wildly popular in Zone 7 and warmer climes. Once, I was thrilled to find one unnamed loropetalum in a nursery; now, there are so many different cultivars, I have trouble keeping up with all the differences among them. There's even one that's rated for Zone 6 (see the Try These section). But I'll tell you a secret—Zone 6 dwellers may be able to grow many of the cultivars of loropetalum in sheltered spots, although they won't necessarily be evergreen, and they'll stay relatively small.*

Botanical Pronunciation

lor-row-PET-a-lum chi-NIN-see

Bloom Period and Seasonal Color

Pink or white flowers in spring and throughout the summer

Mature Height × Spread

6 to 12 feet × 5 to 10 feet

Zones

Zone 7 (most cultivars)

Ninebark

Physocarpus opulifolius

Although you may not be familiar with ninebark, this very hardy deciduous shrub with arching branches is native to Kentucky, Tennessee, and neighboring states. It tolerates a wide range of soil conditions and is very easy to grow. It's also a shrub that provides three seasons of interest in the garden. The characteristic that gave the shrub its common name is the peeling, or exfoliating, reddish brown bark that is prominent during winter. The late spring to early summer flower clusters, which will remind you of spirea, attract butterflies. And the reddish fall fruits are not only of ornamental interest, they will draw birds to your landscape. A bonus is that many cultivars have brightly colored foliage in hues from purple to lime green.

Botanical Pronunciation
fie-so-CAR-pus op-you-lih-FOE-lee-us

Bloom Period and Seasonal Color
White or pink flowers from late spring to early summer; berries in fall

Mature Height x Spread
5 to 8 feet x 4 to 8 feet

When, Where, and How to Plant
Although ninebark adapts to most growing conditions—including clay and rocky soils—the ideal location is in moist but well-drained acidic soil and full sun to partial shade. Plant in spring or early fall. This shrub can grow quickly, so give it enough room that it won't be crowded. See page 191 for directions on the best way to plant shrubs.

Growing Tips
Water weekly when the plant is young if weekly rainfall is less than an inch. After the shrub is mature, you'll need to water only during drought (and often ninebark is drought-tolerant). Fertilize in early spring with a slow-release shrub fertilizer, applied according to label instructions.

Care
Ninebark doesn't have any insect or disease problems of note. It will develop suckers at the base; dig them out as desired to keep the shrub contained. To renew an older plant and improve its appearance, cut the stems to ground level in early spring and let it grow back. Or, to renew the shrub more gradually, you may cut one-third of the stems to ground level each year for three years. Do any other pruning soon after flowers have faded. Watch out for deer.

Landscape Design
Ninebark is ideal for a garden that's planted to attract birds, butterflies, and small wildlife. It makes a nice addition to a native plant garden and is often used as a flowering, deciduous hedge. It's also used to control erosion.

Try These
Coppertina (*P. opulifolius* 'Mindia') has orange-copper foliage in spring; it turns red in summer. 'Dart's Gold' has yellow-gold or chartreuse leaves in summer, showy white flowers beginning in midsummer, and brilliant orange foliage in fall. 'Center Glow' has purple leaves that are gold in the center. Summer Wine (*P. opulifolius* 'Seward') has purplish bronze foliage on a shrub that grows only 3 feet tall and has pinkish white flowers. 'Nanus' is a dwarf (2 feet by 2 feet).

Redvein Enkianthus

Enkianthus campanulatus

When, Where, and How to Plant

Redvein enkianthus thrives in the same conditions as rhododendrons—moist, well-drained, acidic soil that contains ample organic matter. Add peat moss, compost, or finely shredded bark to poor or average soil to improve its humus content before planting. Plant anytime from spring until early autumn in a sunny spot or in an area that receives a few hours of afternoon shade (see page 191 for shrub planting directions).

Growing Tips

In hot summers, redvein enkianthus will suffer if the soil is allowed to dry out. Water deeply at least weekly whenever rainfall is less than an inch over a period of seven days. You may want to place a soaker hose at the base of this shrub unless you have clay soil, in which case you want to be careful to avoid overwatering. Each spring, spread a slow-release shrub fertilizer, according to package directions, in a widening circle around the base of the shrub, beginning 1 to 2 inches from the trunk and continuing to 1 foot beyond the tips of the branches; water in.

Care

Maintain a 2- to 3-inch year-round mulch of organic material such as fine bark, shredded leaves, or pine needles to hold moisture in the soil. These shrubs rarely need much pruning, but if any becomes necessary, do it right after blooming ceases. Redvein enkianthus doesn't usually suffer from diseases or insects.

Landscape Design

Grow them near rhododendrons, deciduous azaleas, mountain laurel, or Japanese stewartia.

Try These

The flowers of 'Red Velvet' are a deeper color than most cultivars; the foliage turns red in fall too. 'Albiflorus' has cream-colored flowers with no veining. 'Red Bells' has two-toned red-and-cream flowers and outstanding fall color; this cultivar grows upright. 'Sikokianus' is a fast grower that has maroon buds opening to red bells streaked with shrimp pink. Its leaves turn maroon with pink markings.

Few of us are able to resist a plant with delicate, bell-shaped flowers. But the flowers on redvein enkianthus are even more appealing because of their unexpected coloration—cream combined with red veining or just a solid red that often attracts hummingbirds—and fragrance. It's quite a showstopper. If that's not enough, you'll find other reasons to buy redvein enkianthus. It's hardy throughout our region, so you don't have to worry about damage from cold winters. Leaves are bluish green in summer, changing to brilliant shades of red, orange, and yellow in fall. Also, its branches are almost horizontal, giving the shrub an arresting appearance in winter. In addition, it grows to a medium size that fits nicely into just about any yard.

Botanical Pronunciation

en-key-AN-thus kam-pan-u-LAY-tus

Bloom Period and Seasonal Color

White, pink, red, cream, or light orange in late spring to early summer

Mature Height × Spread

6 to 15 feet × 4 to 15 feet

Rhododendron
Rhododendron species and hybrids

With rhododendrons, gardeners in Tennessee and Kentucky don't need to be concerned about winter-hardiness; these shrubs are hardy in climates much colder than ours. Instead potential drawbacks include summer heat and humidity (particularly in Zone 7) and the poorly drained clay soil that so many of us have. The good news is that rhododendrons can be grown anywhere in our region as long as the soil is acidic, contains plenty of organic matter, and has good drainage. Rhododendrons also need morning sun or good, bright light all day. Although the roots will rot if kept too wet, adequate moisture is necessary to keep rhododendrons healthy and growing well. These aren't plant-it-and-forget-it shrubs, but their elegant presence and gorgeous flowers make them worth your time.

Botanical Pronunciation
row-doe-DEN-dron

Bloom Period and Seasonal Color
Shades of white, pink, red, lavender, or yellow in late spring

Mature Height × Spread
1 to 15 feet × 18 inches to 12 feet

When, Where, and How to Plant
Taking time to site rhododendrons correctly is one of the keys to success. The first need is outstanding drainage; too much water is almost always fatal. A second necessity is acidic soil that contains or has been amended with an ample amount of organic matter. Grow in a spot that's protected from the wind. Members of the American Rhododendron Society taught me that rhododendrons are not full-shade plants; they need half a day of sun in order to bloom well. Place them where morning sun won't "burn" frozen leaves in the winter, but make sure they aren't in full afternoon sun in summer. To increase drainage, gardeners with clay soil may plant rhododendrons in raised beds, but be aware that if you do, you'll need to water and fertilize frequently. See page 191 for instructions on planting shrubs. Spring is the best time to plant and is also when the most rhododendrons are available.

Growing Tips
Water if weekly rainfall is less than an inch, especially if temperatures are high. Spread a granular slow-release fertilizer on the ground around the shrub, according to label directions, at the end of March.

Care
Trim off winter damage in spring as new growth begins. Prune some each year, right after flowering, to keep the shrubs in shape; pruning an overgrown rhododendron isn't easy or always successful. Many insects and diseases pose potential problems, but if the shrub is properly planted and cared for, few should materialize.

Landscape Design
Make rhododendrons the centerpiece of a woodland garden by planting ferns, deciduous azaleas, and wildflowers around them.

Try These
'Roseum' is absolutely foolproof in any garden, although it often takes several years to begin blooming; it's a large shrub. Also good in Zone 7 are 'Roseum Elegans' and 'English Roseum'. (I always consult members of the rhododendron society near where I live for localized advice on cultivars.)

When, Where, and How to Plant

Plant bare-root roses from late February to late March in Zone 7, and late March to mid-April in Zone 6. You'll know it's time to plant roses when forsythia blooms. Dig a large hole in an area that gets six or more hours of sun, and enrich the soil with plenty of organic matter. Mound a cone of soil in the center of the hole and spread the roots over it so that the bud union (the swelling above where the canes and roots join) is at ground level or an inch above in Zone 7 or about 2 inches below ground level in Zone 6. Holding the bush upright, replace the soil in the hole, packing it down. Water thoroughly and mulch. Set out container-grown roses from early summer until the end of August. Leave 3 to 4 feet between bushes when planting.

Growing Tips

Give roses at least an inch of moisture per week. Fertilize with a granular rose food after each flush of flowers fades. Stop fertilizing by the end of August to avoid tender new growth, which can sustain winter damage.

Care

See page 31 for directions on pruning roses, which should be done each spring. Remove flowers from the bush after they fade. Roses are subject to many insects and diseases. The best way to avoid them is to choose roses that aren't subject to them. The American Rose Society publishes a yearly *Handbook for Selecting Roses,* in which members rank the roses they've grown. I always choose ones that come in at the top. (Visit the ARS website, www.ars.org, to order the booklet.)

Landscape Design

Silver-foliaged *Artemisia* 'Powis Castle' accents roses beautifully.

Try These

'Rainbow Knock Out' has blooms of coral with a yellow center. The red roses on 'Double Knock Out' look just like you think a rose should. 'Munstead Wood' (a David Austin rose) is deep crimson and lightly fragrant.

There's almost no one who doesn't like roses—to look at and to sniff, at least. But many people don't like to grow roses, because they think they're difficult (and truthfully, some of them are). But over the past few years, that objection has pretty much been overcome. There's been a rose revolution. So many easy-care roses have been introduced that anyone can successfully grow roses almost anywhere there's a sunny spot and decent soil, providing they keep the bushes watered. (Knock Out is still the best, but each year more easy-care roses are introduced.) The other development that has made a big difference in rose growing is the introduction of David Austin English roses, which have such a romantic, old-fashioned look and are easy to grow.

Botanical Pronunciation
ROW-suh

Bloom Period and Seasonal Color
Shades of white, pink, red, yellow, orange, and bicolors from late spring until a hard frost

Mature Height × Spread
6 inches to 8 feet × 8 inches to 12 feet

Smoke Bush
Cotinus coggygria

I always shake my head slightly at the idea that smoke bush, or smoke tree, is grown not for the appearance of its flowers at their peak, but for the spectacular show the fluffy flower clusters put on after they've faded. The big, billowing panicles remind me of cotton candy, but the overall effect is of large shrubs covered in pinkish "smoke." If you want smoke bushes with reddish purple foliage, buy plants in mid to late summer to see how they look then, because some have leaves that fade to green. 'Royal Purple' and 'Velvet Cloak' are two that retain their leaf coloration throughout the summer. Seed-grown smoke bushes have variable leaf color, so look for named cultivars. Smoke bush's fall color is usually good.

Botanical Pronunciation
ko-TIE-nus ko-GIG-ree-uh

Bloom Period and Seasonal Color
Yellowish in late spring to early summer; pink to purple "smoke" in early summer

Mature Height × Spread
8 to 25 feet × 10 to 20 feet

When, Where, and How to Plant
Because smoke bush likes loose, fast-draining soil, it is ideal for gardeners with poor, rocky ground, but it grows well in almost any soil, except those that stay wet. Plant from early spring until early fall in full sun. See page 191 for directions on how to properly plant shrubs.

Growing Tips
Smoke bush leafs out late—don't be concerned that it has died over winter when other plants produce their leaves before this shrub does. This is a plant that requires quite a bit of watering when young, so for the first two years, keep the soil evenly moist if rainfall is less than an inch per week. Once mature, smoke bush can tolerate dry soil but may need watering in hot, dry summers, especially in poor soils. Fertilizer isn't usually necessary, but you may want to fertilize purple-leaved cultivars to encourage new growth, which is usually the most colorful. If so, use a slow-release fertilizer for shrubs, according to package directions, at the end of March or April.

Care
Little pruning is necessary or desirable. If the plant develops straggly stems, trim them in early spring. Smoke tree has no serious insect or disease problems.

Landscape Design
Smoke tree is usually grown singly as a specimen shrub, placed where it can be admired. But it's also nice as the centerpiece of a flower border surrounded by plants with pink or purple flowers or silver foliage. And because of its size, it's a colorful choice for screening.

Try These
'Golden Spirit' has yellow leaves all season; it makes a nice contrast with purple-leaved cultivars. 'Grace' has nice purplish leaves in summer but really shines with colorful fall foliage of pink, red, purple, and orange; it grows about 14 feet tall. *C. obovatus* is a native smoke bush (all others are of European and Asian origin); it has green leaves and grows about 20 feet high.

Spirea

Spiraea species and hybrids

When, Where, and How to Plant

Plant anytime from spring until early fall in a sunny or mostly sunny spot. Spirea tolerates any average soil, except those that stay wet and don't drain well. (It adapts fine to ordinary clay.) For best results in poor soil, mix organic matter with the soil in the hole before planting. The ideal planting spot is in moist, well-drained soil. Space plants according to their eventual mature size. See page 191 for shrub planting instructions.

Growing Tips

Most spireas need a moderate amount of water, especially when they're young. For the first two years, water whenever weekly rainfall is less than an inch. Mature plants can usually tolerate dry spells, although you may want to water in prolonged drought. Fertilize in spring with a slow-release shrub fertilizer.

Care

Prune *Spiraea* × *bumalda*, if needed, in late winter or early spring, before growth starts. Shearing the plants right after flowering shapes them and encourages more blooming later. Prune bridal wreath types right after flowering. Rejuvenate overgrown bridal wreath shrubs by cutting one-third of the old stems back to the ground each year for three years. Numerous insects and diseases have an affinity for spirea, but few become real problems. Contact the Extension service for advice if problems arise.

Landscape Design

The small, mounded plants of *Spiraea* × *bumalda* are often massed together as a shrubby groundcover or hedge. One with especially colorful foliage in three seasons is an excellent choice for a rock garden. Try several near the base of smoke bush. 'Limemound' is an attractive edging for a shrub border or along a fence or wall.

Try These

'Fire Light' grows 2 to 3 feet tall and has red-orange new growth; fall color is fiery red. 'Limemound' forms a ball about 2 feet tall by 3 feet wide. *Spiraea japonica* 'Shirobana' has pink, red, and white blooms on the same plant. 'Neon Flash' has bright red flowers.

When someone mentions spirea, do you think of bridal wreath (Spiraea prunifolia 'Plena'), the tall shrub with graceful arching stems that are lined with tiny white blooms in spring and colorful foliage in fall? Or does a low, mounded plant (Spiraea × bumalda) with chartreuse foliage and pink blooms from summer into autumn come to mind? Because the old-fashioned, double-flowering bridal wreath shrub is now considered invasive in Kentucky and Tennessee, you should avoid planting it. But Bumald spirea is excellent for several reasons. It is compact and low-growing, quite adaptable as to light and soil, has colorful leaves in three seasons, and pink flowers in early summer. It's quite cold-hardy and heat-tolerant and so adapts to the winters and summers of our region.

Botanical Pronunciation

spy-REE-uh

Bloom Period and Seasonal Color

White in spring, or pink from spring into fall

Mature Height × Spread

18 inches to 9 feet × 4 to 8 feet

Summersweet
Clethra alnifolia

If I were queen of the world, all flowers would have a light, sweet fragrance. It's one of the first things I look for when I'm choosing a plant for my yard. After all, why shouldn't a plant smell as good as it looks? Summersweet's pink or white flower clusters certainly do—and are as much appreciated by bees as by humans. But a nice fragrance and pretty flowers aren't the only sterling attributes of this native shrub, also known as sweet pepperbush. It thrives in wet places, which so many other plants won't. It also adapts to almost any light—from partial shade to full sun—is both heat- and cold-tolerant, and has excellent fall foliage color. Nicest of all, it's easy to grow.

Botanical Pronunciation
KLETH-ruh al-ni-FO-lee-uh

Bloom Period and Seasonal Color
White or pink from mid to late summer

Mature Height × Spread
4 by 10 feet × 4 by 8 feet

When, Where, and How to Plant

Plant from spring until early autumn in part sun or part shade. Full sun is okay, but the shrub grows larger and blooms better with some relief from summer's hot afternoon sun. Although it's adaptable as to soils, summersweet prefers moist, well-drained, acidic soil that contains abundant organic matter (a soil test can tell you if the pH of your soil is acid, alkaline, or neutral). In the wild, summersweet grows in wet places, so it will tolerate areas that are occasionally wet during the growing season. See page 191 for shrub planting directions.

Growing Tips

Although summersweet can tolerate dry soil, it grows best and produces the most flowers when watered regularly. When the plant is young, keep the soil moist. Fertilize at the end of March or April with a slow-release fertilizer made for shrubs.

Care

Summersweet has few insects or diseases. It flowers on the current year's growth, so do any required pruning in late winter before new growth begins. Little pruning is usually needed, but if it has grown too large for the spot where it's planted, cut back one-fourth of the stems to the ground each year for four years. The plant spreads by rhizomes and suckers; remove unwanted plants at any time.

Landscape Design

Grow with Virginia sweetspire on the edge of a wooded area.

Try These

'Sixteen Candles' has larger flowers than most cultivars, and they last weeks, much to the delight of butterflies; it's low-growing. 'September Beauty' flowers at the end of summer and has good yellow fall leaf color. 'Chattanooga' (discovered at the Tennessee Aquarium) has nice white flowers on a shrub that grows to about 7 feet tall. 'Hummingbird' has white blooms on a compact plant (about 3 feet high) with deep green leaves in summer and clear yellow foliage in fall. 'Ruby Spice' is the cultivar with the pinkest flowers; it's a 6- to 8-foot shrub.

Sweet Shrub
Calycanthus floridus

When, Where, and How to Plant

Buy sweet shrub when it's in bloom to make sure the flowers are fragrant (seed-grown shrubs often have no aroma). Plant in from mid-spring to early summer in any average soil, whether it's acidic or alkaline. Moist, well-drained soil that contains organic matter is ideal. This shrub will adapt to various amounts of light, from full sun to part shade. Sweet shrub doesn't grow as large in a mostly sunny area. In too much shade, it may get leggy or scraggly. It also grows more slowly in dry soil. See page 191 for shrub planting instructions. Spread 2 to 3 inches of organic mulch—such as pine needles, shredded leaves, or fine pine bark—around the base of a shrub, beginning an inch or so from the trunk.

Growing Tips

Keep the soil moist around young shrubs until they are established in your yard (about two years). Water mature plants during the growing season when weekly rainfall has been less than an inch, but don't let soil stand in water. Apply a slow-release shrub fertilizer, according to label directions, in March or April.

Care

Little pruning is usually required. If it's needed, prune in very early spring or wait until just after flowering, as the shrub blooms on new growth as well as the previous year's wood. Dig up suckers as needed. If you like, you may cut off some of the flowers and use them in indoor arrangements. Sweet shrub has no insect or disease problems.

Landscape Design

Plant Carolina allspice where you can appreciate its delightful aroma—next to a garden bench, near a walkway, or beside the patio. It's a good companion in a shrub border.

Try These

'Hartlage Wine' has large, maroon flowers on a large shrub (8 to 15 feet tall and 10 feet wide). 'Michael Lindsey' has superb fragrance, good-looking foliage, and nice yellow fall color.

Sweet shrub—also known as Carolina allspice—is one of those plants that hide their nicest traits behind an unassuming demeanor. It's hardy, deer-resistant, native, and its leaves are aromatic. But the reason I love to grow it is the sweet fragrance of sweet shrub's reddish maroon flowers. It has been described as smelling like strawberries, pineapple, or banana—or all three (for that reason, sometimes the shrub is called strawberry bush). To me, the scent is like pineapple sage. But however you describe it, I think the aroma is heavenly. Sweet shrub's flowers are interesting, although not showy, and the foliage turns a nice yellow in fall. It's also easy to grow and flexible in its soil and light requirements.

Botanical Pronunciation
kal-i-KAN-thus FLOOR-i-dus

Bloom Period and Seasonal Color
Maroon flowers from mid-spring into summer; yellow fall foliage

Mature Height × Spread
6 to 10 feet × 6 to 12 feet

Viburnum

Viburnum species and hybrids

It's estimated that there are about 150 species of viburnum and many more cultivars. So read the plant labels carefully and ask for advice as you choose. If you want fragrance, buy a shrub when it's in bloom—some viburnums have a delightful scent, others don't. The fall and winter berries on all viburnums—much appreciated by birds—may be blue, black, pink, orange, and yellow, as well as red so that adds another element to your decision making. The size and shape of the flowers vary, as does time of bloom, but generally the blossoms are white or pink. Most viburnums are deciduous shrubs, but some are evergreen. The most impressive is double-file viburnum (Viburnum plicatum tomentosum). The snowballs are extremely popular, but do consider others.

Botanical Pronunciation
vie-BURR-num

Bloom Period and Seasonal Color
White or pink in spring to summer; varies by species

Mature Height × Spread
2 to 30 feet × 4 to 15 feet

When, Where, and How to Plant
Because viburnums vary so, it's a good idea to talk with a knowledgeable person at the nursery where you buy your shrub so you can learn the specific soil and light requirements for that particular species and hybrid. In general, you can count on most viburnums being happy in sections of your yard that have six or more hours of sun (evergreens appreciate some afternoon shade, especially in Zone 7). You're probably also safe in choosing an area with slightly acidic, moist, well-drained soil that contains organic matter. Plant evergreen viburnums in spring, deciduous types from spring until fall (see page 191 for how-to directions for planting a shrub). Mulch with 2 to 3 inches of organic material after planting.

Growing Tips
Water when weekly rainfall is less than an inch. Apply a slow-release fertilizer for flowering shrubs, according to label directions, in spring before new growth appears.

Care
The list of potential pest problems on viburnums is long, but you'll be pleased to know that they rarely materialize. If problems do crop up, consult the Extension service to find solutions. Do any necessary pruning just after flowering. Remove water sprouts (vertical growth on stems) as they appear.

Landscape Design
There's a viburnum for just about any shrub use in the landscape—screening, specimen, mixed into a shrub or flower border, or as a hedge. Because of the berries, these shrubs are a must for anyone who wants to attract wildlife. 'Summer Snowflake' (a doublefile viburnum) fits well into a cottage garden.

Try These
Viburnum plicatum tomentosum 'Mariesii' is a beautiful doublefile viburnum that reaches about 8 feet tall and 10 feet wide at maturity. *Viburnum × burkwoodii* 'Mohawk' has dark red flower buds that open to white waxy flowers with red blotches on the back; they have a fragrance similar to clove. *Viburnum davidii* is an evergreen for Zone 7; it has blue berries.

Virginia Sweetspire
Itea virginica

When, Where, and How to Plant

Although Virginia sweetspire is known for its love of wet soils—great news for those who have clay—it nevertheless is relatively drought-tolerant once it's established. So if you don't have any damp or moist places in your yard, plant the shrub in any average soil. It grows largest in full sun but doesn't mind partial shade, making it a nice understory shrub. (I prefer to plant Virginia sweetspire in part shade and soil that's on the dry side so it will stay more compact and not spread as much.) Plant anytime from spring until early autumn (see page 191 for planting directions). Mulch with 3 inches of pine straw or other organic material.

Growing Tips

Water regularly the first two or three years, to keep the soil moist. Once the shrub is established, it will be necessary to water only during dry spells. Water deeply each time you water. Fertilize in spring with an organic fertilizer made for shrubs, following package directions.

Care

Unless the shrub is planted in a wet spot, keep it mulched year-round to conserve moisture in the soil. Do any necessary pruning just after flowering is finished. Insects and diseases rarely bother Virginia sweetspire. If you notice spots on the leaves, they are generally harmless. Remove unwanted suckers at any time; these may be replanted if dug up carefully. If suckers are left in place, the shrub creates a wide colony when soil is good.

Landscape Design

Grow with wildflowers and ferns, or place beside a water garden or stream.

Try These

'Merlot' has deep red fall leaf color. 'Henry's Garnet' is the best-known and most reliable cultivar. It thrives in summer heat and winter cold, and it has excellent flowers and fall color. 'Little Henry' grows only 2 feet tall. 'Saturnalia' is an upright shrub with very good fall color.

I'm a long-time fan of Virginia sweetspire. I think I was first attracted to it because I'm a native Virginian. But when I was living on a shady acre filled with tall trees, I realized what an asset it was to a woodland garden. I appreciated the way it extended the spring flowering season by blooming after most other shrubs had finished. And I enjoyed the two seasons of beauty it produced: flowers in late spring or early summer and then brilliant red fall foliage. It tolerated shade as well as sun and thrived in my dry, rocky ground, although it's supposed to prefer moist soil. I figured that you can't ask much more of a shrub than that, and I've grown it ever since.

Botanical Pronunciation
eye-TEE-uh ver-GIN-i-kuh

Bloom Period and Seasonal Color
White in late spring to early summer

Mature Height × Spread
3 to 5 feet × 3 to 6 feet

Weigela

Weigela florida

For a long time, I didn't see anyone but me growing weigela. I'm sure there were gardeners who stuck with this shrub; I just never saw them. I guessed that weigela was considered old-fashioned, and therefore hard to find at garden centers, which like to carry the latest hybrids. But I liked the rose-colored flowers and the arching form of the bush. Then a number of breeding advances took the quiet, old-fashioned shrub into new territory. New hybrids of weigela began hitting the market, with fascinating leaf colors and a variety of shrub sizes. Not only do these new introductions present an impressive appearance but all of them are hardy throughout Tennessee and Kentucky. I'm pleased to see weigela making a comeback.

Botanical Pronunciation
wie-GEE-luh FLOOR-ih-duh

Bloom Period and Seasonal Color
Late spring to early summer flowers in pink, red, or white

Mature Height x Spread
6 to 9 feet x 9 to 12 feet

When, Where, and How to Plant

From spring to early fall, plant container-grown weigelas in a sunny or partially sunny spot. Although it's quite tolerant of other soils, this deciduous shrub prefers well-drained soil that contains ample organic matter. The shrub produces fewer flowers when grown in shade. See page 191 for directions on proper shrub planting.

Growing Tips

Water deeply in any week when the rainfall is less than an inch; be careful of overwatering in clay soil (don't let the shrub stand in water). Apply a slow-release shrub fertilizer, according to label directions, in spring, beginning the second year after planting.

Care

Prune away winter dieback in early spring or after flowering finishes. All other pruning should be done soon after flowers fade; when you prune in summer, fall, or winter, you'll be cutting off flower buds and reducing the next spring's bloom.

Landscape Design

I like to mix the weigelas with purple foliage with plants that have green-and-white variegated leaves for a nice contrast. Dwarf cultivars of weigela can be charming placed at the back of a bed of perennial flowers or grown near astilbes or peonies. Weigelas with purple or variegated leaves add a colorful note to a shrub border.

Try These

Midnight Wine (*Weigela florida* 'Elvera') has purple leaves and pink flowers on a dwarf, mounded shrub. Hummingbirds like it. Wine & Roses (*W. florida* 'Alexandra') is very similar but it's a larger shrub. The leaves of 'Tango' are purplish on top and dark green on the bottom, the flowers are rosy, and the shrub is very small. French Lace (*W. florida* 'Brigela') has green leaves that have a border of lime green on them and red flowers. 'Red Prince' has deep red flowers, which are lovely against the shrub's dark green leaves. 'Minuet' and 'My Monet' are nice dwarfs that have grown and bloomed well in my yard.

When, Where, and How to Plant

Plant container-grown witch hazels from late winter until early fall in moist soil and in full to partial sun. Witch hazel is a good choice for those who have clay soil. All witch hazels, except the native *Hamamelis virginiana*, can also tolerate alkaline soil. Be sure to read the label to find the mature size of the shrub, and then space it accordingly, as some can grow quite large. See page 191 for shrub planting guidelines.

Growing Tips

Water regularly to keep soil evenly moist. In periods of high temperatures and drought, check twice a week to see if soil is dry, and water deeply as necessary. Fertilize in spring with a slow-release, preferably organic, plant food for flowering shrubs.

Care

Throughout the year, add mulch around the shrub as needed to keep the mulch depth to about 3 inches. In late spring or early summer, do any necessary pruning to control the size of the shrub. At any time you may remove dead wood and dig up suckers. If you do not dig up suckers, the shrub will develop into a large colony. You may enjoy cutting a few budded branches in late winter to place in a vase indoors, where they will soon bloom. Witch hazel has few pest problems.

Landscape Design

Witch hazel is ideal planted near a water garden, but it should always be placed where it can be admired in winter, especially from indoors. Try surrounding yellow-flowered witch hazels with 'February Gold' daffodils and purple-flowered crocus. The native species do well in areas with wet soil.

Try These

'Autumn Embers' has orange flowers and excellent fall leaf color. *Hamamelis vernalis* 'Christmas Cheer' is the earliest witch hazel to flower in my yard. Among the excellent *Hamamelis × intermedia* hybrids, my favorites are 'Jelena', which has copper blooms and 'Arnold Promise', which is still the best yellow I've grown, although I like 'Sandra' too.

January and February aren't months when we think of any shrub flowering. That's why it's so delightful to glance out a window in winter to see a shrub covered with yellow, red, orange, maroon, or copper flowers. Not only is it unexpected, it really lifts your spirits, especially if winter weather is dreary. My experience is that buying one witch hazel frequently leads to planting a few more, since having flowers of various colors and different-sized shrubs (some can easily be trained to become small trees) is fun. But witch hazel doesn't fade into the background once winter is over. Several species and cultivars have excellent fall color. And the new leaves of Hamamelis vernalis are reddish purple, making it interesting in three seasons.

Botanical Pronunciation

ham-uh-MEL-is

Bloom Period and Seasonal Color

Winter in shades of yellow, red, orange, maroon, and copper

Mature Height × Spread

6 to 30 feet × 10 to 25 feet

Trees

Trees make us feel good, and we become attached to them. I can never hear the wind blowing through pine trees without being transported in my mind back to summers I spent as a girl on my grandparents' farm.

But trees offer more benefits than just beauty and pleasant memories. They absorb pollutants from the air and give off oxygen. If planted in the right spot, trees help reduce a home's heating and air-conditioning bills. And everyone knows that outdoors, temperatures are cooler near trees. Trees absorb runoff from excess rainfall, and sometimes they provide privacy and screening. They also attract birds and small wildlife, creating a more natural environment. Besides all that, trees have been demonstrated to increase property values, which even the most practical homeowner will appreciate.

No wonder that one of the first things people do after moving into a new home is to plant a tree or two. But what kind of tree? There are so many different trees, and it may seem difficult to select among them. In your search to find the best tree for your yard, ask yourself a few questions first.

Determine Your Goals

Do you want shade, flowers in spring, or a tree that will attract birds to your yard or produce colorful fall foliage? Do you want one that will serve as a buffer between you, your neighbors, and the outside world, or a tree that will be interesting to look at in more than one season? Many trees have more than one attribute to recommend them. Dogwoods, for instance, flower in spring, have leaves that turn fiery in fall, and also produce berries that are attractive to a host of birds.

*Japanese maple (*Acer palmatum*) landscape*

Do you want or need a deciduous tree (such as an oak), a broadleaf evergreen (a holly tree, for instance), or a needled evergreen—sometimes called a conifer (such as eastern hemlock)? Deciduous trees drop their leaves in autumn, which leads to raking. But it also means that you can position a

Magnolia (Magnolia) *seedpod*

deciduous tree to block the sun from reaching your house in summer, decreasing air conditioning costs, but letting sun through in winter to help warm the house and cut your heating bills.

Evergreens block the sun in summer and winter, and they add a green touch to the yard in cold weather, when everything else looks brown. They are also frequently employed as a screen to block views or foot traffic year-round. As a group evergreens tend to grow more slowly than deciduous trees. This may be helpful or not, depending upon your needs and goals. (Note: Although evergreens never lose all their leaves or needles, they do shed some of them each year. Sometimes homeowners think a pine tree is dying when they see a bunch of interior needles turn brown and fall off. Not to worry; this is how the tree renews itself.)

Do Some Research

Before you make your final selection, find out if the tree develops any messy fruits, seeds, or droppings, called "litter." That can quickly ruin your enjoyment of a new tree. A sweet gum is delightful in fall because of its scarlet leaves, but a nuisance in spring when the little "balls" keep fouling the the lawn mower's blades. And the hard, brown faded leaves of Southern magnolia aren't a pretty sight. But neither of those issues means you have to give up on these otherwise attractive trees. Instead, site them so that their characteristics aren't liabilities. In the case of magnolia, never prune off the lower limbs; they help hide the fallen old leaves. Faded magnolia leaves are also less of a problem when the tree is planted in a mulched bed instead of in the lawn. It's a good idea to plant messy trees at the outer fringe of woods, so the fruits can fall harmlessly to the ground and do not matter. Or, try growing messy trees in the center of a groundcover bed.

How large will that now-small tree grow? Not learning the answer to that question—before buying and planting—is probably the biggest mistake homeowners make when choosing trees for their yard. And either they or the next owners of their house regret it for a long time.

When you don't know the mature size of the tree you're planting, you're all too likely to place it too close to the house, sidewalk, or street. With one-story homes especially, keep perspective firmly in mind. Ask yourself: When this tree matures, how will its size and the size of the house compare? Also, look up: Are there power lines that may interfere with the tree when it reaches its eventual size?

How hardy is that tree? An important question to ask when buying any plant for your yard is: How cold-hardy is it supposed to be? Often people assume that because a plant is for sale in their area, it will grow well there. That's not necessarily so. Always make sure that the tree is rated for your

USDA winter hardiness zone (see page 41). But also pay attention to whether or not the tree can take our heat in August. A fir, for example, is extremely winter hardy, but it languishes in heat and humidity. A tree is a big investment; no one wants one that won't live through one of our hot summers or normally cold winters.

What shape or form will the tree develop as it grows? There are at least nine different shapes that various trees assume as they mature, ranging from columnar (very narrow) to pyramidal to weeping. Employees at a good nursery can tell you the future shape of a tree you're considering. Or, most of the time, the tree's tag will show a photo. Think of the effect that each form will have not only in and of itself, but also in relation to surrounding plantings and structures (house, garage, fence). While a weeping ornamental cherry is a delight in spring, you wouldn't want to fill your yard with all weeping trees; that would dilute the effect. Let the various forms of trees complement and harmonize with the entire yard.

Naturally, you want a tree that grows fast; everyone does. But trees touted as fast-growing often are problem trees: they may have weak wood (limbs break in storms and sometimes even without provocation, destroying the tree's appearance and symmetry), they may be short-lived, their roots may be invasive or large and aboveground, the trees may be insect or disease magnets—well, you get the idea. When you plant the wrong tree, you have to live with it for a long time, and when you finally get rid of it (which can be expensive), you have to start over. In the end, it's simpler and quicker to start with a problem-free tree that grows moderately.

The keys to success with any plant are to select one that likes the conditions of the location you select and then plant it carefully. If the spot where you want to plant a tree is shady and has wet soil, but you plant a tree that requires full sun and fast-draining soil, it isn't going to look good or live very long. Become familiar with your yard—the soil type, the pH, the amount of light that falls on various sections (at all times of the day), and even whether there is good air circulation. Then learn about the trees you're considering—and be a matchmaker.

How to Plant a Tree

The recommended way to plant a tree has changed from what you may have been used to. Extensive tests have shown that your tree is more likely to easily establish itself if you do *not* add organic matter to the soil when you plant. (That may seem wrong, because we are advised to amend the soil of most other things we plant, but studies showed that amendments either didn't help or were harmful to a tree's growth.)

Here's how to plant container-grown or balled-and-burlapped trees:

1. Water the tree and the proposed planting area several hours before planting.
2. Carefully remove any burlap (which is generally not an organic material now) and discard, or remove the tree from its container. Many garden centers have a program to recycle those plastic pots. Pick up a tree only by its rootball, never by its trunk.

3. Dig a hole that's twice as wide as the rootball and just about as deep (but no deeper).

4. Place the tree in the hole at the same level it grew before. Trim off roots that completely circle the rootball and rough up the sides of the rootball a little to encourage root growth.

5. Replace one-third of the soil you removed from the hole back around the rootball. Water well and pat the soil down to remove air pockets. Do this twice more. Or, experts say, it's fine to replace all the soil at once, pat it down, and then water.

6. Fashion a ridge (berm) of soil on the top of the ground around the tree, to capture water. Water again.

7. Mulch with no more than 3 inches of organic material—pine needles, shredded leaves, pine or hardwood bark—making sure that the mulch doesn't touch the trunk. Whatever you do, *don't* create deep mounds of mulch around trees. Yes, you may see plenty of others do that, but it's not good for your trees (see pages 25 to 27, and page 231).

8. Don't fertilize at planting time or during the tree's first year in your yard.

Care: Watering, Fertilizing, and Pruning

Most newly planted trees need about a gallon of water per week for every inch of height—6 gallons for a 6-foot tree, 4 gallons for a 4-foot tree, but no more than 10 gallons total each week. Soaker hoses are a good way to ensure the water is distributed evenly at the root level.

How do you tell if a tree needs watering? Test the soil by inserting a thin stick to see at what level the stick becomes damp. Other signs include leaves look dull or grayish instead of shiny or bright, leaves yellow or drop off, or leaves wilting. If this happens, it may be too late to save the tree.

Fertilizing trees is a subject open to debate, but a good rule of thumb is to fertilize young trees yearly (after its first year), and then switch to feeding mature trees only once every three to four years.

Pruning a tree should be to enhance its shape or to prevent damage to the tree. Pruning is also done to remove tree limbs that are damaged or diseased. It's not complicated, but it's important to remember that working in tall trees is a job best left to experienced professionals.

A tree is a long-term investment. Many can easily live for several generations, so it's important to select the right tree for your yard and take care of it properly so it lives up to its potential.

It's easy to see why it's almost impossible to imagine a beautiful landscape without trees. Trees not only increase the value of your property, as studies have shown, but they create a sense of permanence and comfort. In the following pages, you'll find the right tree for any spot in your yard.

American Holly

Ilex opaca

Because it doesn't lose its leaves, an evergreen tree is a real asset in your winter yard. That goes double for an evergreen, such as American holly, that produces bright crimson (or orange or yellow!) berries to accompany those always-green leaves. No wonder a holly tree is treasured at Christmastime—it looks like a naturally decorated tree outdoors, and it doesn't mind having branches cut for long-lasting indoor arrangements. But this native tree's colorful beauty lasts months before and after December. And at the end of the season, those bright berries are often much appreciated by hungry migrating birds. The tree's pyramidal shape is appealing to many people. It's slow growing, but eventually can reach 50 feet tall, although smaller cultivars are available. Spiny leaves provide protection from dogs and intruders.

Botanical Pronunciation
I-lex o-PAY-kuh

Bloom Period and Seasonal Color
Insignificant white or cream blooms in spring; fall and winter berries in red, orange, or yellow

Mature Height × Spread
15 to 50 feet × 8 to 30 feet

When, Where, and How to Plant
American holly trees prefer moist, well-drained, acidic soil, but are tolerant of a wide range of conditions. In their native habitat, they are sometimes found growing beneath trees whose lowest limbs start 20 feet off the ground, but that produces a very open growth habit that most people don't like. These compact, pyramidal trees grow in full sun or mostly sunny sites. Avoid windy locations. For every three to six female hollies (which produce berries), plant a male that blooms at the same time for pollination; they can be up to 100 feet apart. In spring, dig a hole as deep as the rootball and twice as wide. Place the tree in it, and fill in with the soil dug from the hole. Mulch well.

Growing Tips
Water when weekly rainfall is less than an inch. In early years, apply an organic fertilizer formulated for hollies, according to label directions, at the end of March or April.

Care
Prune lightly anytime except fall to maintain the pyramidal shape. American holly is resistant to most diseases and insects, but may be troubled by holly leaf miner (which leaves "trails" in the leaves), scale (which looks like tiny brown bumps on the stems and undersides of leaves), spittlebug (recognized by the foam it leaves behind), and leaf spots. If any of these appear, ask the Extension service to recommend controls.

Landscape Design
Place American holly where it can be seen from the street and from indoors in winter. Plant several for screening or as a windbreak.

Try These
One objection to American holly is that its leaves are dull, not shiny, so I like the large glossy leaves of 'Satyr Hill'. Its berries are big too. This tree is a vigorous grower and quite hardy. Its eventual height should be about 30 feet, but at fifteen years it will be maybe 7 feet tall.

American Hornbeam

Carpinus caroliniana

When, Where, and How to Plant

Because of transplanting difficulties, it's best to choose a container-grown American hornbeam rather than one that's balled-and-burlapped. Plant in spring. The ideal location will have moist but well-drained acidic to neutral soil and be in partial shade. But hornbeam is versatile—it will also grow in wet soil and in full sun. It grows more densely in sun than in shade, where its growth is more open. Avoid alkaline soil. See page 228 for directions on how to plant a tree.

Growing Tips

Water during dry spells, especially in hot weather. If your soil is good, fertilizer will probably not be needed. In poor soil, apply half the recommended label rate of a high-nitrogen tree fertilizer in late winter or early spring before new growth begins. Do this the second to the fifth years.

Care

Keep a wide circle of mulch around the tree to avoid trunk damage from mowers and string trimmers. Because its lower limbs will droop downward, you may want to remove them (in winter) so that people can walk beneath the tree. But since the hornbeam tree's wood is very strong, do leave the lower limbs if there are children in the family; it makes a good climbing tree. Winter is also the time to prune to a single trunk if you prefer the tree that way. Few insects or diseases affect American hornbeam.

Landscape Design

Because of its size and its tolerance of pruning, hornbeam is an excellent selection for screening and as a hedge. It also makes a good street tree and does well along streams and near water gardens. (And it's a climbing tree for kids of all ages!)

Try These

Although there are many European and Asian hornbeans on the market (including columnar and weeping varieties), it's difficult to find cultivars of American hornbeam. I pick out the tree I want in autumn, looking for one that has attractive and showy leaf color.

Hornbeam is an attractive small tree that's also known as ironwood and musclewood (both names refer to the tree's gray fluted or ridged bark.) It may be grown as a multiple-trunked tree or trained to a single trunk. Hornbeam is especially useful to homeowners because of its versatility—it grows in shade or sun and doesn't mind wet soils. In fall, the tree's leaf color is excellent and interesting clusters of fruits attract gray squirrels and a wide variety of birds, from cardinals and goldfinches to grouse and quail. Also of interest to gardeners who like to attract wildlife to their yards, American hornbeam's small flowers are a source of larval food or nectar for eastern tiger swallowtail and striped hairstreak butterflies.

Botanical Pronunciation

car-PIE-nus car-oh-lin-ee-A-nuh

Bloom Period and Seasonal Color

Inconspicuous flowers in spring; fall leaves in red, yellow and orange and hanging clusters of brown nutlets

Mature Height x Spread

20 to 30 feet x 20 to 30 feet

American Yellowwood
Cladrastis kentukea

For some reason, this tree isn't often considered by homeowners. Its name may draw a blank look. But you probably have seen it flowering at the edge of wooded areas along area highways. It's hard not to notice— and admire—this tree's long clusters of creamy flowers. Those flowers alone are reason enough to grow American yellowwood, but the tree contributes many other fine traits to a landscape—bright green leaves in summer that turn yellow in fall, smooth gray bark that adds winter interest to the yard, an ability to grow in either alkaline or acidic soil, and extreme winter-hardiness.

Botanical Pronunciation
klad-RAST-iss ken-TUK-ee-uh

Bloom Period and Seasonal Color
Late spring fragrant flowers in cream, white, or pink followed by yellow fall foliage

Mature Height × Spread
30 to 60 feet × 40 to 50 feet

When, Where, and How to Plant
Yellowwood adapts to sun or shade and either acidic or alkaline soil. Container-grown plants are preferable. Plant in spring in well-drained soil. The tree goes more slowly in sun than in part shade. Dig its hole as deep as the rootball and twice as wide, place the tree in the hole, and water. Refill the hole with the soil you removed from it and water again. Mulch around the tree. (Find more detailed planting instructions on page 228.)

Growing Tips
If you want this tree to grow fast, regularly water and feed it. Keep the soil moist when the tree is young; established trees tolerate some dryness. Fertilize with 1 pound of granular 19-0-0 formula per inch of trunk diameter in late autumn or early spring. Or spread an organic tree fertilizer, according to label directions, in a wide circle beneath the branches after the leaves have fallen.

Care
Pest problems are insignificant. The limbs and trunks of American yellowwood trees often join at a narrow angle, instead of at a wide angle. These narrow crotch angles become weak when bark in the crotch dies; they can split or break in storms. Remove limbs with narrow crotches when the tree is young, or have an arborist do it. Prune away storm damage as soon as possible after it occurs, but do all other pruning in summer, as this is a tree that "bleeds" sap (which is messy and disturbing to watch, although not harmful to the tree). Don't be concerned by the occasional absence of flowers; yellowwood trees may not flower until they're ten years old and afterward don't always bloom every year.

Landscape Design
Grow American yellowwood as a shade tree or a focal point in your lawn.

Try These
'Rosea' (also called 'Perkins Pink') has fragrant, light pink flowers. Japanese yellowwood (*Cladrastis platycarpa*) is a small tree that would be good for Zone 6 gardens.

Bald Cypress
Taxodium distichum

When, Where, and How to Plant

Plant in early fall or in spring in a sunny spot with acidic soil. Be careful to give it plenty of room to grow—wide and tall—and watch out for overhead power lines. This tree is ideal for a boggy spot, but bald cypress tolerates almost any type of soil, as long as it isn't alkaline. Plant it in a hole the same depth as the rootball and twice as wide, replacing the soil dug from the hole around the tree's roots. Water deeply. Mulch well with no more than 2 to 3 inches of organic matter, such as pine needles or fine pine bark, keeping the mulch 2 inches away from the trunk.

Growing Tips

Water weekly for the tree's first two years in your yard. After that rainfall is usually ample, although you should water during dry spells. In poor soil, encourage better growth by fertilizing lightly twice a year—in February and late spring—with an organic fertilizer. Spread the fertilizer over the ground beneath the tree all the way to the dripline (the outer edge of the tree's branches), according to package directions.

Care

Yellowing "needles" probably mean the soil isn't acidic enough; spray with chelated iron and use a fertilizer for acid-loving plants. Pick off any bagworms at dusk; spray the tree with water if spider mites cause needles to turn brown anytime except fall. Prune dead branches anytime. The knobby growths at the base are normal in wet sites; they're called "knees."

Landscape Design

Place the tree where its exfoliating bark can be admired. It's ideal for swamps and along lakes or streams, but I've seen this impressive tree growing in a shopping center parking lot!

Try These

'Pendens' can make an unusual street tree, not prone to damage sidewalks or curbs. 'Apache Chief' grows 60 feet tall, tolerates some shade, and has red, peeling bark.

Bald cypress is one of the most unusual trees you'll ever grow. It has needles, but unlike pines and other needled evergreens we're familiar with, it's a deciduous tree. Its needles turn a bright cinnamon color in the autumn and then fall off; in spring green needles grow back. Bald cypress is one of a group of trees called deciduous conifers, which makes it a plant that will draw interest to your yard. But it also has another characteristic that makes it very useful in our region: it thrives in wet soil, although it grows just fine in sandy or ordinary soil. It's also hardy throughout Tennessee and Kentucky. Among bald cypress's other advantages are soft needles and a pyramidal shape. This tree lives for a very long time.

Botanical Pronunciation

tax-O-dee-um DIS-ti-kum

Bloom Period and Seasonal Color

No flowers, but distinctive cinnamon-colored needles in fall

Mature Height × Spread

50 to 120 feet × 18 to 65 feet

Black Gum
Nyssa sylvatica

Black gum, also known as sour gum and black tupelo, is worth growing just for its bright red fall color. It's usually planted in home landscapes as a shade tree but is also excellent to attract birds and small wildlife, which make a banquet of the small fruits that appear on the tree in fall. It's also tolerant of wet soil. It's an attractive tree, with reddish new leaves, glossy, dark green summertime foliage, and attractive bark. It isn't ideal for cities, though, since an urban environment tends to slow its growth. It's not easy to locate black gum in garden centers because its long taproot makes it difficult to transplant (it's usually grown from seed in containers), so try nurseries that specialize in native plants.

Botanical Pronunciation
NIS-uh sil-VAT-ih-cuh

Bloom Period and Seasonal Color
Insignificant flowers in spring; bluish black fruits in fall

Mature Height x Spread
30 to 65 feet x 20 to 35 feet

When, Where, and How to Plant
Because of the tree's long taproot, buy a container-grown plant rather than one that's balled-and-burlapped. Plant only in spring, in a sunny spot and moist, acidic soil, although the tree will tolerate wet soils. Clay soil is okay but avoid alkaline soil because that causes slow growth, yellowing leaves, and eventual death. (See page 228 for details of how to plant a tree.)

Growing Tips
When the tree is young, keep the soil moist. At its maturity, water during dry spells. If caterpillars defoliate the tree in spring, fertilize the following winter by spreading an organic tree fertilizer, according to package directions, on the ground in a wide circle around the tree; water in.

Care
Black gum has few insect or disease problems beyond occasional leaf spots. Rake up affected leaves and destroy them. The lower limbs will droop and may need to be removed in winter so people can walk beneath the tree.

Landscape Design
Grow wherever in the yard that you need a nice shade tree, but plant a groundcover beneath to catch the falling fruits in fall and the occasional mess from the birds as they dine on the fruits. It's a tree that makes a nice focal point. A nice companion is dogwood, which is a member of the same family. When using the tree in a garden planted for wildlife, consider growing black gum with the shrub winterberry, *Ilex verticillata* (see page 201). The same birds and wildlife that like black gum's fruits will appreciate winterberry's crop too.

Try These
'Red Rage' comes from an arborist at Louisville's Seneca Gardens Arboretum. 'Wildfire' changes leaf color several times during the year. Its fall foliage is very colorful. 'Autumn Cascade' is a weeping selection.

Carolina Silverbell
Halesia carolina

When, Where, and How to Plant

Plant in spring or early fall in the same type of spot in which you would plant a dogwood: moist, acidic soil that drains well and contains lots of organic matter. Part shade is best, but Carolina silverbell will also be happy in half a day of sun in Zone 6a. Buy these trees in containers, rather than balled-and-burlapped, because container-grown Carolina silverbells transplant best. Dig a hole as deep as the rootball and twice as wide, place the tree in it, and fill in around the roots with the soil removed from the hole. Water thoroughly and spread 2 to 3 inches of organic material, such as pine needles or pine bark, over the soil; don't let the mulch touch the trunk.

Growing Tips

Water the tree enough to keep the soil moist; don't let it dry out. Fertilizer probably won't be necessary, but if you feel the tree needs it, spread a high-nitrogen fertilizer for trees in a wide circle around the trunk in late fall (after the leaves have fallen off in autumn) to early spring (just before new growth starts).

Care

Renew mulch as needed each year. Begin training this tree to a single trunk when its young; otherwise, it will become a large shrub, which isn't as attractive as the tree shape. Prune—never removing more than one-fourth of the growth in one year—in spring, after flowering. This is a very insect- and disease-resistant tree.

Landscape Design

Try to situate Carolina silverbell on a hill or slope so that the flowers can be viewed from below. It's a nice understory tree beneath pines and looks attractive with evergreen azalea, rhododendrons, and other spring-flowering trees.

Try These

The flowers on 'Arnold Pink' are larger than those on the species. They start out rose-pink and fade to pale pink; both colors are attractive.

If you enjoy the spring beauty of redbuds and dogwoods, why not add a more unusual (but just as easy to grow) flowering tree to your landscape? Carolina silverbell is a charming native tree that provides three seasons of interest: graceful white or pink bell-shaped blooms hanging in delicate clusters along the branches in mid to late spring before the leaves appear, fruits that last into cold weather, and white furrowed bark in winter. It's a good substitute in areas where dogwoods aren't grown because of anthracnose disease but it's also an excellent companion to dogwoods where they thrive. You may find this for sale as Halesia tetraptera; that's the previous botanic name but it's the same tree. By whichever name, it's a lovely tree that will brighten your spring.

Botanical Pronunciation

huh-LEE-zi-uh care-o-LINE-uh

Bloom Period and Seasonal Color

Spring flowers in white or pink

Mature Height × Spread

30 to 50 feet × 20 to 35 feet

Chaste Tree
Vitex agnus-castus

Chaste tree can be grown either as a small tree or very large shrub, but I prefer it grown as a multitrunked tree, which has an airy look welcomed in summer. Whichever way you train it, fast-growing chaste tree belongs in your yard because of its easygoing disposition and its spectacular 6- to 18-inch fragrant, blue or purple (also pink or white) flower spikes that cover the tree at the end of summer and into fall. And it's considered deer-resistant. Chaste tree thrives in hot summers, but regrettably, it isn't always winter-hardy north of Zone 7. If you live in Zone 6, however, look for Vitex agnus-castus var. latifolia, which will be hardy for you.

Botanical Pronunciation
VIE-tex AG-nus-KAS-tus

Bloom Period and Color
Blue, lavender, white, or pink, from late summer to early fall

Mature Height × Spread
8 to 25 feet × 15 to 30 feet

Zone
6b to 7

When, Where, and How to Plant
Although tolerant of many situations, chaste tree grows and blooms best in moist but well-drained soil and full sun; flowers won't be as numerous or colorful in part shade. If you don't plan to prune it to a tree shape, place a chaste tree 20 feet from other plants. In early spring, dig a hole as deep as the rootball and twice as wide, place the tree in it, refill the hole with the soil removed from it, and water. Mulch with 2 to 3 inches of organic material (see page 228 for more about planting).

Growing Tips
During a chaste tree's first two years in your yard, water whenever weekly rainfall is less than an inch. From then on, the tree can tolerate dry conditions but it will grow best if watered regularly. Fertilizer isn't usually necessary; if needed to encourage growth, use 1 pound of 10-10-10 formula at the end of March or April.

Care
Remove some lower limbs in very early spring to train to a multitrunked tree shape. Prune to remove winter damage at the same time. After an especially cold winter, or in colder climates, chaste tree may die back to the ground; it should grow back from the roots. In very rainy weather, leaf spots may appear. While affecting the tree's appearance, they usually aren't serious. Few other insect or disease problems should trouble chaste tree. Removing faded flowers encourages the plant to bloom more.

Landscape Design
Chaste tree's small size, interesting foliage, and late-season bloom make it a natural patio tree. It's often included as part of a shrub border. A row of them is spectacular when they're in flower.

Try These
'Abbeville Blue' has deep blue flowers that will be the centerpiece of your garden. 'Montrose Purple' has rich violet-colored flowers on a tree that grows only 8 to 10 feet high. *Vitex negundo* is reliably hardy in Zone 6.

Dogwood
Cornus species and hybrids

When, Where, and How to Plant
Although flowering dogwoods grow beneath taller trees in their natural habitat, they can tolerate quite a bit of sun. But if you have a choice, put a dogwood in partial shade. In Zone 7, morning sun and afternoon shade is fine. The ideal soil is acidic, moist, and well drained, containing plenty of organic matter. Avoid poorly drained soil. Actually, dogwoods don't like very dry or very wet soil. Plant in spring, in a hole twice as wide and the same depth as the rootball, refilling the hole with the dirt that was in the hole. Mulch well with pine straw. (See page 228 for more advice on planting.)

Growing Tips
Dogwoods are shallow-rooted and shouldn't be allowed to dry out; water when rainfall is less than normal—especially when temperatures are high. Fertilizer probably won't be necessary, but to encourage growth in young trees, you can spread a granular high-nitrogen fertilizer for trees, according to label directions, in late fall.

Care
Maintain a 3-inch mulch of pine needles or shredded leaves around the tree. Prune right after flowering, if necessary, but leave lower limbs on trees to protect the trunk. Dogwoods are susceptible to many diseases and insects. The most serious—besides anthracnose—are borers (which often enter through holes in trunks caused by lawn mowers or string trimmers and which kill the tree), leaf spots during wet springs (which can usually be ignored since they're just cosmetic), and mildew (which looks like white powder on the foliage). Check with the Extension service for advice about insects or diseases. To avoid future problems, rake up any diseased leaves that fall from the tree and destroy them.

Landscape Design
Dogwoods are a good patio tree. Underplant with evergreen azaleas and daffodils or tulips for a great look.

Try These
Cornus kousa 'Gold Star' has striking yellow variegation down the middle of green leaves; flowers are white. Its fall leaves are two shades of red.

Flowering dogwood (Cornus florida) is such a well-loved sign of spring that it needs no introduction. But dogwood anthracnose, a fungal disease which has killed so many trees, caused gardeners to turn to other dogwoods. Kousa (Cornus kousa), for instance, which flowers up to a month later than the native dogwood and has a distinctive branching pattern. Pagoda dogwood (Cornus alternifolia) is a small, very hardy native tree with layered branches. Its yellowish white flowers, produced in late spring or early summer, are extremely fragrant, but the fall color is nothing to write home about. The berries are black. But here's very good news: Tennessee researchers discovered a cultivar of C. florida that resists anthracnose. It's called 'Appalachian Spring'. It has white flowers and excellent fall color.

Botanical Pronunciation
KOR-nus

Bloom Period and Seasonal Color
Spring in white, pink, and red; some cultivars have great fall color

Mature Height × Spread
15 to 40 feet × 20 to 30 feet

Eastern Hemlock

Tsuga canadensis

Eastern hemlock, also known as Canadian hemlock although it's native as far south as Alabama, is a needled evergreen that's popular with homeowners because it grows in the shade. And it's one of the few conifers that thrive in Tennessee and Kentucky's normal warmth and humidity. If you've moved here from a colder climate and long for the spruces and firs of your former region, this tree will deliver the look you want. The outer branches of this slow-growing, long-lived tree weep slightly, producing a graceful appearance that's much appreciated in home landscapes. The low-to-the-ground branches persist even when the tree is old. In the warmest parts of the region, consider Carolina hemlock (T. caroliniana), a smaller species that doesn't mind summer heat.

Botanical Pronunciation
TSOO-gah can-uh-DEN-sis

Bloom Period and Seasonal Color
Evergreen needles

Mature Height × Spread
40 to 90 feet × 25 to 35 feet

When, Where, and How to Plant
Hemlocks won't survive either lack of water or too much moisture in the soil over winter, so their soil—preferably containing lots of organic matter—must be moist but well drained. Partial shade is ideal and full shade is okay. In early fall or spring, carefully remove the burlap from around the rootball of a B&B tree and plant in a hole that's as deep as the rootball and twice as wide. Water well and mulch with 2 to 3 inches of organic material such as pine needles or pine bark.

Growing Tips
Water regularly to keep the soil moist, especially during a hemlock's first two years in your yard, when it's getting established. Also water during dry spells. After the first year, a tree may be fertilized lightly with an organic tree fertilizer anytime from late fall until early spring (just before new growth begins). However, it's important to avoid high-nitrogen fertilizer if woolly adelgids, insects that look like aphids, have been seen on the tree or nearby. Fertilizer can encourage their growth and survival, or even make the tree more susceptible to this pest.

Care
If you're using eastern hemlock trees as a hedge or screen, shear in late spring or during summer for a formal look. While large numbers of pests are potential problems, most have little effect on well-maintained trees. In some areas of Kentucky and Tennessee, woolly adelgids have become a big problem, killing many eastern and Carolina hemlocks. If you notice little white sacs, immediately check with the Extension service for the latest research and control recommendations.

Landscape Design
Eastern hemlock is often used as a tall hedge or screen. It grows nicely with shade-loving shrubs, such as evergreen azaleas, rhododendrons, mountain laurels, and oakleaf hydrangeas.

Try These
'Golden Splendor' is a slow-growing, yellow-needled cultivar. 'Sargentii' is a weeping tree that grows approximately 10 to 15 feet, but about twice as wide; its branches reach the ground.

Eastern Redbud
Cercis canadensis

When, Where, and How to Plant

Young trees transplant best; plant in spring or early fall in a sunny spot or partial shade. Redbuds adapt to acidic or alkaline soil and can grow in nearly all types of soil, except those that stay wet all the time. They prefer moist, well-drained soil that contains organic matter. Dig a hole that's as deep as the rootball and twice as wide, and place the tree in it. Water and refill the hole with the soil that was removed from it, packing it down; water again. Apply a 2- to 3-inch mulch of organic material in a circle extending several feet from the trunk. (See page 228 for more about planting trees.)

Growing Tips

Regular watering and fertilizing are the keys to success with redbud. During the growing season, water when weekly rainfall is less than an inch. Fertilize in late fall or early spring with 1 to 2 pounds of granular 19-0-0 formula per inch of trunk diameter or with a high-nitrogen tree fertilizer, applied according to label directions.

Care

Redbud trees have thin bark that's easily damaged by string trimmers and lawn mowers, creating holes for borers and disease to enter. The best way to prevent this is to maintain a wide mulch of organic material, such as pine needles, around the trunk. Control caterpillars organically with Bt. Minimize pruning to lessen the chance of disease. If pruning is necessary, do it in winter or right after flowering.

Landscape Design

Plant redbud in your front yard so the early blossoms can be admired by everyone. Most of the plants I grow with redbuds have white flowers.

Try These

Cercis chinensis 'Don Egolf' is a redbud shrub. 'Forest Pansy' produces purple leaves. 'Appalachia' has red and neon pink flowers. 'Ruby Falls' is a weeping tree with purplish foliage, and 'Tennessee Pink' has pink flowers on a tree that grows 20 feet tall and as wide.

When I moved away from Tennessee for 10 years, one tree I really missed when spring arrived was the redbud. I'm not sure why it wasn't planted much in the other states I lived in, since it's hardy from Zones 4 to 9, grows in about any type of soil, and can tolerate wet or dry soil conditions. Other advantages include its small size, heart-shaped leaves, graceful branches, zigzag twigs, and an abundance of fuchsia-colored flowers before the leaves appear. It's also a native plant. I like redbud because it extends the spring flowering season by blooming before dogwoods. Not everyone likes the brown pods that hang on the branches some winters. Some birds do, though. Soon, I'll be planting a new redbud in my yard.

Botanical Pronunciation

SER-sis can-a-DEN-sis

Bloom Period and Seasonal Color

Fuchsia, pink, or white flowers in spring

Mature Height × Spread

20 to 35 feet × 15 to 35 feet

Flowering Cherry
Prunus species and hybrids

It's true that flowering cherries aren't in bloom for very long, but, oh, that ephemeral beauty is so enchanting. One way to extend the number of weeks that flowering cherries enhance the spring landscape is to plant different species that bloom at different times and have different appearances. Yoshino cherry (Prunus × yedoensis) has fragrant pink or white clusters of early blooms that appear before (or sometimes with) the leaves. Prunus serrulata 'Kwanzan' (usually just called Kwanzan cherry) is known for large, double, rosy flowers and leaves that are reddish when new and bronze in fall. Prunus subhirtella 'Pendula' is a medium-sized weeping tree that produces single pink blossoms. Rosy-flowered Sargent cherry (Prunus sargentii) makes an excellent fast-growing shade tree in Zone 6.

Botanical Pronunciation
PROO-nus

Bloom Period and Seasonal Color
White or pink in spring

Mature Height × Spread
6 to 40 feet × 8 to 30 feet

When, Where, and How to Plant
Plant in spring or early autumn in full sun and fast-draining soil. The trees will appreciate soil that contains organic matter. In clay, consider planting flowering cherries on soil mounds or in raised beds to avoid the possibility of root rot. Dig a hole as deep as the rootball and twice as wide, place the tree gently in the hole, water thoroughly, and fill in around the roots with the soil that came from the hole. Water well and mulch lightly. (See page 228 for more detailed planting advice.)

Growing Tips
Water when weekly rainfall is less than an inch, but be careful not to overwater in clay soil. In late fall, apply a high-nitrogen fertilizer for trees, according to label directions.

Care
When the tree is in bloom, it's fine to cut small branches to use in indoor arrangements. Do any necessary pruning as soon as flowers fade. Maintain a light mulch around the base of the tree—from the trunk to the ends of the branches—to prevent trunk damage from lawn equipment. Insects and diseases are drawbacks with flowering cherries, which tend not to be long-lived trees. If problems appear, consult the Extension service for causes and cures.

Landscape Design
If you ever wanted a Japanese garden, these trees will give you the perfect start. Underplant with spring-flowering bulbs.

Try These
My favorite Yoshino cherry, 'Akebono', has double, soft pink flowers. I planted 'Cascade Snow' for its disease-resistance, but also enjoy its attractive white flowers and dark green leaves that turn orangish in fall. *Prunus campanulata* 'Okame' is an excellent ornamental cherry tree, but not always hardy in the coldest winters. It has terrific fall color, grows quickly, and offers interesting bark that shows up well in winter. Its flowers are also a deeper pink than those found on many cherry trees. It will grow to about 30 feet tall.

Fringe Tree
Chionanthus virginicus

When, Where, and How to Plant
In the wild, fringe tree—also known as Grancy graybeard because its fringelike flowers somewhat resemble the beard of a wise old man—is adaptable to light and soil requirements. But in the home landscape, it will grow and bloom best in full or filtered sun and moist, well-drained, acidic soil that contains some organic matter. (If you don't know whether your soil is acidic, have a soil test done.) Don't plant fringe tree near where deicing salt is spread, since it is not salt-tolerant. In early to late spring or early fall, dig a hole the depth of the rootball and twice as wide, and place the tree in it. Water, and then refill in the hole with the dirt that was removed; water again, and mulch with 2 to 3 inches of organic material. (See page 228 for more about tree planting.)

Growing Tips
Water when weekly rainfall is less than an inch. Spread compost or rotted leaves around the base of the tree each fall to feed it lightly.

Care
Fringe tree leafs out late, so don't worry that something's wrong if foliage doesn't appear when it does on other trees. Possible pests include borers (which enter through the trunk; be sure to keep lawn equipment away from the tree) and scale (little brown "dots" on stems and underneath leaves; see page 34 for controls). Other pests are rarely a problem, but consult the Extension service for advice if necessary. To grow as a tree rather than a shrub, train to one main trunk. Do necessary pruning immediately after the tree flowers.

Landscape Design
Fringe tree is an excellent choice for small yards and sites under power lines.

Try These
Chinese fringe tree (*Chionanthus retusus*) has smaller flowers than the native fringe tree, but produces them a little earlier. It's often grown as a large shrub, and the two planted together are quite an eye-catching combination.

I'm such a big fan of spring-flowering trees and shrubs that I love to have one type or another blooming just as long as possible. Native fringe tree, which develops large, lacy clusters of fragrant white flowers in late spring, is an excellent choice for extending the season. It has waxy leaves, is fragrant, and begins blooming when quite young. There are male and female fringe trees, although they aren't often sold that way. The males bloom somewhat better, but if you're landscaping to attract wildlife, you may prefer a female, since it produces bluish drupes or berries favored by birds and small wild animals. Fringe tree may be grown as a large shrub, but I like it better as a multitrunked small tree.

Botanical Pronunciation
ki-o-NAN-thus ver-GIN-i-kus

Bloom Period and Seasonal Color
Late spring to early summer blooms in white; bluish berries in late summer

Mature Height × Spread
12 to 30 feet × 10 to 25 feet

Ginkgo
Ginkgo biloba

The common name of ginkgo is maidenhair tree. Look at the lovely fan-shaped leaves and you'll immediately see the resemblance to maidenhair fern. Now imagine a large tree covered with clear yellow fan-shaped foliage in fall—that's the appeal of a ginkgo. You might also like that the tree's leaves often drop all at one time, making raking much easier. When young, a ginkgo tree has a gangly appearance, like an adolescent who's all arms and legs. But as this "ugly duckling" ages, it grows wider and more graceful, becoming one of the most rewarding shade trees available. Be sure to read the warning under When, Where, and How to Plant about why you should buy only male trees.

Botanical Pronunciation
GING-ko bi-LOW-buh

Bloom Period and Seasonal Color
Insignificant green blooms in mid-spring; spectacular yellow fall foliage

Mature Height × Spread
25 to 50 feet × 15 to 40 feet

When, Where, and How to Plant
Buy only named cultivars of gingko, as these will be male (female trees develop awful-smelling, messy fruits, which you'll want to avoid). Plant in spring or fall. Soil may be alkaline or acidic, but it should be loose and well drained. (Ginkgo will tolerate clay soil as long as it's well drained.) Dig a hole that's the same depth as the rootball and twice as wide, place the tree in it, water well, and replace the dirt removed from the hole. Mulch with about 3 inches of organic material. (See page 228 for more advice about planting trees.)

Growing Tips
Regular watering after transplanting is important to get the tree off to a good start. Once it's established, the tree won't need watering except during long dry spells. Fertilize when the tree is young, if you like, with 1 pound of 19-0-0 per inch of trunk diameter, or with an organic tree fertilizer, according to package directions, in late autumn after the leaves fall.

Care
Young trees may need to be staked to hold them upright. Make sure stakes aren't attached to the tree too tightly and are removed within one year. Insects or diseases are rarely a problem. Prune in winter, if necessary.

Landscape Design
The most impressive gingko trees I ever saw were a pair placed just to the left of the entrance drive to the Baylor School in Chattanooga. Against a backdrop of tall pines, those two ginkgoes seemed to glow in fall—they looked as if they were made of gold leaf. So if you have the room, follow this example and plant two against a solid-colored background, in a place where they'll be noticed, and let them show off your good taste.

Try These
'Autumn Gold' is a slow-growing, spreading ginkgo with brilliant fall foliage. 'The President' (also called Presidential Gold) develops a wide-branching form sooner than other cultivars.

Japanese Cryptomeria
Cryptomeria japonica

When, Where, and How to Plant
While Japanese cryptomeria is adaptable in most respects, it should be placed where it's sheltered from strong winds. Plant in a sunny or partly sunny spot in early spring or early fall in acidic soil that's rich and moist, but well drained (a soil test will tell you the pH—acidity or alkalinity—of your soil). Dig a hole that's twice as wide as the rootball and just as deep. Place the tree carefully in the hole. Water and refill the hole with the soil that came out of it. Water again. Mulch with 2 to 3 inches of organic matter. (See page 228 for more detailed planting advice.)

Growing Tips
This is a tree that needs ample moisture. Water when weekly rainfall is less than an inch. Fertilizer isn't usually needed, but a granular high-nitrogen tree fertilizer may be spread at its base in late fall (1 pound per inch of trunk diameter).

Care
Japanese cryptomeria needs little pruning, except to remove wayward growth. In early years, pinch the tips of the stems in early summer to encourage denser growth. Insect and disease problems should be few, but if any appear, or if the tips of stems or branches suffer dieback, consult the Extension service for possible causes and cures. Don't worry when the reddish brown barks starts peeling off in strips. That's natural. Some will consider it messy, but others think it's one of the tree's beauties.

Landscape Design
Japanese cryptomeria makes an excellent hedge or screen. It's also a fine specimen tree where an evergreen presence is needed in a prominent place in the yard, and, of course, it's ideal for an Oriental garden. Space 10 to 16 feet apart for a screen.

Try These
The "needles" of many cultivars of Japanese cryptomeria turn plum or bronze in winter, a look that many people like. But since I don't, I gravitate toward 'Gyokuryu' and 'Benjamin Franklin', whose needles tend to remain deep green.

Even though this fast-growing conifer is often called Japanese cedar, it isn't really a cedar. It's a member of the same family as dawn redwood, giant sequoia, and bald cypress, and therefore certain to delight those who like plants that are different. One unusual touch: The tree has what botanists officially call "leaves", but they'll look just like needles to you. And the branches are arranged in tiers. Unlike most needled evergreens, which prefer climates with cold winters and mild summers, Japanese cryptomeria is right at home in our summer's heat and humidity. This can be a big tree, but dwarf cultivars are readily available. So are cultivars with white- and yellow-variegated needles—uh, leaves. 'Yoshino' is reportedly the hardiest.

Botanical Pronunciation
krip-toe-MEER-ree-uh ja-PON-i-cuh

Bloom Period and Seasonal Color
Evergreen foliage; will turn purplish in winter

Mature Height × Spread
1 to 60 feet × 2 to 30 feet

Japanese Maple

Acer palmatum

Because Japanese maples aren't inexpensive, it pays to spend quite a bit of time shopping for exactly what you want, since trees vary in size (from a tiny mound to a tall tree) and form (upright or cascading, for example), and the leaves come in a range of shapes (lobed or dissected) and sizes. There's also the important question of seasonal color—do you want a Japanese maple tree that has green foliage from spring until fall, red leaves from spring until fall, or green foliage in spring and summer and red in fall? The choices seem endless. These are beautiful trees that are especially valuable to homeowners because they're at home in shade gardens, many are small, and they're very decorative.

Botanical Pronunciation
Ace-er pall-MAY-tum

Bloom Period and Seasonal Color
Insignificant purple blooms in late spring; colorful foliage spring to fall

Mature Height × Spread
6 to 40 feet × 8 to 30 feet

When, Where, and How to Plant

Seed-grown Japanese maples will cost less than named cultivars, but you won't know what their eventual size, form, or seasonal color will be. If you want a Japanese maple whose leaves remain red in summer, buy one in the summer so you can see for yourself. Plant young trees from spring until early autumn in a partially shady spot—dappled shade beneath tall trees is ideal (in full shade, the plants grow very slowly; in sun, the leaves are likely to fade color or burn). Japanese maples like moist, well-drained soil that contains organic matter. The planting hole should be the same depth as the rootball and twice as wide. Don't amend the soil, but instead use only the soil that was removed from the hole to fill in around the tree's roots. (See page 228 for more advice about tree planting.)

Growing Tips

Don't let a Japanese maple's soil dry out. It's especially important to keep the soil moist when the plant is young and during droughts. Spread a granular high-nitrogen tree fertilizer, according to package directions, in late fall.

Care

Maintain the mulch year-round. Don't prune off lower limbs, which add grace and charm to the tree. There are few pest problems. Too much sun or wind and too little water can "burn" the leaves; correct the conditions that cause the damage.

Landscape Design

No longer just the pièce de résistance of Oriental gardens, elegant Japanese maples have become the focal point of many partially shady yards. Those with cascading branches add appeal near a water garden.

Try These

'Bloodgood' is the most tolerant Japanese maple I've grown; it endures extreme heat and cold, sun and shade, while retaining a consistent red leaf color all year. 'Waterfall' has cascading branches covered with finely dissected (threadleaf) leaves that are green in summer and gold or yellow in fall.

Japanese Pagoda Tree

Sophora japonica

When, Where, and How to Plant

In spring, plant Japanese pagoda in a sunny or partially sunny spot that has moist, well-drained soil, although the tree is quite adaptable to poor soil, particularly dry soil. It even tolerates compacted soil. Dig a hole as wide as the rootball and as deep (no deeper). Water the tree well and place in the hole. Refill the hole with the soil removed from the hole, patting it down to remove air pockets. Water thoroughly and then spread 2 to 3 inches of an organic material such as pine needles or pine bark over the planting area. (See page 228 for more about how to plant a tree.)

Growing Tips

Keep the tree watered regularly if rainfall is low the first two years the tree is in your yard. Mature trees can survive drought, but if you're able to water during long dry spells, the tree will be healthier and grow better. Fertilize in late fall after leaves have fallen or in very early spring before new growth starts, with an organic tree fertilizer or a timed-release fertilizer.

Care

Gardeners in the coldest parts of the region may experience some limb dieback in bad winters; if so, prune back to live wood in spring. Remove storm damage right after it occurs. The tree has some potential insects and diseases; if problems arise, talk with the Extension service about possible causes and cures. If the tree doesn't flower when young, don't be concerned; that's normal. It may take up to 10 years (usually it flowers faster in warmer climates than in colder ones). You will need to rake up dropped twigs, flowers, and fruit in fall unless the tree is mulched or planted in a groundcover bed.

Landscape Design

Japanese pagoda tree is good for urban areas, because it tolerates pollution. It should *not* be used as a street tree however, because it drops flowers and seedpods.

Try These

Sophora japonica 'Regent' is fast-growing and begins flowering earlier than the species. It has glossy, dark green foliage.

Not only is Japanese pagoda tree—also known as Chinese scholar tree, or just scholar tree—attractive, but mature trees tolerate heat and drought once they are established, a trait that has become increasingly important to us all. Just as nice for those who like flowering trees, it blooms at the end of summer when few, if any, other trees are in flower. Japanese pagoda trees can even stay in bloom for as long as a month, depending on the weather. It makes a nice lawn tree, because it casts only light shade, allowing grass to grow beneath it. However, the seedpods can stain sidewalks, and they and other parts of the tree are reportedly poisonous if eaten.

Botanical Pronunciation

sew-FOE-ruh ja-PON-ih-cuh

Bloom Period and Seasonal Color

White flowers in late summer; yellow seedpods in late fall and winter

Mature Height x Spread

30 to 70 feet x 40 to 60 feet

Japanese Zelkova
Zelkova serrata

Homeowners love the idea of a fast-growing tree. Gardening experts are generally wary of them, because trees that grow rapidly usually develop problems that you don't need (see page 228). But here's a tree that's in good graces with horticulturists and with people who want a good-looking, strong, and well-mannered tree that will grow tall before their children have grown up and left home. Japanese zelkova is a shade tree that may grow several feet a year when it's young and doesn't have bad habits that make arborists shudder. It has foliage similar to elm's and attractive bark that's reddish when young, gray and mottled on mature specimens. Zelkova trees also tolerate wind, heat, air pollution, drought, and urban conditions. Fall leaf color can be variable.

Botanical Pronunciation
zel-KO-vuh ser-RAY-tuh

Bloom Period and Seasonal Color
Insignificant spring blooms

Mature Height × Spread
50 to 90 feet × 40 to 50 feet

When, Where, and How to Plant
Plant anytime from spring through fall in full sun. Soil may be acid or alkaline, but is preferably moist and well drained. Dig a hole as deep as the rootball and two times as wide. Carefully place the tree in the hole, removing synthetic burlap and string from balled-and-burlapped plants. Water well and pack the soil dug from the hole around the tree's roots. Water again and mulch lightly with pine straw, shredded leaves, or fine pine bark. (See page 228 for more detailed advice on tree planting.)

Growing Tips
Water deeply but regularly in its early years to establish a deep root system that can tolerate drought later. If placed in the proper growing conditions, Japanese zelkova grows well without fertilizer. However, if young leaves were killed by a late spring frost, you may want to fertilize in late fall with an organic fertilizer made for trees, spread in a circle around the base of the tree according to package directions or with 1 pound of 19-0-10 granular fertilizer per inch of trunk diameter. Water in well.

Care
In exposed spots, spring frosts may damage the leaves of young trees. They will grow back. Do any necessary pruning in winter, including removing crowded branches. While the tree may occasionally suffer from disease or insects (especially beetles), these are usually not serious. Consult the Extension service if you need any advice.

Landscape Design
Japanese zelkova is a good shade tree in urban areas, as it is quite pollution-resistant. It's often on lists of good street trees, but I can tell you from personal experience living in downtown Boston that the roots of large, mature Japanese zelkovas tear up sidewalks.

Try These
Myrimar (*Zelkova serrata* 'ZSFKF' Myrimar) withstands heat and drought. 'Green Vase' grows especially fast and has more consistent fall color than many zelkovas. The leaves of 'Autumn Glow' turn dark purple in fall.

Kentucky Coffee Tree
Gymnocladus dioicus

When, Where, and How to Plant

Avoid planting anywhere the pods will fall onto a lawn, patio, driveway, or street, or where children or animals may consume them. These trees typically grow along rivers and streams in their native habit; give them moist soil, if possible. They tolerate most conditions, however, even urban locations, alkaline soil, and drought. Spring is the best planting time. Dig a hole as deep as the rootball and twice as wide. Remove any burlap before placing the tree in the hole. Water, and refill the hole with the soil removed from it. Water again and mulch the top of the soil with 2 to 3 inches of organic material, such as fine bark. (See page 228 for more advice on planting trees.)

Growing Tips

If you have planted in a spot with moist soil, you may not have to water. But it's important to keep the soil moist for the tree's first two years. After that, it can withstand drought, but since the tree grows slowly, you may want to water regularly when rainfall isn't adequate, especially when temperatures are high. For the same reason, you may want to apply an organic tree fertilizer or 19-0-0 in winter or early spring according to label directions.

Care

This tree leafs out very late in the spring (maybe May), so don't think it's dead or ailing if the foliage doesn't appear when most other trees begin to green. Prune in late winter. Kentucky coffee tree has few pest problems. Rake up pods in spring.

Landscape Design

This is a tree for large properties and for planting along the edges of woods. When possible, position it so that its scaly and ridged bark can be seen and admired.

Try These

'Espresso' has a lovely vase shape and no pods to mess up the yard, in addition to a perfect name for a coffee tree! 'Stately Manor' has dark green foliage throughout the season.

Imagine a tree with leaves 2 feet wide and 3 feet long that are pinkish purple when they appear and gradually turn bluish green in summer. A tree with showy flower panicles a foot in length and reddish brown pods 10 inches long in fall and winter. That's Kentucky coffee tree, which was widely used by American Indians and isn't known nearly as well nowadays as it should be. It's a nice native tree for those who like its historical association or just want something different from the run-of-the-mill trees planted everywhere. But anyone who appreciates a tough, adaptable tree that can tolerate a wide range of conditions will want it. It's hardy throughout the region. Caution: The pods, seeds and leaves are considered poisonous.

Botanical Pronunciation

jim-NOCK-lad-us die-oh-EYE-kus

Bloom Period and Seasonal Color

Female trees bear 8- to 12-inch-long greenish white panicles in late spring and reddish brown seedpods in fall and winter; (male trees have smaller flowers in May or early June and no pods)

Mature Height × Spread

40 to 75 feet × 40 to 50 feet

Lacebark Elm

Ulmus parvifolia

Would you plant a tree simply because it has handsome bark? I doubt that's among your top considerations when you look for a new tree. Instead you're more than likely looking for colorful flowers, attractive foliage, and a size and shape that fit into your landscape. But once you've seen lacebark elm's shedding and mottled trunk, you may become a convert. Certainly you will never again think of bark as dull! But lacebark elm has some other qualities to recommend it: it's tough, adaptable, fast-growing, and has reddish purple fall foliage. It's also resistant to Dutch elm disease and Japanese beetles. Just don't confuse this tree, which is sometimes called Chinese elm, with Siberian elm (Ulmus pumila), an invasive tree that should be avoided.

Botanical Pronunciation
UL-mus par-vi-FO-lee-uh

Bloom Period and Seasonal Color
Small flowers in fall; interesting bark year-round

Mature Height × Spread
40 to 50 feet × 30 to 50 feet

When, Where, and How to Plant
Plant in fall or spring in a spot that is in sunshine all day. Lacebark elm will tolerate most well-drained soils and doesn't mind if it's acidic or alkaline. But the best results and fastest growth will be obtained in moist soil that contains organic matter. Remove any synthetic twine or burlap from around the roots and discard. Place the tree in a hole that's as deep as the rootball and twice as wide. Water with a transplanting solution, and refill the hole with the dirt that was originally in it. Mulch with 2 to 3 inches of organic matter.

Growing Tips
To get the tree off to a good start, water regularly when weekly rainfall is less than an inch. In good growing conditions, fertilizer usually isn't necessary; as the mulch rots, it will gently feed the tree.

Care
Insects and diseases are not likely to be a problem, as lacebark elm is relatively disease-free and is subject to few insects. After the tree has grown to a moderate size, remove one or two of the lower limbs each winter for three or four years until the lowest limbs are at least 8 feet off the ground. This will enable the tree to show off its bark and allow you to walk beneath it. A fun project, especially with kids, is growing lacebark elm from seed. The tree flowers and forms fruits in late summer or early fall. Collect the seeds when they ripen (November) and plant outdoors right away in a 1-gallon container or where you want them to grow.

Landscape Design
Lacebark elm is a good choice to plant near the street or a pathway, where the bark can be admired.

Try These
Allée (*Ulmus parvifolia* 'Emer ll') resembles American elm and is good for urban areas because it is resistant to Dutch elm disease.

When, Where, and How to Plant

Plant oaks in full sun, preferably in late winter when they're dormant. White oak and willow oak tolerate many situations, but perform best in moist, well-drained, acidic soil. Pin oak will do fine in those wet spots in the yard, but will also thrive in moist, well-drained soil. Pin oak must have acidic soil; its leaves turn yellowish in alkaline soil. Remove any twine and burlap before planting in a hole that's as deep as the rootball and twice as wide. Water, and replace the soil that came from the hole around the rootball. Water again and mulch. (See page 228 for more about planting trees.)

Growing Tips

Water young trees deeply when rainfall is lacking. Fertilizer generally isn't needed, but if your soil is poor, spread an organic tree fertilizer in late fall the second, third, and fourth years.

Care

Sudden oak death is an increasing problem. Signs include tip dieback, leaf blight, and oozing cankers on the trunk. Call the Extension service immediately if you notice these or other problems with your tree. Also consult the Extension service for advice about gypsy moth, a problem in some areas, and oak wilt. Construction damage (when heavy equipment runs over the roots and knocks into the trunks) often kills mature trees three to five years later.

Landscape Design

Because of their size, oaks aren't for small yards. Pin oaks are often used as street trees.

Try These

When I was a kid and my dad went hunting, he would bring me tiny nuts from the chinkapin oak (*Quercus muehlenbergii*), a native that's ideal for Zone 6, although it grows in Zone 7 too. Scarlet oak (*Quercus coccinea*) has glossy green leaves in summer that turn a nice red in fall. The new growth of nuttall oak (*Quercus nuttallii*) is reddish purple and leaves are red in fall. Its leaves fall off in autumn—no having to rake in fall *and* spring!

Oaks are strong, stately trees that give a feeling of permanence to your landscape. Luckily, quite a few oaks live happily in Tennessee and Kentucky. Southern red oak (Quercus falcata) tolerates poor soil. White oak (Quercus alba) is slow-growing and usually has good fall color. Neither is widely available at nurseries; most people have them growing in their yards because the trees were on the property when they moved there. But if you look, you'll eventually find the oak you want (try specialists in native plants and plant sales at nature centers). More readily available in garden centers and nurseries are pin oak (Quercus palustris), which thrives in wet soil, and willow oak (Quercus phellos), which has leaves that look like a weeping willow's.

Botanical Pronunciation
KWER-kus

Bloom Period and Seasonal Color
Some species have colorful fall foliage

Mature Height × Spread
40 to 80 feet × 25 to 60 feet

Paperbark Maple
Acer griseum

From its name, you know this is another of those trees that have interesting trunks. Even if you can't get excited about bark, think of the winter interest it provides when nothing much is attractive in the yard. In this case the bark is cinnamon-colored and peels off the tree naturally in thin sheets (horticulturists call this "exfoliating"). But that's not the only reason you'd want to grow a paperbark maple. It's a 25-foot tree that has a striking vase-shaped silhouette in winter, scarlet leaves in fall, and small flowers that develop into decorative winged seedpods. It also has a delicate texture in summer and is the right size to fit into almost any yard, even small ones. Plus, it's easy to grow.

Botanical Pronunciation
Ace-er GRIS-ee-um

Bloom Period and Seasonal Color
Inconspicuous blooms in spring; great fall color

Mature Height × Spread
25 to 30 feet × 12 to 30 feet

When, Where, and How to Plant
Plant in spring in a sunny area where the trunk's bark will be noticed in winter. This tree is adaptable to types of soil and pH, but it will be more successful if it's grown in moist, well-drained soil that contains humus and is alkaline to slightly acidic (you can learn your soil's pH from a soil test). It will also grow in clay. Dig a hole twice as wide as the rootball and as deep, and place the tree in it; water; refill the hole with the original soil. Water again, and mulch with pine straw. (See page 228 for more detailed directions for tree planting.)

Growing Tips
To do well, paperbark maple requires moisture—so don't let the soil dry out. Water regularly if the soil isn't naturally moist and weekly rainfall is less than an inch. The tree is naturally slow growing (less than a foot a year), so in late fall you may want to apply 1 pound of 19-0-0 granular fertilizer per inch of trunk diameter or feed with an organic tree fertilizer applied according to label directions. Spread either in a widening circle around the tree, beginning 6 inches from the trunk.

Care
There are no serious pest problems with paperbark maple. It also rarely needs pruning. If any pruning is required, do it in winter. Maintain a year-round mulch that's 2 to 3 inches deep, to keep moisture in the soil.

Landscape Design
Plant paperbark maple as a patio tree or the focal point of a small yard. They look good when they're grown in small clumps, the same way river birch is grown. It also fits nicely into a shrub border.

Try These
I haven't found many cultivars available, but I expect that will change, since this has become a popular tree. Two cultivars I've seen are 'Gingerbread' (also known as 'Ginzam') and 'Cinnamon Flake'. Both are excellent.

Red Maple
Acer rubrum

When, Where, and How to Plant
Plant in in a sunny spot in early spring. In the wild, red maples grow in low, wet areas, so they will certainly do the same in your yard if you have a difficult wet area. But if you don't, the tree is quite adaptable. The ideal soil is a moist, well-drained, slightly acidic soil, but average soil should be fine as long as it isn't alkaline (determine your soil's pH, acidity or alkalinity, through a soil test). Plant no closer than 15 feet to a septic system. Place the tree in a hole that's twice as wide as the rootball and as deep, water, and fill in with the soil dug from the hole. Water again, and mulch with a couple of inches of organic material. (See page 228 for more detailed tree planting instructions.)

Growing Tips
Red maples need moisture from spring until fall. Water deeply if weekly rainfall is less than an inch. Fertilizer isn't usually necessary, especially if the tree is growing in the lawn and you fertilize the grass. The best time to fertilize is from late fall to early spring. I use an organic fertilizer made just for trees.

Care
Red maples may occasionally be subject to disease, borers (which enter through the trunk), and leafhoppers (which cause the leaves to look mottled and bleached or browned and curled along the edges). Knock leafhoppers off with a strong stream of water, and spray young trees with insecticidal soap. Red maples need little pruning.

Landscape Design
Red maple is a good choice wherever you need a shade tree that's attractive in three seasons. Place it where it can be seen in spring and fall from indoors or the street.

Try These
'October Glory', which has good heat tolerance, and 'Red Sunset' are easy to find in nurseries and have *fabulous* fall foliage. 'Brandywine' has deeper color and produces no seeds.

Most people assume that red maple was named because its leaves turn red in fall. Actually, it comes from the early spring flowers, which give the tree a fiery glow. Sometimes red maples have excellent fall color and other times they don't. If you want spectacular fall foliage, you can't count on unnamed red maples. Instead, you'll have to pay a bit more to buy named cultivars bred for their consistent autumn hues. Or you can buy a red maple in fall, when its leaf color is evident. It's a native tree that grows quickly, tolerates wet soil, and isn't damaged by storms—traits homeowners value. It's also a good substitute for sugar maple, which is sensitive to heat, and silver maple, which has many problems.

Botanical Pronunciation
Ace-er RU-brum

Bloom Period and Seasonal Color
Red flowers in spring, followed by usually colorful fall foliage

Mature Height × Spread
40 to 90 feet × 40 to 45 feet

River Birch
Betula nigra

Everyone admires the bark of white birch trees, but they can't be grown in this area because summer heat and humidity lead to attacks of birch borers, which kill the trees. But you can get a similar look in river birch, a native tree that's well adapted to Tennessee and Kentucky and even farther south. It's cold-hardy, heat-tolerant, and has beautiful, exfoliating (peeling) bark in shades of salmon and cream. If your yard has clay soil or areas that flood occasionally or stay wet all the time, river birch is just right for them. Despite the "river" in its name, this birch also lives happily in average or even drier soils. (They're so versatile that I've even grown them in sandy soil.)

Botanical Pronunciation
BET-u-la NIGH-gruh

Bloom Period and Seasonal Color
No flowers; grown for colorful, exfoliating bark

Mature Height × Spread
40 to 90 feet × 30 to 60 feet

When, Where, and How to Plant
Plant in fall or spring in a sunny or mostly sunny place that has acidic soil; alkaline soil causes yellow leaves (a soil test will tell you the pH—measure of acidity or alkalinity—of your soil). River birch prefers moist soil but will adapt to most fertile soils, especially if you water it. Place in a hole as deep as the rootball and twice as wide, water with a transplanting solution, and refill the hole with the soil that was dug from it. Mulch if soil is on the dry side. (See page 228 for more detailed planting instructions.)

Growing Tips
When the tree is young, keep the soil moist during spring, summer, and fall. For mature trees, provide water during drought or long dry spells. Fertilizer probably won't be needed, but if it is, spread a granular organic fertilizer for trees in early spring, just before the tree leafs out.

Care
In dry soils, maintain a 3-inch mulch. Prune river birch in summer; its sap "bleeds" if a branch is cut in spring or winter. While not harmful, the running sap is messy and discolors the bark. Aphids, which suck the sap out of the leaves and leave a sticky substance behind, may appear on tender young growth. Hose them off with a hard blast of water, and spray with insecticidal soap. River birch has few other insect or disease problems.

Landscape Design
River birch is right at home next to a pond or stream. Although it can be grown alone as a specimen tree, you usually see a clump of three trees planted together in the same hole, which highlights their graceful silhouette. Some nurseries sell them this way.

Try These
'Heritage' river birch is a fast-grower and, unlike many river birches, develops pleasingly yellow leaves in autumn. 'Dura-Heat' is never bothered by high temperatures and rarely loses leaves in summer.

Saucer Magnolia
Magnolia × soulangiana

When, Where, and How to Plant

Despite its exotic appearance, this is a good tree for urban areas, since it tolerates pollution. When planting, be sure to give it plenty of room, because it has spreading branches. Young trees transplant best. Plant in spring in a mostly sunny spot with moist, well-drained, acidic soil that contains organic matter (a soil test will tell you if your soil is acidic). The tree will also grow in partial shade and full sun although some break from the afternoon sun is a good idea in summer. Dig a hole as deep as the rootball and twice as wide. Place the tree in it and water. Refill the hole with the soil that came from the hole; water again, and mulch with pine straw or fine bark. (See page 228 for more about tree planting.)

Growing Tips

Water deeply whenever weekly rainfall is less than an inch. Fertilizer generally isn't needed.

Care

Maintain a mulch to keep moisture in the soil. Insects and diseases should not be much trouble. The most likely problem is one that's out of the gardener's control—unseasonably warm weather in late winter or early spring that encourages blooming, then a hard frost occurs, and the flowers are killed. Another difficulty is that sapsuckers like to peck holes in the bark, which can cause quite a bit of damage. Prune the tree just after flowering, as needed, to develop a tree form (one trunk with four or five main branches starting a few feet above ground level).

Landscape Design

Give saucer magnolia a place of honor in the front yard. Or choose several, with varying flower colors, and place them in different areas.

Try These

'Lennei' is an oldie but goody that is easy to grow. Its late-appearing flowers are deep wine colored on the outside and white inside. 'Big Pink' is a vigorous grower with deep rose-colored blossoms.

Saucer magnolia is one of the "eager beavers" of the plant world. Not only does it bloom early in spring, encouraged by any winter warm spell, it also begins flowering at a very young age. It's not at all unusual to see a 3-foot saucer magnolia covered with full-sized pink and white or purplish flowers—and it only gets better as it grows older. The tree is hardy throughout Kentucky and Tennessee, and actually can be more satisfactory in colder climates because it isn't as likely that the flowers will be killed by late frosts, a problem in Zone 7 (avoid that issue by choosing late-flowering cultivars such as 'Verbanica' or 'Candolleana'). Although it can be grown as a shrub, saucer magnolia is showier as a tree.

Botanical Pronunciation
mag-NO-lee-uh sue-lan-gee-A-nuh

Bloom Period and Seasonal Color
Pink, purplish, or white blooms in early spring

Mature Height × Spread
10 to 30 feet × 15 to 25 feet

Serviceberry
Amelanchier species and hybrids

Serviceberry's flowers are small and white, and, while pretty, they admittedly are fleeting. So why is this tree worthwhile? I think for its heritage (serviceberry is a staple in Appalachian forests), memories (for anyone who's lived in the country or tramped about the woods in spring), and for that lift your spirits get when you first spy serviceberry in bloom—a quiet signal that winter is finally over. This native plant has many common names, including shadbush, shadblow, sarvisberry, sarvis tree, and Juneberry, because of the small, dark fruits in early summer (supposedly good for jam; I wouldn't know, as the birds always get mine). Amelanchier arborea is the tree species most commonly available to gardeners, although Allegheny serviceberry (Amelanchier laevis) is often found in the wild.

Botanical Pronunciation
am-e-LANG-kee-er

Bloom Period and Seasonal Color
White flowers in early spring

Mature Height × Spread
15 to 30 feet × 20 to 30 feet

When, Where, and How to Plant
Plant container-grown or balled-and-burlapped trees in spring or fall. Be sure that you buy a tree form instead of a large shrub (which will take up a lot of room.) Although tolerant of many types of soil, serviceberry prefers moist, acidic, well-drained soil and partial shade or sun. Pay attention to eventual spread if you decide to grow it as a multistemmed shrub instead of a tree.. The planting hole should be as deep as the tree's rootball and twice as wide. Place the tree at the same depth it grew before, and refill the hole with the soil that was removed from it. Water well and mulch with shredded leaves. (See page 228 for more detailed directions on planting trees.)

Growing Tips
In early years water when weekly rainfall is less than an inch. Later the tree should be able to cope with mild dry spells, but water deeply during droughts. Serviceberry grows moderately fast and doesn't usually need fertilizer.

Care
Usually little pruning is needed, but if required, prune in spring after blooming has finished. Maintain the mulch year-round, (it helps protect the tree during dry weather). Serviceberry has few insects or diseases.

Landscape Design
This tree is a must if you're planting your yard to attract wildlife. The perfect spot for it is along the border of woods filled with spring wildflowers. Consider growing it near shadbush (*Amelanchier canadensis*), a shrub form of serviceberry that grows has excellent fall color.

Try These
'Trazam' (sold as Tradition) is a nice tree form that has early flowers and good fall color. *Ameliancher × grandiflora* 'Autumn Brilliance' has very red fall foliage and grows fast. 'Princess Diana' is also worth growing for its spectacular red leaves in autumn, as well as larger flowers and fruit.

Snowbell
Styrax species and cultivars

When, Where, and How to Plant

Because snowbell typically leafs out early in the season, place it on the north side of the house to delay leaf emergence slightly and therefore avoid frost damage. Be careful to plant snowbell where you want it to grow permanently, since it doesn't transplant well once it's larger. Start with a container-grown plant rather than one that's balled-and-burlapped. Snowbells grow in full sun or light shade and like moist, acidic, humus-rich soil (if you're not sure if your soil is acidic, have it tested). Put it in the same sort of area in which you'd plant a dogwood; snowbell is an excellent understory tree like dogwood. Dig a hole twice as wide as the rootball and just as deep. Place the plant in the hole and fill in around the roots with the soil removed from the hole, packing it down to remove air holes. Water thoroughly and mulch with 2 to 3 inches of organic material. (See page 228 for detailed directions on how to plant a tree.)

Growing Tips

Regular watering is important in the first two years the plant is in your yard. Keep the soil moist but not wet. After that, water during dry spells. In early spring, apply an organic or slow-release fertilizer made for flowering shrubs.

Care

You'll encounter few insect or disease problems. Remove volunteer (self-sown) seedlings that grow from dropped fruits.

Landscape Design

This is a good tree for small gardens. Grow near a red-leaved Japanese maple. A grouping of the different kinds of *Styrax* is attractive and extends the bloom season, since they flower at different times. Plant Lenten roses at its base for a lovely spring show.

Try These

The pink, fragrant flowers on slightly weeping branches make *Styrax japonicus* 'Pink Chimes' a standout. *Styrax japonicus* 'Emerald Pagoda' is a vigorous grower with large, starlike flowers and consistent yellow fall color; it's for Zone 7. 'Pendula' is a graceful weeping form.

There are several different kinds of snowbell, all of which are worth growing for their numerous clusters of lovely white or pale pink, bell-like spring flowers. Styrax japonicus is Japanese snowbell, the one you're most likely to encounter in nurseries, but it's not always hardy when Zone 6 winters are colder than usual. Styrax americanum, the native tree, is more cold-hardy and generally shorter; it's often grown as a large shrub. Styrax obassia is called fragrant snowbell; its exfoliating (peeling) bark gives the tree winter interest. This is a slow-growing tree you'll want to place where its hundreds of flowers can be seen close-up in spring. Snowbell's fall color isn't much, but it more than makes up for that with its spring show.

Botanical Pronunciation
STY-racks

Bloom Period and Seasonal Color
White or pink bell-shaped flowers in spring; silvery green fruits in late summer

Mature Height x Spread
8 to 30 feet x 10 to 30 feet

Sourwood

Oxydendrum arboreum

Sourwood has such an exotic appearance that it's easy to imagine it was discovered in some inaccessible place on the other side of the world. Instead, it's an easy-to-grow American native that most of us take for granted. At every season, sourwood calls attention to its unusual beauty with its pyramidal shape and its 10-inch clusters of creamy, bell-shaped flowers in summer followed in autumn by ivory seed capsules that hang down like splayed fingers from the tips of the branches—and the most brilliant scarlet foliage in the forest. Sourwood does not transplant well from the wild, so gardeners should buy container plants (which were started from seed) from botanical gardens, nature centers, or nurseries that specialize in native plants.

Botanical Pronunciation
ox-ee-DEN-drum ar-BO-re-tum

Bloom Period and Seasonal Color
Creamy flowers in summer, followed by brilliant fall foliage

Mature Height × Spread
25 to 50 feet × 15 to 20 feet

When, Where, and How to Plant

Sourwood trees don't transplant well from the wild, so start with a container-grown tree. Sourwood prefers acidic soil that's well drained. In early fall or in spring, plant it in a spot that has full or at least partial sun. Sun is important, because, although sourwood tolerates some shade, it generally won't bloom as well or have fall foliage as colorful as it would in sun, and you want to encourage the flowers and spectacular fall leaves. Dig a hole as deep as the rootball and twice as wide, and place the tree in it; water, then refill the hole with the soil that was removed from it, and water again. Mulch with pine straw or shredded leaves—but don't let the mulch touch the trunk. (More detailed planting instructions are on page 228.)

Growing Tips

When sourwood is young, water it regularly during dry spells. Once it's mature, it can tolerate some dryness, although you should water small- and medium-sized trees during droughts. Fertilizer probably isn't needed. But if the tree isn't growing well, fertilize with a high-nitrogen tree fertilizer in autumn after the leaves have fallen off, or in early spring. Note, however, that slow growth is normal for sourwood.

Care

Little pruning is needed, and the tree has few serious insect or disease problems.

Landscape Design

Place sourwood in a prominent location where it will show off its exotic looks and early autumn color. I have a small grove of sourwoods at the edge of the woods just before my driveway, where they're the first thing visitors see.

Try These

Few cultivars are available. 'Chaemeleon' (also spelled 'Chameleon') is a kaleidoscope of fall color—leaves turn from green to yellow, red, and purple. Often you'll find all those colors on the tree at the same time. The leaves of 'Mt. Charm' begin coloring earlier in fall than those of the species.

Southern Magnolia

Magnolia grandiflora

When, Where, and How to Plant

Plant in early spring in a spot that's in full sun most of the day. Ideal soil conditions are rich, moist, acidic, and well drained. If possible, provide protection from winter winds. Place the tree in a hole twice the diameter of the rootball and as deep, using the soil dug from the hole to refill the hole. Mulch with 2 to 3 inches of organic matter. (See page 228 for more advice on planting trees.) Southern magnolia is excellent for urban locations—where there's room—because it isn't bothered by air pollution or salt spray.

Growing Tips

Water deeply when rainfall is below normal. Fertilizer isn't necessary, but if you need faster growth, spread a high-nitrogen tree fertilizer around the tree in late fall.

Care

Don't remove the lower limbs; it detracts from the tree's graceful appearance and gives falling plant debris (such as old leaves and seedpods) nowhere to hide. Do any necessary pruning in very early spring. The tree has few insect or disease problems. In severe winters, the sun shining on the frozen leaves will often "sunburn" them. It looks ugly, but those leaves will fall off and new ones will grow. Leave old leaves hidden beneath the tree to provide nutrients as they rot. You may cut the flowers and float them in a shallow bowl of water indoors.

Landscape Design

This is a handsome specimen tree. I've also used a trio of Southern magnolias for screening since they're attractive year-round and grow much faster than most people think they will, especially if watered and fertilized regularly.

Try These

'Victoria' has long-lasting ivory flowers about 6 inches in diameter. 'Bracken's Brown Beauty', which grows about 20 feet tall, is a beautiful old Southern magnolia that's cold-hardy to minus 20 degrees Fahrenheit. 'Edith Bogue' has the same cold-hardiness and is the Southern magnolia that's least likely to sustain snow damage. 'Teddy Bear' is a dwarf.

As evergreen trees go, this one is a true grande dame, so much associated with the South that no one here calls it anything but just "magnolia." You may admire its thick, glossy leaves and large white flowers but think the tree isn't for your yard, for one reason or another. Think again. There are dwarf cultivars for small yards, and cold-hardy cultivars for those who live in the chillier parts of the region. The solution to the "messiness" of old leaves and seedpods is to plant in a mulched bed and never remove the tree's lower limbs. Besides its stately appearance and charming blossoms, the advantages of this native tree include red seeds enjoyed by birds and tolerance of intermittently wet soil.

Botanical Pronunciation
mag-NO-lee-uh gran-di-FLOOR-uh

Bloom Period and Seasonal Color
White in late spring and early summer; red seeds in fall

Mature Height × Spread
20 to 80 feet × 20 to 50 feet

Sweet Gum

Liquidambar styraciflua

Sweet gum has interesting five-pointed leaves that develop impressive fall coloration. Despite that, some people dislike this native tree. The reason? Its prickly "gumballs" or "burr balls"—beloved by preschool teachers and crafters and muttered about by those who tend the lawn. Evade the problem by choosing a cultivar that doesn't develop fruits (see Try These, below). Another option is to site the tree carefully—making sure that it's not planted in the lawn or near a sidewalk, driveway, or street, where the balls will make a mess. By placing the tree at the edge of woods or in an island bed where the fruits can fall into a groundcover or mulch, you avoid aggravation while enjoying some of the longest-lasting fall color.

Botanical Pronunciation
lick-wid-AM-bar sti-rah-see-FLOW-uh

Bloom Period and Seasonal Color
Tiny greenish flowers in spring; long-lasting reddish purple or clear red fall foliage

Mature Height × Spread
60 to 80 feet × 30 to 50 feet

When, Where, and How to Plant

Sweet gum, which likes sunny sites, grows fastest in moist or wet, acidic soils. If soil is alkaline, its leaves will turn yellow. Plant in spring. (See page 228 for detailed tree planting instructions.)

Growing Tips

Sweet gum may take a year or two to get established. Keep the soil moist until it begins growing well. After that, water whenever weekly rainfall is less than an inch. As with all trees, don't fertilize the first year after planting, but in the second and succeeding years, you may spread 1 pound of 19-0-0 granular fertilizer per inch of trunk diameter in a wide circle beneath the tree's limbs in late autumn after leaves fall or very early spring before new growth begins. Or, use a granular organic fertilizer made for trees.

Care

Sweet gum needs little pruning, but winter is the time to do whatever pruning is required. Pests are most likely to be caterpillars (dust or spray with Bt), aphids (dislodge them with a strong stream of water from the hose or spray with insecticidal soap), or scale (tiny dots on the undersides of leaves), which can be smothered with a light horticultural oil (sometimes called sun oil). There's a growth regulator that can be sprayed on the tree to eliminate the formation of the pesky balls, but it may not be easy to time it right, and it's hard for a homeowner to spray a big tree. There are fruitless varieties though.

Landscape Design

If one is a standout, two or three planted in a group as a small grove are dazzling. Remember, this is not a tree for lawns or small yards.

Try These

'Palo Alto' has reddish orange fall color. Among cultivars that generally don't develop the balls for which sweet gum is famous, I prefer 'Cherokee' (*Liquidambar styraciflua* 'Ward') over the well-known 'Rotundiloba', because its leaves are much prettier, and the tree is hardier.

Tulip Poplar
Liriodendron tulipifera

When, Where, and How to Plant
Place tulip poplar in an area where it has plenty of room to grow, away from power lines and buildings. It prefers full sun and moist, well-drained soil that's slightly acidic. Moisture is essential; without it, leaves scorch and fall off, which can be messy given their size. In spring plant in a hole as deep as the rootball and twice as wide, water, refill the hole with the soil that was removed from it, and water again. Mulch with organic matter, such as shredded leaves or pine needles. (See page 228 for more about planting a tree.)

Growing Tips
Without adequate water, tulip poplar's leaves often drop prematurely, making a mess. This often happens in September after a very dry August. To avoid the mess, keep soil moist at all times, but particularly when the tree is young and in dry weather. Don't fertilize unless the tree is not growing well.

Care
Potential insect and disease problems are numerous. Aphids are most common, producing a sweet secretion that is often followed by sooty mold (a brown-black fungus that covers the leaves and may cause them to turn yellow). Use a hose-end sprayer to try to wash off the mold, and then spray the tree with insecticidal soap or a light horticultural oil ("sun oil") to get rid of the aphids. Make sure the tree is well watered when it is suffering from insect or disease infestations; dryness will only make the problem worse. If your tree doesn't flower, it may be because it's not old enough yet; some don't flower until they're more than six years old.

Landscape Design
Plant tulip poplar as a specimen tree where it can be admired and has room to live up to its potential.

Try These
Smaller cultivars include 'Little Volunteer' and 'Compactum'. Columnar, upright forms include 'Arnold' and 'Fastgiatum'. Both have excellent yellow fall foliage and are good for screening.

You may want to grow this tree because of its beautiful flowers, or simply because it's the official state tree of both Kentucky and Tennessee. Another reason to grow tulip poplar (also called tulip tree and yellow poplar) is its exfoliating bark, which adds interest to the yard in winter. This native tree is tall and majestic, the flowers are mildly fragrant, and the leaves turn yellow in autumn. But there's one problem—tiny tulip poplar tree seedlings are often given away to homeowners who have no idea how big they will grow. This is one of the largest of our native trees, suitable mostly for large properties. If it's a favorite of yours, look for some of the smaller cultivars now becoming available.

Botanical Pronunciation
leer-ee-oh-DEN-dron two-lih-PIF-er-uh

Bloom Period and Seasonal Color
Cream to yellow flowers in late spring to early summer

Mature Height × Spread
70 to 100 feet × 35 to 55 feet

Water Gardens

Nothing is more tranquil and soothing than the sight and sound of water. That's one of the main reasons that ponds, decorative pools, streams, and fountains have become some of today's most popular backyard gardening projects. The nicest part is that they can be as simple or as elaborate as you like or have room for. But many homeowners have started out planning a small water garden and discovered that they enjoyed it so much that they wanted something bigger—room for koi, a fancy fountain or waterfall, and plenty of plants in and around the new water feature.

A water feature is a popular backyard project.

The first thing to do is decide where to put the water garden, how deep to dig it, how to line it, and what kinds of plants and, possibly, fish you'll need. After that, you'll discover that planting in a water garden—no surprise!—varies greatly from planting corn or crocus, and so does routine maintenance. How do you fertilize a plant that's growing in water? How do you keep the water clear? And what do you do when temperatures fall below freezing?

Think Before You Dig

When you're going to dig a big hole in your yard, careful planning is a must. If you put it in the wrong place, it's not easy to rectify the mistake. Here's what you need to consider:

- If possible, choose a spot where you can see and hear the water from inside the house or at least from a porch or deck. That gives you the maximum enjoyment possible.

- Sun or shade? The idea of a little pool in the shade beneath a tree is very appealing, but it's rarely a good idea. Sure, it will look cool and inviting—until autumn arrives and you have to remove all those falling leaves from the pond. (Not only do the leaves disrupt the balance of the water, too many of them can kill your fish.) Another reason to favor a sunny site is that waterlilies don't like much shade. Most need a minimum of six hours of sunshine to bloom well. An aquatic plant dealer should stock some waterlilies that will do well in about four or five hours of direct sun, but the selection won't be as large as for sun-loving varieties. A few hours of afternoon shade are fine for your water garden, but avoid completely shady spots—and trees.

- A level spot is best. If the only available area you have for a water garden is on a hill, get professional advice before installation.

Water gardens can be landscaped just as beds are, bordered by ornamental grasses and other plants.

- Do you want a formal or informal style? Most water gardens today are informal, in keeping with our lifestyles and our houses, but you may prefer a more formal look—brick or concrete edging, for instance, instead of rocks and straight lines instead of circles.
- If your yard is rocky, do some preliminary digging to make sure your chosen site isn't home to one or more big boulders that are going to be difficult or impossible to remove. Or have a Plan B, a second site that meets your requirements in case the first one turns out to be hard to dig.
- Before you dig, check for any underground utilities that might interfere (call 811).
- Also check with your local government to see if there are any building codes that affect your project.

Lining a Water Garden Is Important

After determining where the new water garden will go, you'll need to decide how to line it. Yes, farm ponds aren't usually lined, but they're much deeper than what you'll be digging. A drawback of an unlined residential water garden is that water can easily leak out and create a muddy mess. Among your choices for liners:

- Preformed units come in various sizes and shapes (fiberglass that's ¼-inch thick is best). They're usually for smaller gardens and may have a more formal appearance. Make sure they're at least 2 feet deep if you plan to introduce goldfish or koi.
- Concrete can crack when it freezes, so it's often smart to hire an experienced professional to install a reinforced concrete-lined water garden rather than doing it yourself.
- Flexible liners are most common and versatile. Rubber lasts the longest, is easiest to install, and is most expensive. Polyethylene is least expensive and least durable; you'll have to buy twice the recommended amount so you can double it to increase the thickness. My recommendation is 32-millimeter, two-ply PVC, which is in the medium range of cost and durability.

What size flexible liner do you buy? Get out your calculator or pencil and paper and do the math: Measure the length and add twice the depth to that number. Then measure the width and add twice the depth. Add one foot to both those figures to take care of the liner overlap. As an example, if your pool is 7 feet long, 5 feet wide, and 2 feet deep, select a liner that's 12 feet by 10 feet.

*Cattail (*Typha *species)*

Then gather some equipment: a shovel or machine to dig with, a measuring stick, and a carpenter's level. You'll also need sand to line the hole and, if you're using a flexible liner, some soft material to go under the liner to prevent punctures from rocks or tree roots. This can be old carpet, carpet padding, lots and lots of newspapers, or a nonwoven underlayment fabric, which prevents the liner from coming into contact with the soil.

Getting Started

Now you're ready to start construction. For a pond with a flexible liner:

1. Take a garden hose or thick rope and form it into the shape you want your water garden (you can also use flour or sprayable chalk to outline the desired form on the ground). Once you're satisfied with the shape and size, remove all the grass. Then invite a few friends to help you, so the project will go faster and be easier.

2. As you dig the hole, occasionally place a 2-by-4 across the top, and set the level on it, to make sure you're staying even. Remove all rocks and other sharp objects.

3. Pour an inch of sand in the bottom of the hole, tamping it down and making sure it's level.

4. Then cover the sand and the sides of the pool with carpet, thick layers of newspapers, or whatever underlayment you decided to use.

5. Install the liner on a warm day, and lay it out, open, on the ground in the sun to let it heat up so it will be easier to work with.

6. Working with at least one other person, if possible, place the liner in the hole, folding and pleating it as necessary to get it to fit the shape of the hole. Let about 18 inches to 2 feet of the liner spill over the top of the hole and place rocks or other heavy items on top to hold it in place.

7. Fill the pond with water to within 2 inches of the top.

8. Remove the excess liner around the edge so it's about 1 foot wide. Anchor it with rocks or special pins.

9. Edge the pond with rocks or other natural materials, if desired. Or place plants around it.

Installing a preformed pool is a little less work. Here's how to do it:

1. Place the form where it will be installed, and pound stakes at 1-foot intervals around it, following the contours of the form.

2. Dig a hole that's 2 inches deeper than the form, to accommodate the sand that goes under it. Remove all rocks and other sharp objects, and then level the bottom of the hole. Save the removed soil in a pile nearby; you will be using some of it soon. It's helpful to keep the soil on a tarp so it doesn't make a mess on your lawn.

3. Pour a 1-inch layer of sand into the hole, tamp down, and level again.

4. Place the form in the hole, making sure it's level all the way around. (Remove the form to level as needed.)

5. With a hose, run 4 inches of water into the form in the hole and begin using the soil removed from the hole to backfill around the sides of the form. When you've added 4 inches of soil, run 4 more inches of water into the form, and then backfill with 4 more inches of soil, continuing in this way until the sides have soil all the way around them to the top and the form is filled with water to within a few inches of the top.

6. Install edging, if desired.

Whichever lining you choose, buy a water testing kit at a water garden retailer or pet store, and test the water to make sure that it's the proper pH and is suitable for plants and fish (the kits explain how to do this and what information you need to know).

Wait a couple of days after testing and treating the water before you add plants and wait ten to fourteen days before introducing fish. This allows chemicals in the water to dissipate.

Selecting the Best Aquatic Plants

Now it's time to think about plants. Although naturally you will want waterlilies—the beauty queens of the water garden—you actually need a variety of aquatic plants. The least assuming but most valuable of these are called *submerged*, or *oxygenating*, plants. You've probably never heard of *Anacharis*, *Cabomba*, or *Myriophyllum*, but they're valuable supporting players that silently and out of sight go about their work of absorbing minerals and giving off oxygen, thus helping prevent algae in your pond. Water garden retailers sell them by the bunch, and you'll need one bunch for every two to three square feet of water surface. Since several different plants may be sold under the name *Anacharis*, be sure to ask what you're getting; some may be invasive.

Waterlilies come in two types: hardy, which are perennial, and tropical, which are killed by hard freezes.

It might seem obvious that in Kentucky and Tennessee, where our winter weather rarely approaches tropical, hardy waterlilies are the way to go. And you may want the majority of them to be hardy—but not all—because tropicals have some wonderful advantages.

Tropical waterlilies look more spectacular than hardy ones—they have larger, more impressive flowers in a wider array of colors. And they continue flowering up to six weeks longer in the fall. The typical hardy waterlily

Many homeowners begin with a small water feature and discover they want a more elaborate one.

*Pickerel weed (*Pontederia cordata*)*

finishes blooming about the end of September or the first of October, but you can have tropical waterlilies in flower at Thanksgiving, even after a cold spell or two (since it takes repeated freezes to kill them).

Hardy waterlilies usually finish flowering about 3 p.m. (they open in the morning when the sun hits them). So if you work nine-to-five, you probably won't get to enjoy the show, except on weekends. But tropicals—which are divided into two groups: day-blooming and night-blooming—are ideal for those who are away from home during most of the day. Day-bloomers stay in flower until about 6 p.m. Night-bloomers, whose flowers begin opening when the sun goes down, stay open till 10 a.m. or even noon the next day, making them a real conversation piece for evening parties on the patio and a color greeting for early risers on their way to the office.

It's easy to go overboard on buying waterlilies, because they're so appealing. But remember that they spread. In the beginning, aim to have plants covering no more than half the water's surface. Later, when they've filled about two-thirds of the pond's surface, you should begin to remove some.

"Planting" the Water Garden

Many people are surprised to discover that water garden plants are grown in pots, instead of on the bottom of the pond. This makes maintenance much easier. Water garden retailers and some nurseries carry plastic tubs or fabric pots made especially for aquatic plants. But old metal dishpans, wooden buckets, and heavy plastic pots—with *no* holes in the bottom—will work fine too. Avoid redwood, new lumber, and half barrels that smell of whiskey. The most useful all-purpose size when you're starting out is about 12 inches wide and 6 inches deep.

If you have clay soil, your water garden pots are the place for it, mixed with heavy loam. The reason you don't use packaged potting soil, as you would with other container plants, is that it's so lightweight it will float away in the water. For the same reason, avoid manure, wood chips, and any kind of fertilizer except the tablets sold specifically for use in water gardens.

Wet the soil and fill the container two-thirds to three-fourths full. Then follow the directions on the next page for how deep to plant specific plants and how deep to place them in the water. After planting, poke three fertilizer tablets into the soil, following label directions, and then cover the soil's surface with a layer of pea gravel. Set the pots on bricks to bring them to the correct height. Some water gardeners like to place the pots 6 inches deep at first and then, as the plant grows, lower them to the recommended level.

Lotus: After the weather has warmed up in spring, plant in a tub that's about 16 to 18 inches in diameter and 10 or 11 inches deep. Be sure the green or white tip (the growing tip) is about a half inch above the soil. Place a flat rock on top of the root to prevent it from floating, but make sure the rock doesn't touch the tender growing tip. After inserting a fertilizer tablet into the soil, place pea gravel on top of the soil; avoid touching the growing tip. Lower the container into the pond so that it is covered by 6 to 18 inches of water. Position it so that the plant will be in full sun, if possible. A few hours of afternoon shade are fine.

*Lotus (*Nelumbo *species)*

Waterlily: Plant hardy waterlilies when the chance of frost has passed; you can continue planting into summer. For tropical waterlilies, wait until temperatures are reliably warm (about the time you plant melons or okra). Both prefer a sunny location, but you'll be able to find some varieties that will do fine in 5 or 6 (occasionally 4) hours of direct light. Cover tropical waterlilies with 6 to 12 inches of water; place hardy ones about 18 to 24 inches deep. Waterlilies need calm water; don't place them at the base of a waterfall or a fountain.

Seasonal Care

Each month during the growing season, lift the pots from the water and add two or three new fertilizer tablets. Also remove any damaged leaves or faded flowers. In fall, after the plants have stopped blooming, remove the bricks from beneath the containers of all aquatic plants except tropical waterlilies and let them sink to the bottom of the pool; this will protect them from freezing. Tropicals can be discarded after they've been killed by cold, or you can try to overwinter them indoors. To do this, first allow the

Waterlily
*(*Nymphaea *species)*

tubers to dry, and then place them in a plastic tub between layers of damp sand. Keep the container in a frost-free place over winter, and check occasionally to make sure the sand hasn't dried out.

Should You Add Fish?

Everyone enjoys watching koi, but the colorful Japanese fish don't always mix well with water garden plants. In one garden, koi may munch a waterlily down to the soil level. In another, they may root through the pots your plants are growing in, looking for worms and small crustaceans—a messy business! If you have the latter problem, use larger gravel on top of the soil and visit a water garden dealer to pick up netting to place around the pots.

Yes, water gardening is definitely different from other kinds of gardening, but the results—the tranquil pond, the refreshing sound of water cascading from a fountain—make it one of the most satisfying backyard projects you can undertake. Think of it as growing memories.

Bibliography

Armitage, Allan M. *Herbaceous Perennial Plants*. Champaign, Illinois: Stipes Publishing, 1997.

Bender, Steve, editor. *The Southern Living Garden Problem Solver*. Birmingham, Alabama: Oxmoor House, 1999.

Darke, Rick. *Color Encyclopedia of Ornamental Grasses*. Portland, Oregon: Timber Press, 1999.

Dirr, Michael A. *Manual of Woody Landscape Plants*. Champaign, Illinois: Stipes Publishing, 1998.

DiSabito-Aust, Tracy. *The Well-Tended Perennial Garden*. Portland, Oregon: Timber Press, 1998.

Heriteau, Jacqueline, and Marc Cathey, editors. *The National Arboretum Book of Outstanding Garden Plants*. New York, New York: Simon & Schuster, 1990.

Hoshizaki, Barbara Joe, and Robbin C. Moran. *Fern Grower's Manual*. Portland, Oregon: Timber Press, 2001.

General Reading

Bender, Steve, and Felder Rushing. *Passalong Plants*. Chapel Hill, North Carolina: The University of North Carolina Press, 1993.

Hodgson, Larry. *Perennials for Every Purpose*. Emmaus, Pennsylvania: Rodale Press, 2000.

Holmes, Roger, editor. *Taylor's Guide to Ornamental Grasses*. Boston, Massachusetts: Houghton Mifflin Co., 1997.

Ogden, Scott. *Garden Bulbs for the South*. Dallas, Texas: Taylor Publishing, 1994.

Roth, Susan A. *The Four-Season Landscape*. Emmaus, Pennsylvania: Rodale Press, 1994.

Sedenko, Jerry. *The Butterfly Garden*. New York, New York: Villard Books, 1991.

Xerces Society, The, and The Smithsonian Institution. *Butterfly Gardening*. San Francisco, California: Sierra Club Books, 1998.

Photography Credits

Cool Springs Press would like to thank the following photographers and illustrators for their contributions to *Tennessee & Kentucky Garden Guide*.

Bill Adams: Page 161

Steve Asbell: Pages 48, 120

Liz Ball: Pages 100, 231, 233, 234, 246, 255

Cathy Barash: Pages 139, 200

Heather Claus: Pages 13, 23

Dr. Mike Dirr: Pages 117, 232

Le Do: Page 44

Tom Eltzroth: Pages 6, 8, 47, 52, 56, 57, 60, 61, 62, 64, 70, 72, 76, 91, 92, 93, 94, 96, 102, 105, 107, 108, 112, 124, 125, 126, 136, 140, 141, 144, 149, 150, 153, 157, 159, 160, 164, 165, 166, 171, 174, 176, 177, 179, 183, 188, 189, 194, 198, 204, 206, 210, 211, 213, 218, 219, 224, 226, 236, 238, 239, 245, 249, 265 (bottom)

Katie Elzer-Peters: Pages 10, 16, 18, 19, 24, 26, 27, 29, 30, 31, 34, 35, 36, 37, 40, 50, 80, 95, 128, 129, 130, 135, 191, 192, 208, 227, 235

Pam Harper: Pages 109, 115, 243

Index

Latin Index

Meet Judy Lowe

Judy Lowe has had a lifelong love of gardening and has been writing about it for more than twenty-five years. She learned to love gardening from her mother, who could grow anything. Although Judy had no idea that she would ultimately use her horticulture education professionally, her early interest inspired her to study horticulture in college while majoring in English. Thus began her garden writing career.

Professionally, Lowe has been the garden editor of several newspapers including the *Chattanooga Times-Free Press* in Chattanooga, Tennessee, and most recently at *The Christian Science Monitor* in Boston, Massachusetts. She has been very active in the Garden Writers Association, a garden writers group consisting of more than 2,000 members, and served on the board for fourteen years, as president for two years, and as a frequent judge for industry events. She was elected to the prestigious GWA Hall of Fame.

Lowe's eleven previous books include these for Cool Springs Press—*Herbs! Creative Herb Garden Themes and Projects*; *Tennessee & Kentucky Gardener's Guide*, and *Month-by-Month Gardening in Tennessee and Kentucky*—as well as *Ortho's All About Pruning*. Judy has been honored numerous times by the Garden Writer's Association, the National Garden Bureau, and many other groups.

Judy and her husband have lived and gardened throughout the United States (and even overseas). This has provided her wide personal experience growing in a multitude of zones and growing conditions. They live part of the year in South Carolina and part of the year in Tennessee. But everywhere, Judy continues her mission of helping gardeners.